MAKING SENSE OF MANAGEMENT

SAGE has been part of the global academic community since 1965, supporting high quality research and learning that transforms society and our understanding of individuals, groups and cultures. SAGE is the independent, innovative, natural home for authors, editors and societies who share our commitment and passion for the social sciences.

Find out more at: **www.sagepublications.com**

MAKING SENSE
OF MANAGEMENT

A CRITICAL INTRODUCTON

MATS ALVESSON & HUGH WILLMOTT

SECOND EDITION

Los Angeles | London | New Delhi
Singapore | Washington DC

Los Angeles | London | New Delhi
Singapore | Washington DC

SAGE Publications Ltd
1 Oliver's Yard
55 City Road
London EC1Y 1SP

SAGE Publications Inc.
2455 Teller Road
Thousand Oaks, California 91320

SAGE Publications India Pvt Ltd
B 1/I 1 Mohan Cooperative Industrial Area
Mathura Road
New Delhi 110 044

SAGE Publications Asia-Pacific Pte Ltd
3 Church Street
#10-04 Samsung Hub
Singapore 049483

© Mats Alvesson and Hugh Willmott 2012

First published 1996
Reprinted 2004

This second edition published 2012

Editor: Kirsty Smy
Editorial assistant: Ruth Stitt
Production editor: Rachel Eley
Marketing manager: Ben Sherwood
Cover design: Emma Harris
Typeset by: C&M Digitals (P) Ltd, Chennai, India
Printed by: MPG Books Group, Bodmin, Cornwall

Library of Congress Control Number: 2011939471

British Library Cataloguing in Publication data

A catalogue record for this book is available from
the British Library

ISBN 978-1-84920-085-1
ISBN 978-1-84920-086-8 (pbk)

Summary of Contents

Contents

About the Authors

Mats Alvesson is Professor of Business Administration at the University of Lund, Sweden, and a part-time professor at the University of Queensland Business School. He has published a large number of books on a variety of topics, including *Reflexive Methodology* (with Kaj Skoldberg, Sage, 2009, 2nd edn), *Understanding Organizational Culture* (Sage, 2012, 2nd edn), *Understanding Gender and Organization* (with Yvonne Billing, Sage, 2009, 2nd edn), *Knowledge Work and Knowledge-intensive Firms* (Oxford University Press, 2004), *Changing Organizational Culture* (with Stefan Sveningsson, Routledge, 2008), *Interpreting Interviews* (Sage, 2011), *Qualitative Research and Theory Development* (with Dan Kärreman, Sage, 2011) and *Metaphors We Lead By* (edited with André Spicer, Routledge, 2011).

Hugh Willmott is Research Professor in Organization Studies, Cardiff Business School, having previously held professorial positions at the Universities of Cambridge and Manchester, and is currently a Visiting Professor at the University of Technology Sydney. He has a strong interest in the application of social theory, especially post-structuralist thinking, to the field of management and business. His books include *Understanding Identity and Organizations* (with Kate Kenny and Andrea Whittle, Sage, 2011), *The Body and Organization* (with John Hassard and Ruth Holliday, Sage, 2000), *Management Lives: Power and Identity in Contemporary Organizations* (with David Knights, Sage, 1999), *Fragmenting Work: Blurring Organizational Boundaries and Disordering Hierarchies* (ed. with M. Marchington, D. Grimshaw and J. Rubery, Oxford University Press, 2004), *Organizational Analysis: Essential Readings* (with David Knights, Cengage, 2010) and *Organization Theory and Design* (with Richard Daft and Jonathan Murphy, Cengage Learning, 2010).

Preface

Why *Making Sense of Management*? Because we believe that management is too important to be left to management gurus and the recyclers of the received wisdoms distilled in standard textbooks. The purpose of this book is to provide an integrated and distinct perspective on management that is at once broad and critical. Broad in the sense that the theory and practice of management is examined in relation to the emergence of modern capitalist society; and critical because assumptions underpinning the world of management are subjected to scrutiny, rather than being unacknowledged or disregarded.

As with the 1st edition, the book is intended to be of value to anyone – students, teachers, practitioners and others – who is concerned or curious about management, and who is interested in developing a more challenging and reflective understanding of it.

Given the expansion of managerial and organizational control over human life, and the parallel growth of business schools and management education, the critical scrutiny of business, management and organizations is more important than ever. In addition to providing a useful sourcebook and pointers for further reading and research, *Making Sense of Management* is intended to introduce and further stimulate an alternative approach to management theory and practice. In this approach, the subjection of received wisdom to critical interrogation is regarded as a valuable, practical quality, rather than being dismissed as irrelevant or treated as heresy.

The production of this 2nd edition is the latest outcome of a collaborative project that began in the late 1980s when critical work in the field of management was in its infancy. In 1992, we published two texts that proved to be influential in forming what, over the years, has developed into a diverse and comparatively well established body of work identified as 'critical management studies' (CMS). An edited collection titled *Critical Management Studies* (Alvesson and Willmott, 1992) arose from a workshop that aimed to explore the relevance of critical thinking, and of Critical Theory more specifically, for examining various areas of management (e.g. accounting, marketing, etc). The term *Critical Management Studies* now serves as an umbrella label for critical, non-mainstream scholarship and research in the rapidly expanding fields of management and organization.

'CMS' was initially centred in the UK but has quickly become established in other parts of Europe, in Australia and New Zealand, and to a significant but lesser extent in North America. Much research in the area has been presented initially at the Critical Management Studies Conferences held bi-annually since 1999. In the past decade, CMS has continued to spread to Latin America, South America, Asia and Africa (see, for example, *Critical Perspectives on International Business*, 2010). Also, in 1992, we published an article titled 'On the idea of emancipation in management and organization studies'. This appeared alongside several other critical contributions to a Theory Development Forum in the *Academy of Management Review*. Together with the other contributions to this Forum, the paper signalled the arrival of 'CMS' to a mainstream audience. Chapter 7 is a substantially revised and expanded version of that article.

Since the appearance of the 1st edition of this text in 1996, a huge volume of 'CMS' work has been published as books and edited collections as well as journal articles. We have worked hard to incorporate as much as this as possible. But an exhaustive consideration of this rapidly expanding field is beyond the scope of what is intended as a comparatively short text whose (sub-titled) aim is to provide a 'Critical Introduction'. Readers seeking a more comprehensive coverage of specific topics, areas and issues are encouraged to consult the *Handbook of Critical Management Studies* (Alvesson et al., 2009). Other substantial contributions that have appeared since the publication of the first edition include *Key Concepts in Critical Management Studies* (Tadajewski et al., 2011), *An Introduction to Critical Management Research* (Keleman and Rumens, 2008) and *Critical Management Studies at Work* (Wolfram Cox et al., 2009).

This book is a thoroughly revised edition of *Making Sense of Management*, with very little of the earlier text remaining unchanged. Our intent has been to make this edition even more relevant, accessible and clearly focused. In updating the text, we have incorporated references to contemporary economic, social and organizational developments as well as to innovations in scholarship and research. We have also restructured parts of the text. Notably, there are several new sections, including those on HRM and leadership, that pay more attention to the various management specialisms. The process of revision, like the preparation of the 1st edition, has been very much a joint project, with each of us being involved in the development of all the chapters. Inevitably, however, the balance of contribution differs between the chapters. Chapters 1, 2 and 6 bear a stronger imprint from Hugh Willmott whereas Mats Alvesson has the stronger influence in Chapters 3 and 4, with the remaining chapters being more equal in their balance of contributions.

Since so many colleagues have helped us in diverse ways with our intellectual development leading to this project, it is perilous to single out individuals for acknowledgement. Nonetheless, we would like to extend particular thanks to Paul Adler, Karen Ashcraft, Yvonne Billing, Stan Deetz, Peter Edward, Chris Grey, Dan Kärreman, Bjørn Kjønstad, David Knights, Richard Laughlin, John Mingers, Glenn Morgan, Jenny Owen, Michael Power, Andre Spicer, Stefan Sveningsson, Richard Whittington and Edward Wray-Bliss, a number of whom provided us with comments on draft chapters. We are also indebted to Angela Cox, Agneta Moe, Katie Sullivan and Rachel Waldo for help with chapter preparation, language checking and compilation of the References.

Mats Alvesson and Hugh Willmott
September 2011

Introduction

Management is simultaneously a target of celebration and complaint, of denigration and recurrent demands for better organizational functioning. Many hail management as a 'holy grail' that will deliver well-functioning institutions and uninterrupted wealth creation. Yet, management is also charged with serial failures with respect to ethics (e.g. bullying, excessive salaries and bonuses), self-aggrandizement (e.g. empire-building, narcissism), recklessness (e.g. unsustainable expansion, excessive cost-cutting) and poor husbandry (e.g. environmental damage). In response, the popular remedy is more management, often of much the same kind but, of course, 'better'. The paradox reflects a drug-like dependence upon 'management'. We expect it to be effective, we complain when it fails, and we repeatedly demand an increase in the dose to restore our confidence.

In the face of its recurrent failures, repeated calls are made for a revitalization of management – notably, by strengthening leadership and/or by flattening hierarchies in which employees are expected to be self-disciplined and self-motivated as they are urged to collaborate in self-organizing teams led by managers capable of harnessing the potential of these human resources. Such initiatives are invariably dressed up in the language of innovation and the liberation of human potential from restrictive practices and outmoded structures. Yet, these initiatives rarely lead to radical change. Social divisions, global inequalities and damaging ecological consequences tend to be intensified, not reversed. There is talk of empowerment and responsibility – notably, with regard to the husbandry of human and natural resources. Yet, with few exceptions, such talk remains tightly harnessed to business priorities that routinely trivialize, exploit or override any deep or sustained commitment to emancipatory change.

In effect, more sophisticated forms of control (e.g. through culture, team working, branding etc.) are presented as liberating media for the development of ostensibly enlightened, progressive forms of management. As management monopolizes control, other organizations (e.g. unions) dedicated to articulating and defending the concerns of employees, consumers and citizens are rendered redundant. This contemporary, totalizing, neo-paternalistic conception of management extends beyond the workplace to the environment where, as Bavington (2010: 4) observes, discredited management thinking is enlisted to address ecological degradation and crisis (see also Parker, 2002):

> Despite proclamations by environmental scholars about worldwide crises, patho-
> logies, and even the end of management itself, managerial interventions remain
> firmly mapped across the face of the Earth and stand unchallenged as the domi-
> nant legitimized response to a host of social, political, economic and ecological
> problems.

Despite mounting crises – of energy and food as well as finance and ecology – contemporary business, management and working life continue to be presented in a highly positive, celebratory light. We are told that we live in a 'knowledge society' (which has advanced rapidly from a service society to an information society before becoming a knowledge society). We are led to believe that the application of advanced knowledge, in the form of sophisticated technical fixes organized by good management, will extricate us from the crises that now envelop us. The knowledge workers, notably managers, are identfied as the key to our salvation.[1] In this narrative of salvation, it is widely taken for granted that 'the foundation of industrial econo-mies has shifted from natural resources to intellectual assets' (Hansen et al., 1999: 106) and it is frequently claimed that 'many sectors are animated by new economics, where the payoff to managing knowledge astutely has been dramatically amplified' (Teece, 1998: 55). Management in the era of the knowledge society is, we are told, about developing competence, innovation, networking, developing corporate cul-tures and working with branding, not about controlling and exploiting the labour force. Most employees who are subject to 'managerial competence' do not find this credible; nor do we.

The representation of a 'new paradigm' of management – from the exploiters of labour in bureaucracies to the coaches of creative knowledge-workers in post-bureaucracies – is paralleled in the realm of consumption where consumers are increasingly conceived as co-constructors of value. They are seen not only to engage in forms of self-service and internet shopping but also in the co-creation of an 'affective intensity, an experience of unity between the brand and the subject' (Arvidsson, 2006: 93). Whereas 'old' management 'sought to discipline an unruly workforce into adapting certain pre-programmed forms of behaviour' (2006: 41), today, Arvidsson claims, 'in almost every case, it is the other way around'. Today, management respects and engages 'the freedom of the employee, aligning his or her self-realization with the interest of the organization' (2006: 42). There are, of course, some plausible elements in this view, insofar as greater responsibility is placed upon employees to exercise their 'freedom' in a manner that is value-enhancing for the organization. In the absence of such elements, the claim would be widely regarded as improbable rather than enticing. For readers who are attracted to this alluring image, this book will either be totally unappealing – or it will present an interesting challenge.

That an overwhelming majority of academics, consultants and business journal-ists make reassuring claims about management does not mean that they must be uncritically accepted, at least not without some qualifications and reservations. Such positive claims, we will suggest, are motivated partly by self-serving concerns to lend legitimacy to management practices that are socially divisive and ecologically destructive. Flattering images of management operate more successfully as ideology than they do as convincing, nuanced descriptions of contemporary business, working life and its trends. They form a key part of the 'knowledge worker/society' narrative that contains grains of truth presented as sizeable, indisputable rocks. As Thompson et al. (2001) argue, key growth areas of employment – insofar as these exist at all following the faith placed in the managers of investment banks are in low level service jobs, such as serving, guarding, cleaning and helping in health, personal and care services. In these sectors, organizations and work tasks are more convincingly likened to 'McDonaldization' (Ritzer, 1996), where each operation is bureaucratically specified and checked, than to the flowering of a knowledge society. Likewise, more systematic studies and reviews of the degree of debureaucratization in contemporary organizations show only modest support for the idea of its demise, let alone its abolition (Alvesson and Thompson, 2005; McSweeney, 2006). The 'audit society', with growing layers of unproductive surveillance and checking, is perhaps a more compelling characterization (Power, 1999). Understood in this light, references to 'post-bureaucracy' act more effectively as a means of legitimating change and marketing new ideas than as credible indicators, or even as desirable features, of changing forms of work organization (Willmott, 2011a), let alone debureaucratization. Such ideas and references reflect a strong premium placed by academics as well as by consultants and practitioners on labelling and investigating what is perceived to be novel (Alvesson and Thompson, 2005). They are a manifestation of a managerialist obsession with justifying the existence of management by asserting and celebrating its central importance in championing and implementing innovation and change.

These are complex issues that call for on-going debate and critical scrutiny. Various elites and other groups are eager to sell positive messages about an improving world of work, or an even brighter future. By promoting such casual sophistry, they hope to induce a positive, up-beat message. But any serious interest in knowledge issues calls for sharper and more sceptical assessments of truth claims and their effects. One of the greatest strengths of social science is that it offers resources for exercising critical judgment. What, then, do we mean by management? For us, management is a set of techniques and disciplines that promises to address problems that are defined as soluble by the technical solutions that it provides. In the modern era, management is a medium of technocracy where experts, in the guise of managers or executives, are assumed to possess a monopoly of expertise relevant for problem-solving. By definition, non-experts – workers, citizens, consumers – are deemed to lack such expertise and therefore can, at best, play a marginal role in addressing problems, or in assessing how problems are framed, or what solutions are to be given priority. And, yet, as Bavington (2010: 116) reminds us, when considering the application of management to the husbandry of fish stocks, and the unintended consequence of their prospective annihilation,

framing the world as a set of problems amenable to fixing helps to sustain the illusion that solutions to all problems are to be found a more determined application of rationally organized expertise encapsulated in management theory and practice. John Ralston Saul warns us that, 'in a civilization that has mistaken management techniques for moral values, all answers are a trap'.

We believe that the theory and practice of management is poorly served by books that lack a critical perspective on the challenges and dilemmas currently confronting those working and managing in modern organizations. As social and ecological problems pile up in the global economy, there is an eerie sound comparable to deckchairs being rearranged and repaired on the *Titanic*. Instead of addressing more fundamental questions about the defensibility and sustainability of our wasteful and divisive global economy, attention is focused upon ostensibly novel ways of maintaining them by regenerating management practice – for example, by advocating 'corporate social responsibility' (CSR), and by commending the potency of certain (e.g. transformative) types of leadership. Commercial concerns about the inflexibility and poor responsiveness of established organizational practices have resonated with expressions of disillusionment with the effectiveness of established (e.g. bureaucratic and post-bureaucratic) means of organizing. But very little consideration has been given to the rationality and/or accountability of contemporary management theory and practice in relation to fundamental values and goals. This should perhaps come as no surprise with regard to management in the private sector when, as Crouch (2011: 172) observes, 'Exercises of nepotism and favouritism that attract strong criticism in the political sphere pass as normal behaviour in business.'

Where, then, do we turn for ideas that can provide a different and challenging understanding of management theory and practice, and that may supply the basis for an alternative to its present forms? We have already indicated that traditions of social philosophy and social science – especially those which have questioned received wisdoms – can provide an important, yet largely neglected, source of guidance and inspiration. Notably (but not exclusively), the tradition of Critical Theory (see Chapter 2) and associated currents of thought have relevance for such a project. Why Critical Theory? Because it is interdisciplinary and not doctrinaire; and because it has been wrestling for decades with issues concerning management that are now increasingly acknowledged to be problematical for human well-being – such as the mindless equation of scientific development with social progress, the destructive effects of consumerism and commercialization, and the tendency of the modern state to equate policies (e.g. deregulation) intended to enhance and/or legitimize capitalist accumulation with the development of a more civilized, caring and just society. At the very least, such critical thinking can place in question a benevolent image of management by situating its formation and representation in a wider context of relations of inequality and domination – economic, gendered and ethnic – that managers endeavour to stabilize so that they can be perpetuated.

In drawing upon critical traditions of social science, such as Critical Theory, we make no claim to provide comprehensive coverage of all issues relevant for making sense of management. We have not sought to offer a more wide-ranging view of the political and economic contexts of management which, in any case, has been developed by those who are better equipped to produce such an account (e.g. Kellner, 1989; Harvey, 1991; Davis, 2009). Our more modest ambition is to present an introductory sketch of management which, we hope, can assist in the process of questioning and transforming practices that are needlessly wasteful, harmful and divisive.

Knowledges of Management – Conventional and Critical

Doubts about the value of established management ideas and practices have coincided with an acceptance and expansion of management as a subject of academic study. In combination, these developments have supported the emergence of innovative ways of making sense of management that depart from conventional assumptions and prescriptions, often by drawing selectively upon ideas developed within the social sciences.

Scientific thinking has been venerated in modern societies even if most people have very limited knowledge of science, despite becoming better educated. In effect, this relation to (or ignorance of) to science establishes the normality of relying upon a cadre of 'experts', or technocrats, as an alternative to engaging in collective self-determination. In the sphere of organization and work, it is widely accepted that the most taxing and recurrent problems are people-centred rather than technical in character. It is not surprising, therefore, to find social scientific ideas being used to diagnose and address these problems and, in particular, to inform the theory and practice of management. This role of reason (in the guise of forms of social science) in renovating managerial practice raises an interesting question. What kind of social scientific knowledge has most relevance?

This question cannot be answered without first determining *who* it is relevant for. If what counts as relevance is decided by the 'experts' – e.g. managers – then the adoption of social scientific knowledge will be quite limited and narrow. It will exclude knowledge that questions the expertise of management and, especially, knowledge which deconstructs or challenges the legitimacy of managerial prerogative. In other words, if a managerialist conception of relevance is assumed, the scope for critical reflection on management is impoverished. For it is restricted to what is self-serving, or what can be selectively adopted to increase the power, control and/or prestige of management. When it serves a technocratic order in which experts are the 'rulers', forms of critical reflection are emasculated and domesticated. In effect, the potential for critical reflection to foster democratic self-determination is suppressed.

So, can critical thinking reach beyond forms of knowledge that provide consultants and managers with a swirling pool of ideas and findings for addressing *only* those problems that are defined or predefined by managers and consultants? We believe that it can. In this book, we argue that reason can, and should, have a role that is not confined to its use as a resource for identifying and legitimizing technologies of management control. It is indefensible to restrict reason to the (instrumental) task of refining the means of accomplishing existing ends (e.g.

by eliminating needless effort and waste from current organizational practices). For reason can also contribute to questioning whether *the existing ends routinely generate needless waste, divisiveness and destruction* (see Chapter 2). Reason should of course be mobilized to refine the means of pursuing established ends. But, more crucially, it can also be deployed to scrutinize the rationality of the processes through which the ends themselves are determined. To return to our earlier reference to the study of fish stocks, and the role of 'managerial ecology' in addressing the issue of how to preserve them, Bavington (2010: 132) notes how

> Managerial ecology in the cod fishery is inseparably tied up with industrial modernity [and instrumental rationality], and ultimately this whole way of thinking, imagining, and living will have to be called into question if we are to move beyond the deadly consequences of management.

A basic problem with current theory and practice of management is that a narrow, instrumental conception of reason has largely eclipsed a broader critical appreciation of the emancipatory power of reason. An irrational consequence is that what have appeared to be effective solutions to managerial problems have actually produced even bigger social and ecological problems (see Chapter 1). Only by standing back from immediate pressures to produce a technical fix to pressing problems is it possible to appreciate how a given problem comes to be framed and addressed in a particular way and that, potentially, it could be diagnosed differently; why particular kinds of goals and solutions are routinely favoured when other goals and solutions could be pursued; and what changes are necessary if we are to confront, rather than merely displace, pressing social and ecological problems. As Thomas (1993: 12) has suggested, when contemplating the role of critical reflection in problematizing established management theory and practice, the value of such reflection 'lies ultimately in its ability to enhance our freedom, even to increase our chances of survival'. Critical reason cannot be equated with, or reduced to, its contribution to social engineering, troubleshooting or empire-building. Had such reason been applied at BP, it is highly likely that the Deepwater Horizon disaster, involving untold ecological damage as well as the loss of life of 11 employees, would have been averted. As the official report into the disaster noted (published by the US Bureau of Energy Management, Regulation and Enforcement):

> 'The loss of life at the Macondo site on April 20, 2010, and the subsequent pollution of the Gulf of Mexico through the summer of 2010, were the result of poor risk management, last-minute changes to plans, failure to observe and respond to critical indicators, inadequate well control response and insufficient emergency bridge response training by companies and individuals responsible for drilling at the Macondo well and for the operation of the Deepwater Horizon' (see http://www.boemre.gov/pdfs/maps/dwhfinal.pdf).

That the vast majority of textbooks and guru handbooks on management pay little or no attention to the relevance of *critical reason* to understanding and diagnosing the theory and practice of management is, in our view, a lost opportunity and a matter of much regret. A preoccupation with the acquisition of techniques and ideologies of problem-solving is mirrored in the view that management is only about current 'practice' or prevailing ways of 'getting things done'. This view trivializes the significance of management and, in effect, inhibits its scrutiny by prescribing the kinds of knowledge that have relevance for its study and appreciation. As Thompson and McHugh (1990: 28) have ruefully observed, in most literature on management, consideration of 'many deep-seated features of organizational life – inequality, conflict, domination, subordination and manipulation' is neglected or suppressed in favour of 'behavioural questions associated with efficiency and motivation'. There is a reluctance to question the 'sacred' role and prerogative of management – a position that is routinely protected by the defensive understanding that the purpose of such questioning is to 'knock' management rather than to stimulate debate about its role and legitimacy.

An interest in developing *critical* knowledge of, and for, management, it is worth stressing, does not imply that a technical problem-solving orientation is worthless or bogus; or that it becomes irrelevant when a broader view of management is developed. On the contrary, both technical and critical orientations are legitimate, and we welcome the forging of closer links between them (Willmott, 1994b). Technical problem solving is an integral aspect of managing complex organizations; it does not become redundant – though it is likely to be radically questioned and reformulated – with the development of less irrational, and less socially divisive, forms of management theory and practice. Reflection upon conventional wisdom can and should extend well beyond the technical role of providing more effective diagnoses and 'fixes' for managerial problems, as managers narrowly define them. Our intention in this book is to make the insights of critical thinking more widely accessible without patronizing readers by 'dumbing down' or 'sugar-coating' their contents. Our hope is that this second edition will continue to be thought-and-action-provoking for a wide audience of management teachers and practitioners.

Plan of the Book

Chapter 1 clears the ground for the rest of the book. It introduces various themes that are expanded in the later chapters. Its basic purpose is to suggest that management is very much a social and organizational activity – in the sense that it involves unstable and unpredictable interactions between people. To represent management as something akin to engineering, as is frequently done, is highly misleading. For the process of managing necessarily is a medium and outcome of a complex field of politico-economic, cultural and moral relations. Social theory therefore provides a relevant resource for understanding and reflecting critically upon the organization and dynamics of management practice. Critical Theory, we argue, is sufficiently open, broad and self-questioning to address issues spawned by social and economic change, and to accommodate the contributions of other strands of critical thought.

Chapter 2 is concerned with setting our 'critical introduction' to management in its intellectual context. We directly confront the argument that management can be, or should be, 'scientific' – in the sense of aspiring to base management upon objective, scientific knowledge that would thereby remove subjectivity and politics from management practice. We challenge the view that knowledge of society, including knowledge of management, is – or ever can be – value-free. Taking the side of Critical Theory, we argue that the purpose of scientific knowledge is to expose dogmas, including those that support domination, and not to replace them with seemingly unassailable (scientific) knowledge. We deploy Burrell and Morgan's (1979) model of different paradigms of knowledge generation to illustrate the diversity of social scientific knowledges and also to locate Critical Theory in relation to analyses of management inspired or influenced by other critical traditions. Finally, we present the Critical Theory of the Frankfurt School, the principal intellectual inspiration for this book, before signalling some limitations of Critical Theory – a concern to which we return in Chapters 7 and 8.

In Chapters 3–6, we examine the study of management and its sub-specialisms. Chapter 3 considers and illustrates a number of alternative conceptualizations of management and organization. Among other things, we explore the ways in which management can be understood as a form of technocracy, as a process of mystification and as a colonizing power. In Chapters 4–6, we turn our attention to the various sub-disciplines of management. In Chapter 4, we consider the comparatively 'soft' or 'qualitative' specialisms of organization theory, leadership and human resource management where we present a brief overview of the focus and variety of perspectives within each specialism. We then explore the contribution of studies that challenge or overturn conventional wisdom within each specialism, especially those studies that are directly indebted to Critical Theory and other streams of critical thinking. Chapter 5 addresses marketing and strategic management specialisms that stand in between the soft and the hard areas of management. Chapter 6 considers accounting, operational research and information systems – the comparatively 'hard' or 'quantitative' disciplines. Following a similar pattern to Chapter 4, Chapters 5 and 6 share the purpose of reviewing and illustrating relevant contributions in order to make critical sense of these specialisms.

Chapters 7 and 8 present a series of reflections upon the relevance and value of the approach to making sense of management presented in the previous chapters. Chapter 7 explores the scope for bringing together elements of conventional understandings of management with insights drawn from its critical study. This entails some questioning of the practical relevance and accessibility of Critical Theory – something which, in principle, is consistent with its commitment to self-reflection and autocritique. In particular, we suggest the need to concretize its abstractions, and indeed to 'pollute' the purism of Critical Theory. To this end, we sketch some ideas for the fruitful merging of the insights of Critical Theory and the recurrent preoccupations of management and organization studies. Chapter 8 is more directly concerned with the practice of management as we consider possibilities for the development of management practice that is more defensible, ethically and politically.

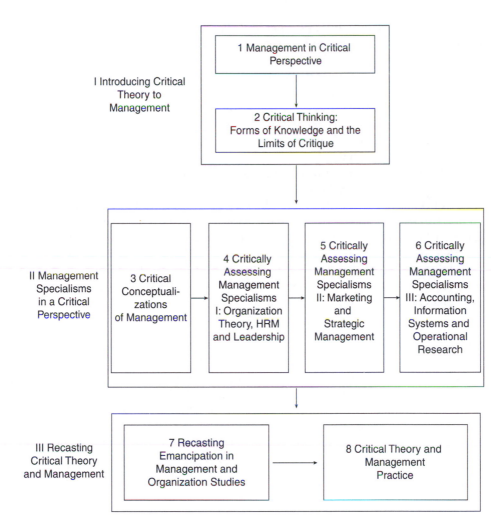

Figure i.1 *Overview of chapters*

Overall, then, the chapters are structured in a way that allows our approach to be introduced and elaborated in Chapters 1–2, then illustrated in Chapters 3–6 and finally reflected upon and developed in Chapters 7–8 (see Figure i.l).

To benefit from this structure, the book is probably best read in chapter order. Nonetheless, we anticipate that some, perhaps most, readers will prefer to look first at sections that are of most immediate interest to them. As we anticipate a readership with varied backgrounds, knowledge and concerns, we have written the book in a way that makes it possible to read each chapter without reference to the others. To assist non-linear readings, we have provided many cross-references to indicate where related arguments are expanded, and we have resisted the temptation to remove minor repetitions.

This book steers away from recycling the clichés and recipes found in most textbooks that have been prepared for management students and in handbooks written for practising managers. We would like the book to be read by practitioners as well as by students; and it is not just the hope of royalty cheques that stimulates this desire! We firmly believe that forms of analysis developed within the critical traditions of social theory are actually more pertinent and insightful for making sense of the everyday tensions, irrationalities and dilemmas encountered by practising managers than are the tired ideas and superficial prescriptions contained in most management textbooks and guru handbooks.

Unlike most management texts, we make no promises of recipes for the solution of everyday managerial problems, or even that the contents will directly advance the reader's managerial career (though it is by no means incompatible with such an outcome). Rather, our hope is that the book will contribute to the development of less superficial and destructive forms of management theory and organizational practice. Through processes of critical reflection and discussion, we believe that ways can be found, individually and collectively, to identify and reduce the needless waste and divisiveness in modern organizations over which mainstream theory and practice of management so unapologetically presides.

 Note

1 To this end, higher education is a 'must' for a growing proportion of the population, responding to a labour market in which a degree is, apparently, a necessity for anything but a 'dead end' job. The rapid expansion of management education and the explosion of business schools are symptomatic of this development, although many of its graduates now find themselves without a job or doing work (e.g. in call centres) for which a degree is largely irrelevant.

PART I

INTRODUCING CRITICAL THEORY TO MANAGEMENT

1

Management in Critical Perspective

In all societies, people are involved in the complex process of organizing their everyday lives. Sometimes our routines run smoothly and we can forget how intricate they are, and how we are continually engaged, in 'managing' their operation. When our routines are disrupted – by others' unpredictability, our indiscretions or ill-health, for example – we are reminded of the fragility of what we take for granted. Each one of us engages in a daily struggle to accomplish ordinary tasks, maintain normal routines and deal with the unexpected. In the context of modern societies, however, responsibility for many organizing activities has been delegated to, or appropriated by, experts. Amongst them are managers hired to shape and regulate so many aspects of our lives – as employees but also in other spheres, such as areas of leisure and the provision of personal services (Hancock and Tyler, 2009).

Forms of corporate and public management exert a pervasive influence over diverse aspects of modern life that previously were organized within communities and by households. Education, health, consumption and the arts as well as work have become objects of management knowledge and control. The application of ostensibly rational, impartial forms of calculation and control, including control exercised by managers, is pervasive (Grey, 1999). In sum, experts in managing have assumed the role of 'improvers' of established ways of doing things and ways of life.

At the same time, modern societies have become increasingly risk and crisis-prone – to, for example, financial meltdown, terrorist threats, nuclear annihilation, ecological degradation, global warming. In addition, there are many less dramatic but nevertheless problematic aspects of modern society, including a widely felt loss of a sense of meaning and purpose in working life (Sennett, 1998, 2006). In affluent or even 'post-affluent' societies, there is a slavish preoccupation with materialism and the acquisition of property – something that is manifest in the emphasis placed upon the production, and especially the marketing, of goods and services. Often, consumption has more to do with boosting status and self-esteem – by keeping up, or ahead of, one's immediate or global neighbours – than with human well-being or flourishing. Economic activity and need satisfaction exist in what has become an increasingly ambiguous, if not perverse, relationship. In contemporary capitalism, greed, superficiality and hedonism dominate; and in these circumstances many people find it difficult to develop a sense of well-being or fulfilment. We are bombarded by images and messages which declare that our lives will be bettered (only) by acquiring more things, finer titles, more impressive careers. We then find ourselves caught up in a 'rat race' where insecurity, anxiety and suffering are temporarily suspended but unaddressed and so effectively reinforced (Alvesson, 2012b). Since management is deeply complicit in the organization and development of modern societies, making sense of management, as a key locus of expert control, is critical. It is critical not only for our self-understanding but, more grandiosely, for the future of modern societies and their sustainability.

Seductions of Capitalism and the Limits of 'Progress'

When contemplating the achievements of the modern era, it is reassuring to believe that advances in science, and the expertise attributed to its enlightening powers, has swept away much dogma and prejudice. In the Western world dogmas of religion and superstition have indeed been widely challenged and debunked, at least by the more educated of their populations. But they have been superseded by modern, secular myths – such as the belief that science and related forms of knowledge guarantees progress, that markets ensure freedom and efficiency, that affluent consumption is the route to happiness, and that experts know best. In this process, values and practices other than those that contribute directly to economic growth and consumption, and so increase private wealth, have become marginalized and neutralized. Nonetheless, and mainly at the fringes of society, there have been repeated eruptions of disenchantment and recurrent efforts to fashion new values and practices which, as the pressures placed upon resources by globalizing capitalism increase, are set to intensify.

The modern world is shaped by varieties of capitalism in which scientific and technical knowledge has been applied to extract profits from the production and marketing of every conceivable product and service. As a distinctive politico-economic system in which wage labour is hired to make commodities that can be sold for a profit, the reach of capitalism has extended around the globe to incorporate former state socialist societies (e.g. the Soviet Union and the People's Republic of China). Capitalism has gained legitimacy by absorbing and then promoting pressures to support the public supply, and subsequent privatization (Grimshaw, Vincent and Willmott, 2001), of a basic level of public goods, in the form of housing, health care and education. The provision of these goods has facilitated an important measure of political stability and, with it, mass consumption as an engine of economic growth. Conversely, any withdrawal of these goods, or slowing of economic growth, threatens this legitimacy.

With technological progress and wealth creation has come a creeping commercialization and commodification of everyday life. Most recently, its advance has developed the 'new' markets of entertainment, leisure and, increasingly, the premium pricing of ecological correctness (e.g. organic and other green or low carbon produce). As the meaning of life has been progressively identified with the pleasures of consuming commodities produced and delivered by capitalist corporations, the governance of modern economic and political institutions has become geared to capitalist expansion. Politics has become preoccupied with the technical task of preserving the status quo as democratic debate about ends is displaced by a techno-cratic focus upon the refinement of means.

Consider the issue of how 'consumer needs' are defined. Marketing techniques play a central role in the formation of these 'needs' – for example, by associating products with enviable lifestyles or cultural heroes. Leading marketing textbooks are largely silent on the issue of how consumer demand is constituted – how anxieties are generated and then exploited or aspirations are fuelled and responded to. There is scant discussion of the relationship between increased consumption and ecological destruction. In the world of marketing, as in other management specialisms, 'the environment' is referred to as if it were something 'out there' rather than an integral part of our lives (Naess and Rothenberg, 1991): it becomes yet another sphere or object of management knowledge and control – equivalent to the markets for entertainment, health and leisure – ripe for penetration and colonization. Growing environmental anxiety among consumers is not addressed directly but, rather, is seized upon as an opportunity for product differentiation and gaining a competitive advantage (e.g. through the so-called greening of products or the building of 'environmentally friendly' or 'sociably responsible' corporate images). From a critical perspective the discourses and practices of marketing, for example, are seen to be propagators and seducers of consumer desire as much as they are articulations of, or responses to, human need (Klein, 2000; Morgan, 2003).

As a counter-image to a dominant view of economic actors being engaged in value creation, one could suggest that many businesses are involved in forms of *value destruction*: cities and landscapes are transformed in environmentally and aesthetically negative ways for commercial purposes; as new images and accompanying aspirations are developed, existing products become out-dated and lose their attractiveness; people are led to believe that what is not novel or fashionable is inferior. It is seldom wanton destruction or even built-in obsolescence. But often the balance between creation and destruction is not self-evident, as attention is given only to the immediate positive aspects of innovation with minimal consideration being given to adverse unintended or long-term consequences. Consider, for example, the notion of 'financial innovation', in the form of securitization, that was at the heart of the financial meltdown of 2008 (Willmott, 2010; 2011a). As Engelen et al. (2011) note, 'the coupling of financializaton and innovation established a normative bias in its favour with the growth of securitization interpreted as engineering which facilitated the efficient marketization of risk.' What it promised was the spread of risk; but what it delivered was its mystification and, paradoxically, its concentration resulting in the drying up of credit and the use of public funds to preserve banks that had evaded the discipline of 'moral hazard' by becoming 'too big to fail'.

The strength of attachment to capitalist values (e.g. individualism expressed in the form of maximization of self-interest, as exemplified by the financial sector) and priorities (e.g. private accumulation and mass consumption) means that responsibility for social division (e.g. foreclosures, unemployment) and ecological destruction (e.g. Deepwater Horizon 'accident') is more likely to be attributed to industrialization, science, weak regulation, irresponsible companies or some combination of such factors. By focusing upon such elements, there is a tendency to disregard their shared development within a politico-economic system founded upon domination and exploitation where costs are routinely 'externalized' or treated as 'acceptable business risks' to be covered by insurance. Exploitation is systematically built into capitalism. The creative capacity of human beings, hired as employees, is harnessed to produce wealth that is appropriated privately by the owners of capital, which takes the form of factories, service firms, intellectual property (e.g. patents), etc. Domination is an integral feature of capitalism in the form of institutions (e.g. education) and ideologies (e.g. liberalism) that naturalize its features and/or represent them as congruent with 'human nature' or most consistent with the preservation of 'freedom', 'equality', 'democracy', and so on. In such ways, divisiveness and destructiveness are downplayed as capitalism is commended as the means of overcoming such problems.[1]

Despite their eager professing of green credentials, politicians and industrialists struggle to provide leadership as they remain preoccupied with 'managing' the survival and growth of their (capitalist) economies and businesses. Their priorities have been dramatically demonstrated during the 'Euro Crisis' of 2011 which is unfolding as we complete this book. Remarkably, the problems (e.g. of Greece and Italy) have been widely diagnosed in terms of national profligacy and 'sovereign debt', and the 'bailing out' of these nations. Yet, arguably, it is the banks that have been content to lend to these nations that are, once again, being 'baled out' by ordinary taxpayers – of Germany or through the European Central Bank. We, it seems, have become the captives of (financialized) capitalism, unwilling or unable to debate and renew the meaning of modern ideas of freedom, community and democracy, and reluctant to face up to the question of how an espoused commitment to these ideas can be translated into substantive action and appropriate forms of governance and planetary husbandry. Of course, politicians and companies are also to a degree captives of voters and lobbyists. They are pressured by demands for a continuing flow of inexpensive and accessible goods and services, and resist making the material sacrifices necessary to reduce gross inequalities and secure sustainability. Such demands are fuelled by huge investments of firms in promoting the appetite for material goods, and the promises of politicians to maintain economic growth and thereby 'improve' the material standard of living.

Failure or refusal to recognize the interconnectedness of social and ecological problems spawns remedial action that is limited to interventions where quick wins can be made. The excesses and gross inequalities of capitalist development, nationally and globally, go largely unchallenged, and, at best, state provision addresses only the most shocking, de-legitimating manifestations of destructiveness, deprivation and neglect. Billions have been found almost instantly to bail out the banks but, in the years following the financial crisis, many countries are experiencing great difficulties in sustaining core welfare programmes. These have been assessed to be too expensive and/or the services have been contracted to the private sector where labour conditions are generally inferior with regards to employment security, trade union representation, pensions, etc., and so costs are lower. While bankers continued to pay themselves billions of dollars in bonuses, the withdrawal of the services and benefits (in order to reduce the deficit produced by the financial crisis and its impact upon growth) has been justified on the grounds that such benefits breed a culture of fecklessness and dependency. Experts operating in the financial markets completely failed to make prudent assessments of the risks inherent in the use sophisticated financial instruments (e.g. CDOs, CDSs). Yet, following the crisis, it is the experts in financial markets to whom states are beholden, since a collapse of their currency and/or a crippling rise in interest charges on loans to service the debts in part incurred in bailing out the banks is threatened if they continue to borrow for social purposes (Tett, 2010).

What Then of the Managers?

Managers form a heterogeneous group whose members work across a variety of sectors – e.g. public, private, voluntary – and in diverse organizations where they undertake a wide variety of tasks. They occupy different specialisms (e.g. marketing) and work at different levels in organizational hierarchies. They manage in uncertain conditions and are in possession of imperfect information; and they are under pressure to be responsive to a plurality of demands. This diversity and dynamism makes it far from easy to generalize about what management is and what managers do. Our ambition is to cover management and managerial work fairly broadly, but we concentrate primarily on management of business (and so have comparatively little to say about public sector and third sector forms of management) because it is 'business' rather than public management or social enterprise that most strongly shapes and influences the theory and practice of management. Our focus is also limited principally to managers with significant influence, i.e. above the level of supervisory or junior levels of management.

We justify this selectivity on the grounds that, in our assessment, practices of corporate management developed in the private sector have conditioned its application across other sectors. The form of management developed within larger capitalist enterprises has been taken up in other contexts as a model to be emulated, albeit in modified form. Whilst its relevance and appropriateness for other, not-for-profit contexts is very debatable, its 'market-orientated' logic, in particular, has been widely diffused – most notably, in the development of 'new public management' which is distinguished by the incorporation of private sector disciplines and performance measures.

Amid confusions and uncertainties about managers, and their collective activity as 'management', there is a tendency to privilege one single, *technical* meaning: management as a universal process comprising a number of functions, such as planning, coordinating, and so on. Ignored in this conception is the embeddedness of the managers performing these functions, individually and collectively, within relations of power and domination. These *social* relations are crucial as it is through them that the functions ascribed to management are defined, allocated and undertaken. Management is inescapably a *social practice* (Reed, 1984) as it is embedded in social values, politics, interests and relations of class, gender, ethnicity, etc. As such, the mean-ing and activity of management are most 'intimately bound up with the social sit-uation of the managing group' (Child, 1969: 16). The nature and significance of management depend upon the historical and societal context(s) in which it emerges and takes shape (Wilson and Thomson, 2006). The decision making of (senior) managers increasingly shapes these contexts (Scarborough, 1998).

The 'social situation' in which modern management has developed is one of specifically capitalist economic relations and the rise of the modern state within diverse societal contexts. This is important because, when the historical and cultural embeddedness of management is appreciated, it is no longer plausibly represented as a set of universal functions. Instead, it is more compellingly understood as 'an out-growth of disparities in socio-economic power, the acquisition or initiation of work processes by private capital or the state, and the desire for control which flows from that' (Hales, 1993: 6). Management is conditioned by the specific, local contexts in which it develops and which it shapes. It comprises diverse practices that develop within institutions established by private capital and the modern state and which are conditioned by disparities of socio-economic power. In these institutions, managers are delegated responsibility to exercise discretion in a manner that secures the control and reproduction of established, yet inherently fragile, relations of power. Their work involves reforming these institutions in order to sustain them. To this end, managers develop and apply whatever technologies – coercive and seductive – that are believed to be effective and legitimate. Yet, while managers are empowered *inter alia* to raise funds, generate revenues and allocate resources, the nature and extent of the rise and influence of management – what Burnham (1941) called the 'managerial revolution' – is restricted as well as enabled by wider relations, of patriarchy and ethnicity as well as capital and the state within which management decision making is embedded.

This assessment begs the question of why, in textbooks, management is so widely presented as a universal and neutral activity. One answer, as we suggested earlier, is that the authority of management depends, at least in the business sector, upon a covering over of the exclusion of democratic control over decision making – including the raising of funds, the generation of revenues, and the allocation of resources, within work organizations (Deetz, 1992a). This is no coincidence as disparities of ownership, income and opportunity have been secured by delegating control to management whose task it is, in the private sector at least, to deliver profitable growth by ensuring productive effort and containing dissent. The institution of management has ensured that privately owned work organizations are largely exempted from any form of democratic accountability to employees or a wider citizenship (Khuruna, 2002). Top management alone, enabled as well as constrained by corporate governance regulation, is expected to exercise control over organizational matters, although there are many formal and informal expressions and modifications of this prerogative. Notably, there are some differences between countries as a consequence of legislation that incorporates some representation of labour and sources of countervailing power from unions, professional employees, pressure groups and so on.

Managers are intermediaries between those who hire them and those whom they manage. Managers are employed to coordinate, motivate, appease and control the productive efforts of others. These 'others' do not necessarily share managerial agendas and might otherwise be inclined to be productive in ways that would not accommodate the 'overhead' of managerial salaries and the dividends and capital growth that accrue to shareholders. As management becomes a separate activity undertaken by a specific, comparatively privileged group, any notion of work organization comprising a community of interest with shared goals invites a sceptical assessment. A 'them' and 'us' division is invited and can easily widen; and one key task of management is to address and minimize such a possibility. The situation is complicated, however, as managers are themselves salaried employees with their own sectional (e.g. empire building and defending) agendas, even if they are more directly accountable than other employees to major shareholders or, in the case of public management, to political elites and ultimately to electorates. Almost all managers are subordinates, and most are perhaps more subordinates than superordinates (although, as we have noted, our focus is primarily upon middle and senior rather than junior managers).

The critical study of management unsettles conventional wisdoms about its sovereignty as well as its universality and the impartiality of its professed expertise. It is therefore worth stressing that the critical study of management is by no means 'anti-management'. The purpose of 'critical management studies' (CMS), as we conceive of it, is not to commend, or participate in, the Utopian project of eliminating all forms of hierarchy, removing specialist divisions of labour or even abolishing the separation of management from other forms of work.[2] Rather, in addition to challenging received wisdoms about management, such as its impartial professionalism and political neutrality, the critical study of management aspires to foster less socially oppressive forms of organizing and managing. The (for us) desired democratization of managerial activity may result in divisive work organizations being replaced by collectives or cooperatives in which there is a focus *inter alia* upon social objectives, green forms of work and a reduced vertical division of labour. It is also highly likely that some vertical as well as horizontal divisions will be retained, albeit ones that are accountable to diverse stakeholders rather than shareholders or fund managers interested primarily or exclusively in securing or enhancing the return to investors. It is envisaged that social divisions will be justified through processes of democratic contestation, and not by executive elites whose decision making is supported by spurious, self-serving assertions about the rationality, impartiality or effectiveness of their rule. The demand here is not for an end to management but for the harnessing and redirection of management to more democratically determined and accountable ends.

Beyond the Understanding of Management as a Technical Activity

Recognizing the political context and social organization of management leads to the understanding that problems of management cannot be adequately addressed purely by developing more efficient and effective forms of technical control. Wherever this is assumed, problems (e.g. gross inequalities, ecological destruction, diminishing planetary resources) that are fundamentally social and political in organization come to be interpreted as amenable to solutions using purely instrumental forms of reasoning.

Blindness to the social conditions and media of management restricts awareness of how the human difficulties and challenges associated with organizing everyday tasks are compounded by major social divisions – manifest in differences of values, objectives and resources, and clashes of interests.

Exhibit 1   An Etymology of Management

The origins of the term 'management' can be traced to the Italian word *maneggiare,* which means 'to handle a horse'. This semantic root is instructive in its portrayal of the social divisiveness of management as a contradictory process: a process in which a person simultaneously takes responsibility for and seeks to control a valuable, yet recalcitrant, resource. Given the importance of securing cooperation from wilful, potentially resistant 'human resources' it might be assumed that managers would wish to gain total control of employees. However, total pacification is unlikely to be secured in the absence of the kinds of regime envisaged by Huxley in *Brave New World* (and even there, it was not fully effective). In any event, it is doubtful whether total subjugation would be unequivocally advantageous.

The limits of total conformity are dramatically exposed when use is made of the stratagem of 'work to rule' – that is, doing precisely what is required without exercising any discretion (or extending any goodwill). Working to rule demonstrates the dependence of managers upon the judgment and goodwill of employees as it simultaneously mocks and subverts the exercise of management control. On the other hand, allowing employees a measure of autonomy, however carefully controlled (e.g. through the strengthening of corporate cultures), exposes managers to the risk that employees will 'abuse' or redefine this autonomy for their own purposes. Managers want employees to develop and deploy initiative. But managers also want employee initiative and discretion to be exercised in managerially acceptable and disciplined ways. For this reason, managers seek to manage the meaning of work and employment. It has been observed that:

> a crucial variable in the construction of reality lies in the *management* of meaning: actors compete to contrive and propagate interpretations of social behaviour and relationships . . . The management of meaning is an expression of power, and the meanings so managed are a crucial aspect of political relations. (Cohen and Camaroff, 1976: 102, cited in Gowler and Legge, 1983: 198, emphasis in original)

Given the challenges encountered by managers in organizing people, it is not difficult to understand why the metaphor of horse handling was adopted. It lucidly

(Continued)

(Continued)

articulates the demanding task of marshalling and channelling the energies, habits and desires of potentially stubborn, unruly and headstrong suppliers of labour who are capable of developing competing definitions of the situation, including an unflattering assessment of their bosses.

The *maneggiare* metaphor also conveys the understanding that managers form an elite group or stratum that is different from, and superior to, those they 'handle'. The metaphor does not endorse the idea of management as just one, technical element in a specialized division of labour. Rather, it highlights the *social division* of the 'handlers' (from the 'horses' who supply the labour) and the managerial skills applied to them: labour is 'broken in' – by teachers in schools and colleges if not by managers in factories and offices – and continuously monitored and developed in order for its profitably productive potential to be realized.

Managers are of course well aware of many of the conflicts, pressures, uncertainties and even the contradictions that beset their work (Clarke et al., 2009; Jackall, 1988). They may frequently feel frustrated and oppressed by systems that they supposedly at least partly control; and they may bemoan the difficulties encountered in gaining cooperation and commitment from their managerial colleagues as well as from their subordinates (Watson, 1994). Such difficulties and dilemmas are not well addressed by received managerial wisdom. This wisdom ignores or denies the social formation and power–invested purposes of managerial work, as it conceives of management and managing as universal functions accomplished by applying a 'best practice' set of tools, techniques and systems. The most pressing challenges are addressed by resort to managerial mantras of 'organizational restructuring', 'improved communications' or more 'effective leadership' in the hope that these will provide relevant remedies for more deep–seated problems of social division, normalized domination, routinized exploitation and ecological destruction.

The education of managers routinely excludes or marginalizes ideas that are, potentially, most relevant for diagnosing and addressing the pressures and contradictions of managerial work (Ghoshal, 2005; Khuruna, 2007). Management education and training continues to encourage managers to understand themselves as depositories of impartial expertise who privilege the claims of technical, instrumental reason. When the limits of a technical understanding of management are acknowledged, managers are seen to juggle competing demands for resources and recognition – demands that come from more senior managers as much as from their subordinates. That said, a narrow focus upon intergroup politics can deflect attention from an appreciation of how managerial work is deeply embedded in wider social divisions (Willmott, 1987; 1997a). As we noted earlier, managers act to intermediate between those who deploy resources to dominate or exploit others, and others who are subordinated in such processes. We now outline briefly the main theoretical inspiration for this way of making sense of management.

Critical Theory and Modern Society

Since time immemorial, and certainly since the Enlightenment, human beings have exercised powers of critical reasoning to doubt and change established customs, ideologies and institutions. In the modern age, practices of witchcraft and slavery, and, more recently, patriarchal practices, have been subjected to critical scrutiny. Varieties of critical thinking, including Critical Theory (CT), build upon this legacy. The intent is to promote reflection upon oppressive and exclusionary practices, and thereby to facilitate the extension of greater autonomy and responsibility. By autonomy is meant the capability of human beings to make informed judgments about values, ideals and paths that are comparatively unimpeded by dependencies and/or compromised by a subordination to inequalities of wealth, power and status. We are not here invoking a fantasy of full sovereignty conceived of the individual human being who exists in splendid social isolation. To the contrary, we assume that as humans we are always formed by social relations, cultural understandings and unconscious processes that often impede or conflict with our capacity to be reflective, to use our knowledge, to exercise our intellectual skills and to engender a sense of morality. Nonetheless, in contemporary society, such capacities remain significant; and their development can be facilitated through education and research. By responsibility we mean a developed awareness of our social interconnectedness and, thus, a realization of how our collective responsibilities extend to our husbandry of the planet. In the light of its commitment to the expansion of autonomy and responsibility, critical thinking doubts the rationality and necessity of forms of acquisitiveness, divisiveness and destructiveness that accompany globalizing capitalism. These characteristics are manifest where nation states compete with each other to produce the most favourable conditions for investment, and where corporate executives are incentivized and disciplined by shareholders to pursue every avenue for maximizing profitability. Since management theory and practice are implicated in these developments, they are highly appropriate targets of critical analysis.

The Capacity for Critical Reflection

The intent of critical thinking, and of CT more specifically, is to challenge oppressive institutions and practices where there is little or no meaningful democratic account-ability and/or where there are significant harmful consequences. An example of such a challenge is the influence of feminism and the women's movement in disrupting a range of (chauvinistic) values and practices and so combating their normalization. A related ideal is for the development of social relations, including employment relations, in which oppressive pressures to acquire and display gendered identities, including the expectation to act and feel as a 'real' man or embrace 'true' female values, are dissolved. To be clear, this emancipatory move does not advocate a narrowing of gender differences, where men and women become culturally indis-tinguishable. Rather, it calls for the removal of oppressive gender relations in which there is pressure to conform to gender stereotypes or ideals promoted through the media for purposes of consumption and/or control. This could lead to much less predetermined and varied ways of 'doing' or 'non-doing' gender than established practice routinely permits.

The resistance to such emancipatory movements is not difficult to recognize. Despite the considerable strides made by feminism, its radical values and practices are marginalized in most countries, and diluted if not excluded in most organizations. Even the basic principle of equal pay for equal work has yet to be established in all workplaces. Women remain woefully underrepresented in processes of managerial knowledge development and dissemination. In recent years, a conservative ideology of individualism (see below) has tended to blunt the radical edge of feminism as neo-liberalism has elevated the individual above more collective and progressive considerations. Gender issues have tended to become reduced to issues about promoting women's careers, thereby further reinforcing a strong focus on careerism, and so displacing other values – for men as well as women – in life, including meaningful, comparatively stress-free forms of employment. In short, this brief reflection upon the influence of feminism, and its colonization by conservative ideologies, provides a cautionary illustration of how critical ideas can become domesticated and instrumentalized for other purposes. There is no reason to believe that insights and demands associated with critical management studies are not subject to the same influences, and thus face the prospect of selective recuperation through mainstream theory and practice (see Boltanski and Chiapello, 2007; Willmott, 2012).

The ideology of individualism encourages us to assume that we are each sovereign, self-determining beings, and that our life chances – including access to education, health services and so on – are attributable to our individual talents, application or good fortune. 'Success' in gaining grades at school, 'winning' jobs in the labour market or even 'acquiring' sexual partners is attributed to some winning trait that the individual is deemed to possess, and not to their circumstances. Without denying that human beings differ, the development and elevation of specific attributes is a product of history and culture, and is not solely or even mainly the sovereign work of individuals.

Critical reflection casts doubt on the dominant, received wisdom of modern, capitalist societies in which individualism, fuelled by narcissism, is pervasive (and perhaps most apparent in the cult of celebrity that applies no less to CEOs of large, publicly recognized firms than to the transient 'stars' of reality TV shows). In this regard, a condition and a consequence of autonomy and responsibility, as contrasted to individualism and fame, is the flourishing of democracy – which is not the same as a society that boasts nominally democratic political institutions. Nominal democracy can easily degenerate into largely formal and stage-managed processes where parties converge on the 'middle ground', and participation in democratic institutions drains away as it seems to make little difference which party or politician is elected. The risk is that dogmatism ('there is no alternative' to the middle ground) displaces debate and critique. The measure of a democratic society is not reducible to the existence of particular, formal institutions but is reliant upon the strength of its members' everyday commitments to, and the upholding of, democratic values in all institutions, including its workplaces. As Deetz (1992a: 350–1) has observed of workplace democracy:

> it is a moral political issue, not one of greater productivity and satisfaction ... We know something of civic responsibilities, and we need to take them to work ... The moral foundation for democracy is in the daily practices of communication ... The recovery of democracy must start in these practices.

Fully democratic decision making occurs when individuals are able to think and act autonomously and responsibly, as dicussed earlier, in ways that acknowledge and support their interconnectedness, rather than striving to control and exploit interdependence for sectional or self-aggrandizing purposes.

These are laudable aims. Not surprisingly, some critical thinking is sceptical of the possibilities for democracy and emancipation – on the grounds, for example, that it is not possible to adjudicate rationally between the truth claims of competing ideologies. We will return to this issue in Chapters 2 and 7. For the moment, we note that forms of critical thinking, including Critical Theory, observe that emancipatory progress has been made in the past – with regard to slavery, for example – and, potentially, can be made in the future. Contemporary struggles to overthrow despots and thereby develop more democratic forms of government provide other examples – even though such advances may be compromised, precarious and subject to reversal. Or to offer another, widely recognized example, there has been significant progress regarding gender issues in many countries over recent decades. Today, there is less inclination to regard nature as an unproblematic resource that can be exploited without regard to the consequences. As in the other cases, there are no guarantees of a progressive outcome for emancipatory campaigning, and critical reflection is a necessary but insufficient condition of such change. It is a necessary element as it challenges established ideas and practices in which diverse, institutionalized forms of oppression are harboured and normalized. But emancipation requires the embodiment of critical thought in practice. To the extent that this step is ignored or marginalized, critique contains traces of what it seeks to challenge and eliminate.

Reconstruction and Critique

In Critical Theory (CT) a distinction is made between abstract and concrete 'moments' of reflection. The abstract moment of reconstruction mobilizes critical reason to diagnose prevailing conditions. For example, reconstruction identifies and analyses the presence of elements of patriarchal thinking within the ostensibly impartial and functional disciplines and neutral techniques of management (Collinson and Hearn, 1996). When re-constructing such received wisdoms, the analyst acts comparatively cerebrally and dispassionately as an observer (whilst in principle acknowledging the limitations of such efforts). When engaging in critique, in contrast, responsibility is taken for tackling the problems in a way that involves a commitment to participating in changing the 'objects' of (reconstructive) analysis (e.g. in respect of one's everyday practices, by campaigning for their transformation, etc.). Critique involves a move beyond reconstruction to incorporate critical self-reflection articulated as praxis. Critique fuses reflection with transformative practice that must be actively struggled for.

When employed in an organization or indeed when studying at university, it is not unusual to experience some twinges of discomfort about aspects of 'management' that are disquieting or mildly offensive. Particular actions or demands may violate a sense of propriety, fairness or reasonable conduct – for example, behaviour that is considered to be excessively punitive or divisive. Consider the example of a group of senior managers studied by Watson (1994). Following interviews with their new managing director, Paul Syston, who was suspected of being hired as an axeman to 'rightsize' the organization, each of the managers feared for their own job[3]. Such unnerving occasions may potentially stimulate reflection on the structures (e.g. of ownership and control) that make such episodes possible and render those subjected to them mute and/or deferential. If reflection is to move in the direction of critical reflection, however, there must be some theory, whether simple or sophisticated, that can provide a way of reconstructing such experiences of managerial work.

In the light of our earlier reference to the ideology of individualism, it is under-standable that the managers studied by Watson were preoccupied with Syston's motives, his personal style and his inclinations. They did not engage in reconstructive reflection upon the conditions – notably, the control exercised by dominant share-holders – that make it both possible and legitimate for bosses like Syston to treat fellow managers as expendable human resources, and to interact with them in a cor-respondingly distant, intimidating manner. Had the managers engaged in a process of reconstructive reflection, they might have understood their treatment by Syston to be symptomatic of their occupancy of a contradictory position within capitalist organizations – a position in which they are simultaneously made responsible for organizational performance, and yet are mere sellers of (comparatively well remuner-ated and prestigious) labour who fear being side-lined or losing their jobs.

Instead of personalizing the problem with Syston in terms of his style, or his appearance as 'a bit of a miserable sod' (ibid.: 103), these managers could have reflected on how the hierarchical relationship – and associated social distance – between managing directors (Syston) and senior managers operates as a potent mechanism of control. And beyond that, they might have reflected on how this parallels their own relationship to their subordinates, and the difficulties they encounter in being more 'personal' with their staff without being manipulative and/or hypocritical (Roberts, 1984). Arguably, it is the structural arrangement of subordination, and not only or even mainly Syston's personality *per se*, that inhibits senior managers in asking their boss directly about his plans or suggesting their own ideas – in other words, to initiate a form of praxis.

Turning to Syston, his status permitted him to assume an intimidating persona as a way of distancing and defending himself in relation to senior managers. The temptation for those who occupy elite positions is to develop a non-communicative, intimidating or 'bullying' style. When looked at in this way, Syston's frosty impersonality is an understandable response to the pressures and associated anxieties that *he* experiences in a position of superordination. By refusing to enter into any kind of personal relationship with his senior managers, Syston excluded or denied any moral relationship to them, and was therefore more readily able to treat them not as human beings with families and so on, but as commodities to be bought (hired) and sold (fired) at will. In doing so, it could reasonably be argued that Syston was not being sadistic or bullying, but was actually being more direct and 'realistic' (and not paternalistic) about the nature of his relationship to the senior managers, even if this did little to endear them to him or elicit their support.

To move from reconstructive diagnosis to critique would require the senior managers to reflect critically upon their anxieties in response to Syston's silence about his plans for the company, and perhaps to recognize them as symptomatic of a hierarchical relationship acted out either aggressively or openly by Syston, depending on one's interpretation. In which case, the senior managers might have directly addressed their anxieties and collectively overcome them, at least to the point of engaging Syston in a discussion of 'his plans', rather than being intimidated into silence by his style.

This shift to critique is, however, difficult to imagine in the absence of any depth of solidarity amongst the senior managers and a collective preparedness to be assertive, rather than deferential, in relation to their boss. Acting as self-contained individuals, they were reluctant to admit and share their anxieties and vulnerability. Critical self-reflection was therefore inhibited, or at least individualized. In principle, a process of critique, as contrasted with cathartic personality bashing ('miserable sod') could have surfaced, reduced their anxiety, and so enabled the managers to confront their new boss instead of being intimidated by him. Instead of deciding to 'wait and see' or agreeing to work on the assumption that Syston was listening and willing to be persuaded (Watson, 1994: 104–5), their sessions with Syston could, in principle, have prompted a process of mutually supportive critique amongst the managers. More practically, the managers could have resolved to develop a more open and democratic form of corporate governance in which those occupying managerial positions (e.g. managing directors but also themselves) became more accountable to fellow employees – a shift that, logically, requires managers to seek out, challenge and change diverse autocratic, antidemocratic practices, including the way managers at all levels tend to relate to their subordinates. Such a shift, it is worth stressing, would foster not only procedural changes in corporate governance but also substantive, embodied changes in how managers make sense of their responsibilities and undertake their work. People who are inclined to 'wait and see' rather than to 'reflect and act' are viewed, in the light of critical analysis, as simultaneously the victims and the perpetrators of the situations from which, ostensibly, they desire to escape. This diagnosis flows from the embrace of a critical tradition of social scientific enquiry that strives to foster an emancipatory transformation of modern institutions through the development of reconstructive analysis but ultimately through engaged critique.

Of course, people in positions of dependency – like the subordinates of Syston – have learned to be deferential to their bosses and so are inclined to be cautious, and are generally eager to safeguard their positions. Apart from the issue of whether passivity is typically the best tactic here, the wisdom of striving to hold down or retain the job at all costs must be questioned. Many people understandably stick to their jobs mainly because they have become dependent upon a given level of pay and status, and so cling to their job regardless of the personal (e.g. stress) and social (e.g. relationship) costs, so long as alternatives on the labour market seem inferior. But pay and status are perhaps overvalued, as becomes clear when people feel released rather than destroyed by redundancy or early retirement. Without underestimating the material and symbolic benefits of work, and pressures to follow conventional working and career patterns, more holistic considerations may motivate people to give priority to other considerations, such as opportunities to be creative, to undertake more fulfilling (e.g. community building) activities and/or to have more positive work relationships.

Critical Thinking and Management Practice

We have noted how mainstream views of management represent it as a technology of goal achievement (Macintyre, 1981). In textbooks and in training courses, management disciplines and skills (e.g. those of selection and appraisal ascribed to Human Resource Management professionals, see Chapter 4) are presented as neutral techniques that guide and empower individual employees to work more effectively.

A major problem for making sense of management is this: 'whether a given manager is effective or not is, on the dominant view, a different question from that of the morality of the ends which his [sic] effectiveness serves or fails to serve' (MacIntyre, 1981: 71). The authority ascribed to managerial techniques and skills acts to exclude subordinates from the opportunity to participate fully in decisions that directly or indirectly affect their working lives. Often obscured by a technical preoccupation with designing and operating systems and procedures, however, are the lives, and life worlds, of employees. In these worlds, moral evaluations – about the trustworthiness of managers' promises (e.g. those made by Syston to his senior managers, see above) – motivate and condition behaviour. In working life, moral judgments are repeatedly made about the acceptability or reasonableness of others' behaviour, including their expectations and their judgments. Explicit and implicit references to moral notions of 'fairness' and 'reasonableness' are routinely invoked by both managers and managed in order to manage expectations and gain a workable measure of agreement. In practice, management unavoidably relies upon a moral (normative) base of understandings that is ignored or obfuscated when wrapped up in the rhetoric of technical rationality, yet is rarely if ever eliminated (Boltanski and Chiapello, 2007).

Management practices assume, promote and reward certain values and behaviour as they frustrate and punish the pursuit of other, competing agendas. When, for example, managers assume the moral virtue[4] and/or effectiveness of particular motivational techniques directed at improving individual performance (e.g. performance-related pay), competitive and egoistic forms of behaviour tend to be induced (Perrow, 1986), often with adverse, unanticipated consequences for morale and cooperation, especially when rewarded individuals (e.g. traders in financial markets) do not pay for the downside of their actions (e.g. major write-downs). Techniques that reward individualistic behaviour perversely fuel the desire for ever more potent ways of feeding the egoism that they breed; and, in this process, the application of those techniques tends to have effects which undermine any efficiency gains that they initially produce (Roberts, 1984). An emphasis upon such techniques also deflects attention from moral–practical concerns about how more rational forms of management and organization might be developed – for example, with respect to the collective nurturing, husbanding and allocation of scarce resources for the improvement of education, housing, health care, etc., as well as to a widening of access to materially and symbolically valued goods.

In critical management studies (CMS), 'best management practice' is not a matter of identifying the most technically rational means of achieving current ends (e.g. profitable growth). Rather, 'best practice' is evaluated in terms of its contribution to the realization of the progressive objectives of social justice, greater autonomy, responsibility, democracy and ecologically sustainable development. In countering apathy and fatalism, critical analysis envisions the possibility of extending emancipation from the overcoming of past domination and oppression (e.g. slavery, employment discrimination, etc.) to address institutionalized forms of oppression within workplaces where there is little or no democratic accountability for how resources are applied; how the divisions of labour are determined; and how tasks are designed, allocated and rewarded. When framed in this way, the responsibility of management is not equated with preserving or improving structures and processes for a better realization of a given, narrow set of objectives. Instead, this responsibility is conceived as a collective task, guided by processes of critical self-reflection concerned with the identification and realization of alternative values and practices that are humanly (and ecologically) more fulfilling and less degrading.

By championing ideas about 'social justice', 'autonomy', 'responsibility', 'democracy', 'sustainability' and 'ecological balance', critical thinking engages in an ongoing struggle with competing views that are hostile to its diagnoses and aspirations. By struggling to mobilize the emancipatory power of human reason, barriers to human cooperation and collective well-being can be brought to consciousness, debated and collectively lowered. Whether or not people, organizations and societies are responsive to the challenges of critical, emancipating thinking is partly a test of the persuasive eloquence of its advocates. The challenge of translating these aspirations into practice is to act in ways that disrupt and counter the dominance of means–ends rationality and the pervasiveness of conservative and reactionary thinking.

When set in this context, this book can be interpreted as an expression of hope: it assumes that more thoughtful organizational practice is possible by pursuing progressive ends and adopting means consistent with their realization. With this aim in mind, diverse traditions of critical thought – including the ideas of Foucault, feminists, labour process analysts and poststructuralists – are welcomed in the process of reflecting upon and fermenting progressive forms of change in contemporary management theory and practice (e.g. O'Doherty and Willmott, 2001; 2009). We do not believe that any particular tradition, such as Critical Theory, has all the answers. Nor would we claim that it can provide more than a partial, supplementary view on issues of management and organization which also involve ongoing efforts to generate positive means–ends relationships and improve technical rationality. The lack of a blueprint for a good 'ratio' between technical and emancipatory concerns and progressive change is perhaps frustrating or disappointing. However, it is consistent with an emphasis upon the self-determination of ends through critical self-reflection, rather than reliance upon an 'authority' – in the form of a technocrat or a charismatic leader – to identify and arrange their delivery.

The Challenge of Change and the Vision of Democracy

The destruction of ecosystems by the dynamism and instability of capitalism stimulates critical reflection and radical action. The globalization of communications has been instrumental in heightening and spreading awareness of the increasing division between the global North and South and the related deterioration of the ecological system. More generally, in the most technologically advanced of modern societies there is a growing 'recognition that science and technology are double-edged: they create new parameters of risk and danger as well as offering beneficent possibilities for humankind' (Giddens, 1991: 28). There is a gathering sense of unease about the avowed rationality of scientific and technical fixes to human problems, including the sophisticated financial engineering at the centre of the global economic crisis of 2008 and, as we noted in the Introduction, the deep drilling for oil resulting in the loss of 11 human lives and ecological disaster visited upon the marine population and communities in the Gulf of Mexico in 2010 (see also Exhibit 2). Economic growth and consumerism trigger not just enthusiasm but also suspicion and opposition. With a measure of scepticism and disillusionment, there has emerged a greater openness to other, diverse sources of authority, including the alternative perspectives fostered or supported by critical social theory and movements for sustainability and global justice.

Exhibit 2   Failure of Management Blamed for BP Gulf of Mexico Blow-Out

A US presidential commission blamed industry failures for last April's rig explosion which killed 11 people and caused one of the worst oil spills in history – also warning they were likely to recur without major reform. BP, Halliburton and Transocean, the three key companies involved with the Macondo well, made

(Continued)

(Continued)

individual decisions that increased risks of a blow-out, but saved significant time or money, the report said. 'Most of the mistakes and oversights at Macondo can be traced back to a single overarching failure – a failure of management,' it concluded. 'Better management by BP, Halliburton and Transocean would almost certainly have prevented the blow-out.'

Source: http: //www.oilspillcommission.gov/chief-counsels-report

It is when the experience of daily living is felt to contradict business practices and values, such as cost cutting which compromises safety, that efforts to question inequalities, injustices and irrationalities are stimulated. Values (e.g. of fairness, meaningful work, community) nurtured in civil society are mobilized to problematize and transform aspects of a system (e.g. exploitation, domination, careerism) that frustrate the realization of those values. Individuals then become collectively mobilized and engaged in struggles to exert control over their future. The principal media of those struggles are social movements:

> Social movements ... are the principal agents in the contemporary struggle for participatory democracy. The emergence of these movements – ecological or 'Green' movements, feminist movements, progressive trade union movements, neighbourhood control movements, consumer cooperatives and worker ownership movements, and so on – represent an uncompromising call in contemporary society for democratic participation and self-management. As alternative movements, they have identified the technocratic system and its apolitical decision-making strategies as primary targets of their countercultural opposition. (Fischer, 1990: 355–6)

For example, following the pollution of the area produced by the blow-out of the BP rig in 2010, Greenpeace activists mounted a protest by scaling another deepwater oil rig, 'Centenario', located in the Gulf of Mexico. They gained media coverage by deploying banners that read 'Stop Deepwater Oil Drilling' and 'Go Beyond Oil'.[5] Despite the difficulties and obstacles encountered in fostering emancipatory change, social movements demonstrate possibilities for promoting moral and political renewal. In these processes, managers can also play a part by supporting all forms of progressive development, in either a professional or personal capacity. It is far too simplistic or convenient to exclude them on the grounds that they are the architects of oppressive, undemocratic practices and/or that they are responsible only to corporate and shareholder priorities. The position and subjectivity of many managers is much more complex, contradictory and open than is suggested by one-dimensional conceptions of their work and allegiances. This is not to deny, as we noted earlier, that managers in the private sector are hired to organize work processes in ways that realize a profit for shareholders or that in the public sector managers are comparatively constrained by budgets and targets. But, as comparatively privileged employees, they nonetheless experience the stress and oppression associated with the controls to which *they* are subjected (e.g. budgets, appraisals, targets, etc.), even if this means that their resistance to socially divisive and ecologically destructive practices, especially in the workplace, is likely to be weaker and (even) more covert.

What managers often lack – and do not find in conventional management textbooks – is a way of making much sense of uncomfortable and/or contradictory experiences – such as the treatment of senior managers by Paul Syston commented upon above. Their limited capacity to make sense of management as a social practice can result in managers becoming hardened, finding rationalizations for their actions or becoming bewildered in the face of employee reactions to their interventions. Consider the example of a plant manager at a major chemicals company described by Nichols and Beynon (1977: 40–3). After reading a leaflet in which managers were called 'pigs', a manager is reported to have said to a fellow colleague: "'*Us* they mean … It's us they're talking about. I'm no pig. I bloody well *care* about what I'm doing"'.

What the manager found hard to bear was being required, as a consequence of a decision made in Head Office, to make a number of workers redundant. He found this difficult – not only because he knew 'that redundancy can be "fucking awful"' (ibid.: 43), but because it led, or forced, him to think of employees as numbers who had to be cajoled or subtly pressured to leave voluntarily. "'You see you find yourself counting: That's fourteen gone. That'll give a bit of space in the system. One of them's changed his mind – the bastard! I don't think I'm like *that* – but you certainly find yourself doing it"' (ibid.).

This manager experienced his work, or at least this aspect of it, as 'a moral problem' although he also found himself translating it into a technical one of fulfilling the quota of volunteers for redundancy. He was confused about the extent of personal responsibility that he bore for 'counting numbers'. In an effort to solve the conundrum, he asked himself what those being made redundant thought. Did they think that he was responsible? "'The thing is I don't think they think it's *me*. I don't think it's *my boss*. They think it's *them*. But we're them. But it's not us. It's something *above* us. Something up there"'.

Nichols and Beynon report that this manager concluded his soliloquy by gazing up at the ceiling. He was at a loss to understand his actions and the extent to which he should take personal responsibility for them. The problem with conventional management textbooks is that such issues are, for the most part, ignored or avoided or consigned to the sub-field of 'business ethics'. In 'business ethics' very little attention is paid to the bigger picture of systemic exploitation and domination. Instead, the focus is upon codes of conduct that, in effect, suggest that complying with the code exhausts manager's responsibility for their actions, and so contributes to a withering of moral sensibility rather than its enhancement. Management is represented as a set of techniques, including codes of conduct and structures of governance, that are presented as functionally necessary forms of 'best practice'. Instead of confronting the positioning of management with capitalist relations of production, the focus is upon the *design* of systems rather than their effects, and upon the *techniques* that professional managers should acquire to ensure their smooth operation, including the procedures and the 'cooling out' scripts to be followed when making employees redundant. The emphasis is upon ensuring the smooth(er) running of 'the machine' by minimizing the likelihood of legal or moral challenge. In short, mainstream textbooks make sense of management as a technology, and not as a social relation involving fundamental political and ethical issues. When confronted directly with his work as a social relation, the plant manager described above was simply at a loss to make sense of it (see also Exhibit 3).

Exhibit 3   Example of Guidance Given to Headteachers Conducting Redundancy Interviews with Staff

... (9) How Much Needs to be Said?

In conveying the decision the Headteacher should be brief and to the point. Don't beat around the bush. Make the opening as clear as possible, perhaps beginning on the basis that 'I am afraid that I have some bad news for you', and then explain exactly what the position is. In doing so it is very important to stress that it is the job which is redundant and not the person. Explain why redundancy is necessary and what selection formula has been used, but do not go into background detail about the circumstances leading up to the decision.

(10) The Length of the Interview

Ten minutes is about right. Experience shows that people are rarely able to take in all of the details immediately anyway, and if there has been effective communication within the Department there will already be a background awareness that redundancies are likely. It is absolutely essential that the employee concerned does receive written details of his or her financial and job position, together with an assurance that they can return for a further interview after the initial shock to clarify any questions they may then have.

Source: Isle of Wight, nd

Over the past two decades or more, much managerial work has itself been intensified and/or rendered increasingly insecure as hierarchies have been somewhat flattened, and restructurings have occurred with ever greater frequency. Career paths have become more uncertain as the comparative safety of specialist, functional 'chimneys' are eroded. In this context, it becomes more apparent that many managers are 'victims' (in terms of additional stress and job loss), and not just 'perpetrators', of the control systems that they design, operate and control. In many cases, insecurity produces greater compliance although, in the context of continuous change, a passive response becomes riskier. Experiences of tension and conflict may also promote critical reflection upon conventional, managerialist diagnoses of, and prescriptions for, managerial work and an associated interest in doing things differently. Such differences of orientation may include challenging and removing oppressive forms of organization, enabling more meaningful forms of employment, and reducing the carbon footprint of organizations.

Making Sense of Management: Unpacking the Received Wisdom

Received wisdom assures us that, as a consequence of processes of rationalization and modernization, contemporary organizations are managed on an ever more rational basis. Managers are portrayed as the heroes of this transformation: 'No job is more vital to our society than that of the manager. It is the manager who determines whether our social institutions serve us well or whether they squander our talents and resources' (Mintzberg, 1975: 61). With the current fashion for leadership, it is now often claimed that 'leaders', and not managers, are the ones who undertake the vital tasks in organizations, even though those doing the leadership are invariably managers or 'executives'. In dominant views, there is very little recognition of leadership in organizations not exercised by managers. The manager–leader distinction is fuzzy, not least for managers (Carroll and Levy, 2008; see also Chapter 4); but it has a rhetorical appeal to the vanity of managers. Representations of managerial work as 'leadership' often reinforce managerialism as an ideology in which knowledge of how to organize is understood to be distilled in the expertise ascribed to managers. The expertise of managers (whether they are referred to as leaders or not), this soothing doctrine of managerialism continues, establishes them as competent and trusted mediators between the claims of a plurality of stakeholders and interest groups – consumers, suppliers and employees as well as employers. Management education, including leadership training, is supposed to equip managers with the specialist expertise required to make decisions that ensure the efficient and effective fulfilment of the needs of organizations and society. Management – especially if it is beefed up or anointed with 'leadership' – provides the golden key to the good society.

The idea that managerial work is guided by the rational calculus of management theory is expressed in the representation of management knowledge as 'science', or at least academically respectable forms of knowing.[6] The linking of management to science and in particular university education, has great ideological appeal as it implies neutrality and authority (see Chapter 2). Strong links to universities and in particular business schools assist in securing the exercise of managerial prerogative without any wider social accountability. The so-called sciences of management are abstracted from the cultural and historical contexts of their conception and application. Teachers and practitioners of management are then spared the unsettling realization that the very formulation of 'scientific' management theories, as well as their implementation, occur within politically charged, value-laden contexts. When managers are considered to have access to the academic body of knowledge for managing complex systems, as distilled in business degrees, the logical conclusion to be drawn is that they must be allowed to apply this knowledge without much hindrance.

Yet, paradoxically, it is precisely inexact, contextually sensitive forms of knowledge that are often most valued and celebrated by practising managers who are sceptical about forms of knowledge that claim to have universal applicability. A premium is placed upon 'gut knowledge' and 'feel' that lacks or defies 'scientific' justification. Texts that are attentive to the trickier aspects of practice – such as the politics of management – are often deemed to be most 'realistic' by practitioners, as long as they embrace a managerialism agenda, and so not reflect too deeply on the legitimacy of managerial prerogative.

But most management texts – textbooks, pop-business writings but also many research texts – disregard the trickier aspects of practice. As Susman and Evered (1978: 584) have observed, 'Many of the findings in our scholarly management journals are only remotely related to the real world of practising managers and to the actual issues with which members of organizations are concerned, especially when research has been carried out by the most rigorous methods of the prevailing conception of science.' In a similar vein, Bedeian (1989), when speaking as the President of the American Academy of Management, has referred to the mountain of 'mindless research' that 'often restates the obvious'. If management academics persist in being mindless, he concludes, they 'will continue to deserve the criticism so commonly sent our way by the popular press' (ibid.: 14). If, as the observations of Bedeian indicate, much academic research on management has little immediate practical relevance for managers, it is relevant to ask why such 'mindless' research continues to be funded by government and business.

In addressing this question, it is relevant to note how, as areas of academic enquiry and as forms of social practice, management and organization are not only fuzzy and ambiguous but also continuously under (re)construction. They are shaped and changed by shifts in the social and economic conditions that form the corporate landscape over time (Boltanski and Chiapello, 2007). Such changes are brought about in part by the diffusion of management knowledge. As management knowledge is taken to be authoritative, it has truth effects as new social realities are produced. As a consequence, it is most unlikely that studies of management will deliver precise or stable results. In our view, this limitation does not imply that little can be learned from empirical studies or from theories. On the contrary, these can inform, enrich and challenge our understanding, but only when we maintain a critical distance from their claims. It is important to be aware of how, in most areas of management, a diversity of perspectives and theories have been developed that commend different and contradictory diagnoses and recipes for change. Appreciating the significance of debates and productive conflicts about management knowledge is integral to developing a critical perspective (Palmer and Hardy, 2000).

Advocates and sponsors of research carried out using what are regarded as 'the most rigorous methods of the prevailing conception of science' (Susman and Evered, 1978: 584) may believe that, eventually, their findings will justify the investment by delivering universal truths and reliable recipes for success. Evidence of resistance to such knowledge by managers (and by scholars who are less bullish about their knowledge claims) may be interpreted by its producers as evidence of 'pre-' or 'un-scientific' or 'unprofessional' thinking for which the obvious remedy is additional research and better training. A rather different interpretation of why research based upon a conception of science attributable to the physical sciences continues to attract support from funders and the gatekeepers of management scholarship is not simply because of a naïve belief in its emulation of the physical sciences but because the scientization of management bestows upon management a valuable – even magical – aura. In doing this, it conveys the image of impartial experts whose prerogative is strongly associated with, if not as yet firmly founded upon, scientifically respectable bodies of knowledge (Thomas, 1993). As Pfeffer has commented:

> It is certainly nobler to think of oneself as developing skills toward the more efficient allocation and use of resources – implicitly for the greater good of society as a whole – than to think of oneself as engaged with other organizational participants in a political struggle over values, preferences and definitions of technology. (1981: 12)

Much, even all, academic research on management is disdainfully viewed as useless mumbo-jumbo by practitioners who see little that is relevant or meaningful in its baroque representation within the most highly regarded academic journals. Such research is nonetheless supported, or at least tolerated, because its association with science, and in particular with the university (and the business school), however spurious, provides the 'expertise' of management with a valuable veneer of authority and respectability. Just as reports by management consultants serve to legitimize decisions by executives whose impartiality might otherwise have been questioned, 'scientific' research in management lends legitimacy to the work of managers and serves to justify managerial prerogative and privilege. This is not to deny that some managers may find some management research of relevance to their careers. But, in general, it seems to be valued only when it is packaged and presented in a manner that renders it accessible, and its lessons are formulated in less abstract and cautious ways, e.g. in pop-management texts with brash titles such as *In Search of Excellence* or *From Good to Great*, offering easily digested blueprints for delivering corporate peak performance(s). What remains problematic, however, is the conversion of academic research into usable, managerially acceptable techniques that, aside from their preoccupation with providing quick fixes for practitioners, take little account of the particular contexts and wider consequences of their application.

Making Sense of Management: Sketching a Critical Perspective

In response to our criticisms of mainstream accounts of management, it could be objected that they present a comparatively easy target for critical analysis. Our defence is that reputable textbooks and journals are the basic storehouses of contemporary understanding of management, so they are important and legitimate targets of criticism. That said, it is necessary to acknowledge and address conceptions of management which diverge, in various ways, from the received wisdom. In this section, we concentrate upon work that begins to take into account how management theory and practice are shot through with ideology and politics.

'Progressive' Conceptions of Management and the Extension of Technocracy

A conventional criticism of established, classical conceptions of management is that they fail to recognize how, in practice, management decision making is 'bounded' by limited information, limited brain power and by pressures to reach 'closure' before all options are thoroughly subjected to rational scrutiny and evaluation (March and Simon, 1958). This criticism usefully draws attention to the practicalities of managerial work in which the ('rational', 'scientific') process of reaching optimal decisions is compromised by the intrusion of 'realities' that will not wait for the optimal solution.

Later studies have extended this criticism to argue that decision making is affected by managers' particular allegiances, preconceptions, preoccupations and hunches (Pettigrew, 1973). It is their recipes and 'biases' that, in part, compensate for lack of timely information and a limited capacity to process information, and so are seen to account for deviations from the formal, rationalist logic of classical management theory.[7] The role of 'hunches' and 'gut feel', is, from a rational standpoint, symptomatic of an 'unscientific' legacy, and this invites a redoubling of scientific efforts to place decision making upon a sound basis. However, it may be doubted whether it is ever possible to cleanse such processes and remove such influences considering that management is a social, not a technical, practice. From this perspective, managerial decision making is seen to be 'an essentially political process in which constraints and opportunities *are functions of the power exercised by decision-makers in the light of ideological values*' (Child, 1972: 16, emphasis added).

Studies that pay attention to the politics of organizational decision making and the conditioning of managerial work by ideological values, including the self-preservation of managers, provide a valuable counterbalance to the over-rationalized textbook picture of management. Yet, studies that focus upon the micropolitics of management are often limited in their critical penetration as they proceed as if the question of 'management for what?' were either self-evident or beyond debate. Their limitations become evident when they simply extend the technocratic range of management theory to the rational control of values. Their technocratic message to managers is that they should learn to become more aware of how values shape their perceptions, and/or appreciate the operation of organizational politics, as this would enable them to act more effectively. As Pettigrew (1985: 314–6, emphasis added) writes:

> Changing business strategies has to involve a process of *ideological and political change* that eventually releases a new concept of strategy that is culturally acceptable within a newly appreciated context. In the broadest sense, this means, prescriptively, that step one in a change process should be to improve and build upon any natural processes of change by tackling questions such as how existing processes can be speeded up, how the conditions that determine people's interpretations of situations can be altered, and how contexts can be mobilized toward legitimate problems and solutions along the way to move the organization additively in a different strategic direction.

Analysis and prescriptions for managerial work may pay some attention to what Pettigrew terms 'ideological and political change'. All too often, however, such attention is narrowly focused upon 'ideological and political' aspects of organizing simply as a means of smoothing a process of top-down change. Established priorities are on the whole assumed to be legitimate. Proposed 'change' addresses means but not ends.[8] Insights into the context and dynamics of organizational change are not prized for their capacity to stimulate debate upon the legitimacy of current priorities. Instead, these insights are selectively developed and engaged as a technology geared to minimizing conflict associated with taking 'a different strategic direction'. The emphasis is upon bolstering established means and recipes of management control (e.g. bureaucratic rules and procedures) through the strategic (re) engineering of employee thinking and values in line with the 'new concept of strategy' and the 'legitimate problems and solutions' – as identified by top management or their consultants and mainstream academics. It might be asked: 'what is wrong with that?' Our answer is that it is inadequate insofar as it disregards the wider context of institutionalized power relations in which management practice is embedded. It also perpetuates a philosophy of management in which an expedient concern to maintain the status quo (e.g. by managing the values of employees) displaces any concern with the transformation of work organizations in the direction of increased democracy and collective self-determination.

The Case of 'Tech'

The mobilization of cultural means of controlling employees (including managers) is studied in depth by Gideon Kunda (1992) in his research on 'Tech', a company celebrated by commentators for its creativity and progressive, people-oriented style of management. The following excerpt is illustrative of how employees at Tech are surrounded by, and continuously subjected to, a distinct and integrated corporate culture:

Tom O'Brien has been around the company for a while; like many others, he has definite ideas about 'Tech Culture'. ... But, as he is constantly reminded, so does the company. When he arrives at work, he encounters evidence of the company point of view at every turn. ... Inside the building where he works, just beyond the security desk, a large television monitor is playing a videotape of a recent speech by Sam Miller (the founder and president). As Tom walks by, he hears the familiar voice discuss 'our goals, our values, and the way we do things'. ... As he sits down in his office space, Tom switches on his terminal. ... On his technet mail he notices among the many communications another announcement of the afternoon events: a memo titled, 'How Others See Our Values', reviewing excerpts on Tech Culture from recent managerial bestsellers. ... In his mail, he finds *Techknowledge*, one of the company's newsletters. On the cover is a big picture of Sam Miller against the background of a giant slogan – 'We Are One'. He also finds an order form for company publications, including Ellen Cohen's *Culture Operating Manual*. ... The day has hardly begun, yet Tom is already surrounded by 'the culture', the ever-present signs of the company's explicit concern with its employees' state of mind (and heart). (ibid.: 50–2)

This passage conveys the idea of Tech as an institution in which employees are continuously bombarded by positive images of the company and messages about what is expected of them. Employees are not, however, necessarily submissive participants in processes of corporate brainwashing. Unlike the automatons portrayed in Orwell's *Nineteen Eighty-Four* or Huxley's *Brave New World*, employees bring alternative values and priorities to their work. Through processes of distancing and irony, Tech employees are able to expose and deflate the use of high sounding corporate rhetoric and thereby counteract the strategic engineering of norms and values. That said, Kunda's study also discloses a darker side of Tech's corporate culture. Tech culture readily accommodates and exploits a degree of employee wilfulness and resistance – in the form of the parodying of values and expectations. Indeed, Tech employees were not discouraged from interpreting tolerant ridiculing of Tech ideology as a confirmation of the company's ostensibly liberal ethos.

   The most pervasive and insidious effect of Tech culture was its repressive tolerance of dissent (Marcuse, 1964). Tech's capacity to accommodate and disarm its critics, Kunda suggests, was more effective in stifling organized forms of resistance than a more coercive, heavy-handed approach that would have aroused resistance: 'in the name of humanism, enlightenment and progress, the engineers of Tech culture elicit the intense efforts of employees not by stirring their experiential life, but, if anything, by degrading and perhaps destroying it' (Kunda, 1992: 224–5). Kunda shows how modern ideologies – humanism, enlightenment and progress – are mobilized, often in subliminal ways, to legitimize demands upon employees (see Fleming, 2009). Yet, despite the repressive tolerance engendered by Tech culture, the frustrations and psychological degradations experienced by its employees prompted many of them to develop and amplify countervailing images of this seemingly benevolent organization. These were, however, seldom integrated into a coherent and clear stance. Instead, employees expressed distance and irony, which functioned more like a safety mechanism, blowing off some steam, while affirming the liberal ethos nurtured by senior management. In effect, Tech employees, including its managers, mainly acted out the corporate requirements of a strong overt commitment to the organization, regardless of what they thought privately. They worked very hard and, on the whole, were resigned to their fate of becoming exhausted and burned-out. (Such 'decaf resistance' (Contu, 2009), pseudo-resistance or faking autonomy is not uncommon – see Fleming and Spicer, 2003; Kärreman and Alvesson, 2009.)

Management control is rarely based entirely upon seeking the active consent, as contrasted with conditional compliance, of the managed. As a consequence, managers develop forms of inducement and punishment through which they strive to minimize forms of misbehaviour, resistance and dissent. Wherever inequalities are not founded upon unforced consent, it is necessary to develop ideologies (e.g. the prerogative of management to manage based upon their superior, impartial expertise) that aspire to justify the exclusion of 'the managed' from participating in making decisions (and meanings) that directly affect their lives. Such ideologies legitimize technocracy – a system of (corporate) governance 'in which technically trained experts rule by virtue of their specialized knowledge and position in dominant political and economic institutions' (Fischer, 1990: 17).

The paradox of post-classical, 'progressive' management texts and ideologies – which emphasize a loosening bureaucratic control and managerial supervision in favour of greater self-discipline – is that they simultaneously go some way towards debunking the rationalist pretensions of conventional management thinking *and* facilitate the application of more sophisticated technologies of control that, in principle, serve to extend the jurisdiction of management. Such ostensibly 'progressive' interventions aspire, and serve, to advance and legitimize an expansion of management's manipulation of elements of culture and identity in order to expand and strengthen systems of control. Their ways of making (sense of) management exclude sustained consideration of how, historically, the objectives and functions of management are defined, refined and pursued through processes of moral and political struggle.

Managers as Agents and Targets of Instrumental Reason

The moral and political dimensions of managerial work are illustrated by Jackall's *Moral Mazes* (1988) which explores how managers deal with dissonance between their personal values and the demands of the corporation to transgress these values (see also Dalton, 1959). The dissonance is routinely attenuated, Jackall argues, by complying with 'what the guy above you wants from you' (ibid.: 6). What (s)he wants is not just compliance with organizational rules or values but a *particular form* of compliance that safeguards their power and status, yet which can be plausibly represented as congruent with corporate rules (accepted techniques and procedures). This compliance co-exists, and often overlaps with, a strong focus on instrumentality: 'technique and procedure tend to become ascendant over substantive reflection about organizational goals … *Even at higher levels of management, one sees ample evidence of an overriding emphasis on technique rather than on critical reasoning'* (Jackall, 1988: 76, emphasis added). In other words, 'what the guy above you wants from you' is privileged so as to curry favour with him or her, but in a manner that affirms its legitimacy in terms of compliance with available techniques and procedures. Actions are then based upon the demands of superordinates and conformity with technical considerations without regard to a wider set of concerns or any ambition to develop independent thinking. It is worth noting how this emphasis upon technique and procedure receives widespread approval from shareholders (and, in the public sector, from politicians). That is because compliance with their procedural requirements promises to limit the otherwise ill-defined boundaries of managerial discretion.

However, endorsement of a technocratic ideology does not place managers in an unequivocally secure position. The logic of neutrality 'demands' that managerial work is to be subjected to the same rationalizing processes that managers visit upon their subordinates (Clarke et al., 2009; Smith, 1990). Even without the development of powerful information technologies, which have eliminated the work of many supervisors and managers, programmes of employee involvement and corporate-culture strengthening require the internalization of supervisory responsibilities among multi-skilled, self-disciplined operatives. As some of the responsibility for managing and checking subordinates' work is devolved to workers, there is less need for managers who have been the targets of de-layering in 'lean', 'reengineered' organizations. Insofar as managers accept and internalize a technocratic ideology, they are ill-prepared to make sense of, let alone resist, developments that pose a threat to their very existence. Management and managing is, in short, bedevilled by tensions and contradictions that mainstream management is largely impotent to acknowledge and address.[9]

Conclusion

Supplying an answer to the question 'what is management?' is by no means as straightforward as many texts on management are inclined to suggest. Received wisdom takes it for granted that the social divisions between managers and managed are either natural (e.g. based upon superior intelligence and education) and/or functionally necessary. Conceiving of management in this way is symptomatic of sense-making that conflates management as a *social* practice with a body of *technical* expertise. As Knights and Murray (1994: 31) observe, 'a great deal of managerial practice constructs a reality of its own activity that denies the *political* quality of that practice.' As we have sought to show, such denial is itself central to the institutionalized politics of management where 'the political' is suppressed by being normalized as the prerogative of experts. In other words, silencing consideration of the political formation and application of management knowledge and practice is integral to bestowing legitimacy upon managers.

When the 'political quality' of management practice is denied, the costs – personal, social and ecological – of enhancing growth, productivity, quality and profit are disregarded. Scant attention is paid to the increase in stress, the loss of autonomy in work, the cultivation of consumerist values or the degradation of the environment – all of which are associated with the drive for 'efficient management'. Indeed, there is a well-rehearsed response to anyone who raises such issues which runs along the following lines: business is responsible for the production of wealth; personal, social and ecological problems are the preserve of individuals and governments; and government has the task of developing viable, effective (and preferably minimal) forms of regulation to facilitate (fair) competition. When some wider responsibility of corporations is acknowledged (e.g. toxic impact, inadequate supervision or inappropriate incentives), it is claimed that many problems have come to light only recently; and that experts will, in due course, ensure their correction. Or that better management – perhaps cultivated by business ethics statements, corporate social responsibility initiatives or moves from 'management' to 'leadership' – will address these concerns.

Conventional wisdom invites us to celebrate the contribution of management to corporate and national wealth and to the satisfaction of people's needs for employment, job satisfaction, goods and so forth. We are urged to regard managerial work as a positive and central feature of modern, pluralistic societies. Management knowledge is equated with rationality as the basis of the good society. Rarely is the darker side of management acknowledged, and then it is presented as an aberrant deviation from a normal, beneficial and sustainable state of affairs. Knowledge of management is overwhelming *for* management, not an examination *of* management.

Of course, it is highly likely that the opposite complaint – namely, that we have little to say about the brighter side of management theory – will be levelled against this text. Critical writing books, like this, are in the genre of tragedies, and paint a gloomy, even depressing view of things (Fineman, 2006). We acknowledge the difficulty of achieving a balanced view of management that is neither simply 'pro' or 'anti' (see also Spicer et al., 2009). The difficulty of attaining such balance, we believe, can be related to the contradictions of management theory and practice discussed earlier. 'Balance' is in the eye of the beholder. From a perspective that values critical reflection as a key resource for democracy, ecological stewardship and sustainability, mainstream management thinking is self-serving for a status quo that systematically subverts these values. Such thinking invites, or provokes, the development of an *antithesis* that is outrightly hostile to management in any shape or form. We have distanced our analysis from what we regard as a utopian position that rejects the possibility of management having any legitimate place in democratic organizations; and that calls for the elimination of management as the only progressive course of action. We are certainly not against management; indeed as senior academics we are to some extent engaged in it and believe it is an important part of contemporary life that we need to think positively *and* critically about. Some ideas intended as a contribution to a *synthesis* are sketched in Chapters 7 and 8. For the moment, it may be helpful to summarize a number of the central understandings, themes and concerns of this text.

- *Management is a social practice.* Its content, both theoretical and practical, is embedded in the historical and cultural relations of power and domination (e.g. capitalism, patriarchy) that enable/impede its emergence and development.

- *Mainstream thinking* represents management practices as objective/impartial/scientific/ technically superior. It normalizes and obfuscates how power relations shape the formation and organization of management.
- *Tensions exist* between the lived reality of management as a politically charged process and its 'official' representation as a set of impartial techniques for directing and coordinating human and material resources.
- *Critical studies of management* recognize, expose and examine these tensions. Instead of seeking to mitigate the tensions through the refinement of techniques, often sanctified by appeals to 'science', 'humanism' and so on, critical studies anticipate the possibility of resolving them through a transformation of social relations (e.g. changing the mind-sets and institutions that foster patriarchal practices or ecological damage).
- *Critical studies are also a product of prevailing relations of power.* The existence of critical studies is dependent upon tensions (see above) which stimulate reflection upon conventional theory and practice. The embeddedness of critical thinking in power relations renders its own claims partial and provisional.
- *Critical studies may reconstruct received wisdom* (e.g. about management). Reconstruction provides an alternative body of knowledge but without any necessary change either in the person (e.g. a manager) who adopts this analysis or in their practical actions.
- *Reconstruction becomes critique* when it inspires and guides processes of personal and social transformation.
- *Critical studies seek to illuminate and transform institutions and social relations* despite being embedded in these relations. Such studies provide alternative frameworks for interpreting the practices of management, and facilitate a process of radical change as envisaged and struggled for by progressive social movements.
- *Emancipatory transformation occurs as people change*, personally or collectively, by changing habits and institutions that impede the development of greater autonomy and responsibility. Responsibility depends upon the practical realization of the interdependence of human beings and our interdependence with nature. Autonomy depends upon the development of institutions in which individualism is problematized and minimized, thereby allowing the unimpeded realization of interdependence.

In the place of self-serving images of managers – as impartial experts, 'go-getters' and 'do-gooders' – it is vital to attend to the pressures that lead management to be in the business of the unremitting exploitation of nature and human beings. Their work results in national and international extremes of wealth and poverty, the creation of global pollution, the promotion of 'needs' for consumer products, etc. Caught in the maelstrom of capitalist organization, managers are urged or induced to emulate, normalize and reward all kinds of manipulative and destructive behaviour. As Shrivastava (1994b: 238) has observed of mainstream management thinking, 'it is widely believed that corporations are generally beneficial, neutral, technological "systems of production" that equally serve the interests of many stakeholders ... This assumption ignores the destructive aspects of corporate activities.' 'Greenwashing', where corporations manage an impression of ecological concern to conceal their destructive impact, is perhaps a particularly nauseating example of the abuse of corporate powers (Jermier and Forbes, 2003). Another is the dedicated follower of fashions, brands and lifestyles, who defines him or herself through commercial and consumerist discourses and is narcissistically preoccupied with a fluctuating and vulnerable sense of self, targeted by ads and promotions pointing at discrepancies between ideals of perfection and glamour, and the imperfections of body and actual appearance.

The capacity of human beings to reflect and think critically makes it possible to question the direction of mainstream management theory and practice and to challenge its self-justifications. In principle, management could be dedicated to providing a basic level of primary goods for the world's population, acting in ways that are ecologically sound and facilitating processes of collective self-determination. All too often, however, the social and ecological destructiveness of contemporary management practice is pursued by appealing to a rhetoric of 'progress', 'efficiency' and, most recently, 'ethics'. This provokes critical reflection in response to pathological consequences of 'progress': the gross exploitation of natural and unrenewable resources and associated pollution; extreme and obscene inequalities of wealth and opportunity, nationally and internationally; and institutionalized discrimination on the basis of gender, ethnicity, age and so on. The contradictory effects of mainstream management theory and practice stimulate alternative visions and struggles for a more rational social and economic order. Precisely because capitalism is so productive in generating wealth, yet systemically incapable of distributing its bounty to those most disadvantaged by its operation, diverse forms of 'critical publicity' continue to be thrown up – most recently by the strength of ecological and 'global-justice' movements.

Integral to the emancipatory intent of critical thinking is a vision of a different form of management: one that is more democratically accountable to all whose lives are affected by management decisions. From this perspective, management and organizations become substantively rational only when governed through decision-making processes that take direct account of the will and priorities[10] of diverse stakeholders who include employees, consumers and citizens – rather than being dependent upon the priorities of an elite of self-styled experts, both financial and managerial. These priorities cannot, however, be taken at face value: key to functioning democracy is ambitious critical reflection and dialogue (Deetz, 1992a). It would be contradictory to anticipate the precise (re)form of management in advance of its development by democratic processes. What can be said with some confidence, however, is that those responsible for developing and implementing its functions will, of necessity, be attentive and accountable to the concerns and values of a much wider constituency than is presently the case.

 Notes

1   The two major strands in the initial development of critical management theory have been Labour Process Analysis (LPA: Thompson, 2009) and Critical Theory (see Alvesson, 1987; Scherer, 2009). In LPA, management is analysed as a medium of control which secures the exploitation of labour by capital (Braverman, 1974;

Knights and Willmott, 1990). In Critical Theory, management is studied more in relation to the domination of technocratic thinking and practices, and the associated emasculation of critical thinking, autonomy and democratic decision making, and not in terms of the logic of the capital–labour relation that makes the organized working class its agent of revolutionary transformation. See Chapter 2 for a fuller discussion of Critical Theory.

2   Hierarchical organization can be of value in coordinating complex, technical divisions of labour when it has a democratic mandate. What is problematical is not hierarchical organization *per se* – to a degree this is necessary and productive, at least in large organizations (see du Gay, 1994) – but there is often unjustifiable reliance upon it (Child, 2009). It is also used to bolster and institutionalize structures of class, gender and ethnic domination.

3   Watson (1994) relates how, following individual interviews with their new boss, Paul Syston, a number of the managers reported that he had said very little and had given them scant indication of his plans.

4   In this case, 'moral virtue' is framed in terms of the justice of ensuring that the highest performing individuals receive the highest rewards, thereby eliminating the morally indefensible payment of 'free riders'.

5   See   http://www.greenpeace.org/international/en/news/features/Activist-occupy-centenario221110/?utm_source=feedburner&utm_medium=feed&utm_campaign=Feed%3A+greenpeace%2Fallblogs+%28Greenpeace+Blog+Aggregator%3A+All+our+blogs+in+one+feed%29.

6   Even where the term 'science' is not explicitly used, or where management is presented as a 'practice' mediated by diverse cultural values and political systems, the basic message is maintained. As Drucker (1977: 25), a leading management guru, expresses this understanding: 'The management function, the work of management, its tasks and its dimensions are universal and do not vary from country to country.'

7   In part, this development was stimulated by the internationalizing of management and the rapid economic growth of Asian economies, which have fostered a growing awareness of how management practices are embedded in and expressive of national cultures. An emergent knowledge of management practices in other countries, notably Japan in the 1970s and 1980s, made it increasingly difficult to believe that practices which appear 'irrational' from a Western standpoint pose any significant obstacle to achieving the conventional goal of profitable growth (see Pascale and Athos, 1982).

8   For example, in business schools, the inclusion of electives in 'business ethics' or the espousal of (pseudo) 'participative styles' of managing tends to exemplify rather than challenge the acquisition and application of abstract techniques and idealized prescriptions.

9   For example, the strengthening of corporate culture, which encourages employees to identify more closely with the mission of their organization, may succeed insofar as a stronger sense of collective purpose assuages individual employees' experience of vulnerability and insecurity. However, there remain underlying

tensions between the collectivist ideas disseminated by the gurus of corporate culture and deeply embedded Enlightenment beliefs in 'individual freedom' and, more specifically, the operation of 'free' labour markets and individual competitiveness. In the West, the use of labour markets to achieve work discipline creates and promotes the moral vacuum and individualistic behaviour that corporate culture seeks to correct without changing the conditions that operate to undermine the effectiveness of this stratagem as a medium of management control. The limits of individualistic Western management thinking and practice are well illustrated by the departure of Japanese companies from a number of Western management's supposedly 'rational' principles. Locke (1989: 50–1) relates the paradoxical success of this deviation to the absence in Japanese history of an equivalent to Western Enlightenment. As a consequence, Locke argues, 'the Japanese worker does not think of himself as engaged in an economic function (being an electrical engineer, a production engineer, lathe operator, accountant, etc.) which is divorced from the firm, an occupational function that can be done anywhere. He is a Hitachi man, a Honda man, and so on, a member of a community' (ibid.). The Western worker, in contrast, lacks a deeply engrained ethic that binds each individual, morally as well as economically, to his or her employing organization.

10 As we argue and elaborate in subsequent chapters of this book, it is also important not to take expressions of this will and its priorities at face value, but to probe more deeply by encouraging critical reflection upon, and communication about, 'needs' and 'interests' attributed to human beings.

2

Critical Thinking

Forms of Knowledge and the Limits of Critique

The development of modern Western societies has been shaped by two dominating powers: capitalism and science. A critical basis for analysing capitalism was established by Marx. His analysis included some reflections upon the historical potency of scientific thinking for capitalist development but it was largely restricted to an appreciation of its applications in industrializing the labour process, and thereby securing the subsumption of labour under pressures for accumulation. Comparatively overlooked or taken for granted by Marx was the revolutionary but *equivocal* role of scientific thinking in 'modernizing' the world by debunking received wisdoms and dismissing knowledge claims that could not be empirically proven as normative or 'ideological'. The power and equivocality of science was addressed more directly by the other colossus of social theory, Max Weber.

This chapter explores the relationship between knowledge, values and power. At its centre are the questions of what counts as scientific knowledge and what are the limits of its authority. We are concerned with such questions because, in modern societies, science has become established as the dominant source of authoritative knowledge. Science also promotes the view that objective, value-free knowledge is attainable. This understanding, which is as dangerous as it is questionable, underpins the technocratic thinking that lends a spurious credibility to managerial expertise, as discussed in Chapter 1. In effect, the aura of science is invoked, more or less explicitly, to inhibit or suppress debate about the value of particular ends as well as the values incorporated in the claimed rationality of the means.

The idea of value-free knowledge deflects attention from how, in practice, what counts as 'scientific knowledge' is the product of value judgments that are conditioned by specific historical and cultural contexts. Whatever grandiose claims may be made for science, its knowledge remains a contingent product of the particular values that give it meaning and direction. It is for this reason that it makes little sense to counterpose 'science' to 'ideology' – as if it were possible to generate impartial, non-ideological knowledge about an independently given world. Instead, the term ideology is more appropriately applied to knowledge that makes (inflated) claims to be neutral, acontextual, 'incontrovertible', etc.

We begin by considering the view that social science is, or should be, value-free. We believe that criticizing this view is important because it continues to have a seductive yet perilous appeal, and not least among management academics who, since the publication of Taylor's *Principles of Scientific Management* (1911), have endeavoured to revise his thinking rather than contest its scientific aspirations. An appreciation of the principled but ultimately misguided advocacy of value-free science, notably by Max Weber, is, we believe, helpful in illuminating key issues and problems that bedevil claims to produce objective knowledge. *Challenging the idea of value-free science is of crucial importance to critical studies of management because, in the absence of this challenge, critical science is dismissed as normative, value-laden ideology.* In place of this binary division, we commend an understanding of how different value-commitments, analysed in terms of contrasting combinations of assumptions about science and society, are productive of different forms of knowledge. To illuminate this stance, we draw upon the influential paradigm framework developed by Burrell and Morgan (1979). We commend their relativization of a single, positivist/functionalist 'paradigm' of organization science but we reject their claim that knowledge can be neatly divided into four watertight, 'incommensurable' paradigms. Instead, we advocate a modified version of Habermas' (1972) theory of cognitive interests. We conclude the chapter by surveying some themes and issues that are central to critical theorizing.

The Limits of Scientific Knowledge

There is a widely held belief that science, including management science, can produce objective knowledge by removing all 'subjective bias' and forms of interference from 'non-rational' cultural ideas. When armed with the objective facts, there is a rational and therefore legitimate basis for organizing and managing people in accordance with scientific, rather than arbitrary or partisan, principles. That Taylor (1911) dubbed his principles of work organization 'scientific' was no accident; he fervently believed that he had identified universally valid principles for eliminating the irrationality of custom and practice from processes of production and methods of management.[1] Many contemporary followers of Taylor (e.g. Hammer and Champy, 1993), called 'McDonaldizers' by Ritzer (1996), have sought to refine his technocratic vision – often by incorporating more sophisticated theories of human motivation and group dynamics – without doubting the wisdom or coherence of the impulse to perfect the scientific control of human productivity.

The use of scientific thinking to promote and legitimize all kinds of 'dehumanizing', divisive and destructive social technologies has prompted critics of such technocratic reasoning to question its presuppositions and effects. The very idea that management can be made scientific – extolled in the notion of 'management science' – arouses anxiety about how scientific knowledge could be (mis)used, by being invoked to 'prove' the objective superiority of particular values and their associated programmes, Taylor's Scientific Management being a case in point.

That said, advocates of science may themselves be ambivalent about its powers. Notably, Weber celebrates science as a powerful, positive force for dispelling myths and prejudices. Its revelations are understood to strip away preconceptions and prejudices to expose what, for Weber, are the unvarnished facts. By drawing upon scientific findings, Weber argues, modern individuals can become less deluded about themselves and their world. With the benefit of factual, social scientific knowledge, people can better calculate how their commitment to particular values may be more effectively fulfilled. In these respects, social scientific knowledge is seen to make a potent contribution to the fulfilment of individual and social responsibility as well as to the quality of life. And yet, Weber was deeply worried by the disenchanting and corrosive effects of scientific knowledge upon established traditions and moral values. For this reason, he insists upon a clear-headed appreciation of the *limits* of scientific authority. Wherever these limits are ignored or inadequately appreciated, he cautions, the debunking power of science is destructive of institutions and practices (e.g. religion, the arts) which are highly fulfilling and meaningful for those who participate in them, even though they lack scientific defensibility. For Weber, what is meaningful, however irrational it appears from a scientific standpoint, is ultimately more valuable than what is scientifically credible. In the absence of this understanding of the limits of sciences, Weber anticipated the development of a narrowly rationalized, disenchanted and dispirited world.

Weber valuably points to the destructive as well as the enlightening aspects of scientific knowledge. Science can be a positive force, he contends, only when its limits are fully appreciated and respected. Accordingly, he insists upon distinguishing sharply between (i) producing facts by investigating the 'portion of existing concrete reality (that) is coloured by our value-conditioned interest' (Weber, 1949: 82) and (ii) making value-judgments about the merits of social institutions. Science, according to Weber, simply produces the facts. It cannot require the individual to accept these facts or to comply with their demands if these contradict the ultimate values to which s/he is committed. This is something that Taylor (see above) and his successors ignore when they regard workers as 'recalcitrant' who fail to comply with 'best practices' that are proven by scientific studies to be efficient or effective. The key point, for Weber, is that values can never be disproved by scientific knowledge. The question of how individuals choose between different possible ends, or value commitments, is 'entirely a matter of choice and compromise. There is no (rational or empirical) scientific procedure of any kind whatsoever which can provide us with a decision here' (Weber, 1949: 67). There is, in other words, no scientific way of adjudicating between competing values and associated norms of behaviour. Views about life 'can never be the products of increasing empirical knowledge' (Weber, 1968: 576; see also Weber, 1948: 143).

Weber connects the value of scientific knowledge to processes of self-formation whereby human beings wrestle with the claims of competing values in an effort to give meaning and purpose to their lives (see Willmott, 1993b). He does not want scientific knowledge to weaken or prematurely terminate this self-formation process – which in many respects parallels that of critical self-reflection (see Chapter 1) but he is primarily concerned with individual maturation rather than collective emancipation. For Weber, scientific knowledge is dangerous when it is (mis)understood to provide the only authoritative answer to how to live, and so displaces the uniquely and fundamental human responsibility for making an informed but ultimately irrational commitment to particular values and associated courses of action. The danger is that scientific knowledge is grasped and applied in a way that short–circuits the process of self-formation – for example, by suggesting that only one way of organizing work is 'scientific' and, by implication, that alternatives are irrational, and so must be rejected. This kind of (technocratic) reasoning is dehumanizing because, as Weber stresses, human actions involve the exercise of (responsible) judgment in relation to competing value commitments – a responsibility that cannot be replaced by scientific knowledge however authoritative it may claim, or seem, to be. From this perspective, science can legitimately inform us about the likely implications of particular choices but it cannot remove from individuals the distinctively human responsibility for choosing between competing ultimate values.

Weber's conception of the nature and limits of science is important because it challenges the (ab)use of scientific (or technocratic) knowledge, including 'scientific Marxism', to support or legitimate particular values or projects (e.g. the replacement of elected politicians, however worthy or scandalous, by technocrats – as is happening in Greece and Italy as we check the proofs of this text). More specifically, Weber's understanding of science questions the legitimacy of technocratic decision making that is (erroneously) justified by allusions and appeals to the scientific authority of experts. It insists that decisions are ultimately political (and ethical), and not technical or scientific, in determination. When commenting upon the common misconception that an accumulation of facts or 'evidence' can resolve choices between values, Weber observes that:

> If the notion that (value-) standpoints can be derived from the 'facts themselves' continually recurs, it is due to the naïve self-deception of the specialist who is unaware that it is due to the evaluative ideas with which he unconsciously approaches his [sic] subject matter, that he has selected from an absolute infinity a tiny portion with the study of which he *concerns* himself. (Weber, 1949: 82, emphasis in original)

We might, for example, think of the manager who, looking at a set of accounts, declares that 'the facts speak for themselves' when seeking to justify the need for additional investment or when making a case for compulsory redundancies. Or we might think of the politician, or the management consultant, who declares that executives intent upon making changes but who lack support 'often have no choice in how they deal with those attempting to impede their efforts' (Hammer, 1994: 47). Such claims are bogus because, no matter how many facts are accumulated about a particular subject (e.g. management), they will be insufficient in themselves to adjudicate between different value-standpoints. The denial of choice is an assertion of power, not of rationality.

An Evaluation of the Weberian Vision

Weber was concerned that scientific knowledge would be enlisted by all kinds of cranks and demagogues to justify and champion their convictions. To address this issue, he insisted that a sharp division exists between values and facts. As we have noted, he argued that scientific facts could *inform* the process of making value-judgments but these facts could not legitimately *prove* or *justify* those value-judgments as this required an (irrational) leap of faith (Weber, 1949: 55). For Weber, Scientific Method can determine the facts; but any amount of facts cannot, in themselves, disprove a value-judgment. The separation of facts and values, Weber believed, or at least hoped, would allow scientific knowledge to progress unhindered by value-judgments. It would also protect science from criticism arising from the potential misuse of scientific knowledge to support particular values. What sense are we to make of Weber's ideas about the possibility of value-free knowledge? Can they withstand critical scrutiny?

We noted earlier how, for Weber, the choice and constitution of the topic of scientific investigation is 'coloured by our value-conditioned interest' (Weber, 1949: 76). What Weber does not appreciate or address, however, is how the very commitment of science to objectivity is necessarily *refracted through diverse sets of value-commitments* — that is, commitments forged within social and political processes that produce *different forms* of 'scientific knowledge'. His argument for value-free science *assumes* a unitary view of science as it fails to recognize that *different value standpoints promote their own distinctive conceptions of science* (Knorr-Cetina, 1999). Of course, Weber acknowledges that the selection of a specific *topic* to investigate depends upon a value-standpoint that renders the topic relevant. Evaluative ideas enable scientists to identify their objects of enquiry *but*, in Weber's conception of science, the particular *value-standpoint(s) of science* is not problematized. For Weber, the choice is either to embrace the specific value-standpoint that renders the production of science meaningful or to become committed to some other value-standpoint. When embracing the specific value-standpoint of science, all the scientist can do is to generate (ostensibly) value-free, factual knowledge of some aspect of the world while avoiding any temptation to invoke scientific knowledge to support or challenge any other, pre-scientific or extra-scientific value-commitment.

Weber's advocacy of the value-free principle is important insofar as it helps counter the irrational, modernist tendency to justify and realize particular value-commitments, including management knowledge, by reference to the (seemingly incontrovertible) authority of science. More positively, by supporting each individual's pursuit of valued ends, the value-free principle can contribute to the development of a more rational society by paying attention to the particular value-commitment of science so that it does not become a universal (technocratic) benchmark of rationality. On the other hand, critics of the Weberian, value-free position have argued that the separation between 'science' and 'morality', or between 'is' and 'ought', is unconvincing. As Giddens (1989: 291–2) has observed:

> I do not see how it would be possible to maintain the division between 'is' and 'ought' presumed by Weber … Whenever we look at any actual debates concerning social issues and related observations, we find *networks of factual and evaluative judgments, organised through argumentation* (emphasis added).

Critical thinking challenges the Weberian claim that the realms of science (facts) and values (judgments) are, in reality, ever separate or separable. For this claim is seen to ignore or deny the practical embeddedness of science within particular (e.g. anthro-pocentric or ecocentric) assumptions. Those persuaded by this claim are seen to be prisoners of an illusion of 'pure theory' (to be discussed below).[2]

Amongst those who stress the inescapable value-ladenness of science are commentators who argue that the adequacy of scientific claims should be judged in terms of their contribution to the (dynamic) project of overcoming socially unnecessary suffering through critique, and not in terms of their (static) reflection of social realities or even the rational reconstruction of them (see Chapter 1). The abuse of science to which Weber points is regarded as inevitable when science is disconnected from the critical task of establishing a good society rather than the application of science in support of the status quo. The emancipatory impulse of critical reflection is not to create or refine scientific knowledge of the world *per se* but, rather, to challenge and transform relationships that foster and pressure forms of ignorance and sustain socially unnecessary suffering.

Science and Critical Theory

A perverse consequence of the doctrine of value-freedom – dubbed by Gouldner (1973b: 63) a 'salvational myth' – has been its succouring of an ideology of *scientism* in which particular knowledge claims produced by Scientific Method are represented as indisputably authoritative. Instead of leaving a space for critical reflection, as Weber intended, scientism inhibits and counteracts processes of self-clarification and the development of responsibility. Where science is equated with value-free knowledge, all other forms of knowledge are obliged to comply with its protocols or become marginalized as unscientific. As Habermas (1974: 264) wryly observes, when 'science attains a monopoly in the guidance of rational action, then all competing claims to a scientific orientation for action must be rejected'. A similar assessment, more colourfully expressed, is made by Collins and Pinch (1998:152) who characterize such 'scientism' as a form of fundamentalism which is defended by 'warriors' who 'seem to think of science as like a fundamentalist religion: mysterious, revealed, hierarchical, exhaustive, exclusive, omnipotent and infallible'.

Critical thinking challenges scientism by attending to how all forms of knowledge are conditioned by relations of power and domination. Notably, Critical Theory (**CT**), as developed by members of the Frankfurt School (to be considered below) emphasizes the possibility of mobilizing human reason to interrogate the authority of scientific knowledge, and not merely to extend or perfect its generation. CT directly presupposes and champions the possibility of a *critical science* that addresses and strives to promote the *rationality of ends* as well as the rationality of means. Whereas the value-free conception of science is preoccupied with refining its methodology for discovering the 'truth' about some portion of reality, CT is concerned with showing how scientific representations of Reality and Truth are conditioned and coloured by the social relations through which truth claims are articulated and accepted – a concern that is paralleled in Foucauldian (1977, 1980) considerations of power/knowledge. Only by transforming these relations, CT argues, is it possible to develop less partial or dogmatic representations of reality – a shift in understanding that can itself create important conditions for social change.

The doctrine of value-free knowledge is an example of what Habermas (1972) terms 'the illusion of pure theory' to which we referred earlier. It exemplifies a belief that perfect, historical, disembodied knowledge can be produced by imperfect, historical, embodied (human) beings. When dazzled by this illusion, it is assumed that (scientific) knowledge can be separated from the politics that impel its production. Belief in this separation of 'facts' from values and interests is, for CT, symptomatic of a forgetfulness of the depth of connection between the production of knowledge and practical, human problems. Distinctively human problems arise from the self-consciousness and self-determination that accompany the 'cultural break with nature' (ibid.: 312); and these problems cannot be suspended even, and perhaps especially, when engaging in scientific activity. For CT, the challenge for science is not to perfect Method that will produce precise empirical description and explanation but, rather, to (marshal and) advance thinking in a manner and direction that contribute to emancipatory change. We now elaborate this understanding.

Three Types of Knowledge

The conception of social science commended by Weber is challenged by Habermas (1972) who connects the production of knowledge to the problems endemic to human beings' distinctive relationship to nature and their (cognitive) interests in addressing problems thrown up by this relationship (see also Willmott, 2003). Human beings are uniquely faced with the challenge of coming to terms with the exceptional openness of their relationship to nature – that is, the *cultural* break with nature. In the process, the production of three basic kinds of knowledge is stimulated. First, there is a *technical* (cognitive) *interest* in gaining greater *prediction and control* over unruly natural and social forces. Guided by this interest, diverse kinds of scientific disciplines and associated technologies have been developed to calculate and master elements of the natural world, including the behaviour of human beings. This type of science, which Habermas characterizes as *empirical–analytic* is manifest, for example, in studies that identify the variables (e.g. motivation, training) that may enable line managers to render employee productivity more predictable and controllable.

The second type of knowledge arises from a human interest in *understanding and communicating with each other*. The purpose of such communication, Habermas contends, is not simply to improve our capacities to predict and control the natural and social worlds (that is, the knowledge prompted by the first cognitive interest) but to develop a fuller understanding of the lifeworlds of other people. This, Habermas maintains, is a scientifically coherent and defensible project in itself: in the form of *historical–hermeneutic sciences*, this cognitive interest is directed at enhancing *mutual understanding*. It seeks, for example, to enrich our appreciation of what organizational work means to different groups of people, thereby improving our comprehension of their world and enabling and enriching our communications with them. In the field of management, knowledge generated by this interest moves beyond a technical interest in, say, the identification of variables believed to condition human behaviour (e.g. employee productivity or brand loyalty). Historical–hermeneutic science seeks to better appreciate what people think and how they feel about, say, their treatment as producers of goods and of services, irrespective of what instrumental use may be made of such knowledge.

The in-depth appreciation and understanding of others' social worlds, such as that provided by Kunda (1992) in his study of 'Tech' (see Chapter 1), can be illuminating and even enlightening. But it may also leave unconsidered and unchallenged the historical and political forces which shape and sustain these worlds. Attentiveness to the exercise of power in the construction and representation of reality is the province of *critically reflective* knowledge which, Habermas argues, is motivated by a third *emancipatory* (cognitive) *interest*. The distinguishing feature of this interest resides in a concern to expose socially unnecessary forms of suffering occasioned by needless domination and exploitation. For example, it addresses connections between experiences of frustration and the existence of patriarchal practices and institutions – practices that can, in principle, be transformed through emancipatory actions, as demonstrated by the suffragettes and feminist activists. *Critical science* discloses such connections by *reconstructing* the processes through which 'relations of dependence' become 'ideologically frozen' (Habermas, 1972: 310) or normalized. Arguing for critical science, in contrast to a hermeneutical concern to provide an illuminating and persuasive account of the field of study, Deetz (1993) observes that:

> The quality of research from a critical theory standpoint is not based on the ability to tell a good tale but on the ability to participate in a human struggle – a struggle that is not always vicious or visible but a struggle that is always present ... [and is rooted] in the right to participate in the construction of meanings that affect our lives. (p. 227)

Critical science is concerned to understand how practices and institutions of management, which include the production and application of all three of Habermas' types of science, are developed and legitimized within relations of power and domination (e.g. capitalism, patriarchy) that, potentially, can be transformed. This concern differentiates critical science from studies which assume that established relations of power and authority are prefiguratively rational, albeit that, as yet, they are imperfectly so (see Chapter 1). Whereas the mission of empirical–analytic research is to produce knowledge of the reality of management so that a more efficient and effective allocation of resources can be achieved without necessitating a radical transformation of the status quo, critical analysis subjects the rationality of such objectives to scrutiny, arguing that conventional management theory and practice act as a 'servant of power' (Baritz, 1960; see also Brief, 2000) insofar as it takes for granted and (pre) serves the prevailing structure of power relations. By default if not by design, much management theory is wedded to values preoccupied with reproducing or refining the status quo, to the detriment of advancing a society in which socially unnecessary forms of domination are targeted and progressively eliminated. To the extent that critical analysis provides insights that provoke and facilitate emancipatory personal and social change, it exemplifies critique. This book aspires to make a contribution to this project.

An Illustration from Identity Research in Organization Studies

Before moving on, we will briefly illustrate Habermas' model of forms of knowledge. Almost any area from management studies could be chosen but the study of identity has attracted considerable interest since the early 1980s (Knights and Willmott, 1985) and has steadily increased during the intervening decades (Alvesson, 2010; Ybema et al., 2009).

The technical interest dominates studies of identity and identification in management and organization research, but to a lesser degree than is common as there is significant representation of interpretive and critical studies in the area. Studies taking a technical cognitive interest explore how identity and identification may be key to a variety of managerial outcomes and thus provide the means of improving organizational effectiveness. Consider, for example, the assumption that 'self-categorization processes are a critical mediator between organizational contexts and organizational behaviour' (Haslam, 2004: 38). By acting upon this intervening variable, it is predicted that particular valued outcomes in terms of efficiency gains, for example, can be facilitated. More generally, much organizational identification research maintains that identification levels affect decision making and behaviour, stereotypical perceptions of self and other, group cohesion (Ashforth and Mael, 1989), and social support (Haslam and Reicher, 2006).

Interpretivist scholarship, associated with Habermas' (1972) second cognitive interest, the 'historical–hermeneutic', seeks enhanced understanding of human cultural experiences, or how we communicate to generate and transform meaning. Contrasted with the technical interest and associated studies, there is little direct concern for the instrumental utility of such knowledge for enhancing organizational performance. Historical–hermeneutic studies focus on how people craft their identities through interaction, or how they weave 'narratives of self' in concert with others, and out of the diverse contextual resources. For researchers guided by this cognitive interest, identity is important for better understanding the complex, unfolding and dynamic relationship between self, work and organization. Typically, studies guided by this interest explore how managers struggle to make sense of themselves and their organizational realities in an ambiguous, often conflict-ridden world (e.g. Beech, 2008; Clarke et al., 2009; Watson, 2008; Sveningsson and Alvesson, 2003).

Finally, studies guided by Habermas' third, emancipatory cognitive, interest focus on relations of power and domination. Their concern is to illuminate how workers or managers struggle against oppressive forces that restrict or compromise their autonomy and/or impede their capacity to organize collectively to overcome deadlocks (Willmott, 2011a) and repressive relations that tend to constrain agency.

Notably, critical scholars have approached identity as a powerful way to analyse dynamics of control and resistance (Collinson, 1992; Ezzamel et al., 2001). Another focus has been on organizational worldviews that, in principle, are intended to subordinate human bodies to managerial regimes, for example, through an individualized narrative of career that cultivates constant entrepreneurial activity and associated forms of self-discipline (Grey, 1994), or as we noted earlier, through the construction of appropriate identities with 'strong' organizational cultures, such as 'Tech' (Casey, 1995). A current strand of interest is the disabling and enabling functions of contradiction in identity constructions – for example, the acute pressures associated with cultural templates or 'scripts' for who and how we ought to be, which co-exist with a multitude of forces that undermine the possibility of living up to such ideals (e.g. Costas and Fleming, 2009; Sennett, 1998).

The Unfolding of Critical Thinking about Management and Organization

Within social science as a whole, and amongst management and organization researchers more specifically, there has been growing scepticism about the relevance and value of empirical–analytical forms of science for addressing and solving the problems of modern society. This weakening of confidence shows through in more progressive texts and commentaries on management and organization (see Chapter 1). Less is heard about 'management/organization *science*'; more is heard about 'management/organization *studies*'. Less is heard about the authority of hard facts; more is heard about the persuasive power of symbols and metaphors, albeit ones that remain preoccupied with enhancing control over a naturalized present. We do not, however, want to exaggerate this 'weakening' since much scholarship remains resolutely 'empirical–analytical', even when it addresses symbols and metaphors. While the rise of neo-institutional theory in the past decade is, on balance, a welcome development from a critical perspective, it has yet to discharge the baggage of empirical–analytical science – a task that is not assisted by a culture of research that is dominated by journals (e.g. the *Academy of Management Journal*) that devote little or no space to unapologetically historical-hermeneutic, let alone critical, scholarship.

Established analyses and prescriptions have not been displaced. But, in scholarly studies of management at least, they are increasingly unsettled by alternative perspectives which, in turn, have unsurprisingly produced some backlash against more controversial (e.g. critical) 'styles' of research. Agendas of theory and practice developed by practitioners and advocates of functionalist theory (see below) have been challenged by those drawn from the broader terrains of social and political theory, including traditions of phenomenology, Marxism and poststructuralism.[3] One response by opponents of such diversification has been to give priority to journal lists where the place of publication (in established journals, with no history of publishing critical work) is more important than the content of the scholarship (Mingers and Willmott, 2011).

Nonetheless, management scholarship is considerably more diverse than it was about 20 years ago, enabled by the appearance of journals dedicated to, or at least willing to include, critical forms of scholarship.

Burrell and Morgan's pathfinding *Sociological Paradigms and Organisational Analysis* (1979) (hereafter *Paradigms*) has been particularly influential in opening up the field. At the heart of *Paradigms* is the subversive idea that differing standpoints, demarcated in terms of their assumptions about society and social science, result in different forms of (organizational) knowledge. In addition to its impact in the broad area of organization studies, *Paradigms* has inspired a series of calls for a broadening of agendas in the specialisms of marketing (Arndt, 1985), accounting (Hopper and Powell, 1985), operational research (Jackson, 1982), etc.

Competing Assumptions about Science and Society

In this section, we outline Burrell and Morgan's four paradigms of social scientific analysis before engaging their framework to locate the distinctive contours and contribution of Critical Theory in relation to a number of other, closely related approaches. To do this, we initially set aside our reservations about Burrell and Morgan's rigid division of social and organizational knowledge into four mutually exclusive paradigms (see Deetz, 1996; Willmott, 1990, 1993b) as we commend its heuristic value. The coherence of the framework is an issue to which we return when we compare and contrast Burrell and Morgan's (1979) conceptualization with Habermas' (1972) theory of cognitive interests, as summarized earlier.

Burrell and Morgan (1979) draw upon diverse traditions of social and organizational analysis to identify four fundamentally different lenses, or paradigms, through which social and organizational realities can be interpreted. Of most direct relevance for the present discussion, Burrell and Morgan contend that each paradigm has a legitimate claim to be accepted as science. So, instead of Weber's single, value-free view of science, Burrell and Morgan identify four distinct paradigms of social science based upon different philosophies of social science and theories of social regulation (see Figure 2.1).

An *objectivist philosophy of science* assumes the existence of a reality 'out there' that, in principle, can be faithfully captured or mirrored by the application of scientific methods. As the nature of the social world is assumed to be similar to, if not precisely the same as, the natural world, it is believed that social phenomena can be observed and measured using equivalent methods. Typically, the favoured methodology involves the careful construction of 'objective' instruments (e.g. questionnaires) that are designed to provide information about the variables (e.g. centralization) that are deemed to comprise key defining elements of the social world – such as the attitudes of employees or the type and variety of roles or functions performed by managers.

A *subjectivist philosophy of science*, in contrast, assumes that social phenomena are fundamentally different from natural phenomena and therefore cannot be mirrored or captured by so-called objective instruments. Unlike the constituent elements of

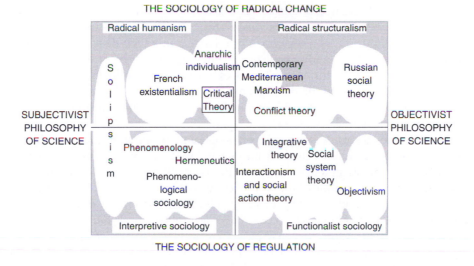

THE SOCIOLOGY OF RADICAL CHANGE

Figure 2.1   *The four sociological paradigms (adapted from Burrell and Morgan, 1979: 29)*

nature, whose properties remain constant for all practical purposes, the social world is understood, from a subjectivist standpoint, to be continuously constructed, reproduced and transformed through intersubjective processes of communication. It is these processes alone that sustain the sense of reality. It is only by being attentive to the meanings through which reality is rendered 'objectively' real to its members, subscribers to a subjectivist philosophy of science contend, that an adequate appreciation of the social world can be developed. Typically, the methodology favoured by 'subjectivist' researchers requires a close involvement with those who are being researched in order to discover how the meanings of concepts – such as 'centralization' – are actually formulated and interpreted by different members of an organization, and how this meaning is negotiated and changed over time.

Turning to consider the vertical dimension of the Burrell and Morgan matrix, theories of social regulation are divided from theories of radical change. *Theories of regulation* assume that modern societies and their organizations are defined more by order than by conflict. Order in organizations and society is interpreted as evidence of a fundamental equilibrium and consensus among their members. Conversely, disorder is interpreted as a temporary imbalance and a necessary means of re-establishing equilibrium. Attention is concentrated upon the issue of how cohesiveness and functional adaptation is accomplished and sustained. Since social order is deemed to be the outcome of an unconstrained accord between the constituents of organizations and society, the focus is upon how mechanisms for preserving social order can be strengthened.

Theories of radical change, in contrast, assume that social relations are conditioned more by contradictory pressures for transformation than by forces of continuity

and integration. Evidence of consensus is associated with forms of social domination that establish order and 'consensus' through direct repression or, in liberal
democracies, through a repressive form of tolerance in which dissenting voices are
at once accommodated and marginalized. The appearance of order and stability
is then connected with, for example, processes of mass subordination to the indi-
vidualizing disciplines of market relations (e.g. economic dependence) and/or
insidious kinds of socialization (e.g. technocratic indoctrination through education
and the mass media).

   From this 'radical change' perspective on people and organizations, the reproduction
(and transformation) of prevailing institutions and routines are understood to depend
upon, and be potentially blown apart by, the contradictory effects of deep-seated,
institutionalized inequalities and injustices. What may appear to be natural or
inevitable forms of authority (e.g. patriarchy) and timeless sources of meaning (e.g.
chauvinism) can, at moments of crisis, become problematical and untenable; and
efforts to restore their authority may, perversely, accelerate their decline and demise.
When diverse sources of tension combine, and prove resistant to suppression or
accommodation, major expressions of rebellion and radical change can occur – such
as the widespread disaffection amongst students and workers in Western Europe in
1968, the liberation of Central Europe during the latter half of 1989 and the 'Arab
Spring' of 2011.[4]

Four Paradigms for Analysing Management

So far we have identified two contrasting conceptions of social science and two
divergent ways of making sense of society. By combining subjective/objective
philosophies of science and regulation/radical change theories of society, four paradigms of analysis are identified. We briefly outline the two 'regulation' paradigms – functionalism and interpretivism – before paying more detailed attention to radical
structuralism and radical humanism as the latter are more directly connected to
critical thinking.

The Functionalist and Interpretivist Paradigms

The *functionalist paradigm* combines an objectivist philosophy of science with a
regulation theory of society. Burrell and Morgan identify this as the dominant
paradigm in the social sciences and comment that it tends to be 'highly pragmatic
in orientation ... problem-oriented in approach ... [and] ... firmly committed to a
philosophy of social engineering as a basis of social change' (1979: 26). In Chapter 1,
we echoed this view when we noted how knowledge based upon functionalist
assumptions has dominated management textbooks and is deeply engrained in the
curricula of business schools. It is also probably fair to say that much of the knowledge production and dissemination undertaken within this paradigm pays little
attention to Weber's concerns about the use/abuse of science.

The *interpretive paradigm* studies symbols (e.g. words, gestures) used to render social worlds meaningful. Conceiving of organizational realities as 'little more than a network of assumptions and intersubjectively shared meanings' (ibid.: 29–31), this paradigm departs markedly from the functionalist treatment of social realities as comprising measurable elements or variables. Disillusionment with the capacity of 'hard', functionalist analysis to get to grips with the complexity and slipperiness of forms of organizational work has stimulated the growth of managerialized versions of interpretivism. At the same time, hardnosed functionalism has been joined, but not superseded by, softer, qualitative forms of neo-functionalist analysis. This quasi-interparadigmatic fusion of functionalist and interpretivist analysis is assisted by a shared reliance upon a regulation theory of society. It is most clearly evident in an inclination to abstract the examination of processes of intersubjective meaning construction from consideration of the relations of power and domination through which, arguably, meanings are socially generated and legitimized. To acknowledge and analyse these relations, it is necessary to turn from paradigms of regulation to the paradigms of radical change.

The Radical Structuralist Paradigm

The *radical structuralist paradigm* is distinguished by its combination of an objectivist philosophy of social science with a radical change theory of society. Organizational behaviour is understood to be conditioned, if not determined, by structures of domination – such as the institutionalized exploitation of labour within the capitalist mode of production. Fundamental to the radical structuralist paradigm is the understanding that what individuals think and do is conditioned more by the operation of structural forces than by their own consciousness or intentionality. As Burrell and Morgan (1979: 378) put it, from a radical structuralist perspective 'the system as a whole retains an undiminished elementality – that is, men [*sic*] may seek to understand it but, like the wind or tides, it remains beyond their control', an assessment that resonates with the objectivism of functionalism. Where radical structuralism departs from functionalism is in its assumption that there are fundamental contradictions in social relations which render their social reproduction unstable. These contradictions are understood to account for the existence of more or less overtly coercive or insidious institutions (e.g. secret police, compulsory state education, mass media) that ensure the continuity of social order. The structural contradictions, it is claimed, also account for the eruption of recurrent conflicts and tensions in organizations and society and contain a potential for radical change that is released whenever prevailing institutional structures are found wanting in their regulation of instability.

Radical structuralists of a Marxism persuasion identify a basic contradiction between the organization of work within capitalist enterprises (socialized production of goods and services) and the appropriation by shareholders of the surpluses produced by employees' labour (private accumulation of wealth). This contradiction, when not effectively massaged by the welfare state, has the potential to erupt in industrial conflict and public disorder. Efforts to contain such contradictions in one area (e.g. fiscal contraction to balance the budget or curb inflationary wage demands, resulting in mass unemployment) are understood to generate increased tensions in related spheres (e.g. fiscal crises arising from a fall in taxation revenues and added expenditure on benefits without the anticipated stimulus to growth required to generate increased taxation receipts). To secure the appearance of order, repressive measures (e.g. reduction in civil liberties, greater powers given to judiciary and police, the installation of technocrats in place of politicians, etc.) may be applied. Such interventions may be effective in re-establishing order in the short term but at the risk of (further) undermining the legitimacy of the capitalist state. From a radical structuralist standpoint, then, the roots of problems and disorder – as manifested in economic, financial and ecological crises, widespread psychological distress, degraded work conditions, poor housing, juvenile delinquency, etc. – lie in the contradictory structures of capitalism. These problems may be moderated through reform. But they can be resolved only through a radical and revolutionary transformation of the capitalist system – a transformation which is propelled principally by systemic contradictions rather than by the efforts of people, either individually or collectively, to hasten its (inevitable) arrival.

Within the field of management and organization studies, Braverman's (1974) *Labor and Monopoly Capital* has been a major source of inspiration for the development of radical structuralist analyses of management and organization. Reviving and updating Marxian labour process analysis, Braverman directly challenged the claims of conventional accounts of work organization and employee consciousness, arguing that findings of studies concerned with job satisfaction, for example, pay minimal attention to how worker expectations are conditioned by wider structural factors. The finding that most workers report that they are 'satisfied' with their jobs, radical structuralists contend, tells us more about how employee expectations have been shaped to accommodate and cope with (deskilled) work than about their degraded experience of employment.

The Radical Humanist Paradigm

In the *radical humanist paradigm*, a subjectivist philosophy of science is combined with a radical change theory of society. In common with radical structuralism, the radical humanist paradigm understands social order to be a product of coercion, rather than consent. But its focus is upon contradictions within consciousness and their control through ideological means of manipulation and persuasion, rather than contradictions within the structures of (capitalist) society:

> One of the most basic notions underlying the [radical humanist] paradigm is that the consciousness of man [sic] is dominated by the ideological superstructures with which he interacts, and that these drive a cognitive wedge between himself and his true consciousness. ... The major concern for theorists approaching the human predicament in these terms is with release from the constraints which existing social arrangements place upon human development. (Burrell and Morgan, 1979: 32, emphasis omitted)

Critical Theory (CT), exemplified in the writings of Horkheimer, Benjamin and Marcuse as well as Habermas, has probably been the most influential of the several approaches located by Burrell and Morgan in the radical humanist paradigm. Bracketed together with the work of other neo-Marxist traditions, such as those associated with Lukacs (1971) and Gramsci (1971), Burrell and Morgan position the contribution of CT 'in the least subjectivist region of the radical humanist paradigm' (Burrell and Morgan, 1979: 283).[5] In contrast to the unmediated materialism of the radical structuralist paradigm, CT takes greater account of *the role of ideas* in the formation and reproduction of consciousness and society. For the radical humanist, the potential for radical change resides in the contradictions between, on the one side, the demands upon consciousness made by dominant (e.g. patriarchal) structures and, on the other side, the capacity of human beings to be creative and self-determining in ways that are fundamentally antagonistic to the reproduction of the status quo.

As the young Marx (1976) argued, the modernizing forces of capitalism exert the contradictory effect of alienating people from each other, from nature and from themselves. Communities are torn apart; industrial work is socially divisive; market relations transform people into commodities; people have limited opportunities for creative and spiritual growth. Through critiques of this kind, radical humanism makes its appeal to *every person* who is *oppressed within, and alienated from, modern institutions,* and not just those who are identified as members of the working class or proletariat. The intent of radical humanist analysis is, first, to raise awareness of how normality is oppressive; and, then, to facilitate the creative and self-determining liberation of individuals from the 'psychic prison' in which they/we are deemed to be incarcerated. Virtually everyone, radical humanists believe, is a victim of systemic oppression – oppression that is so taken for granted that it is routinely viewed as 'life'. Proponents of CT also believe that, when subjected to critical reflection, such experience can spur and inspire opposition to forces of domination.

Within the paradigm of radical humanism, CT is best viewed as a key resource for advancing ideas and practices that share a commitment to the construction of a more rational or, at least, a less irrational society, nationally and globally. Instead of focusing upon the struggle between capital and labour over the control of the labour process and the distribution of surpluses, CT emphasizes the meanings and ideologies through which institutions are established, reproduced and changed. In this respect at least, CT shares with interpretive analysis an appreciation of the central role of meaning in the reproduction of social realities.

Critical Theorists have kept alive the Enlightenment idea that critical reason can be mobilized to transform society, and not just to enhance our knowledge and control of society, or to bolster the authority of an élite. If technology is to enrich rather than impoverish human experience, CT argues, its development and use must be placed under more democratic forms of control. To this end, the values of alternative and intermediate technologies are commended because, quite apart from their ecological benefits, they offer a (decentralized) means of empowering local communities to develop their own solutions and shape their own fate. CT values self-determination in which material and social technologies are deployed in ways that facilitate and extend democratic decision making locally, nationally and globally. At the same time, CT is far from sanguine about the prospects, let alone the inevitability, of radical emancipatory change. A progressive outcome of the breakdown of prevailing structures is by no means assumed. Any substantial and sustained reduction in socially unnecessary suffering is understood to be conditional upon the nurturing and dissemination of critical science in the form of practical rationality. By advancing and applying critical science, CT seeks to realize ends that are *practically rational*, in the sense of being more congruent with the expansion of autonomy and responsibility. From this perspective, the attainment of practical rationality, in contrast to the refinement of technical or instrumental rationality, is a condition and a consequence of the open, democratic determination of ends advocated by CT.

Incommensurable Paradigms and Complementary Types of Science

From the standpoint of Critical Theory, there are significant difficulties with Burrell and Morgan's framework in which an incommensurability of paradigms is assumed. The *Paradigms* framework exemplifies a tendency within social science towards dualistic forms of analysis (e.g. individual v. society; action v. structure, etc.) which Burrell and Morgan cast into a metaphysical principle. As a consequence, the possibility and coherence of studies which refuse the polarization of 'subjective' and 'objective' approaches are denied.

Burrell and Morgan place CT in the subjectivist realm of the philosophy of social science. However, if we examine Habermas' *Legitimation Crisis* (1975), for example, we find that this study is no less concerned with the so-called objective structures of society than are key texts of radical structuralism, even though, as its title indicates, *Legitimation Crisis* is also attentive to issues of ideology and individual motivation that are credited to the radical humanist paradigm. In passing, Burrell and Morgan (1979: 294) acknowledge that their framework struggles to accommodate what they might characterize as CT's 'interparadigmatic' elements. They also acknowledge that despite an attentiveness to the role of language (which marks him as a 'subjectivist' in Burrell and Morgan's eyes), Habermas is 'at pains to stress that the theory of communicative competence must be linked to the fundamental assumptions of historical materialism if it is to be adequate and effective'; and that 'the materialist and idealist strands within Habermas' work are always yoked in a relationship of great tension, and his theoretical orientation aims at their reconciliation' (ibid.: 296).

Having saddled themselves with a dualistic framework, Burrell and Morgan are forced to pigeon-hole CT somewhere and, of course, to diagnose tensions in CT rather than to recognize oversimplifications in their own position that necessitate the diagnostics. They slot CT into the radical humanist paradigm, presumably on the grounds that it is less deterministic and economistic than structuralist

Marxism; and also, perhaps, on the more expedient grounds that, without CT, the radical humanist paradigm box would be embarrassingly bereft of content. Despite such shortcomings as we have shown the *Paradigms* framework provides a useful *heuristic* for recognizing and appreciating differences in analytical positions. It becomes unwieldy, however, when those differences are solidified into four mutually exclusive paradigms.

At this point, it is appropriate to return to Habermas' theory of knowledge-constitutive interests, which we sketched earlier, as it offers a different and arguably more instructive, basis for differentiating diverse kinds of scientific endeavour. By connecting the *production of knowledge* to the materially grounded arousal of cognitive *interests*, Habermas makes more visible their connection. From a CT perspective, Burrell and Morgan's framework lacks a grasp of the connection between science/knowledge and politics/human interests. Most tellingly, Burrell and Morgan (1979) are unreflective or disingenuous about how their representation of the contours of organizational analysis, as four mutually exclusive paradigms, is itself value-laden or interest-guided. The presentation of their framework as if it were a value-free reflection, or map, of the terrain of organizational analysis exemplifies 'the illusion of pure theory' (see above) in respect to the texts that they interpret (rather than the realities that such texts seek to report). CT, in contrast, is directly attentive to the presence of values and politics in shaping forms of knowledge. Instead of appearing to stand outside the process of knowledge production, Habermas' theory of cognitive interests is self-consciously located, as an exemplar of critical science, *within* the terrain that it strives to elucidate and transform.

The Critical Tradition

It is important to emphasize that our attention to Critical Theory does not signal an unequivocal allegiance to this tradition of analysis. We do not believe that CT possesses a monopoly on truth. Nothing is to be gained by denying the important insights and contributions made by other studies of management and organization, such as those of labour process theory or Foucauldian analysis. But, equally, we continue to believe that CT provides a broad-ranging and deep resource for making critical sense of management.

'Critical Theory' refers to the contribution of scholars and commentators who are closely related, or strongly sympathetic, to the work of the Frankfurt School. Central figures of the School include Max Horkheimer, Theodor Adorno, Walter Benjamin, Herbert Marcuse, Erich Fromm and, of greatest contemporary significance, Jürgen Habermas (see Appendix for a brief history). At the core of Critical Theory is a concern to develop a more rational, enlightened society through a process of critical reflection upon the organization and efficacy of existing institutions and ideologies. The considerable diversity of Critical Theory (CT) is integrated around a common desire to mobilize the potentials of critical reasoning to question and transform oppressive features of the modern world by means of 'a non-authoritarian and non-bureaucratic politics' (Held, 1980: 16). Without claiming that their thinking escapes the conditioning of prevailing relations of power, members of the Frankfurt School assume the possibility of subjecting established dogmas to critical scrutiny, and thereby to open up a space for emancipatory change.[6]

Exponents of CT are concerned to remedy the comparative neglect of culture and ideology in critical analysis, without simply making a switch or reversion from Marxian materialism to Hegelian idealism. Orthodox Marxism is criticized for failing to appreciate how forms of culture and communication – in the guise of ideology and the institutionalization of conflict – can serve either to diffuse the potential for dissent or, indeed, may be mobilized for radical transformation. As Habermas has observed with regard to his own shift of focus from production to communication:

> The paradigm-shift ... to communicative action does not mean that I am willing or bound to abandon the material production of the lifeworld as the privileged point of reference for analysis. I continue to explain the selective model of capitalist modernization, and the corresponding pathologies of a one-sided rationalized lifeworld, in terms of a capitalist accumulation process which is largely disconnected from orientations towards use-value. (1985: 96)

This passage underscores the fundamental importance of 'the material production' of the social world. The demands of the capitalist accumulation process, it is suggested, are largely responsible for creating the modern world in which productive activity is directed at the generation of commodities. These commodities have utility principally as a means of exchange, and thus of capital accumulation, rather than being of direct benefit, or 'use-value', for human happiness and development. An adequate understanding of processes of modernization focuses on the 'pathologies of a one-sided rationalized lifeworld'. In turn, this suggests that Critical Theory provides a valuable resource for the development of critical studies of management and organization without adopting it as the sole, or as necessarily always the most fruitful source of critical thinking. This commendation of CT is consistent with the view of Critical Management Studies as a 'broad church' that accommodates diverse traditions of critical scholarship between which there is healthy debate and dissent as well as cross-fertilization (Alvesson et al., 2009).

Some Themes in Critical Theory

A number of themes and issues have been central to Critical Theory and are directly relevant for the study of management and organization. Amongst the most relevant are (a) the dialectics of Enlightenment, (b) the one-dimensionality and consumerism of advanced capitalist societies, (c) the critique of technocracy and (d) communicative action. There are some overlaps between the themes, but it is convenient, for expository purposes, to examine them separately.

The Dialectics of Enlightenment

At the heart of the Enlightenment project is the critique and replacement of earlier belief systems grounded in tradition, common sense, superstition, religion, etc. with ostensibly more rational forms of thought and practice. However, this project can itself encompass new and emergent forms of dogma, dependence and deprivation – notably, when appeals to science are made to establish and legitimize forms of domination. The paradox of the Enlightenment project – that it produces destruction and oppression as well as liberation and progress – is associated in Critical Theory (CT) with the expansion and domination of a scientistic and technocratic consciousness: consciousness that seeks the development of instrumentally rational means for achieving ends that are deemed (by value-free science) to be beyond rational evaluation.

The rosy, positivist view of science, pictured as the benevolent agent of enlightenment, was forcefully challenged by Horkheimer and Adorno (1947a) in *Dialectic of Enlightenment*. Modern civilization, they argue, has become progressively mesmerized by the power of a one-sided, instrumental conception of reason. Beguiled by successes in conquering and harnessing nature, people in modern societies are seen to be trapped in a nexus of scientism and technocracy. This nexus, Horkheimer and Adorno contend, is no less constraining, and is in many ways much more destructive, than the myopia of pre-modern traditions which the advance of a modern, scientific civilization aspired to replace: 'In the most general sense of progressive thought, the Enlightenment has always aimed at liberating men [*sic*] from fear and establishing their sovereignty. Yet the fully enlightened earth radiates disaster triumphant' (ibid.: 3). Perhaps the most obvious symptom of this disaster is the relentless effort to dominate nature, associated with the ruthless exploitation of scarce natural resources and widespread environmental destruction, pollution and climate change.[7]

Whenever scientific knowledge fails to appreciate its historical embeddedness within the contexts of its production, CT argues, it stands in danger of *naturalizing* phenomena in ways which *mystify* their emergence out of a dynamic process of struggle between competing and contradictory forces in society. Where the connection of scientific knowledge to an interest in *emancipation* is lost or forgotten, science becomes an ideology: an instrument of political and economic domination. In the form of technocracy, scientific expertise effectively freezes social reality and legitimizes subordination to what currently exists.

When naturalized, social phenomena are represented as existing 'beyond' human powers, rather than as social and political artifacts. From the perspective of CT, the theory and practice of management must be understood in the context of the way beliefs, ideas and values define and legitimize the social category of managers and management. The production of (management) knowledge is seen to be conditioned by relations of power and domination that enable but also constrain our capacity to reflect critically upon established 'truths' – such as our knowledge of people and organizations represented in management studies, and absorbed by its students and practitioners (see Chapter 1). For CT, much scientific and management knowledge is a *one-sided* expression of a dialectical process in which its authority is naturalized, as an appreciation of its historically embedded production is obscured. The dialectical imagination of CT, in contrast, strives to expose and critique claims that theories are objective and that management practices are substantively effective. In so doing, CT discloses the limits of established wisdoms and 'best practice(s)', and thereby helps to open up the possibility of more rational, less contradictory, pathways of social and economic development.

One-dimensionality and Consumerism

The term 'one-dimensional man' was coined by Marcuse (1964) to emphasize how a dominant social logic effectively produces people that are mesmerized and subordinated to its mode of operating, lacking capacity and motive to think about alternative ideals and ways of being. Marcuse highlights how the organization of advanced capitalist societies effectively frustrates or deflects the emancipatory impulses of oppositional movements. At the heart of Marcuse's analysis is a critique of consumerism. In affluent Western societies, Marcuse argues, people are enjoined to become passive and unreflective consumers who are incapable of imagining forms of life that differ from the present. The USA, in particular, is identified as a society that possesses enormous productive capacities. Yet, instead of being applied to facilitate qualitative improvement in the lives of its citizens, societal development is driven by the logic – or illogic – of capitalism that, in the name of progress and the American Dream, routinely spreads waste, destruction, superficial satisfaction and needless misery.[8]

Proponents of CT directly challenge the conventional wisdom that mass consumption actually satisfies human needs. Instead of regarding needs as objectively given by human nature, CT understands 'needs' to be shaped by powerful forces (e.g. advertising). They are formed in ways that tie people emotionally, as consumers, to the possession of more and more goods, and thereby increase their material and psychological dependence upon the goods society (see Chapter 3). The depth of this dependence, Marcuse (1969) suggests, is productive of a sense of self that is preoccupied, if not obsessed, with consuming as a way of filling what, in the absence of more fulfilling life-projects, is a vacuum of meaning, and is therefore 'opposed to every change that might interrupt, perhaps even abolish, this dependence' (ibid.: 19). For Marcuse, forms of enjoyment provided by mass consumerism are essentially dehumanizing and repressive. Their principal effect is the numbing of human sensibilities, not their refinement or development.

In a similar vein, Fromm (1955, 1976) has argued that *discriminating* processes of consumption could, and should, form an integral part of a happier and more satisfying life. Yet, perversely, an ever-inflating 'need' for more goods subverts the powers of discrimination, and continuously feeds the consumerist habit. The individual 'consumes' sport, films, newspapers, magazines, books, lectures, natural sceneries, social situations and even other people in the same remote and alienated way that everyday merchandise is consumed. The alienated consumer does not participate actively or appreciatively in these activities, but wants to 'swallow' everything there is. By celebrating the freedom of consumption, the conditioning powers of industry fill and control free time that might otherwise be devoted to contemplation, reflection and communication. Still, the mass media are not considered to be irredeemably reactionary or oppressive. If placed under democratic control, rather than being driven by commercial forces that celebrate the values and practices of the status quo, the mass media could be vehicles of education and emancipation. Although an imperfect example, the BBC and similar forms of public service broadcasting demonstrate how a licence fee or sponsorship from subscribers and accountability to the public, rather than to shareholders, can provide a distinctive, comparatively high quality form of broadcasting that incorporates educational and broadly emancipatory values.

The Critique of Technocracy

A distinguishing feature of technocracy is its denial of the relevance of ethics – or moral-practical consciousness (Habermas, 1979: 148) – in processes of individual and societal development. As we argued earlier, the ends of human and organizational existence are taken for granted, are alleged to be self-evident or are deemed to lie beyond rational debate. In the selection of means, ethical considerations are excluded or marginalized as the identification of the best method or procedure is considered to be a purely technical matter. Taylorism exemplifies the technocratic role of experts. Decision making is regarded as the province of managers who, because they are deemed to know best about the field under consideration, can identify the most efficient and/or effective way of achieving (seemingly) given or self-evident ends.[9] To regard these ends as given or beyond rational interrogation and debate is to accept and reproduce the values and priorities of the groups who, through processes of political struggle, have established their ends as *the* ends.

We noted earlier how Weber sought to ward off the technocratic abuse of science by contriving to divide the realm of science (facts) from the realm of values. Habermas, in contrast, differentiates purposive-rational action (oriented towards efficient and effective realization of given ends) from communicative action (oriented towards understanding), *and* argues that the former is always embedded in, and depends upon, the normative framework provided by the latter. As well as providing a basis for his criticisms of Marx's preoccupation with production to the comparative neglect of communication (see above and Habermas, 1974), this assumption guides Habermas' interest in ideas concerned with interaction and the phenomenology of everyday life (Habermas, 1984) that inform his critique of historical materialism:

> I would like to propose the following: the species learns not only in the dimension of technically useful knowledge decisive for the development of productive forces but also in the dimension of moral-practical consciousness decisive for structures of interaction. The rules of communicative action do not develop in reaction to changes in the domain of instrumental and strategic action; but in doing so they follow *their own logic*. (Habermas, 1979: 148, emphasis in original)

Technocracy, Habermas contends, depends and thrives upon a denial, or forgetting, of the embeddedness of instrumental reason in the normative framework of society.

The more that technocratic consciousness contributes to, and dominates, processes of individual and social development, the more obscured and displaced is the moral-practical quality of *all* human interaction, including the production and application of scientific knowledge. Characterizing technocratic thinking as an ideology, precisely because it masquerades as being above ethics when it is not, Habermas (1971: 105–6) notes how the potency of positivist knowledge of the social world resides in its capacity to 'detach society's self-understanding from the frame of reference of communicative action and from the concepts of symbolic interaction and replace it with a scientific model'. As this occurs, Habermas continues, 'the culturally defined self-understanding of a social lifeworld is replaced by the self-reification of purposive-rational action and adaptive behaviour.'

Habermas draws attention here to the contemporary tendency in the West for the normative framework of society to be supplanted, if not absorbed, by a (technocratic) preoccupation with refining the subsystems of purposive-rational action. 'Old-style' politics, which sought its justification by drawing from an established (classical) pool of ethical ideas about the 'good life', are contrasted with modern politics which have tended to become narrowed into instrumental questions about how to maintain or regenerate elements of the (capitalist) system. In this process, a technocratic focus upon means displaces democratic debate about ends. The traditional approach, Habermas argues, was oriented to 'practical goals ... defined by interaction patterns'. In contrast, the contemporary (technocratic) approach to politics is aimed at the functioning of a manipulated system. Formally democratic institutions exist but, in effect, these operate to permit administrative decisions to be made largely independently of the specific motives of citizens. These institutions provide legitimacy for such decisions. But there is minimal substantive participation by citizens in key decision-making processes. It should therefore come as no surprise that so many citizens in advanced Western societies feel so remote from, and disaffected in relation to, the world of liberal democratic politics – a disaffection that threatens to disrupt the conditions upon which technocratic rule relies.

To counter the degeneration of (bourgeois) democracy and its drift into technocracy, Habermas stresses the importance of distinguishing (practical) communicative from (technical) instrumental rationality, and argues that as much – and more – attention must be devoted to the rationalization of the former, by '*removing restrictions on communication*' (Habermas, 1971: 118, emphasis in original), as has been given to the rationalization of systems of instrumental, purposive-rational action. Otherwise, the prospect is for ethics and democracy to be progressively eroded and eventually to 'disappear behind the interest in the expansion of our power of technical control' (ibid.: 113). Potentially, the corrosive effects of technocratic consciousness can be challenged and reversed by promoting and supporting actions that challenge restrictions and open up communications within all spheres – familial, organizational and public – and thereby facilitate the development of a *democratically rational society.* As Habermas, puts it:

> Public, unrestricted discussion, free from domination, of the suitability and desirability of action-orienting principles and norms in the light of socio-cultural

repercussions of developing subsystems of purposive-rational action – such com-munication at all levels of political and repoliticized decision-making processes is the only medium in which anything like 'rationalization' is possible. (ibid.: 119)

To sum up, when decisions are dominated by a technical interest in refining means, fundamental questions about ends, involving questions of politics and ethics, are marginalized. By arguing for the primacy of communicative action, Habermas' thinking problematizes the domination of technocracy as it elevates practical ration-ality as a resource for contesting the restriction of processes of rationalization to the realm of instrumental action.

Communicative Action

The concept of communicative action challenges the conventional understanding that instrumental or strategic rationality is the only, or purest, expression of human activity. Habermas (1984, 1987) contends that all communication presumes and depends upon a structure of understandings – such as the understanding that utter-ances are sincere or truthful – which can nonetheless be doubted in the course of interaction; and that this universal structure makes possible the process of dialogue and argumentation through which a *rational consensus* can, in principle, be reached. Inherent in language use is the understanding that statements include certain validity claims: that a statement is comprehensible, sincere, normatively defensible and true. Participants normally expect statements to meet these criteria, and so respond criti-cally when they believe that they are not met; and then, in principle, ask for justifi-cation and/or for the person behind the statement to clarify or revise the statement made. Embedded in the very structure of communication, Habermas contends, is a 'universal pragmatic' which anticipates a situation in which an *unforced rational con-sensus* about ends is emergent, and appropriate forms of action are pursued. Insofar as this situation remains unrealized in practice, distortions of communication are conceived to generate potent sources of frustration and suffering that place restric-tions upon, and so motivate emancipatory change (to be elaborated below).

Habermas of course realizes that, in everyday life, communications are routinely distorted and break down whenever constraints – in the form of sanctions and repressions – impede the practical realization of the ideal of unforced consensus. Both structures (hierarchies, division of labour, performance pressures) and actors pur-suing their sectional interests in politically conscious ways obstruct or postpone the real-ization of the ideal. Habermas' theory invites the critical investigation of systematically distorted communication, although it should not be mistaken for a readily applicable diagnostic tool or as a foolproof recipe for guiding people to the ideal that it anticipates. Habermasian critique does not harbour the illusion of pure theory (see earlier). Its critical intent is to challenge unreflective, ideological discourse and thereby open up a questioning of ends as well as means, and not to establish a final truth.

The thesis that frustrations and contradictions arising from distortions of communicative action animate the dynamics of emancipatory action can be illustrated by reference to the contemporary emergence of social movements and forms of experimentation – the global justice movement, the ecological movement, the peace movement, the animal rights movement, etc. – where processes of questioning and argumentation have been strongly encouraged and facilitated.[10] Such activism may, from a neoconservative or reactionary standpoint, be dismissed as moral degeneracy or naïve idealism. For Habermas, in contrast, the questioning of standardized patterns of action, and rejection of traditional bourgeois norms, is evidence of a vibrant lifeworld of face-to-face and informal (e.g. texting, social networking) interaction. Despite the pacifying effects of the mass media and pressures to accept received wisdoms, this activism is seen to articulate and expand a capacity for critical reflection and self-determination.[11] Problematizing received wisdom and values (e.g. about the natural environment as an external and limitless depository of waste, or public indebtedness as a sink for the sequestration of private banks' toxic debts) is regarded as a necessary precondition for forging a consensus founded upon communicative ethics. These ethics cannot rely upon established dogmas and formulae. Instead, they must be forged from a process of dialogue and deliberation:

> the need for achieving understanding is met less by a reservoir of traditionally certified interpretations immune from criticism; at the level of a completely decentred understanding of the world, the need for consensus must be met more and more frequently by risky, because rationally motivated, agreement. (Habermas, 1984: 340)

Habermas' optimism regarding emancipatory currents within the dynamics of modernity is, as we have noted, tempered by a concern that the everyday, face-to-face lifeworld is being progressively colonized by technocratic rationality. Experts – professionals, consultants and functional managers – seek to extend their control over more and more areas of social life. In this process, advice-giving moves from friends and colleagues to consultants and counsellors; and leisure becomes informed by the advice and control offered by lifestyle coaches and marketers, etc. To elaborate this concern, Habermas (1987: 151 *et seq.*) distinguishes between 'social' and 'systems' forms of integration. Social integration is accomplished through immediate, communicative interactions between those whose lives it directly coordinates. It involves the active and, in principle, unconstrained engagement of participants in determining the normative order of their lifeworld. Blogging and 'tweeting' by individuals (not corporations) are contemporary, technology-mediated expressions of such communications. In contrast, systems integration induces coordination by requiring participants to comply with a normative order that is imposed upon them at a distance by diverse experts and by impersonal media (money, bureaucratic rules, law, etc.). Systems integration is achieved through the use of inducements and sanctions rather than through the active (and normally face-to-face) consent of participants. Whereas interaction in the lifeworld is attentive to 'cultural tradition, legitimate orders and socialized individuals' (ibid.: 182), the operation of systems media, notably money and power, fosters a:

purposive-rational attitude toward calculable amounts of value and makes it possible to exert generalized, strategic influence on the decisions of other participants while *bypassing* processes of consensus-oriented communication. Inasmuch as they do not merely simplify linguistic communication, but *replace* it with a symbolic generalization of rewards and punishments, the lifeworld contexts in which processes of reaching understanding are always embedded are devalued in favor of media-steered interactions; the lifeworld is no longer needed for the coordination of action. (ibid.: 183, emphasis in original)

The effect of coordination by means of systems integration, Habermas argues, is to devalue and weaken the moral order of the lifeworld. Possibilities for improving and enriching the rationality of the lifeworld, opened up by modernist questioning of the authority of tradition, are impeded by efforts to preserve the system – as when, for example, functional rationality feeds off, and colonizes, the meanings and understandings that are developed and valued within everyday life. Lifeworld values are weakened wherever a set of standards determined by experts is imposed upon citizens/ customers who are encouraged to substitute those standards for what they have developed within the lifeworld. Individuals then become constituted in passive roles – as employee/consumer/client/citizen/etc. – shaped principally by the technical, instrumental rationality of systems rather than by the practical, communicative rationality of the lifeworld. As one friend of ours expressed it, having moved into a more affluent region where consumerist ideals were more salient: 'Before I had a life, now I have a lifestyle'.

When the institutional framework of the lifeworld is colonized by systems rationality, Habermas contends, there is a process of cultural impoverishment, as diverse experts set standards and package opinions. It is a form of degradation that Habermas (1984: 330) attributes, above all, to '*an elitist splitting-off of expert cultures from contexts of communicative action in everyday life*' (emphasis added). However, as we noted earlier, this process of colonization continuously encounters problems of legitimation: 'money and power can neither buy nor compel solidarity and meaning' (ibid.: 363). Systems rationality can, at best, induce dramaturgical compliance with the administrative norms of the new technocracy in which corporate cultures, for example, are managed by human resource professionals (see Chapter 3 and 4), or where traders and managers in financial institutions become progressively removed and remote from the lifeworlds of those for whom their trades have material consequences. This does not foster the trust and mutual respect, and ultimately undermines the very confidence that is necessary, for systems rationality to be translated into effective forms of cooperation. From this it follows that a major task for critical thinkers is to expose the precarious foundations as well as the oppressive effects of the instrumental rationality of systems. Doing so, it is possible to open a space in which the everyday lifeworld is revalued and rationalized – not by experts or other proponents of systems rationality but, instead, by groups or movements that challenge technocracy and champion democracy in ways that at once demand and support the values of autonomy, responsibility and solidarity.

Critiques of Critical Theory

To conclude this chapter without some reference to criticisms of Critical Theory would be inconsistent with the latter's critical intent and self-critical claims. Many criticisms could be considered but, for present purposes, we are highly selective. We return to make additional criticisms in Chapter 7. Here we divide our brief review of critiques into those that are 'external' to CT, and therefore challenge its basic assumptions, and those that are basically sympathetic to CT, but identify difficulties with its project.

External Criticisms

To those who regard social phenomena as neutral objects of investigation, equivalent to the objects of the natural sciences, the claims of CT are, of course, hopelessly 'unscientific', value-laden and 'political'. CT is swiftly dismissed as Leftist propaganda, peddled by disaffected intellectuals who lack the sense and/or scientific commitment to recognize the unbridgeable difference between facts and values. In response, Critical Theorists have urged reflection upon the assumptions which support such dogmatic dismissals. Yet, despite an ever-expanding volume of literature that argues against the neutrality and objectivity of social science (Alvesson and Sköldberg, 2009; Denzin and Lincoln, 2005), many people remain indifferent to, or unpersuaded by, powerful arguments that dispute science's value–neutrality. Or, at least, they are willing to defer to the 'scientific expert' not least because they (we) feel unable to take responsibility for decision making. Failure to defer is assumed to precipitate a fall into the abyss of chaos and/or relativism.

Some of those who share CT's scepticism about conventional images of science and society have not, however, been persuaded by its arguments about human autonomy and processes of historical development. Such claims are criticized for failing to grasp how the engine of history operates largely independently of human consciousness (e.g. Braverman, 1974) or, in the modern era, acts to reduce critical consciousness to a cynicism that 'holds anything positive to be fraud' (Sloterdijk, 1980: 546). Alternatively, CT is seen to appeal to notions of autonomy and democracy that lost their meaning or purchase in the context of modern societies, where the credibility of these nineteenth-century ideas has largely drained away (see also Crook et al., 1992). Luhmann (1982), for example, has suggested that the basis of Habermas' distinction between technical and practical rationality is historical, and that its moment has likely passed – a view which, ironically, is not inconsistent with Habermas' own cautionary observation, cited earlier, that 'we have no metaphysical guarantee' (Habermas, 1979: 188) that the contemporary erosion of the lifeworld as a constitutive force will not continue, and even become total.

Alternatively, the outpourings of CT have been interpreted as the work of a disgruntled group of intellectuals whose privileged class background has impeded their identification with the interests of working people and an associated inclination to identify almost every group as alienated and, therefore, as potential agents of eman-cipatory change. Suspicion of the historical and elitist basis of CT has been expressed by Bottomore (1984) who contends that:

> Reading the Frankfurt School texts on the loss of individual autonomy (and espe-cially the writings of Adorno and Horkheimer) it is difficult to escape the impression that they express above all ... the sense of decline in a particular stratum of society, that of the educated upper middle class, or more specifically the 'mandarins', and the nostalgia for a traditional German Kultur. (ibid.: 42–3)

This objection is related to the criticism that Habermas' (re)formulation of CT has been excessively preoccupied with questions of culture and ideology, to the neglect of the material basis of society (see Roderick, 1986). Habermas is censured for a focus upon communication that tends to deflect attention from its conditioning by the dynamics of capitalist reproduction. When responding to such criticism, Habermas has, as we noted earlier, argued that relations of production are signifi-cantly shaped and mediated by processes of communication and identity formation that are inadequately appreciated in materialistic analysis (see Habermas, 1987: 332 *et seq*.). Needless to say, this defence cuts little ice with those who identify contradic-tions within, and struggles over, the productive process as the principal engine of history and of radical social change.

And feminism?

Another criticism directed at CT is its very limited engagement with feminist theory and minimal appreciation of the significance of feminism as a social movement. That all leading Critical Theorists have been men is probably not unrelated to this critique. The neglect of feminism is particularly disappointing in Habermas' case because he has demonstrated such a willingness to debate with so many other strands of critical social theory. In Chapter 3, we make reference to feminist organization theory. Here we outline some central strands of anti–patriarchal thinking to highlight its affinities with central themes of Critical Theory.

Feminists argue that the very structures of modern society are phallocentric and patriarchal; and that change is necessary if women (and men) are to be emancipated from male domination. There are, however, a variety of feminisms (see Calas and Smircich, 2006), some alien, and some much more closely related to CT. *Liberal feminism* tends to share the basic assumptions of functionalism (see earlier discussion of 'the functionalist paradigm') as it concentrates on promoting a narrow set of equal-opportunity issues, such as the careers of female managers. The basic concern is to make better use of the capacities that women can bring to the world of work. The concerns of *radical feminists* go well beyond the demand that women must be able to compete without prejudice for positions presently occupied by men, and must be enabled to do so by the provision of policies and services, such as child care, that allegedly make this possible. In isolation from other more radical demands, such as the equal valuing of the unpaid work in the home that many women presently do, the winning of equal opportunities is assessed to do little more than legitimize dominant institutions by making them appear ungendered (Collinson et al., 1990). Since it is principally men who have defined and colonized what is acceptably 'feminine', radical feminists seek to change the institutions within and through which their self-identity is constituted.

These concerns echo and support radical humanist thinking insofar as they are critical of the neglect of 'non-economic' forces in radical structuralist analysis. However, a key issue for radical feminists is the limited and marginalized critique of patriarchal structures of domination in both 'humanist' and 'structuralist' variants of radicalism (Walby, 1986). Without necessarily denying the importance of politico-economic forces and contradictions in the organization of modern societies, radical feminists highlight and question the genderedness of modern institutions. In particular, their critiques have drawn attention to how, in these work organizations, men have occupied positions of social and economic advantage, in terms of status, wealth and influence, relative to women, and have therefore been able to shape and solidify (patriarchal) forms of institutional development. The challenge of radical feminism is very far-reaching: it encompasses all manifestations of gendered practices, and not just the right of access to positions which embody patriarchal values (Martin, 2003). The challenge extends to apparently impersonal and neutral terrain, such as nature (Merchant, 1980), science (Harding, 1986) and the market (Hartsock, 1984).

Perhaps the most extreme – or most pure – form of radical resistance to patriarchy, which ostensibly amounts to a total rejection, is *separatist feminism* in which women undertake to create their own institutions. Participation by men is excluded on the grounds that their involvement renders social relationships violent, subordinating and demeaning. Partly as a reaction to what have been regarded as excesses of separatist feminism (which effectively disregard or deny any active role or responsibility of women in reproducing patriarchal forms of domination), *radical postfeminism* has sought to retrieve and re-value aspects of femininity (e.g. motherhood and a logic of care associated with experiences of nurturing and caretaking) that influential strands of radical feminism have tended to neglect, or interpret as symptomatic of female subordination, reflecting traditional divisions of labour. Radical postfeminists are concerned about the unintended, self-defeating consequences of feminisms that impede, rather than facilitate, communication with other groups who are potentially supportive of the feminist goal of dissolving patriarchal institutions (see Gore, 1992). For example, postfeminists more readily place a positive value upon the sensuality and nurturing quality of femininity, whilst also arguing that such qualities are distorted and exploited within patriarchal societies. In some versions, these qualities are identified with a universalistic conception of 'the feminine' (e.g. Marshall, 1993), albeit one to which both sexes have some degree of access. In other versions of radical postfeminism, what counts as 'feminine' or 'feminine values' has no essence but, instead, is understood to be historically and culturally contingent (Flax, 1990b). The latter position, leaning towards poststructuralism (see below) and its antipathy to fixed categories and seemingly self-evident and stable identities (like 'men' and 'women'), opens a space for addressing issues of gender relations in a way that subverts a tendency to regard (and marginalize) 'feminism' as an exclusively women's issue (Flax, 1990a). This stance, which challenges the dualism of masculine/feminine issues, is also more consonant with the Habermasian understanding that different types of knowledge are potentially complementary rather than irremediably incommensurable.

Radical feminism usefully draws attention to a major blind spot in Critical Theory (Fraser, 1987; Meisenhelder, 1989). It highlights the vital importance of understanding patriarchy as a fundamental source of domination; and it identifies the women's movement as an important (yet in CT neglected) source of opposition to oppressive, male-centred values and practices. Postfeminist ideas are potentially of relevance for CT, and especially for Habermas' emphasis upon communication, because they open up awareness of, and communication about, gender-related forms of subjugation. Rather than simply dismissing CT as 'gender blind', it is notable that some postfeminists have drawn upon, and have critically reconstructed, the insights of CT in ways that recognize their mutual concerns and enrich their respective understandings (e.g. Benhabib, 1992; Martin, 2003).

Fraser (1987), for example, reviews and re-works the Habermasian distinction, discussed above, between, on the one hand, 'the lifeworld' – which is closely associated with the domestic and private sphere – and, on the other hand, 'the system' where technical rationality is dominant, and which is identified more closely with the world of work and the public sphere. The distinction between 'lifeworld' and 'system' is found to have '*prima facie* purchase on empirical social reality' (ibid.: 37). At the very least, it acknowledges the common experience of a division existing between the personal sphere (e.g. the family) and the more impersonal realm of economic relations (e.g. paid employment). But, Fraser argues, it is no less important to appreciate how this distinction can obscure the *continuities* between these realms – for example, by masking or marginalizing the extent to which the home is 'a site of labour, albeit unremunerated and often unrecognized', that is largely undertaken by women. If this criticism is accepted, then it is necessary to revise Habermas' analysis in a way that recognizes how the (patriarchal) positioning of men, as heads of family households, is underpinned by their privileged access to money and power, the principal media of the operation of 'the system'. In fact, Habermas does acknowledge the presence and oppressive influence of such media within the sphere of close, interpersonal relations. But, tellingly, these are regarded as a 'colonizing force', not as directly implicated in the constitution of the modern 'lifeworld'. Only in his more recent work is this stance tempered by an acknowledgement of the intertwining of 'system' and 'life-world' elements (see Scherer, 2009). Radical feminists valuably stress the degree of mutual interdependence, interpenetration and male domination of both 'lifeworld' and 'system':

> the struggles and wishes of contemporary women are not adequately clarified by a theory that draws a basic battle line between system and lifeworld institutions. From a feminist perspective, there is a more basic battle line between the forms of male dominance linking 'system' to 'lifeworld' *and us*. (Fraser, 1987: 55, emphasis in original)

Nonetheless, if CT acknowledges its relative gender-blindness, and if radical feminism is prepared to learn from CT, there are possibilities for integrating their respective insights and concerns (Benhabib and Cornell, 1987; Luke and Gore, 1992). Indeed, it has been suggested that this coming together of CT and feminism is necessary if radical feminism is not to become bogged down in the mire of postmodernism/ poststructuralism (Nicholson, 1990), and if CT is to become more fully engaged with contemporary struggles.[12] Within Habermas' communication theory of society, there would seem to be every reason for including gendered structures and norms as a principal medium of distorted communication – not only between, but also within, gender relations as men and women struggle to recognize and emancipate themselves from the oppressive (e.g. 'aggressive'/'submissive') demands of received (and, it might be added, even radical) wisdoms about masculinity/femininity.

And poststructuralism?

In a number of respects, Critical Theory resonates with more politically engaged forms of poststructuralist analysis as they share an antipathy towards (radical) structuralist analysis. That said, poststructuralists have questioned whether knowledge can ever be separated from power, and therefore reject as incoherent and dangerous Habermas' claim to have identified a rational grounding of CT's normative standards (e.g. Foucault, 1980; Lyotard, 1984). Such a claim is *incoherent*, the critics contend, because all forms of knowledge – including the idea of the ideal speech situation and communicative action – are articulations of power and, inescapably, exert a subjugating effect upon those who identify them as truth. The objection here is that CT is insufficiently self-reflective and self-critical about the possible effects of its own preconceptions – notably, the assumption that its ideas about 'autonomy' and 'responsibility' are unequivocally propitious for humankind. Such a view is *dangerous*, poststructuralist critics declare, because it suggests that what is done in the name of humanism and emancipation is somehow exempt from oppressive effects. The risk is one of 'reason' being invoked to deny or mystify forms of subjection that ostensibly it claims to expose and remove. Habermas' response to such criticism has been to concede that CT cannot escape this risk. But he then attempts to turn the tables on the poststructuralists (see Poster, 1989) by inviting them to reflect upon what, for him, are the far more serious consequences of abandoning any basis for differentiating the true from the false, and the rational from the irrational. Serious efforts to ground positions, values and decisions through communicative rationality are, he insists, far better than the alternatives. Otherwise, Habermas (1992: 209) argues:

> *All* validity claims become immanent to particular discourses. They are simultaneously absorbed into the totality of some one [*sic*] of the blindly occurring discourses and left at the mercy of the 'hazardous play' amongst these discourses as each overpowers the other (emphasis in original).

Habermas seems to be responding constructively to the poststructuralist thesis that attention must be paid to the consequences of adopting particular kinds of discourse, and not just to how their claims are grounded. In doing so, CT is defended on the basis that efforts to differentiate the true from the false are less damaging in their effects than either a refusal to do so and/or a commitment to showing how such distinctions are solely 'immanent to particular discourses' rather than in any way being a condition of all forms of discourse (Freundlieb, 1989; see also Power, 1990).

Internal Criticisms

The boundary between internal and external criticisms of CT is weak, and some contributions to feminism and poststructuralism are more like siblings than strangers to CT. Nonetheless it is important to acknowledge critique that is emerging from authors who see themselves as part of, or closely allied to, a CT tradition. Some of them have targeted for criticism CT's attentiveness to cognitive processes, to the neglect of human embodiment. (This has also been addressed by some radical feminists, e.g. Gilligan, 1982.) Cognitive processes, these critics argue, play a comparatively minor role in the practical activity of releasing human beings from oppressive conditions (Fay, 1987; see also Keat, 1981; Lukes, 1982). This criticism resembles the objections of those who argue that CT exaggerates the importance of consciousness in processes of radical social change. However, those who stress the significance of embodiment do not so much question the central role ascribed to consciousness as embed it in corporeal and unconscious processes (McIntosh, 1994). Forces of repression, Fay (1987) contends, exist in the body as well as the mind. Or, as he puts it:

> Changing people's self-conceptions may not be enough to change those perceptions, feelings, and dispositions which are deeply incarnated into their muscles, organs, and skeletons. ... Humans are not only *active* beings, they are also embodied, traditional, historical, and embedded. (ibid.: 207, 209, emphasis in original)

A broadly similar criticism is made or implied by authors who highlight the significance of various forms of cynical consciousness (Sloterdijk, 1980; Fleming and Spicer, 2003). Such objections underscore the point that 'reconstruction' and 'critique' (see Chapter 1) are rather loosely coupled. An individual may be well versed in the (rationally reconstructive) refinements of CT, but this knowledge may exert little practical effect upon his or her conduct. In our view, such criticism is well targeted; and it is applicable to much of the analysis that comprises critical management studies, including our own. It is, however, important to point out that although this criticism of 'intellectualism' is relevant for considering in particular Habermas' work, key writings by Fromm (1976), Marcuse (1964) and others also have an emotional appeal, likely to trigger responses like 'What in hell are we up to?' This may be more likely to lead to some consequences for action and not solely cognitive effects. Habermas, being targeted by critics accusing CT of impotent reflectionism, has responded by underscoring the difference between the two kinds of critical reflection outlined in Chapter 1. There is reflection that operates in the realm of ideas (e.g. about the universal presuppositions of speech and action) which has no *necessary* effect upon broader processes of self-(trans)formation. But there is also reflection that incorporates, but goes beyond, processes of 'rational reconstruction' to dissolve destructive habits of mind and other compulsions that unnecessarily 'restrict patterns of perception and behaviour', and thereby enable 'the subject (to) emancipate himself from himself' (Habermas, 1975: 183). Habermas has less to say on how *reconstruction* is practically translated into *critique*, although his efforts to articulate a theory of deliberative democracy, informed by his 'universal pragmatics' which assume the possibility of reasoned and inclusive public discussion geared to attaining consensual decisions, moves in this direction (see Reed, 1999). Critics have argued that democratic decision making is inherently conflict-ridden and that the idea of reaching an unforced consensus is not only illusory but also damaging of the very pluralism that democracy is committed to respecting and strengthening (Mouffe, 1999b; Edward and Willmott, 2012). This shortcoming relates to another criticism concerning CT's lack of a substitute for the proletariat as the agency of emancipatory social change.

Seeking to learn something from the lessons of modern history, leading advocates of CT have been highly sceptical about the prospects of proletarian revolution without, in most cases, becoming resigned to the prospect of total domination by instrumental reason or becoming wholly sceptical about the possibility of emancipation. As Burrell (1994: 5) observes, Habermas 'stands against all varieties of totalizing critique which lead to despair. For him, the philosopher as "guardian of reason" is also the sentinel of, and for, human hope.' Departing from other, more accessible but arguably cruder forms of critical thinking, Habermas has embraced an abstract and rather hazy idea of gradualist change. For Habermas, change arises from a developing, though uneven, disillusionment with the effects – personal, social and ecological – of modern capitalist society that are increasingly experienced as a destructive disillusionment that finds it positive expression and antidote through the activities and demands of radical social movements. Most recently, however, Habermas seems to have become more doubtful, if not outrightly pessimistic, about the prospects for the emergence of such a cohesive movement for change: 'I suspect that nothing will change in the parameters of public discussion and the decisions of politically empowered actors', he writes, 'without the emergence of a social movement which fosters a complete shift in political mentality.' And he continues, 'The tendencies towards a breakdown in solidarity in everyday life do not render such mobilization within western civil societies exactly probable' (Habermas, 2010: 74). As this book goes to press, there may be the stirring of such a movement in the Occupy Wall Street activism which began in New York's Zuccotti Park and, facilitated by social media, spread rapidly across North America and to many cities around the world (see also endnote 5).

To date, leading proponents of CT have devoted much more attention to the process of rational reconstruction than to the issue of how critical thinking has relevance for, and purchase upon, practical processes of collective self-(trans)formation.

Management and organizations have also been grossly neglected by leading Critical Theorists (e.g. Habermas, Honneth), a neglect that is symptomatic of a tendency to ignore such institutions, despite their centrality to modernity and systems rationality. Nonetheless, any lingering doubts about the practical, emancipatory relevance and potency of CT should not eclipse an appreciation of its role in raising important issues and providing inspiration for critical reflection. Of course, critical reflection upon established routines and habits of mind may merely fuel paralysing doubts and anxieties, especially in the absence of a supportive culture for addressing and dissolving such concerns. But CT may also stimulate and facilitate greater clarity about, and resistance to, forces that place socially unnecessary constraints upon open communication and personal fulfilment. It is important not to expect or demand too much of CT – CT cannot itself do the practical work of emancipation.

 ## Summary and Conclusion

In this chapter we have considered the central role played by knowledge in society: although intellectual understanding is insufficient to create change, knowledge nevertheless informs and justifies how we act. Whenever knowledge is, for all practical purposes, accepted as truth – when, for example, it is taken for granted that managers make the decisions or that women have 'special orientations and skills' – some forms of action are facilitated as others are impeded. In this sense, knowledge is powerful, especially when it is represented and understood as neutral and authoritative (i.e. scientific). Because knowledge is a potent medium of domination, it is necessarily a focal topic of critical analysis.

In the first part of the chapter, we argued that the idea of one, authoritative value-free science acts to devalue and suppress alternative knowledge and conceptions of science. Burrell and Morgan's (1979) *Paradigms* framework was introduced to demonstrate the heuristic value of highlighting the presence of different approaches to the production of knowledge about organizations and management. Their framework also enabled us to locate Critical Theory in the wider terrain of social scientific enquiry. A limitation of Burrell and Morgan's framework is that the production of knowledge is abstracted from its motivation, and Habermas' theory of cognitive interests was commended as a means of correcting this omission. Habermas' formulation of three cognitive interests shows, and encourages, the development of different kinds of science, including the empirical–analytic knowledge generated with Burrell and Morgan's functionalist paradigm, but *within* a broader critical vision of science as a potentially emancipatory force.

From the standpoint of Critical Theory, the central problem in making sense of social reality, including the theory and practice of management, is *not* how to cleanse the scientific method of normative bias but, rather, how to formulate and address *the kind* of normative commitment which should inform the production of knowledge. CT contends that the identification and pursuit of means and ends can be more or less rational, depending upon the openness and symmetry of the power relations through which decisions about ends are reached. Accordingly, the development of less distorted forms of knowledge and communication, which is a precondition for the fuller democratization of modern institutions, is understood to be conditional upon removing institutional and psychological obstacles to achieving greater openness and symmetry.

In seeking to illuminate the focus and scope of critical thinking and to illustrate this by reference to Critical Theory, we have indicated its relevance for critiquing aspects of management and organizations within advanced capitalist societies. CT's attention to consumerism and the influence of mass media, for example, is relevant for analysing marketing as a specialism of management (see Chapter 5); and CT's critique of technocracy and instrumental reason is widely applicable to the contents of management disciplines which are refined and applied for purposes of buttressing instrumental reason or revitalizing the status quo (see Chapters 3–6).

In conclusion, it is worth noting how advocates of CT, and Habermas in particular, have addressed abstract theory and to some extent general political and broader social issues without considering in any detail specific social institutions and practices, such as management and organization. It would therefore seem highly appropriate to complement the theoretical emphasis of Critical Theory with a more direct focus upon the (technocratic) domain of management and organization where, arguably, the media of money and power are most intensively engaged and where system and lifeworld meet and clash.

Notes

1 Whereas established management practice relied upon the vagaries of 'custom and practice', Taylor's scientific principles claimed to articulate the rational specification of managerial and worker behaviour. Taylor took it for granted that everyone has a broadly equal stake in rationalizing productive activity – managers and workers as well as shareholders – and would therefore each accept his principles of organization. Quite apart from the resistance of shopfloor workers who resented the loss of control over the pace and variety of their work, Taylor failed to grasp that managers – the experts – would not be unequivocally unenthusiastic about the additional burden of responsibility that his system placed upon them. Although the realization of his technocratic vision was found to be flawed by its unrealistic assumptions, Taylor's ideas did much to cement the ideal of managerial prerogative and control based upon specialist expertise. Subsequent revisions of management theory have rejected his principles without abandoning his technocratic vision.

2 Pure theory, Habermas (1972: 314–5) argues, wants to 'derive everything from itself, succumbs to unacknowledged external conditions and becomes ideological. Only when philosophy discovers in the dialectical course of history the traces of violence that deform repeated attempts at dialogue and recurrently close off

the path to unconstrained communication does it further the process whose suspension it otherwise legitimated: mankind's evolution toward *Mündigkeit*. *Mündigkeit* can be loosely translated as autonomy and responsibility in the conduct of life.'

3   There have also been criticisms from trade unionists as well as from radicals of both the Left and the Right. Those on the Left have viewed management as agents of capital whose oppressive function is to keep workers in their place. From the Right, management is criticized for building self-serving bureaucratic empires that harbour inefficiency, impede competitiveness and dampen individual initiative.

4   The example of Eastern Europe serves to illustrate how the contradictions of state socialism can be contained through military oppression, routine surveillance and corruption as well as less transparent processes of indoctrination and mystification. The crushing of urban oppositional elements in China in 1989, in Russia during 1995 and 1996, and in Syria in 2011 has illustrated how the use of violence by the state can be sustained and brutally exercised in the face of resistance. The coercive use of the army as well as the police during the Miners' Strike in the UK revealed the iron fist beneath the velvet glove of a modern 'democratic' state. When the Occupy Wall Street protesters were forcefully removed from New York's Zuccotti Park, the media were prevented from witnessing the event. Credentialed members of the media were kept a block away and police helicopters prevented news helicopters from filming the eviction. Many journalists reported being roughly or violently treated (see http://en. wikipedia.org/wiki/Occupy_Wall_Street. Accessed November 17, 2011). As the examples of Eastern Europe indicate, where the coercive grip of totalitarianism is loosened, other, gangster-like forces can emerge to fill the vacuum. In the absence of a well-organized working class, the breakdown of order presents an opportunity for various reactionary ideologies and criminal practices to assert themselves, often with former *apparatchiks* remaining in key positions and/or using these positions to acquire state assets.

5   In this respect, Critical Theory is distanced from other elements of the radical humanist paradigm – such as the traditions of anarchism (e.g. Stirner, 1907) and existentialism (Cooper, 1990) which disregard the historical and material conditions of action. While these philosophies are directly concerned with issues of human freedom, their marginalization of the importance of the historical embeddedness of human experience leads them to become fixated upon what one Critical Theorist has characterized as the self-absorbed jargon of authenticity (Adorno, 1973).

6   For overviews, many of which focus upon the work of Jürgen Habermas, see *inter alia* Jay, 1973; Held, 1980; Friedman, 1981; Honneth, 1991; Kellner, 1989; Rasmussen, 1990; Finlayson, 2005. There are also a number of collections that contain illuminating articles on particular aspects of Critical Theory. See, for example, Thompson and Held, 1982; Wexler, 1991. For a 'purist' critique of our engagement of Critical Theory, see Böhm, 2007.

7   This instrumentalism is closely related by CT to the exchange principle which assumes that everything is translatable into money, an abstract equivalent of everything else. The measurement and quantification of all phenomena, associated with the demands of capitalism for exchange, forces qualitatively different, non-identical phenomena into the mould of quantitative identity. Through the use of standardized, quantifiable instruments, the distinctive orientations and values of individuals are processed and measured according to an apparently objective set of categories or truths.

8   Marcuse's analysis parallels 'the end of ideology' thesis developed by Daniel Bell (1974) who heralds the era of the 'post-industrial society' in which class antagonisms and systematic crises are extinguished. However, whereas post-industrial theorists, like Bell, simply report and effectively endorse this trend, CT is consistently hostile to this development. The 'problem', from the point of view of CT, is that modern, affluent societies are too successful in 'delivering the goods', at least for the majority of their members. Their very success impedes the development of a critical distance from ruling ideologies of consumerism. If not wholly inconceivable, protest or rejection of dominant values and practices becomes, for most people, irrational.

9   In the popular imagination, this is precisely what science is supposed to do, which helps to explains why science, or the popular idea of it, is so readily associated with successive generations of innovative methods of organization and management that are (or claim to be) more productive.

10 This aspect of Habermas' work is particularly well discussed and critically examined in White (1988, especially Chapters 5 and 6).

11 It might be tempting to suggest that Habermas has an excessively romanticized view of such groups, and fails to fully recognize the constraints upon communication that arise from their own identity-securing concerns in which social pressures to comply with various forms of 'political correctness' and to respect tabooed topics impede open debate. While this is always a danger, a reading of his highly sceptical writings on the student protest movement in the late 1960s offers considerable reassurance (Habermas, 1971, Chapter 2).

12 This task has been facilitated by Habermas' movement away from a philosophy of consciousness towards a philosophy of language. Instead of locating the impulse for emancipation in the alienation of an essential – whether asexual, male or female – human *nature*, the philosophy of language focuses upon how *interactions*, including those that are constitutive of gender relations, are routinely forged within asymmetrical relations of power. For a good overview of various shifts and reformulations within Habermas' thinking, see Finlayson, 2005.

PART II

MANAGEMENT SPECIALISMS IN A CRITICAL PERSPECTIVE

3
Critical Conceptualizations of Management

In this and the following three chapters we draw upon the ideas developed in Part I to articulate a critical perspective on management and its specialisms. We introduce this chapter with a discussion of the extensive range of metaphors that have been deployed to understand the world of management and organization. We address metaphors of management that are primarily inspired by Critical Theory (CT): management as distorted communication; management as mystification; management as cultural doping; and management as colonizing power. In each case, we explore the general relevance of these metaphors for making sense of management before indicating their pertinence to the understanding of particular management specialisms. In Chapters 4–6, we focus more directly upon several specialisms of management, paying special attention to CT-influenced understandings of their nature and development.

On Metaphors and Metaphorical Understanding

Everyday and political language, as well as social science, are redolent with metaphors and metaphorical expressions. For example, when Churchill talked about an iron curtain being drawn between West and East Europe after the Second World War, he was, of course, using a politically charged metaphor. The same is the case with the use of phrases like a 'high position' or 'moving upwards' when referring to the authority and conditions of a job or to a career change. Metaphors are widely employed, in more or less self-conscious ways, to represent and/or (re)construct reality: 'the essence of metaphor is understanding and experiencing one thing in terms of another' (Lakoff and Johnson, 1980: 5). However, when the use of a metaphor, for example, becomes taken for granted (e.g. when reference is routinely made to organizational structure as a pyramid), language appears to reflect reality rather than to offer intrinsically imperfect and playful accounts of what it represents as reality. Moreover, when a metaphor is deemed to reflect reality, it exerts a constitutive effect upon reality as well as diminishing the credibility of alternatives. So, for example, use of the metaphor 'iron curtain' conjures up particular kinds of ideas about the Soviet Union that then may have self-fulfilling consequences with regard to, say, foreign policy.

Language and the Mobilization of Metaphors

As the world is interpreted through the medium of language(s), our sense of reality is framed and structured in historically and culturally distinctive ways (see Chapter 2). This framing invariably involves the mobilization of metaphors. Indeed, 'framing' and 'mobilization' are themselves metaphors that serve to articulate our understanding of the metaphorical quality of much communication. By addressing metaphors as a topic *of* analysis (instead of using them as an unacknowledged resource *for* analysis), it is possible to highlight how meaning is managed – for example, by portraying organizations as 'machines', 'communities' or 'battlegrounds'. Directing attention to the presence and influence of metaphors in everyday communication can, in principle, open up an appreciation and discussion of how different metaphors shape, enhance or shift our awareness and actions in much the same way that the appreciation of paradigms can open up the terrain of research (see Chapter 2).

In the field of management and organization studies, a number of metaphors have been widely but unselfconsciously applied. They include metaphors that represent organizations as 'machines', 'organisms' and 'cultures' (for a discussion of these and other metaphors, see Morgan, 1997; Grant and Oswick, 1996). These three metaphors, in particular, have been used by practitioners and consultants as well as academics (e.g. Burns and Stalker, 1961). For reasons discussed in Chapter 1, those who deploy such metaphors are attracted to the idea that the human world should mirror, if not mimic, the seemingly consensual, smooth-running operations of nature (organism), or engineering (mechanism), over which they, as the expert analysts or managers of these 'systems', are uniquely qualified to preside.

Each management specialism (e.g. accounting, marketing) has been drawn to systems thinking as a rhetoric for justifying the key importance, and (systemic) contribution, of its procedures and requirements. So, for example, the authors of the text *Human Resource Management* formulate the Training and Development element of the Personnel/Human Resource specialism using the following terms:

> Training and development (T&D) is a *subsystem* of the HR management system. The primary objective of the T&D *subsystem* is to change the behaviour of people in the company so that performance of the company as a whole is improved. ... *The inputs processed are the employees of the company.* ... You are interested in system effectiveness, that is, the degree to which the T&D system is achieving *system* objectives. You are also interested in the relationship between the benefits and the cost of the system. (Klatt et al., 1985: 337, 370–71, emphasis added)

Individual metaphors might be judged to be more or less sophisticated or more or less novel. But, crucially, metaphors are rooted in particular ideas and assumptions about the world; and they are plausible and popular partly because they legitimize and sustain particular (power-invested) worldviews. In using mechanical and organic metaphors to study organizations, there is a danger and likelihood of using managerialist language and ideas as a resource for studying management and organization when, arguably, they should be its topic (see Bittner, 1965). Moreover, as we stated earlier, metaphors have performative effects: the use of metaphors influences not only how *we understand the world* but also *how we act to reproduce or transform it*. Metaphors invite us to (re)produce the world in particular ways, and not just to frame it in a specific way. In the absence of critical reflection upon their use, researchers, students and practitioners are, by default, conditioned in their thoughts and actions by a few dominant metaphors for making sense of management and organizations.

Pitfalls of Metaphorical Understanding

Lively debates and theoretical work have addressed the use of metaphors in framing social and organizational phenomena (e.g. Alvesson and Spicer, 2011; Brown, 1976; Grant and Oswick, 1996; Morgan, 1980, 1997). A major limitation has been a tendency to focus upon a limited number of metaphors – machine, organism, culture, etc. – without giving much attention to how they are selectively adopted and mobilized. Many metaphors are possible, though comparatively few are widely favoured. When a particular metaphor is deemed to 'capture' some aspect of reality, the attribution of objectivity to a metaphor says as much about the value-orientation (see Chapter 2) and social position of the person or group that makes this attribution as it does about any correspondence between the metaphor and what it aspires to 'capture'. Our point is that the use of metaphors resides at the centre of the politics of management theory and practice. These politics are ignored when linkages between the use of metaphors and bigger issues – concerned with power, knowledge and responsibility in modern societies – are weakly made, if not ignored. This danger is particularly acute when the metaphor concept is packaged in a neat, easy-to-assimilate format.

Morgan's (1997) influential bestseller, *Images of Organizations*, is a mixed blessing in this regard. Positively, it highlights the significance of metaphor and provides an accessible overview of many different, metaphorical orientations – including some which normally escape attention. Unfortunately, it also invites, and tacitly facilitates, an uncritical 'off-the-shelf' attitude: readers are encouraged to sample and combine competing frames of reference to achieve a more 'total' picture of organizational phenomena. Instead of appreciating how metaphors articulate different value-orientations towards management and organizations, Morgan's supermarket approach treats metaphors as elements of a common jigsaw. The suggestion is that the more metaphors one knows about, or masters, the more informed or empowered one becomes. Instead of striving to appreciate the political and historical significance of the use and popularity of particular metaphors (Jackson and Willmott, 1986; Tinker, 1986), Morgan's supermarket approach suggests that a fuller, more comprehensive understanding can be achieved simply by piling the intellectual trolley with additional perspectives (see Reed, 1990).

The supermarket attitude takes no account of how metaphors often stand in a conflicting, or at least inconsistent, relationship to each other (Heydebrand, 1980). For example, the 'root metaphor' view of culture – a paradigm-like, basic understanding of organizations as made up of cultural meanings and beliefs (Smircich, 1983b) – is not readily reconciled with the image of bureaucracies as machines that operate independently of the will of individual members of staff. Machine-like ideas continue to dominate discourses and practices on corporate culture where values and meanings are treated as building blocks in organizational design, to be engineered and controlled by corporate leaders. Thus, Peters and Waterman (1982: 11) have claimed, with regard to the development of their highly influential 7-S framework, that what it 'has really done is to remind the world of professional managers that "soft is hard". It has enabled us to say, in effect, "All that stuff you have been dismissing for so long as the intractable, irrational, intuitive, informal organization can be managed".' In short, the 'soft' elements of the 7-S framework are identified as variables that the insights of postclassical organization theory render accessible to prediction and control (see Chapter 2).

This is not to deny that the use of metaphors can serve valuable purposes. Understanding a company responsible for the provision of public transport as a machine, for example, may highlight and facilitate the careful integration of a very large number of tightly coupled sets of operations that are necessitated in order to carry passengers and their luggage safely and predictably around the world. As passengers, we probably want to be assured that the wheels are securely attached, and that the engine has been properly maintained. But, as staff and as passengers, we probably also prefer not to be treated as mere numbers or commodities that are processed by the system in ways that are contrived to be 'customer-friendly' only insofar as such friendliness is deemed to be consistent with profitability and/or growth. Although perhaps an extreme example, the following endorsement of Business Process Reengineering (BPR) – one of the most influential management-of-change techniques during recent decades – conveys the mechanistic spirit of this manipulative thinking:

> Reengineering is, essentially, saying: this mighty machine (i.e. modern organization) – rebuild it, transform it into something better. And people too, complex instruments, transform them, rewire their emotional and psychological workings, free up new, better connections. (Leigh, 1994: 51)

The problem, from the perspective of Critical Theory, is that metaphors informed by functionalist thinking (see Chapter 2) have been dominant to the point of producing, refining and legitimizing machine-like relationships within and between organizations.

The Dominance of Functionalist Metaphors

Engineering and organic metaphors are strongly associated with the portrayal of organizations as robust, stable, unitary, apolitical and fundamentally conflict-free phenomena. Such functionalist metaphors suppress awareness of the role of organizations as media of social power where conflicts and frustrations are endemic to much organizational life. Functionalist ideas of organizations as machine and/or organism-like downplay the involvement, albeit alienated, of all organizational members in their maintenance and transformation. By disregarding how organizational members define the situation, make choices and act, we represent, and can turn, organizations into something thing-like and depersonalized, and thereby normalize and cement alienation. As Habermas has elaborated this argument:

> With systems theory, the phenomena ... are described in a manner independent of the language and self-understanding of the actors. The objectivating change in stance triggers off an alienating effect, repeated with each individual systems-theoretic description of a phenomenon previously grasped from the participant's perspective. (1991: 254)

A widespread preference for (functionalist) metaphors that reify the operation of systems and privilege their 'survival' may not be accidental as they implicitly assume the legitimacy of the status quo.[1] From a Critical Theory perspective, other metaphors – like totalitarianism, mystification and colonization – are no less apposite and relevant for making sense of modern organizations than are ideas about 'reengineered culture' or the 'turbo-charged machine'. Such disquieting metaphors draw attention to how the theory and practice of management are currently dominated by ways of making sense that ignore or deny its darker features. In marketing, for example, dominant thinking conceptualizes it as a 'need satisfier', as if marketing plays no role in the constitution of the consumer whose 'needs' it claims to satisfy. In order to appreciate this otherwise unacknowledged role, other metaphors must be mobilized, such as marketing as mystification. Conceptualizing organizations as instruments of domination (Hochschild, 1983) or as sites for ecological destruction (Shrivastava, 1993), in addition to Morgan's (1997) metaphor of the psychic prisons, help to dispel the complacency of conventional wisdom where an equivalence is assumed between human and planetary well-being and the profitable growth of corporate capitalism.

To recap, highlighting the existence of diverse metaphors for making sense of management and organization can be instructive. At the very least, it can be helpful for unsettling the apparent naturalness and taken-for-granted domination of widely used metaphors. To appreciate the significance and limitations of any metaphor, it is necessary to reflect upon its inspiration by a particular value-orientation (see Chapter 2). The absence of such reflection upon the connections between power structures, the use of particular metaphors and their presentation as 'product lines' in a metaphors supermarket (e.g. Morgan, 1997) does nothing to counter the preference for familiar metaphors that broadly confirm, rather than unsettle, dominant preconceptions and prejudices. The alternative is to develop metaphors that offer fresh and more challenging interpretations of the realities of management and organization. To be clear, the proposal is not simply to replace a devotion to conventional and dominant metaphors with a similarly uncritical allegiance to critical ones. Instead, we are calling for use of a variety of functional and critical metaphors, facilitating a critical dialogue between alternative understandings. Instead of the supermarket selection of a basket of metaphors, we recommend paradigm-aware critical confrontation.

Critical Theoretic Conceptualizations of Management

Having noted the pervasive presence of metaphors and identified some problems in their use, we now present some counterpoints to dominant metaphors of management. To this end, we identify several metaphors that are broadly informed by a critical perspective on social and organizational reality, as outlined in the previous chapters.

Management as Distorted Communication – Communication and the Instrumentalization of Reason

As we noted in Part I, the theory and practice of management routinely privileges instrumental rationality in which communication is focused upon, and is largely restricted to, the refinement of means. A one-sided emphasis on means easily leads to these becoming an end in themselves. The displacement of debate about goals in favour of the perfection of means occurs when ends are taken for granted and/or when ends are deemed to lie beyond rational debate. We also noted how the perfection of means is coloured, mediated and often displaced by other considerations, such as the sectional (e.g. career) values and priorities of managers. Nonetheless, *official* corporate language is frequently one of monolithic deference to seemingly apolitical, instrumental rationality.

Companies, and to an increasing extent other organizations (hospitals, schools, etc.), are enjoined to function as carriers and supporters of a rhetoric of instrumental rationality. This is most evident in corporate mission statements, press releases and annual reports. With the heavy emphasis on centrally controlled organizational communications often associated with a strong focus on branding, there is an escalation of resources invested in efforts to secure the domination of how people within and outside organizations are supposed to understand them (Klein, 2000). The packaging of an idealized and stylized version of the organization has been expanded to include 'personal branding' which involves an instrumentalizing of the self as a product, in the form of a career facilitating device, that is presented to existing or potential employers (Lair et al., 2005).

To be clear, there is nothing inherently evil or undesirable about instrumental rationality or the metaphors that it favours. On the contrary, as we suggested in Chapter 2, instrumental reason is fundamental to human well-being: it enables us to organize resources – both natural and human – in ways that can reduce needless divisiveness, suffering and waste. When applied with the unequivocal and uncoerced consent of organizational members, the application of instrumental reason mainly improves human welfare, although there can be unintended consequences. In the absence of practical reason – that is, ethically informed judgment – instrumental reason pays little attention to its unintended effects or its neglect of considerations that resist instrumentalization. Negative effects include 'externalized costs', such as the destruction of human communities and the natural environment (Jermier and Forbes, 2003; Shrivastava, 1993). When unchecked by critical reason, instrumental rationality is liable to produce a means–ends dystopia where, over time, even the relevance and value of ends become assessed in terms of what is achievable with the available means. Beliefs and practices that are deemed not to comply with this logic, and are not rendered to make a functional contribution to the efficiency and/or effectiveness of means, are then regarded as useless or passé.

In contemporary society, the dominance of an ideology of instrumental rationality – which is routinely assumed to be superior or more rational when compared to other values, goals and discourses (e.g. democratic, ecological, etc.) – places a major constraint upon the development of practical, as contrasted with instrumental, rationality. Indeed, Deetz and Mumby (1990) have suggested that 'the legitimation of managerial rationality through the dominance of the technical interest necessarily produces systematically distorted communication insofar as all forms of discourse are made sense of (i.e. judged as valid) via the interpretative template of technical-rational knowledge.' In Chapter 2, we noted how Habermas (1984, 1987) has recast and elaborated the critique of instrumental rationality within his communication theory of society. According to this theory, there are four conditions of communicative action: truthfulness, legitimacy, sincerity and clarity. If, for example, the truth and/or sincerity of communication is radically and continuously doubted, then it is difficult and perhaps impossible for communication to proceed. In this sense, the four conditions identified by Habermas are a necessary, though generally taken-for-granted, condition of any form of communication. Without an anticipation of, and respect for, these conditions, communication, and with it practical rationality, soon degrades or breaks down. Communication can thus be assessed and evaluated in terms of its approximation to, or distortion of, these criteria. The issue of whether communication in organizations approximates to dogma (closed communication) or dialogue (open communication) can also be raised. In short, the value of the distorted communication metaphor is that it directly highlights restrictions on free dialogue. As Forester has argued:

> When organizations or polities are structured so that their members have no protected recourse to checking the truth, legitimacy, sincerity, or clarity claims made on them by established structures of authority and production, we may find conditions of dogmatism rather than of social learning, tyranny rather than authority, manipulation rather than cooperation, and distraction rather than sensitivity. In this way critical theory points to the importance of understanding practically and normatively how access to, and participation in, discourses, both theoretical and practical, is systematically structured. (1983: 239–40)

This view emphasizes that organizations do not only produce goods and services. They are also, and more fundamentally, producers and reproducers of media of communication in which employees are often induced to pay attention to a very limited range of organizational activities and outcomes (see Chapter 1). From this perspective, modern corporations can be perceived as proto-totalitarian institutions insofar as the value and relevance of employee contributions is assessed predominantly in terms of the monolithic 'template of technical-rational knowledge' (Deetz and Mumby, 1990).

Instead of actively enabling communicative interaction, and thereby encouraging more differentiated worldviews and dissolving traditional hierarchical forms of authority, the reproduction of the modern corporation tends to require and preserve communications that are systematically distorted (Deetz, 1992a, 1992b), and not least by policies that promise or advocate forms of 'teamwork', 'empowerment' and open communication whilst impeding their realization.

The case of Business Process Reengineering

Common to most recent major ideologies and techniques for improving corporate performance (e.g. Excellence, TQM, Balanced Scorecard) has been the contradictory championing of empowered employees and strong leadership. This circle is squared by the claim that the discipline of firm leadership is productive of greater autonomy. Or, as Peters and Waterman (1982: 322) make this case, 'a set of shared values and rules about discipline, details and execution can provide the framework in which practical autonomy takes place routinely.' In other words, the individual employee is free to do what he or she wishes as long as this is what the boss wants the employee to wish (Willmott, 1993a).

Consider the case of Business Process Reengineering (BPR). Business Process Reengineering is distinguished by its identification and promotion of new information and communication technologies as a means of radically transforming work. For example, reengineered work may enable customers to deal with a single representative/VDU operator who responds to their requirements simply by activating the relevant databases and networks and then monitoring progress. Instead of designing organizations as a production line with production and service work being completed by a series of employees undertaking a sequence of tasks, BPR aspires to turbocharge the productivity of labour by moving to parallel processing. In principle, all activities are then dramatically speeded up and unproductive duplication is eliminated (Willmott, 1994b; Grint, 1994).

Despite the lip service paid to concepts like 'empowerment' and 'teamwork', there can be little doubt that the intent of BPR is to impose and sustain a top-down totalizing solution. Hammer and Champy (1993), the leading advocates of BPR, contend that:

> It is axiomatic that reengineering never, ever happens from the bottom up. ...The first reason that the push for reengineering must come from the top of an organization is that people near the front lines lack the broad perspective that reengineering demands. ... Second, any business process inevitably crosses organizational boundaries ... some of the affected middle managers will correctly fear that dramatic changes to existing processes might diminish their own power, influence and authority. ... *Only strong leadership from above will induce these people to accept the transformations that reengineering brings.* (ibid.: 207–8, emphasis added)

Most recent recipes for improved corporate performance, such as Excellence, TQM and Balanced Scorecard, have been couched in the velvet language of humanism and employee involvement. BPR, in contrast, is couched in engineering language and charges senior management with the task of imposing its recipe for revolutionary change upon employees who are to be 'induced' into accepting its requirements. Senior managers may 'carry' those wounded by reengineering for a little while but they must '"shoot the dissenters!"' (Hammer in Kalgaard, 1993: 71). Hammer and Champy brazenly identify the need for 'Czars' (not champions) who will ruthlessly push through reengineering programmes without regard for the personal, social or even the economic costs involved in such a coercive approach to organizational change (Grey and Mitev, 1995). Top management and senior staff, aided by BPR consultants, are assumed to know best. Any suggestion that their knowledge may be imperfect or even wrong, and/or that their decisions are based on self-interest, is suppressed.

From a CT perspective, such developments are interpreted as nascent technocratic totalitarianism. Whatever is deemed by experts to be effective in terms of gaining a competitive advantage or maximizing output, however insidious or demeaning, is regarded as legitimate. Leaders committed to change, it is argued, 'have no choice in how they deal with those attempting to impede their efforts' (Hammer, 1994: 47). When instrumental rationality is elevated to rationality *per se*, it becomes an ideology. With this elevation the value-based ends and the value-laden means for attaining these ends are shielded from reflection and critical evaluation.

Technocratic totalitarianism in Human Resource Management

Human Resource Management (HRM) elaborates a battery of 'objective' techniques for managing the selection, motivation and promotion of employees (Steffy and Grimes, 1992; Townley, 1993) which, in principle, are yoked to the strategic objectives of the organization (Legge, 1995). Advocates of HRM claim that its new approach and accompanying set of practices replace old-fashioned personnel management (see also Chapter 4). With sufficient investment and resources, the well-run HRM machinery is designed to deliver a qualified and highly motivated work force. Human capital is increasingly used as a metaphor for people in organizations. Common distinctions involve soft and hard HRM systems that are targeted, and productive of, high- and low-commitment workforces, respectively. Soft- or high-commitment HRM is characterized by long-term relationships, caring and personal development. Hard- or low-commitment HRM is characterized by exploitative and short-term relationships. The latter is exemplified by business-focused and calculative aspects of managing 'headcounts' in a rational way. Some critics have used the phrase 'inhuman resource management' (Steyaert and Janssens, 1999) to describe the treatment of employees as expendable, manipulable commodities (Legge, 1999). Often the ideology of HRM one-sidedly emphasizes and exaggerates the soft- or high-commitment version of HRM, claiming that this is the key to success. But this account presents an idealized and limited picture. There are, as Watson (2004) points out, reasons to avoid overplaying the soft/hard distinction, as a calculative view of personnel cannot be avoided wherever employees are treated as commodities sold in labour markets, so that there is always a tension with efforts to incorporate a more long-term and development-oriented approach.

HRM specialists do not go to the root of the problem which, we contend, would require the removal of constraints that impede employees discovering for themselves what is meaningful for them. Instead, they contrive to design and reward work in ways that circumvent this issue by introducing measures to increase employee motivation, flexibility and productivity. Standardized forms and procedures such as appraisal talks, often structured in a specific way and institutionalized to take place at prescribed intervals, are part of HRM systems, following a quite different logic than employee-initiated, emergent talks with colleagues, friends and managers about their work, performances, ambitions (or lack thereof), etc. The latter would not necessarily be better than formal, managerially led appraisal talks, but strict HRM regimes may easily reinforce and monopolize a managerially dominated, instrumentalized version of conversations about work and development. A communicative action logic would proceed more strongly based on the employee's initiative and agenda setting and involve relations other than the manager–subordinate one.

Within HRM discourse, employees are understood to be 'motivated' so long as they are productive – regardless of whether their work is experienced as personally meaningful. In this sense, as Sievers (1986) has argued, the idea of motivation is a 'surrogate for meaning' in a world where experts dominate decisions about how organizations and jobs should be designed, and work frequently lacks any deeply valued purpose or significance. A basic problem of increasingly large parts of contemporary working life in 'affluent societies' is that it comprises tasks that have a remote and questionable relationship to what is intrinsically meaningful to, or personally valued by, people. It is one thing to do something clearly related to people's needs, another thing to produce something that increases their status – which by definition is at the expense of others, as status is a zero-sum game (see Alvesson, 2012b). A lack of meaningful work is a consequence of, and is compounded by, the production of products and services primarily to accumulate personal wealth rather than as a response to social demands (e.g. affordable health care, housing, clean environment, meaningful education, etc.). In turn, producing for profits distributed to personal and institutional investors rather than need requires intensive marketing and selling efforts to construct people as consumers for whom consumption provides only temporary and superficial satisfaction.

In HRM, the idea of making work more motivating serves to legitimize piecemeal social engineering. As a surrogate for meaning (see above), the literature on motivation allows non-meaningful work to be interpreted through a technocratic lens so that 'the human resource becomes a manipulable object of management control' (Rose, 1990). Through the systematic design of programmes of selection, induction and training, the province of management is expanded by Human Resource specialists to include teaching employees how to think and feel about their work, as well as how to do it more productively. The aim of such programmes, often guided by consultants, is to place under systemic control the potentially disruptive extra-organizational values that employees bring with them into employment (see Chapter 1 and below). Likewise, marketing specialists have for some time promoted the idea of 'internal marketing' and 'relational marketing' – developments that aspire to provide a technology for forg and sustaining social ties (see Chapter 5), while accountants represent their specialism as 'the language of business' and themselves as its impartial 'score-keepers' or 'map-makers' (see Chapter 6).

As we noted in Chapter 2, money and power provide the media for designing and redesigning the norms that regulate interaction between employees and their internal and external customers (Wilkinson and Willmott, 1995a). As reason is instrumentalized, albeit in the name of empowerment, important questions concerning ends, values and ethics are excluded from the corporate agenda or trivialized by it. Managers become preoccupied with career goals and organizational politics (Jackall, 1988; Knights and Murray, 1994). And yet management is routinely and publicly represented as if it is fundamentally a matter of impartial professionalism, not of politics. A technocratic ideology is developed in which management is viewed as the dispassionate response by experts to 'objective' factors. Communication from and about management is distorted as issues are represented in terms of the application of neutral expertise – competences, skills and techniques which are assumed to be dedicated to the realization of a common social good (see Chapter 1). There is a heavy emphasis on top management and staff experts as architects and champions of policies, structures, programmes, rules and steering techniques. This focus upon how changes should be managed and how individuals ('human capital stock') should be targeted for development excludes, or at least marginalizes, the possibility of mobilizing employees as active participants in dialogue. Reliance on instrumental rationality and a technocratic orientation to decision making narrows and constrains communicative action – which is ironic, given the former's inescapable dependence upon the latter.

Management as Mystification – the Selective Constructing and Confusing of Needs and Understandings

The mystification metaphor is used to draw attention to the ways managers strive to construct a favourable image of themselves and/or their organization through the careful arrangement of symbols and ceremonies (Alvesson and Deetz, 1996; Rosen, 1985). The mystification metaphor, it is worth stressing, does not necessarily imply that researchers or other analysts enjoy privileged access to an 'objective' reality behind the mystique (though some may fall victim to this delusion). Rather, the metaphor of mystification is understood here to draw attention to how management contrives to shape the way people – employees, consumers and citizens – make sense of the social world and participate in it. It understands management as an institution whose agents mould and influence people's beliefs, meanings, values and self-understandings.

Liberation and creativity are fashionable ideas promise to 'liberate' managers and employees from the drudgery of traditional patterns of work by promising a flattening of hierarchies and increased empowerment. But, in effect, these ideas impose a new set of disciplines upon employees who are encouraged to equate processes of liberation and creativity with unequivocal dedication to corporate values and objectives, as they induce employees to regard fellow workers as their customers (Oakland, 1989). 'Soft' versions of Total Quality Management, in particular, incorporate Human Resource thinking as they proclaim that: 'Total quality management is part of a holistic approach to progress … there is a tremendous unlocking of energy in management and the workforce … liberating people at work to become more truly themselves and more creative' (Bank, 1992: 195). This seemingly liberating move, with the desired outcome that people become 'truly themselves', is misleading as it assumes that the 'true self' is somehow identifiable independently of the cultural attributions that are made about it; and, relatedly, that a 'true self' will be affirmed by such techniques (Fleming and Sturdy, 2011). Another, related problem with such claims is that they assume emancipation and creativity to be gifts that can be bestowed upon employees by managers. Arguably, however, these are not gifts but outcomes of individual and collective struggles to overcome forms of dependency. In the absence of such struggles, it is others – e.g. managers – who decide how and when people are 'truly themselves' and what counts as being 'more creative' (Willmott, 1993a).

Human resources thinking aspires to operate as a cultural filter that 'embraces the uncertainties of employee existence, imposes order and meaning on them and provides the employee with a predictable, secure and carefully projected and rewarded understanding of organizational life' (Keenoy and Anthony, 1992: 243; see Alvesson and Kärreman, 2007 for a case illustration). However, organizational life is not (yet) the only source of symbolic or cultural meaning. Not only are occupational and professional subcultures likely to be resistant to the demands of human resource thinking, but employees bring to the workplace (moral) notions of fairness, justice and so forth that are not necessarily compatible with either the content of human resource policies or with the procedures used to implement them. Effective management, Keenoy and Anthony (ibid.: 249) contend, is dependent upon the maintenance of community bonds of a more substantial and more coherently moral nature than can be constructed by human resource consultants and practitioners. In other words, to translate this criticism of human resources thinking into Habermasian language, the systems logic of impartial professionalism is likely to collide with 'lifeworld' understandings of equity and legitimacy. This tension/collision may be avoided by employees who develop defences (e.g. indifference or cynicism) that impede rather than facilitate the kind of commitment that is sought by policies aimed at increasing employee involvement and unlocking creativity.

Mystifying the hierarchy

In contemporary management theory and practice, there is much talk about the flattening of hierarchies and the reduction – if not the removal – of middle management. Consider, then, the following example (taken from Alvesson, 1995). In a Swedish IT consultancy company, top management expended considerable time, energy and financial resources in encouraging its staff to adopt the norms and values of the company. Employees were repeatedly told that the hierarchy was extremely flat, with only two grades – subsidiary managers and consultants – and no intermediate levels. In general, social relations within the firm were represented to staff as non-hierarchical, close, friendly and family-like.

One consultant in this company was asked to compare it to his former workplace. In doing so, Joe repeated many of the themes contained in the corporate ideology, especially the lack of an extended hierarchy. At his previous place of employment, this consultant had a group manager as his immediate superior whereas, in his present workplace, there was a flat structure. 'My only boss is Alf (Subsidiary Manager)', he said. Later in the same interview, he was asked about possibilities for exerting some influence in the allocation of assignments. It turned out that Joe's last assignment had been given to him by Sten, without his being asked whether he was particularly interested in it. The researcher then asked if Sten, a consultant, had managerial responsibilities and received the answer: 'Yes, he works directly under Alf'. In practice, then, it seemed that Sten functioned as a middle manager with semi-formal status as second-in-command. As far as the interviewee was concerned – a graduate engineer with several years of working experience – there was no doubt that Sten was his superior, even though he had earlier identified Alf as his only boss.

This example suggests that Joe had not fully reflected upon the plausibility of the official representation of the organization as 'flat'; or, at the very least, that he was willing to disregard the anomaly by regurgitating, without qualification, the official view that Alf was his only boss. Certainly, the direct reference to Sten's managerial responsibilities seems to contradict directly Joe's earlier description of the company. Yet he revealed no awareness of the discrepancy.[2] The example illustrates how continuous exposure to a dominant set of ideas can produce an unreflexive regurgitation of their content and, indeed, can operate to dull sensitivity to experiences that could potentially disrupt and debunk their authority.[3]

Mystifying the customer

Perhaps the area of management where the mystification metaphor is most obviously applicable is marketing, and especially its role in selectively constructing how, as consumers, our 'needs' are identified and satisfied. Marketing represents itself as a technically rational apparatus for closing the gap between producers and consumers as its claim is to identify 'customer needs'. 'Marketing is all about mutually satisfying exchange relationships for which the catalyst is the producer's attempt to define and satisfy the customer's need better' (Baker, 1987: 8). And yet, arguably, the nature and extent of human need is something that is socially ascribed and negotiated rather than objectively given (Knights and Willmott, 1974/5). Marketing is thus implicated in the constitution and mystification of what human need is, rather than simply reporting upon, and responding to, given needs.

Consider advertising images. Very often, these function as ambiguous symbols, capable of containing various sorts of meanings and stimulating various kinds of impulses and desires (Klein, 2000; Leiss, 1983). Commercials for cars or cigarettes are displayed against a picture of unspoiled wilderness, or a bottle of spirits is set in a farmhouse room full of handcrafted furniture. The fluidity of the symbolism that surrounds these products acts to encourage us to associate the purchase of these goods with a satisfactory level of 'need satisfaction' – not for a means of transport or a fix of alcohol but for status, identity confirmation, self-esteem, etc. Marketing in particular, but also management in general, is engaged in processes of myth-making as it exploits ambiguity and insecurity (e.g. about identity) to procure and expand its influence, often and increasingly by promising to enhance our sense of identity or 'lifestyle'.

Techniques of mass persuasion developed to shape and control processes of consumption are now being applied to the task of 'internal marketing' within organizations. Within the sphere of production, Total Quality Management programmes seek to induce employees to identify themselves as customers within a supply chain (Wilkinson and Willmott, 1995a). Such programmes are at the centre of contemporary efforts to increase productivity, quality and flexibility by securing control of the 'soul' of each employee (Rose, 1990) – for example, by directly intervening in the design of work cultures through which a sense of work identity is acquired. Their intent is that employees should derive self-esteem from the service given to the next person in the value chain, as their 'customer', rather than from the personal meaning or pleasure associated with the work they do. Here, the idea of a fellow producer as a 'customer' to be satisfied is the preferred surrogate for meaning. Metaphors drawn from outside the sphere of production, such as 'team' and 'customer', are mobilized in ways that mask and mystify, more or less intentionally, their embeddedness in and contribution towards relations of domination and control (Kerfoot and Knights, 1994).

In sum, the metaphor of mystification highlights ongoing processes of influencing how people make sense of ambiguous phenomena (arrangements, changes, acts, product qualities, etc.). They draw attention to how critical evaluations are denied, normalized or counteracted, and how 'positive' perceptions and attitudes are developed. To explore further this aspect of mystification, we introduce the metaphor of cultural doping, as it is suggestive of processes that penetrate deeply into the formation of self-identity. Doping is a matter of ensuring that people have the 'right' orientations.

Management as Cultural Doping – the Corporation as a Socialization Agency

The cultural doping metaphor represents management as a socialization agency. Socialization is the process through which humans acquire, and identify with, the values, customs and aspirations of the social groups in which they live and grow up. Socialization can also be defined as cultural learning. In induction and development programmes, employees are told – more or less explicitly – how they must perceive and relate to organizational reality, and how they should participate in organizational rites where the 'correct' values, virtues and ideals are communicated. Often the influence is exercised on a subconscious level, making it difficult for employees to recognize it and subject it to critical scrutiny (for critical discussions, see Kunda, 1992; Willmott, 1993a).

The dominant, technicist orientation inculcated into management education is an example of such doping (see also Chapter 8). Much education and training of managers is about acquiring the 'right' (i.e. self-assured and 'positive') orientations towards managerial work. Personnel specialists, for example, are increasingly encouraged to adopt the jargon and orientation of Human Resource Management – a term and slogan that suggests and legitimizes an equivalence of human beings and other factors of production, as it further erodes the traditional, welfare-oriented role of the personnel specialist who, in principle, subscribed to an ethos that paid attention to the well-being of employees (Watson, 1977; Keenoy and Anthony, 1992). In the marketing field, the cultural doping metaphor highlights how people are brought up to be, above everything, 'sovereign' consumers, to such an extent that a great deal of a person's subjectivity – values, feelings and thinking – is associated with, and evaluated in terms of, the level and content of consumption.

To own and consume becomes a core element in affluent societies. With the segmentation of markets, and the increased emphasis upon the acquisition of lifestyles, marketing has tended to grow in appeal and influence, and not least when it appears to pay for public goods, for example, through the sponsorship of sport and through its contribution to entertainment or good causes, such as education and ecology. In the commercialized process of educating people about how to make sense of life, corporations and marketers have strengthened their position while parents and cultural traditions have lost ground (see Lasch, 1979). In the USA, the typical child is now 'immersed in the consumer marketplace to a degree that dwarfs all historical experience' (Schor, 2004: 19). Even before starting school 25 per cent of all children have a TV in their bedroom and they are exposed to massive efforts by advertisers to shape their awareness and preferences. The typical first grader can evoke 200 brands.

The effect of the expansion of marketing and consumption has been illustrated by historical studies of the changes in 'people production' during the last century (see especially Rose, 1990). Fromm (1941) and Riesman (1950) identified the market-oriented, 'other-directed' person as an increasingly common character type in the USA. The attributes of such a person include flexibility, dependence on other people's opinions and a willingness to adapt to fashions and social changes. Lasch (1979, 1984) has characterized the historical personality type of Western capitalist societies, pre-eminently the USA, as comprising a combination of unstable self-esteem and recurrent self-doubt – a volatile mix concealed from self as much as from others beneath an outward appearance of gregariousness, self-confidence and conviction (see also Goffman, 1959). Such a person – labelled as narcissistic by Lasch – believes (or desperately wants to believe) in the favourable appearance that s/he contrives to present to others. However, the schism between self-confidence and self-doubt, which lies at the centre of narcissism, is keenly felt as an experience of alternation between (publicly expressed) feelings of satisfaction and grandiosity, on the one hand, and (privately repressed) feelings of emptiness and vulnerability, on the other. Advertising and images of consumption are understood to normalize narcissism as they stimulate grandiose fantasies which simultaneously arouse feelings of unhappiness and inadequacy, and then provide a compensatory solace for them. The outcome, Lasch argues, is an increase in feelings of resentment and self-contempt. As he puts it:

> *Modern advertising seeks to promote not so much self-indulgence as self-doubt. It seeks to create needs, not to fulfil them*; to generate new anxieties instead of allaying old ones. By surrounding the consumer with images of the good life, and by associating them with the glamour of celebrity and success, mass culture encourages the ordinary man to cultivate extraordinary tastes, to identify himself with the privileged minority against the rest, and to join them, in his fantasies, in a life of exquisite comfort and sensual refinement. Yet the propaganda of commodities simultaneously makes him acutely unhappy with his lot. By fostering grandiose aspirations, it also fosters self-denigration and self-contempt. (1979: 180–1, emphasis added)

Empirical support for this claim comes, for example, from studies which indicate – perhaps unsurprisingly – that people looking at beautiful models who so frequently act as human hoardings for products and services tend to be more dissatisfied with their own looks afterwards (Kasser, 2002).

The metaphor of marketing-as-cultural-doping (socialization) draws attention to how, when marketers influence the demand for products, they are affecting not only tastes, wants, understandings and needs; they are also involved in producing and governing people, insofar as personal identity becomes more closely associated with, and dependent upon, what they own and consume. Current marketing talk about tailoring products and services to the profile or specifications of individual customers proclaims that niche marketing and the customization of goods will enable modern consumers to express and secure their individual identities without discrediting the framework of mass consumption (e.g. McKenna, 1991; Pine, 1993). However, as Lasch (1979) emphasizes, programmes and techniques that seek to exploit or colonize the lifeworld are inherently problematical and unstable. Instead of developing a less precarious basis for processes of self-formation and reproduction, these interventions can compound the precarious and fluid nature of (modern) identities and stimulate the development of resistance (e.g. social movements and protest groups, as well as individual 'down-shifting') that challenge their legitimacy.

It should not be assumed, however, that people are passive receptacles into which forms of 'dope' are poured. Aside from resistance – for example, 'Adbusting' (see http://www.adbusters.org/) – satire and irony are widely deployed to debunk and deflate the grandiose claims made for products and services. Given the ever increasing level of consumption and strength of investments for regulating demand for new products and services the impression is that resistance is exceptional compared to affirmation and celebration of consumerist orientations and identities. Often 'resistance' is reduced to the expression of some awareness – e.g. about fashion-following and paying over the price for the right brand – of the effects of power and manipulation, while actions do not follow this awareness, but is instead compliant with strategies for managing employees and customers. This is referred to as cynical consciousness (Fleming and Spicer, 2003). Whether the planet can continue to accommodate the demands placed upon natural resources by current and rising levels of global consumption is another matter. One could hope for nature, at some point, putting up a much stronger barrier of resistance than we human beings often seem to be capable of doing.

Management as Colonizing Power – the Erosion of the Lifeworld

Colonization describes the way that one set of practices and understandings comes to dominate and exclude other practices and discourses. Consider 'lifeworlds' (e.g. the family) where human beings develop a sense of being purposive, wilful subjects with distinctive social identities (as discussed in Chapter 2). Instead of understanding social phenomena from the perspective of the participants in such lifeworlds, instrumental reasoning represents the world as impersonal, interchangeable elements of the system. 'The system' conceives of the social world in terms of the operation of more abstract and formal structures of relations, governed in the modern era by money and (formally based) power. Within the rationality of the system, individuals are treated as numbers or categories (e.g. grades of employees determined by qualifications, or types of clients by market segment) and, more generally, are viewed as objects whose value lies in reproducing 'the system'. Most work organizations, Habermas (1987: 309) contends, 'not only disconnect themselves from cultural commitments and from attitudes and orientations specific to given personalities; they also make themselves independent from lifeworld contexts by neutralizing the normative background of informal, customary, morally regulated contexts of action'. 'The system', Habermas argues, poses a corrosive challenge to the sense of self-identity and value that develops within 'the lifeworld'. This is a tendency to which each of the three metaphors discussed in the previous sections of this chapter draw attention in different ways. The colonization metaphor can be seen to pull together their insights into a broader framework for interpreting contemporary developments.

When pointing to the colonization of the lifeworld by systems thinking and values, Habermas is concerned that, in advanced capitalist societies, the primacy and significance of the lifeworld becomes devalued as it is when regarded as an irrational impediment to the perfection of systems' properties; or when it is viewed purely as a resource for breathing new life into tired bureaucratic structures (Willmott, 1992). This devaluation of lifeworld properties is perverse because the instrumental rationality of the system depends upon the communicative rationality of the lifeworld, even though it appears to function independently of lifeworld understandings and competences. At the very least, 'systems' depend upon human beings who are capable of communicating effectively and who are not manipulated and demoralized to the point of being incapable of cooperation and productivity. It is when the connection between 'system' and 'lifeworld' is denied or distorted that a marginalization and erosion of the normative and ethical sensibilities developed within the lifeworld occur. Current talk of 'business ethics', corporate social responsibility and the strengthening of corporate culture to facilitate empowerment, trust and teamwork can be seen as a – largely synthetic and perverse – 'system' response to its own corrosive effects upon lifeworld values and practices.

Perhaps the most obvious case of colonization occurs in the sphere of consumption where individuals are encouraged to identify with 'system' images and packages of 'the good life' or 'life-style'. Obliged to consume in order to exist, we are exhorted by assorted advertisers and experts to realize how our lifeworld should be ordered, including leisure and even sexual identity. The space for face-to-face formation and control of the lifeworld is progressively reduced. Processes of defining the meaning and identity of the self are colonized by techniques developed by 'expert' promoters and packagers of goods and services, including education and training programmes that encourage employees to substitute 'systems' values (or, at least, learn how to manage the appearance of doing so) for those of the lifeworld (see Chapters 1 and 8). Engineered, top-down meanings are intended to replace the bottom-up meanings which employees and consumers bring from the lifeworld. Investments in these colonization projects within and outside organizations are extensive and pervasive.

Each of the management specialisms currently competes to demonstrate their relevance and effectiveness to processes of colonization. Accounting has historically established itself as the specialism of management control by providing impersonal, quantitative measures of individual and organizational performance. Accounting academics and professionals have been busily promoting its relevance for brin-gacademics and professionals have been busily promoting its relevance for bringing 'value-for-money' to public sector organizations, such as hospitals and schools. Similarly, Information Systems (IS) has been commended as something that must be introduced with the utmost urgency into all spheres of production and consumption so that computers now mediate and control many aspects of our day-to-day transactions and communications.[4] Within organizations, the rise of 'knowledge management' means that the experiences and knowledge of people are being targeted for codification and storage, and so become part of organizational property. Knowledge is decoupled from experience, insight, reasoning and reflexive judgment as it is turned into something that is stored in a warehouse-like knowledge management system (Alvesson, 2004). Databases organized and managed using computers are often deemed to be 'better' or 'more authoritative' as well as quicker, just as television news is widely deemed to be more neutral as well as immediate than the equivalent newspaper coverage. However, the use of new technology is not unremittingly colonizing. Satellite communications (e.g. mobile phones) and especially the Internet are as yet largely unregulated (and, indeed, are very difficult to regulate or censor effectively), and are therefore actual and potential carriers of all kinds of subversive 'life-world' material and person-to-person communications (e.g. use of social networking sites and texting to mobilize forms of activism that are difficult to police).

The complete subjugation of employees and consumers to 'system objectives' may be an unstated, and perverse, aspiration of managerial theory and practice, including – and especially – its 'progressive' variants that advocate 'empowerment' and 'self-actualization'. But it is highly doubtful whether this (totalitarian) vision can ever be realized. This assessment is illustrated by the following quotation from an employee in one of the biggest UK supermarket chains. The employee, who has been trained to smile at customers – at her workplace, posters at all entrances to the shop-floor were emblazoned with the injunction 'Smile, you're on stage' – commented, 'the company has to be realistic … it's alright for someone to tell you to smile but you can't smile at someone who's calling you a stupid bitch' (Ogbonna and Wilkinson, 1990: 12). The company's expectation that its employees will be civil towards customers is, of course, consistent with established values of the lifeworld in which cold, impersonal, off-hand behaviour is expected to be the exception rather than the norm.[5] Lifeworld values (e.g. of quality and care) are selectively invoked in corporations to introduce and legitimize programmes of 'customer care', 'total quality' and the like, in an effort to project the idea that the customer is valued as a person, and is not being 'cared for' simply as a means of retaining market share and increasing profitability. However, the tactic meets its limits when employees are required to sustain a smile even when customers are deemed, according to lifeworld values, to be unreasonable or even personally offensive (see also Van Maanen, 1991). A polite, diplomatic attitude towards rudeness and hostility at all times may be consistent with the 'system' priority of retaining customers. But it violates lifeworld values where the very personal quality of relationships allows for emotions – negative as well as positive – to erupt. More generally, as Habermas has suggested, the exploitation, abuse and colonization of lifeworld values is productive of tension and resistance:

> The new conflicts arise along the seams between system and lifeworld … the inter-change between the private and public spheres, on the one hand, and the economic and administrative action systems, on the other … it is institutionalized in the roles of employees and consumers, citizens and clients of the state. It is just these roles that are the target of protest. Alternative practice is directed at the profit-dependent mobilization of labor power. … It also takes aim at the monetarization of services, relationships, and time. (1987: 395)

Compliance with demands by employers to be polite and diplomatic, even under the severest provocation, is likely to be grudging as well as insincere ('I smile because I'm told to') (see Hochschild, 1983). It is compliance that may wear very thin and turn to resentment when, for example, the injunction to be a smiling shop worker is placed in the contradictory context of being understaffed, overworked and under-valued by customers and employer alike. Not unusually, front-line employees find themselves in the firing line of frustrated customers for failings over which they have no direct control. Where processes of self-formation and social integration are undermined, goodwill and morale is sapped, with the associated risk of crises of motivation and legitimation (Habermas, 1975, 1987). Successive interventions by management – from Scientific Management through Total Quality Management to Business Ethics – are intended to render organizations more effective (in 'systems' terms) by extending the managerial sphere of governance from bodies (the design of jobs) to souls and minds (the socialization of employees). That the demand for new techniques of management control remains buoyant suggests that the colonization of the lifeworld by experts who manage 'the system' is far from assured or complete.

Conclusion

In this chapter, we have considered four metaphors (or metaphor-like conceptuali-zations) – management as distorted communication, management as mystification, management as cultural doping and management as colonization – as a way of pro-viding a provocative alternative to metaphors more commonly used to characterize organizations and management phenomena.

We do not claim that metaphors, singly or in combination, perfectly reflect or fully illuminate what organizations and management are about. In some specific cases, they may offer minor insight, but arguably they often give an eye-opening perspec-tive on management and organizational phenomena. Metaphors provide alternative ways of making sense of social reality. Our counter-metaphors attend to issues that, we contend, are unacknowledged or poorly appreciated by self-serving, mainstream representations of management.

Whilst appreciating the appeal and persuasiveness of metaphors, we have also stressed that processes and forms of mystification and cultural doping offer only tempo-rary and partial solutions to problems and anxieties of self-formation. As Giddens has remarked, when challenging a tendency to exaggerate the extent to which people are passive, helpless victims of the power of media images that colonize their consciousness:

> In assessing the prevalence of narcissism in late modernity, we have to be careful to separate the world of commodified images ... from the actual responses of indi-viduals ... powerful though commodifying influences no doubt are, they are scarcely received in an uncritical way by the populations they affect. (1991: 178–9)

Each of our metaphors provides a springboard for further theoretical and empirical work. By challenging the authority of conventional wisdom, they can be deployed to inspire and promote more critical understandings of modern work organizations,

Table 3.1

Metaphor	Key issue	Problem	Effect	Critical challenge
Distorted communication	Domination of instrumental reason	Technocratic consciousness	No space for political and ethical communication	Appreciate primacy of communicative rationality and limit space for instrumental rationality
Mystification	Construction of needs	Power-defines needs and wants	Neglect of alternative wants and objectives	Critical reflection on needs and wants
Cultural doping	Socialization	Dominance of one source of norms and orientations	Restricted value set	Broaden sources of value
Colonization	Conflict of logics	Domination of system logic (formal power and money codes dominate)	Marginalization of meaning-making work	Engagement in grounded (experience-based) meaning-making

and thereby contribute to processes of emancipatory transformation. It is relevant to recall how, historically, imperialistic colonizers sooner or later have encountered local resistance to their oppressive ambitions. It is to be hoped that a comparable process of opposition and revolt will develop within modern societies where 'lifeworld' values are being colonized and degraded by 'systems' priorities; and that this challenge to 'systems' colonization will be supported by diverse social movements and protest groups whose members are also antipathetic to the erosion and distortion of communicative rationality by an overbearing instrumental rationality. This is a common thread that, potentially, could bring together alliances of oppositional groups around a political agenda of global justice and radical change.

Notes

1 The very idea of *survival* is strongly associated with natural selection theory. Like many words that appear to be neutral and innocent, the concept of survival is not. For it evokes ideas about the natural world, where adaptation has nothing to do with sectional interests and is unmediated by *socially constructed* (and transformable) divisions of class, gender and ethnicity. Likewise, reference to 'organization' and even 'organization studies', rather than to (the study of) diverse organizing discourses and practices, tends to marginalize consideration of issues of action, conflict and oppression (Willmott, 1996c).

2 It is also possible that Sten was aware of the discrepancy but was only partially successful in concealing this awareness. If this interpretation is favoured, then there is the difficulty of reconciling a tendency or pressure to hide this awareness with the espoused corporate ideology of open communications, even with external researchers.

3 An example of dulled sensitivity that is closer to home for British academics concerns the comparatively recent rating of the research and teaching performance of all university departments. Though initially viewed with scepticism and hostility, these rating exercises have become progressively institutionalized, with the tendency for academics to evaluate departments in terms of reified categories rather than their localized knowledge of their distinctive strengths, quirks and weaknesses. See Willmott (1995a, 2011c), Prichard and Willmott (1997) and Mingers and Willmott (2011) for a fuller discussion of these developments. There is an irony here since one of us (Willmott) accepted an invitation to be a member of the panel charged with evaluating the 'research excellence' of UK business and management departments.

4 For example, it has been found that customers purchasing travel and insurance products are much more likely to be persuaded of the reliability and genuineness of 'deals' if they are flashed up on a computer screen rather than presented in glossy brochures.

5 As was demonstrated by Garfinkel's (1967) notorious breaching experiments in which students living at home were instructed to take on the role of lodgers.

4

Critically Assessing Management Specialisms I

Organization Theory, HRM and Leadership

In this and the following two chapters we address a number of management specialisms.[1] In this chapter, we consider organization theory, HRM and leadership. Of course leadership can be seen as a subcategory of organization theory, but it has also emerged as a distinct field and so it warrants attention at a time when managers are so keen to represent themselves as leaders, and where there are broad expectations that leadership will solve all sorts of problems. These specialisms are concerned with the 'softer', human side of management. In general, they are less preoccupied with quantification and with avowedly objective forms of measurement. In Chapter 5, we turn to the specialisms of marketing and strategic management. These share some concern with human issues but are also often informed by approaches drawn from economics and psychology where the emphasis is on constructing and measuring variables, thereby transforming aspects of organization and management into something that is unrecognizable as human. (Leadership studies also often favour quantification, despite numerous incisive critiques of this approach.) Then, in Chapter 6, we examine the fields of accounting, information systems and operational research where a technical approach and a reliance upon quantitative data are often more in evidence, and people issues are pushed to the margins.

Of course, it is difficult to make a sharp distinction between the respective domains and orientations of the various management specialisms. Service management, for example, incorporates elements of marketing and organization theory. Within more quantitative disciplines (e.g. accounting and operational research) there has been some significant broadening and 'softening' of approach as behavioural (organizational) elements are incorporated. Contemporary trends towards 'multidisciplinarity' in management studies, as well as teamworking and networking in management practice, are intended to encourage closer cooperation between specialists and foster the development of 'hybrid' managers (Ezzamel and Willmott, 1998). Increased collaboration between suppliers and customers in joint ventures on product development, for example, creates pressures for more fluid, networked arrangements, rather than the preservation of specialisms and departmental silos, such that 'hybridity' becomes more valued (see Boltanski and Chiapello, 2007). In general, it would seem that social and organizational skills associated with the behavioural dimension of management are exerting an increasing influence on the development of knowledge of, and practice within and across, specialist fields of management.

Our aim in Chapters 4–6 is to offer a broad indication and discussion of contributions to each specialism, and thereby provide a source of inspiration for radical rethinking of conventional understandings. Our objective is not to present a comprehensive review of critical studies of the management specialisms or even of those studies that resonate most deeply with the concerns of Critical Theory. (For such reviews, see the contributions to Alvesson et al., 2009.) To reprise what we said in Chapter 1, we view our commentary as a stimulus to emancipatory forms of management theory and practice, and not as anything remotely approaching a definitive statement on how each of the specialisms has been subjected to critical scrutiny.

Organization Theory

We regard organization theory as the most fundamental and pervasive of the management specialisms. That is not entirely surprising as every aspect and specialism of management is 'organized'. Organizing is endemic to all the specialisms and, indeed, is not infrequently identified as the very medium of management (e.g. Hales, 1993). Organization theory is also the richest of the specialisms in terms of theory, research and generation of ideas and perspectives. It is the most important for critical management theory as it most readily accommodates diverse currents of critical thinking and has had the greatest influence on the development of other specialisms.[2] As we address organization theory in many parts of this book, in the following section we treat it fairly briefly.

Beyond Classical Organization Theory

The basic outlines of the critique of mainstream (functionalist) organization theory and practice were sketched in Chapters 1 and 2, and we will not repeat these here.[3] Instead, we briefly review three trends that have shifted organization theory away from its classical formulation in the writings of Taylor (1911) and Fayol (1949). *First*, there has been a renewed interest in varieties of thinking associated with Human Relations (Mayo, 1949) and Socio-Technical Systems (Emery and Trist, 1960) approaches, where sentiment is identified as an untapped resource for securing improved levels of commitment and productivity. The attainment of corporate objectives is understood to be secured by responding to individual employee needs, with self-esteem and self-actualization being championed as 'key motivators'. The recasting of such thinking is evident, for example, in prescriptions for building strong corporate cultures where self-esteem and self-actualization are carefully managed through the development of more 'organic' organizational systems (see Chapter 3). Associated with this managerial focus upon culture and symbolism is a growing attentiveness to corporate identity, branding and image management

(Alvesson, 2012a; Hatch and Schultz, 2004; Kärreman and Rylander, 2008; Kenny et al., 2012). There has been a keen interest in possibilities for encouraging employees to identify more closely with the organization, including the seemingly paradoxical injuction to 'just be yourself' (Fleming and Sturdy, 2009). In this way, corporate characteristics and ideals are used as guidelines for how employees (should) define themselves. By managing how employees regard themselves in rela-tion to their corporate membership – in a manner that parallels the external mar-keting of images to consumers – managers hope to create commitment and what is seen as an appropriate mindset and productive behaviours (see Alvesson and Willmott, 2002).

A *second*, related shift incorporates this focus on employees' values, mindsets and identifications but points towards a broader and, in principle, more integrated and totalizing set of regulatory mechanisms. Elements of hierarchy, bureaucracy, stan-dardized procedures and results measurement are retained but combined with a 'post-bureaucratic' emphasis upon new forms of flexibility. In such ways, the range of means of control are broadened and increasingly

> ... include cultural and ideological controls (emphasizing the importance of cus-tomer service, quality and image; affirming the business enterprise as an arena for heroic or spiritual accomplishments), structural controls (continuous measure-ments and benchmarking, flatter organizational hierarchies), technological controls (electronic surveillance of unimaginable sophistication) and spatial controls (open-plan offices, controlled access). (Gabriel, 2005: 17)

One key element here is the adding of the consumer as a key player in the exercise of organizational control (du Gay and Salaman, 2002) so that, for example, employees are urged to regard themselves as providers of service to customers and to imagine what, as consumers of services and products, they would wish to experience:

> in the past 30 years or less, the consumer, the abstract individual who seeks hap-piness in buying choices and offers no account or explanations for them, has entered the world of organizations, transforming the old dyad – workers and manag-ers locked into their long-standing feud – into a *ménage à trois*. (Gabriel, 2005: 20)

The addition of these 'softer' forces and means of control does not simply involve the application of a further layer of control or an additional restriction upon employees. Teamworking, for example, requires some integration and slackening of highly frag-mented divisions of work and direct forms of supervision, but it also involves an increased level of peer (or 'concerted') control that can be highly oppressive (Barker, 1993; Ezzamel and Willmott, 1998a; 1998b). The internal complexities and dynamics of organizing, especially in rapidly changing market or technological conditions, mean that ambiguity and uncertainty are ubiquitous. In such circumstances, employ-ees face a broader set of pressures and demands but these can also present opportunities for slipping away from, and producing resistance to, new variants of control (Fleming and Spicer, 2007).

The *third* shift away from classical theory is a move from an assumption that organizational members share identical interests (e.g. in deriving benefit from applying the principles of scientific management) to understanding that organizations comprise a plurality of stakeholders – such as employees, consumers, suppliers, government, the law, the local community, as well as providers of finance. Organizations are increasingly understood to attend to, or disregard, the needs of a plurality of groups; and the task ascribed to professional managers is one of ensuring that the diverse needs of these groups are recognized, that conflicting interests are regulated, and that a dynamic equilibrium is maintained. Contemporary organizational analysis has done much to highlight the presence of different forms of rationality and even 'irrationalities' (Brunsson, 1985) as well as hypocrisies (Brunsson, 2003). An emphasis upon diversity may, however, imply that power relations between stakeholders are more or less equal, if not wholly symmetrical.[4] Overlooked is the extent to which plural rationalities are a medium and outcome of institutionalized inequalities of wealth and influence, and are a product of ongoing conflicts between various groups (see Chapter 1).[5] When plural rationalities are situated in a wider context of inequalities and asymmetrical power relations, the establishment of a strong corporate culture, for example, is interpreted less as a means of improving the balance between a plurality of stakeholders than as a stratagem for disregarding differences of income and opportunity by encouraging conformist attitudes and values.

In order to illuminate the limitations of pluralist understandings of organizations, it is necessary to shift to a more radical standpoint, such as those developed within the Marxist and radical feminist traditions which we introduced in Chapter 2.

Gendered Organization Theory

Initially, interest in gender and management emerged from a liberal feminist position and concentrated on women managers (e.g. in terms of leadership style and other problems. compared to male managers). It included consideration of difficulties experienced by women in attaining managerial positions because of prejudices and resistances that acted as barriers to women making careers (e.g. Eagly and Carli, 2007; Marshall, 1984). As we noted in Chapter 2, such an approach is rather restricted: it concentrates on those organizational and psychological conditions that are of immediate relevance for women aspiring to function as managers and climb up the organizational career ladder. While the liberal feminist position challenges male-biased practices and beliefs, it does not question the wider institutional arrangements or the overall logic of corporate organizations (Alvesson and Billing, 2009; Calas and Smircich, 2006; Collinson et al., 1990).

A broader and deeper gendered vision of organization understands all aspects of modern organization to be infused with values, rules, priorities and orientations that are also gender-saturated. It notes, for example, how corporations and public bureaucracies have traditionally been, and remain, dominated by males (Mills and Tancred, 1992). Because women have taken primary responsibility for the reproductive sector – child care and other 'logics' that are developed within the reproductive sphere (Gilligan, 1982) – many features of organizations are assessed to be comparatively alien and frustrating to women. Moreover, when women adapt to organizational conditions and managerial demands, there is the risk that 'conformity and the abandonment of critical consciousness are the prices of successful performances' (Ferguson, 1984: 29).

As we noted in earlier chapters, there are similarities between Critical Theory (CT) and a number of the more critical versions of feminist thinking, including their respective critiques of (the dominance of) instrumental reason (Alvesson and Billing, 2009; Martin, 2003). However, while CT contends that the dominance of instrumental reason is problematic irrespective of gender, radical feminists contend that 'the feminist case against bureaucracy goes beyond ... (the "traditional" critique of CT and Marxism) because it constructs its alternative out of concrete and shared experiences of women, rather than out of a romantic vision of precapitalist life or an abstract ideal of "human nature"' (Ferguson, 1984: 27). To this, a CT response might be that many men share with many women similar experiences of frustration in relation to bureaucracy, and that while men generally may be more at ease in the impersonal culture of bureaucratic organizations, this is a mixed blessing; and that it is a relatively small elite of men who are the primary material beneficiaries of contemporary forms of work organization. One could also challenge the idea that the experiences and values of women are uniform. Women vary considerably, not only in political opinions and career interests, but also in experiences of dissatisfaction in organizations (Billing and Alvesson, 1994). Drawing attention to what is most acute for female workers may obscure what are common concerns and grievances among many employees, irrespective of gender. In this respect, at least, there is scope for a closer dialogue between feminism and Critical Theory (Martin, 2003).

Indeed, in recent years there has been a growing challenge to the idea of the dichotomy between males and females as robust categories (Butler, 2004). It has been questioned whether this dichotomy mirrors, rather than constitutes, two distinct groups corresponding to biological sexes. It is also doubted whether the dichotomy adequately grasps complex socialization patterns which fix the meaning of, and ideas about, men and women. There has been an increasing interest in how masculinity and femininity are socially constructed and transformed. Instead of being fixed by nature or history, gender identities and relations are seen as precarious and unstable. Associated with this deconstruction of gender is an interest not only in women but also in men and masculinity (Collinson and Hearn, 1996), and in the social and organizational processes through which forms of femininity and masculinity are produced within corporate settings. For example, sexual imagery and jokes (Collinson, 1992; Hearn et al., 1989), and discourses about corporate strategy and leadership, are understood to involve strong elements of masculinity that act to strengthen male identities and thereby reproduce asymmetrical gender relations in organizational life (Calas and Smircich, 1991). Here possible tendencies towards a 'de-masculinization' of management and organization that, for example, places less emphasis upon heroic forms of leadership, invite consideration.

Critical Organization Theory

When discussing the four paradigms of organizational analysis identified by Burrell and Morgan (1979) in Chapter 2, we overviewed a number of strands of critical thinking in the study of organizations (see also Casey, 2002; Grey, 2008). Here we expand upon the contribution of Critical Theory (CT) to organizational analysis. Analysis informed by CT, it will be recalled, aspires to go beyond the historical–hermeneutical project of seeking to appreciate members' interpretations of organizational phenomena. In so doing, it interrogates the conditions that support, and perhaps impede, the capacity to develop and articulate particular interpretations. CT-guided studies move away from the idea that researchers can 'objectively' capture others' interpretations without placing their own gloss upon the meaning of such findings. The CT researcher is not a passive observer but, instead, is much more of a 'reconstructionalist' who does not simply record organizational members' interpretations of their experience but discerns within them articulations of the narrowness and managerialism of organizational ideologies (Steffy and Grimes, 1986). In turn, this critical reconstruction of conventional wisdom can stimulate the development of a dialogue with organizational members and/or the (mainstream) architects of managerial ideology and culture. In this dialogue, the question of how interpretations are conditioned by forces of which the individuals involved are often only dimly aware, is brought to light and subjected to critical scrutiny. In such ways, CT seeks to open up radically new understandings of organizational life that have a potential to give voice to, and promote, critical reflection and autonomy, informing both carefully-thought-through and communicatively and democratically grounded modes of work and organization (see Benson, 1977; Böhm, 2005; Burrell, 1994; Willmott, 2003).

There are two broad variants of organization theory inspired by CT. One approach focuses upon the alienation of individual consciousness, and understands emancipatory action in the context of the conflict between an essential human freedom and its negation by oppressive social institutions. A second approach, which Habermas' work has inspired since the early 1970s, proceeds from the pragmatics of communication whose violation is understood to provoke emancipatory action.

On the alienation of human consciousness

A major concern for leading Critical Theorists (e.g. Marcuse) has been the way people can become psychologically dependent upon, and 'imprisoned' within, modern institutions. Workaholism and the psychological (as contrasted with material) anxieties associated with the loss of employment or lack of promotion are symptomatic of such dependencies. Careerist obsessions leading to the structuring of self, partner and friendship relationships into a career-facilitating project seem to be increasingly common (Grey, 1994; Lair et al., 2005). As we have suggested above and in previous chapters, managerial interest in topics like corporate culture, organizational identity and corporate branding can be interpreted as moves to exploit employee anxiety (e.g. about self-esteem) by contriving to provide corporate antidotes for it.

This interpretation can be contrasted with traditional psychoanalytic theory in which the irrationalities of the human psyche are viewed as intrinsic to human nature. From the latter perspective, reason is regarded as a precarious accomplishment, always vulnerable to the play of unconscious motives and fantasies (Freud, 1917) that are only marginally affected by the dampening or amplifying influence of social and cultural conditions. CT, in contrast, contends that culture plays a significant role in the development of the human psyche – for example, by increasing the conflict between libidinal drives and the standards and restrictions of civilization, and/or by reinforcing the power of immature fantasies (Marcuse, 1955; Fromm, 1970). The neurotic and narcissistic character of the modern individual is, according to this view, much more a function of a particular form of civilization than it is a reflection of a woman or man's essentially problematical psychology (cf. Lasch, 1979; see also Chapter 3).

From a CT perspective, then, the confusion, anxiety and emotional turmoil that impedes the process of organizing personal and social life in accordance with so-called 'rational' ideals is, in large part, socially and organizationally produced (Sennett, 1998; Sveningsson and Alvesson, 2003). Authoritarian social relations, degraded conditions of work and low discretion are all understood to be detrimental to employees' well-being. Strongly non-democratic and non-egalitarian relations between superiors and subordinates are understood to induce more or less conscious feelings of dependence, anxiety and vulnerability. It is for this reason that efforts to counteract hierarchical and authoritarian relations can be deeply threatening. The (unconscious) tendency is to comply, albeit with repressed feelings of resentment, with their demands (Knights and Willmott, 1989; Sennett, 1980). Jobs that provide little discretion and little intellectual stimulation are linked to rigid attitudes towards life, passivity and broadly conservative and authoritarian opinions (Kohn, 1980). Instead of striving for clarification of the life situation, and then engaging in action to change it, there is a tendency for passive adaptation, clinging to the status quo and compensatory consumption to be pursued and endorsed (see Chapter 3).

This does not mean that the development of the human psyche works solely against emancipation or that it necessarily acquiesces to the status quo – however problematic. On the contrary, the tensions associated with the restriction of autonomy and responsibility provide the basis of personal and collective resistance to forms of domination. Marcuse (1955) argued that human instincts, which are mostly unconscious, stand in potential opposition to the oppressive disciplines of modern organization and society (see Chapter 2). According to Marcuse, contradictions arise between, on the one hand, the modern ego administration that programmes people – through education, training and mass media – to produce and consume; and, on the other hand, libidinal drives that repeatedly call for pleasure and satisfaction. Libidinal impulses recurrently present a challenge to the status quo and may, therefore, foster emancipatory change[6] – when they do not fall foul of repressive desublimation, or where forms of pleasure are pressed into the service of corporations (e.g. 'hoopla' in the guise of competitions, parties, prizes and 'gongs' for performance) (Burrell, 1992), and are intended to work as a distraction from more fundamental, routinized and constrained work conditions (Fleming and Sturdy, 2011).

Habermas, in contrast to Marcuse, is sceptical about placing too much emphasis upon instinctual impulses towards emancipation, arguing that the ascription of instinctual impulses is itself historically and culturally mediated. Or, as he puts it, the concept of instinct is 'rooted in meaning structures of the lifeworld, no matter how elementary they may be' (Habermas, 1972: 256). Instead of a focus upon the alienation of human consciousness – produced by either loss of control of the means of production (Marx), or the denial of instinctual impulses (the id) by the formation of the super-ego (Freud) – Habermas turns to *language* as the medium of all human understanding and the source of human autonomy and responsibility:

> the human interest in autonomy and responsibility is not mere fancy, for it can be apprehended *a priori*. What rises out of nature is the only thing that we can know: *language*. Through it structure, autonomy and responsibility are posited for us. Our first sentence expresses unequivocally the intention of universal and unconstrained consensus. (ibid.: 314, emphasis in original)

In his later work, Habermas endeavours to make good this claim by seeking to show that communication could not proceed without making the (unarticulated) assumption that human beings are autonomous and responsible, and that an unconstrained consensus is anticipated (see also Chapter 2). We now turn to analysis of management and organization that has been influenced by 'the linguistic turn' in Critical Theory.

Organizations as Structures of Communicative Interaction

The analysis of organizations as structures of communicative action, rather than sites of psycho-social imprisonment, is symptomatic of a (Habermasian) shift in CT from a focus upon the alienation of individual consciousness to a consideration of distortions in intersubjective communication. Instead of assuming that humans possess an essential autonomy that is frustrated and deformed by the demands of oppressive organizational structures, the focus upon communication sidesteps the question of what is essential to human nature in favour of an understanding of the fundamental conditions of human communication. The critical issue then becomes whether particular structures of communication allow these fundamental conditions to be fully realized; or how relations of power – in the form of capitalism, technocracy, consumerism, sexism, racism, etc. – systematically impede this possibility by, for example, representing such impediments as natural or functional rather than social and enslaving.

Drawing upon Habermas' ideas on communicative interaction and rationality, Forester (1983, 1989, 1993) has identified four kinds of misinformation or communicative distortion that are of particular relevance for understanding organizational work (see also Kemmis, 2000). Forester addresses two dimensions. The first concerns the *inevitable/socially unnecessary* character of the distortion. Some distortions are almost

Contingency of distortion	Autonomy of source of distortion	
	Socially *ad hoc* (person-bound)	Socially systematic/ structural
Inevitable distortion	*Cognitive limits:* complexity, random noise, idiosyncratic personal traits disrupting communication (1)	*Division of labour:* information inequalities due to legitimate divisions of labour, problems in the transmission of meaning (2)
Socially unnecessary distortions	*Interpersonal manipulation:* deception, bargaining, wilful unresponsiveness (3)	*Structural legitimation:* monopolistic distortion of exchange, ideological creation of needs (4)

Figure 4.1   *Types of communicative distortion (adapted from Forester, 1982)*

impossible to avoid, while others follow from circumstances that can be changed, and the source of the distortion abolished. The second concerns the question of whether the distortion is *ad hoc* (where it is more connected to individual action than a reflection of social structure) or *structural/systematic* (where it is inherent in a particular social order). Combining the two dimensions leads to the model shown in Figure 4.1. Even though all sources of communicative distortion must be considered, a focus on communicative interaction suggests that square 1 (cognitive limits) is of least interest and that square 4 (structural legitimation) is of greatest significance for analysing the theory and practice of management and organization.

While drawing attention to forms of communicative distortion that, in principle, can be counteracted, the model acknowledges the significance of universal problems for the emancipatory project. For example, the emotional and cognitive state of human beings places limits upon communicative rationality (square 1), as do the unpredictable dynamics and ambiguities of social life (square 2). The proposed means of uncovering the link between power and distortion, and thereby facilitating emancipatory change is, first, to evaluate empirical phenomena by considering their immediate character in terms of their necessary or unnecessary bounds; and, second, to examine their structural or non-structural character in a given social context. When phenomena are discovered to be socially unnecessary and structurally based, the consistent response is to question and reach some grounded agreement upon how things are, and how they should be, prior to acting to facilitate the emancipatory change of the existing structures. As Forester (1988: 9) puts it, the idea is to challenge 'any perceived "necessity" or "natural" or reified character of such constraints. Here we have the link between a tradition of ideology critique and political action and a previously altogether depoliticized understanding of administrative and planning rationality.' The same critical logic could be applied to other articulations of organizational ideology that evade critical scrutiny.

Habermas' communication theory encourages a readiness to say 'no' to statements with problematic validity claims, and a preparedness to engage in communicative processes of challenging such statements when deemed necessary. The criteria for rationality and legitimacy is the degree to which statements indicating standpoints about values, goals and means can be probed in a process of dialogue to warrant their 'truth' (are statements well grounded in what we recognize as facts?), their 'legitimacy' (do they express acceptable values and norms?), their 'sincerity' (are they referred to in a sincere or manipulative way?) and their 'clarity' (are they diffuse – could they be clarified?) (Forester, 1993). It is possible to conceive of a strong and a weak version of critical organization analysis guided by Habermas' theory of communication. The strong version suggests that the truth, legitimacy, sincerity and clarity of statements can be decisively tested through a process of critical scrutiny. In doing so, there is a risk that one pays insufficient attention to the contingent conditions of the judgments that are made, and so slides into authoritarianism or elitism, lacking in modesty about how far one can go in testing the statements in (undistorted) dialogue. Relatedly, and as poststructuralists (see Chapter 2) have warned, the strong version of Habermas' communication theory does not encourage reflection upon the disciplinary effects of its own presuppositions.

It is therefore important to explore how Habermas' ideas may be used in a 'weaker', critically pragmatic way, where the working principle is not to try to get rid of all communicative distortions or indeed to anticipate an ideal speech situation, but to open up a space for increased communicative action with regard to beliefs, consent and trust, thereby challenging and reversing the tendency of work organizations to devalue, corrode or appropriate the values of the lifeworld (e.g. family, neighbourhood, voluntary associations). This can to some extent be combined with a pragmatic view of poststructuralism (Deetz, 1992a; 1992b; see also Chapter 7). A developed capacity to question and discuss the rationality of significant statements can consequentially alter the way that these discourses act to maintain the position of a ruling, managerial elite. This capacity to question can also provide a basis for the critique and transformation of organizational practice (Alvesson, 1996; Forester, 1989, 1993, 2003). Support for this endeavour can be derived from studies which show that, despite an official rhetoric of purposive rationality, 'interactions are still connected via the mechanism of mutual understanding' (Habermas, 1987: 310). Not only is there considerable scope for so-called 'informal behaviour' in which processes of mutual clarification and adjustment are incorporated, but the effective operation of organizations is, in practice, heavily dependent upon such processes. Habermas makes this point: 'If all processes of genuinely reaching understanding were banished from the interior of organizations, formally regulated social relations could not be sustained, nor could organizational goals be realized' (ibid.). Without such 'informal behaviour' any sense of meaningfulness, urge to clarify meanings and to improve mutual understandings would be impaired or lost. Space for such behaviour tends to be reduced and weakened when priority is given to system imperatives associated with formal objectives, plans, structures and techniques for regulating behaviour at work – for example, through job designs, performance indicators, HRM-based people improvement procedures, etc. Tensions and identity crises associated with the separation between formal systems and a sense of personal meaning are, *inter alia,* understood by Habermas to stimulate, and resonate with, processes of critical reflection that challenge and counter the tendency for an overbearing systems logic to devalue and displace lifeworld values, including those fostered outside of the workplace in the family and community.

Summary

Organization theory guided by CT shares with postclassical organization theory (e.g. (neo) human relations) a concern to highlight the perverse effects of suppressing the contribution of lifeworld values (e.g. sentiment and tradition). In each case, there is an effort to resist the reduction of human beings to appendages of the corporate organizational machine or system. That said, postclassical thinking has the instrumental purpose of oiling the machinery to make it function more effectively. It does so by exploiting human sensibilities and mitigates their resistance to mechanical forms of control. CT, in contrast, places in question the instrumentalization of human beings. It analyses how relations of power in organizations operate to impede open communication – for example, by introducing more or less subtle incentives and veiled forms of coercion. From a CT perspective, the purpose of studying organizations and organizing practices is not simply to 'map' their contours, to appreciate the diverse meanings attributed by actors to their organizational conduct, or even to identify means of raising productivity by countering forms of dissatisfaction and poor morale. Rather, its purpose is to encourage and contribute to a dialogical process of exposing, challenging and removing forms of oppression. More specifically, it involves exposing and questioning relationships, discourses and practices that impede rather than promote greater personal and collective autonomy and responsibility.

 ## Human Resource Management

Human Resource Management (HRM) is an area of practice that, to some extent and selectively, applies ideas developed in organization theory (Watson, 2007), although it also draws upon work psychology and personality theory (e.g. Guest, 2002). Its theoretical base is often weakly articulated and its content is frequently focused upon administration and techniques that are becoming increasingly pervasive as boundaries between work and life and inside/outside the organization are becoming blurred (Costea et al., 2008), as well as by communication technologies (email, cellphones, etc.). We have touched upon HRM issues in Chapter 3. Here we give it a more systematic and integrated treatment in which we focus principally upon its more critical elements.

In common with proponents of other contemporary knowledge areas and occupations, exponents and students of 'HRM' have been engaged in a mobility project in which they have sought to upgrade its status and significance for organizations and the broader economy. They have done so by distancing it from, and seeking to elevate it over, the established specialisms of Personnel Management, Industrial Relations and Organization Theory. As the term HRM suggests, it is a managerialized version of more pluralistic conceptions of employees and workplaces. In mainstream HRM, human beings are conceived as resources, and the objective is to render them pliable in ways that maximize performance – for example, through the construction of High Performance workgroups. A basic pitch of HRM is that 'people are the most important assets of an organization' which, of course, suggests that HRM is the most important area of expertise. The recasting (or rebranding) of Personnel Management as HRM illustrates Habermas' point about the instrumentalization of knowledge. The explicit identification of people as 'resources' is suggestive of their equivalence to other factors of production – a status that exemplifies the application of a 'systems' logic to human beings.

The past couple of decades have witnessed an increased interest in knowledge work and claims that the post-industrialized knowledge economy is well established – a development that has supported calls for (even) greater investment in 'human resources' and the honing of their 'competences' (Newell et al., 2002). There is, however, considerable variation in the meaning and significance attributed to the 'knowledge economy' and the 'knowledge workers' within it. Some argue that 'knowledge workers' comprise only a relatively small, although expanding, element of the workforce who possess advanced knowledge and intellectual or symbolic skills (Alvesson, 2004; Thompson et al., 2001). It is also debatable whether all or most organizations in the so-called knowledge-intensive sector of economies are particularly interested in making substantial investments in 'HRM'. There is great variation and, while companies that make such investments tend to attract the greatest publicity, there are many examples of knowledge-intensive firms in which competence development receives very limited top managerial attention or resources (Fosstenløkken, 2007).

In the academic literature, HRM tends to be presented as a core strategic activity (e.g. Boxall and Steeneveld, 1999; Steffy and Grimes, 1992). It is deemed to be 'strategic' insofar as it takes care of 'the most important asset' – with regard to recruitment, training, staffing, career planning and development, compensation, labour relations, and so on. HRM is considered to be fully 'strategic' when every facet of the employment relationship is managed in a manner that contributes optimally to the achievement of organizational goals. There are differing interpretations of strategic HRM. It may, for example, be viewed as oriented, or tailored, to the business strategy of an organization. In which case, depending on the work and the kind of labour needed, HRM activity might focus on the recruitment of a low-commitment, high-turnover workforce when this approach is assessed to be most consistent with a low-cost market niche. Or HRM may be interpreted as providing a 'best practice' portfolio of approaches to recruitment, training, etc. by, for example, facilitating the recruitment, development and retention of highly committed staff with the potential to collaborate successfully and learn quickly. Many academic advocates of HRM are inclined to reserve the label for the latter approach, in which case HRM is said to be

> a distinctive approach to employment management which seeks to achieve competitive advantage through the strategic development of a highly committed and capable workforce using an array of cultural, structural and personnel techniques. (Storey, 2001: 6)

As we noted in Chapter 3, HRM advocates are inclined to make bold claims about how large-scale investments in people produce better performance and better work(places) (see Hesketh and Fleetwood, 2006). In making such claims, there is a 'cherry picking' of attractive practices that associates HRM with investments in processes of recruitment, training and development staff, and distances HRM from downsizing, outsourcing and redundancies. Critical studies of HRM, in contrast, tend to substantiate and reinforce observations about the partiality of HRM. These studies describe the theory and practice of HRM in unflattering terms, taking issue with its narrow and simplistic prescriptions – which say how things should be, rather than endeavouring to discover how things are and what makes them that way. The theory and practice of HRM are generally more concerned with the refinement of tools and techniques than with nuanced explanations (e.g. of employee resistance to 'cultural, structural and personnel techniques'; see also Boxall et al., 2007), let alone with advancing a deeper understanding of employee relations. In-depth qualitative studies of HRM practices are quite rare, with the exception of a few studies that have focused upon particular forms of HRM activity or technique, such as appraisal, where it is typically shown not to work as intended (Alvesson and Kärreman, 2007; Townley, 1999). In contrast, much HRM research is preoccupied with investigating and endeavouring to prove that heavy investment in HRM pays off (Huselid, 1995; Pfeffer, 1994), and thereby justifies the strategic position to which advocates of HRM aspire (see also Keenoy, 2009). This mainstream focus on the normative and descriptive has rendered the area atheoretical as well as lacking in rich and deep empirical studies of HRM practice (Schneider, 1999; Steyaert and Janssens, 1999). Its critics complain that HRM research is 'narrow, technocratic and managerialist' (Keegan and Boselie, 2006: 1508) in its exclusion of broader concerns, such as how people practically relate to, and are affected (if at all) by, HRM arrangements and practices. Their complaint is that HRM research incorporates very limited reflexivity – that is, efforts to consider its position, priorities and practices in a self-critical way (Janssens and Steyaert, 2009).

There is, nonetheless, a small but growing stream of critical HRM studies, some of it inspired by Legge (1978, 1995; see also Fox, 1974; Keenoy, 1990, 1999; Watson, 2004) which aims to

> offer counter images to those put forward in dominant discourse – drawing attention to hidden and less desirable aspects of HRM practices, offering alternative

readings, giving voice to those marginalized, discriminated against or silenced, and offering innovative or insightful ways of interpreting employees' experiences of HRM. (Keegan and Boselie, 2006: 1508)

Two important areas of such critical work are (i) the scrutiny of assumptions informing mainstream HRM research and scholarship; and (ii) the role of HRM, as ideology, in legitimizing managerial interests by presenting positive views that effectively provide a smokescreen for the darker, contradictory aspects of how 'human resources' are managed in contemporary organizations.

Assumptions

We have already noted how mainstream HRM research is criticized for being technocratic, positivist and lacking in reflexivity. One aspect of this orientation is the preoccupation with a narrow conception of (financial) performance that is strongly associated with a (top) management perspective. Janssens and Steyaert (2009) have argued that a broader attentiveness to a range of 'outcomes', including those that are unintended and unflattering to management, must be adopted if HRM research is to escape its stultifying indebtedness to a managerial frame of reference. More specifically, Janssens and Steyaert commend the development of HRM research in a direction that is attentive to the political nature of the employment relationship – where priorities and preferences between employers and employees may overlap but are not necessarily shared or reconcilable. Janssens and Steyaert also recommend that more attention is paid to employees' legal rights in a manner that makes HRM specialists more directly and systematically attentive to the promotion and defence of such rights. In doing so, HRM researchers are invited to recognize and explore how HRM practices are embedded in 'broader patterns of culture, power and inequality' (ibid.: 146).

Another assumption of many HRM researchers is that employees are essential, fixed subjects (e.g. within a hierarchy of needs) that are amenable to be worked upon by HRM initiatives and techniques. The instrumentalization of people as 'assets' is consistent with this understanding and it sustains a 'systems' form of thinking that excludes, or at best narrows, any ethical concern with regard to how employees may be negatively affected by job stress and insecurity that routinely accompany forms of work intensification (Keegan and Boselie, 2006: 1508). The counter-assumption is that people are more processual, context-dependent, hard to 'pin down' and therefore difficult to 'sum up', and generally not 'object-like'. They are engaged in making sense of their world, actively interpreting it and acting on the basis of emergent constructions of themselves and their intentions in a complex and often dynamic world. Such understandings are common in forms of interpretive and poststructuralist analysis but are absent from mainstream HRM. As a consequence, mainstream HRM research may be unthreatening, if not particularly instructive, to HRM practitioners. It may also appear naïve and subservient to those who, through critical reflection, have come to adopt a more challenging standpoint. The latter standpoint suggests that the employee-as-resource is fostered (e.g. by managers and HRM more specifically), rather than discovered, through participation in employment practices (Deetz, 2003; Townley, 1993). On this view, HRM practices and practitioners participate in the creation of what they allegedly merely discover and contrive to manage.

Ideology Critique

Ideology critique generally circles around claimed discrepancies between rhetorics and reality. For example, appealing claims about new initiatives, such as the creation of a 'high performance workforce', are seen to exist in a relation of some contrast and tension to actual practices. Such claims have ideological and legitimizing effects (e.g. in terms of career advancement) for HRM practitioners and academics who promote or endorse them. Three overlapping aspects of the critique of HRM-as-ideology can be outlined:

- *The boosting of (traditional concerns of) personnel management, and packaging it as HRM as if it is something quite different and unquestionably superior.* There is a kind of ideological upgrading of personnel administration that is seen to lack any credible anchoring in organizational practices (see Guest and King, 2004). HRM is simply 'talked-up' as an approach as it assumes an alignment of employer and employee interests by 'putting people first' and investing in their competences.
- *The making of HRM into something 'strategic'.* The 'talking-up' of HRM frequently involves its association with what is 'strategic' in a way that disregards or denies the less glamorous 'non-strategic' aspects of HRM. This forms part of a more general inflation of mundane, operational activities as a discourse of strategy becomes dispersed and deployed to redefine work as strategy-focused, rather than mere administration and management. In other words, the 'halo effect' of an association with 'strategy' serves to boost status more than it offers any credible indication of what actors actually do, or accomplish. In sum, the association of HRM with strategy becomes an ideologically inflected representation of practice in a way that conflates contemporary reality with a projected but never-to-be-realized future (see Berglund, 2002).
- *An excessive use of positive-sounding representations of how work organizations now value and will treat personnel.* In 'talking up' HRM (see point above), competence, development, high performance, trust, alignment of interests, human capital, investment in people, etc. are widely and repeatedly rehearsed terms. Yet, in most organizations, there is at best a complicated and unstable mix of highly selective, longer-term investment in people and their careers together with much expedient treatment of employees as expendable assets who are expected to focus upon their short-term employability, not their employment security. Not unusually, there is a marked and widening differentiation between a small and shrinking elite of employees who enjoy comparatively good conditions and prospects, and a mass who are temporary and/or poorly remunerated. All employees are subject to the vagaries of market volatility and the impacts of acquisition or failure; but the elite are generally much better cushioned

from cost–cutting, outsourcing and so on. In an economic climate that demands flexibility, and where pressures to deliver shareholder value make executives eager to save costs through rationalizations, the promise of high-commitment HRM has greater resonance as an alluring discourse of legitimation than as a blueprint for foreseeable practice. As Guest and King (2004: 412), leading advocates of HRM, have conceded:

> It seems that when organizations are making money they are too busy to implement best practice HRM and feel that in any case they are doing well enough without it; and when they lack money, they can't afford to implement it.

When scrutinized from a critical standpoint, contributions to the study of HRM are seen to be much stronger on rhetoric, ideology and the legitimation of people management than on influencing or explaining why corporate practice typically falls short of its promises. An alternative, critical conception of HRM has been advanced by Delbridge and Keenoy (2010) who sketch a number of directions that would take HRM 'beyond managerialism':

1 Contextualize the practices of HRM 'within the prevailing socio-economic order and its associated discourse of market individualism' (ibid.: 10). A key focus would be the institutions of employment regulation, including the law, formal and informal negotiations, and so on. This would extend to a consideration of the role of the state and the involvement of unions.
2 Denaturalize 'the taken-for-granted categories and assumptions which typically inform the mainstream analysis of HRM' (ibid.; see above also).
3 Include the voices of those who tend to be excluded from mainstream accounts of HRM, such as 'those in non-standard forms of employment, minority workers and those working outside the Western industrialized economies' (ibid.).
4 Incorporate the study of HRM outside of larger corporations, including 'small and medium sized organizations, and the public and third sector, as well as explore alternative forms of organization such as cooperatives' (ibid.: 11).

In a companion paper, Delbridge (2010) has argued for a form of critical HRM that is broadly equivalent to what Burawoy (2004) terms 'public scholarship'. Its intent is to engage a wide audience (e.g. of practitioners as well as scholars) in a 'dialogue on matters of political and moral concern' (ibid.: 4). Much (mainstream) HRM proceeds with 'a specific problem defined by a client', often in the real or imagined form of senior management. In contrast, a task of critical HRM is to scrutinize 'the values under which research in [such policy-oriented or consultancy-inspired research endeavours] is conducted' (ibid.). To do this, Delbridge (2010: 6) suggests that proponents of 'critical HRM' should adopt and adapt central elements of the agenda of CMS, a number of which have been outlined above: questioning the taken-for-granted; moving beyond instrumentalism and an associated preoccupation with performance; embracing a concern for reflexivity and a focus upon meanings in research; and challenging structures of domination.

Leadership

The Leader-Driven Organizational World?

Nowadays we hear about the importance of leadership in nearly every sphere of human endeavour. The leader has become one of the dominant heroes of our time. When faced with major crises, cries ring out for better leadership. Almost regardless of the problem, leadership is presented as the solution. Leadership is repeatedly associated with what is necessary and advantageous. It has always been an important area of management, but interest in leadership has exploded during recent years. Managers are increasingly referred to as leaders; earlier efforts to make a distinction between managers and leaders are less common today.

Leadership is, according to received wisdom, like motherhood and apple pie – unequivocally good: 'leadership is vital for healthy organizations' (Western, 2008: 5). It is deemed to be crucial for the functioning of all institutions – not only firms but schools, hospitals, welfare agencies, NGOs, etc. Advocates and apologists for leadership declare that 'a leader is responsible for direction, protection, orientation, managing conflict and shaping norms' (Heifetz and Laurie, 1994: 127). Implicitly, it is assumed that other people in organizations lack the qualities needed for such 'responsible' work. Leaders are vital, others rather less so. This is a powerful message in very many studies, including education and corporate practice, which address leadership.

It seems that nearly everyone, from politicians to priests, wants to acquire and parade leadership abilities (Storey, 2011). Certainly many students graduating from business schools are eager to make a career as a leader, perhaps seduced by persuasive accounts of researchers and lecturers who are eager to make students feel positive about their prospects, and thereby receive upper-quartile course evaluations. But how many students have the ambition to become a good subordinate or follower? It appears that few are satisfied with such a modest goal in life. Instead, the world is full of leader-wannabees. Such expectations and aspirations are destined to lead to many avoidable frustrations and disappointments (Alvesson and Spicer, 2011).

There are several ironies in the heavy emphasis on leadership. One is that today's society is often said to be a knowledge economy with well-educated people who are individualists. This suggests that the challenge for those with an ambition to lead are greater than ever, as so few people are inclined to define themselves as followers waiting to be led. Another is that, despite the increasing numbers of people who see themselves as leaders in organizations, the great majority of people are in subordinate positions – or they work as professionals or knowledge-workers without necessarily being dependent upon leaders to inspire or motivate their activity. The space for leaders doing leadership (in any ambitious and systematic way) is rather limited. A third irony is that although almost everybody studying and practising leadership emphasizes its importance, people define it in varied, vague and often contradictory ways. A fourth is that while questionnaire studies and interviews with leaders often confirm positive views of leaders obtaining good results, in-depth studies seldom confirm this picture. In such studies, leadership is seen to take the form of a grandiose fantasy, rather than as something that plausibly describes what managers do and accomplish. So-called 'leaders' are mainly engaged in administrative and operative work, and specific leadership acts are often difficult to detect (Alvesson and Sveningsson, 2003a; Sveningsson and Larsson, 2006).

There is an expanding sceptical literature on leadership, which questions a range of dominant assumptions (see Collinson, 2011). These include the idea of leadership having a strong influence upon results (Pfeffer, 1977), the sole leader (Gronn, 2002), the passive follower (Collinson, 2006), the coherence and 'realness' of leadership (Alvesson and Sveningsson, 2003b), the ideological celebration of the positive, indeed heroic, leader (Yukl, 1999), the monologic (as different to dialogic) character of leadership (Fairhurst, 2001; Ladkin, 2010), and idealized notions of the moral superiority of the good or authentic leader (Alvesson, 2011b). Sceptical students of leadership have drawn attention to the masculine nature of conceptualizations of the leader and leadership (Alvesson and Billing, 2009) and leadership as involving social domination (Knights and Willmott, 1992), with some forms of leadership producing cult-like phenomena (Tourish and Pinnington, 2002).

We will not elaborate on all forms of critique but instead focus on leadership as ideology before addressing how Habermasian ideas may be used to develop more progressive forms of leadership.

Leadership as Ideology

Although some leadership literature takes seriously the contextual and relational aspect of leadership, most studies express a strong *leader-centric* view. The division between leader and follower is usually taken for granted. The leader is assumed to be the key agent while the follower is conceived to be a more or less passive receiver of influence. There is limited recognition of how, in mainstream leadership studies, social relations are very partially and inadequately understood: it is assumed that the leader almost omnipotently defines a social relation and that others simply follow. And yet, what is described as 'leadership' is a matter of interactions occurring in a broader set of institutional arrangements, mediated by ideologies and values which condition what people occupying managerial and authority positions do and don't do (Collinson, 2006; Knights and Willmott, 1992). Often behind a specific managerial behaviour, there are conventions and routines that prescribe how and what managers 'do' in order to demonstrate 'leadership' – meaning that so-called leaders are rather led by discourses (e.g. of leadership) which constitute them as leaders, and who find themselves under pressure to act in line with what is defined as leadership (Alvesson, 2011a). Leadership ideals operate to control and discipline managers as 'leaders' and their subordinates as 'followers'. That said, and as we have emphasized, the constitutive effect of discourse is not necessarily as strong as some of the most pessimistic commentators are inclined to presume. In the case of managers, they are often mired in administration and preoccupied with hitting targets and 'deliverables' – so employees are not easily persuaded by their efforts to 'pass' as leaders.

Another feature of much leadership thinking is its emphasis on the positive, power-free influence of leaders, in contrast to management where formal authority means that subordinates are more or less forced to obey. Leadership thinking presents and encourages a *romantic* view of workplace relations as conflict-free, in which, when led rather than managed, authentic individuals interact positively and productively. Underpinning such claims is an assumption of shared meaning and a harmonious integration of experiences based on positive relationships that nurture good and successful outcomes. Lurking beneath most popular formulations of leadership and many academic approaches, like charismatic and transformational leadership, there are strong resonances with popular mythology – notably, the American Dream and Hollywood blockbusters – where heroic individuals showing true grit transform a bunch of unpromising followers who 'deliver' as the leader intended. This is most evident in pop-management writings that target a mass market of managers eager or anxious to become, or to be seen as, leaders, but it also frames many academic leadership studies. Here we find slightly more modest versions of Hollywood mythology, but the narrative is largely unchanged. The leader – the strong, powerful, superior individual – enters the situation and transforms worried, selfish, bewildered followers into self-confident, committed and focused employees who are now empowered to do what is expected of them, or preferably much more than that. This is, for example, salient in ideas of transformational and charismatic leadership (Burns, 1978; Sashkin, 2004):

> Transformational leaders cause followers to become highly committed to the leader's mission, to make significant personal sacrifices in the interest of the mission, and to perform above and beyond the call of duty ... (Shamir et al., 1993: 577, cited in Tourish and Pinnington, 2002)

The powerful influence attributed to leadership really calls for a larger-than-life character, and so appeals more to fantasy and wishful thinking. Leadership researchers produce long lists of impressive things that leaders should do for, and with, their subordinates (e.g. Mumford et al., 2002), including to 'define the parameters of the corporate culture' (Kets de Vries, 1994: 78).[7] Many leadership studies have a strong messianic overtone (Alvesson, 2011b). In time of moral uncertainty, doubts and/or worries, leadership offers comfort. According to authorities in the field, leaders are not only powerful: they are powerful in the right, moral way. Effective leadership is married to integrity, a deep connection which, as Palanski and Yammarino (2009) write, has become almost an axiom in leadership studies. So, if leaders are domineering, it is only for the good of the organization. True leaders are authentic; they have integrity and a sense of moral purpose making them capable of raising the moral standards of followers, and thereby enhancing commitment and performance. The transformational leader 'must incorporate moral values as a central core' (Bass and Steidlmeier, 1999). In this sense, leadership is a bastion against moral uncertainty. In earlier times, we went to the church and prayed, now we go to leadership development programmes and chant the salvational mantra: leadership, authentic leadership. The true leader is a saint-like figure, a moral peak performer (Alvesson, 2011b). Many people – practitioners and students of management – are keen to preserve and promote a pure and idealized notion of the leader, and thereby exclude, or at least impede, the application of critical thinking to its sphere. To the extent that a view of true leadership, as involving superior performance and moral supremacy, is embraced, there is no need to think independently. The message is: believe the vision, follow the values of the leader, feel inspired by his/her way of being and so refrain from acting autonomously at work. Or, better still, conflate automony with conformity. As Salaman (2011) has observed, this reliance upon the 'inspirational' leadership of individuals rather than the predictability of organization carries with it substantial risks, not least of which is the rise of leaders – of major corporations, financial institutions and regulatory bodies, for example – who are inclined to 'believe in their own inviolability' and 'suppress, neutralize and undermine the frameworks and systems of governance that should have constrained and challenged them' (ibid.: 66).

A Habermas-inspired View of Leadership: Beyond Pure Critique

Critical students of management have taken limited interest in leadership, and when doing so have tended to be rather dismissive, as indeed we have, in pointing at it as seduction (Calas and Smircich, 1991), social domination (Gemmil and Oakley, 1992; Knights and Willmott, 1992) and/or triggering follower resistance (Collinson, 2005). It is seen to reinforce elitist ideas and legitimize management and managers. Critical researchers have begun, however, to accept that leadership cannot be ignored but invites ways to critically and constructively engage with it (Alvesson and Spicer, 2011; Western, 2008). Fryer (2012) suggests the use of a Habermasian framework for examining leadership in which ideas about communication action are engaged. His analysis draws upon Habermas' thesis, discussed above and in Chapters 2 and 3, claiming that unconstrained forms of speech, where various claims (about norms and truths) can be scrutinized, provides a counter-factual basis for identifying well founded, shared agreements. This thinking can be loosely connected to popular ideas of participatory and transformational leadership, where autocratic forms are criticized, and leader-led employee involvement in some low-key decision making is considered to play a role. But the Habermasian approach goes well beyond these ideas as it is directly connected to *democratic* decision making about key issues of resource allocation, not mere involvement, consultation and/or participation. It, at least in principle, resonates with ideas that are more or less commonsensical in the context of democracies where it is believed that the force of the better argument made by rival parties should override the social background or cultural capital that each party may possess and mobilize. Most people do not believe or expect the manager to have a monopoly on superior insights and arguments.

At the same time, the Habermasian approach is not without its difficulties. As Fryer (2012) points out, it is perhaps overreliant on rational argumentation; accomplishing a consensus is problematical; and not only managers but also people in subordinate positions may be unwilling to engage in open dialogues. These difficulties may be exacerbated by the authority or expertise attributed to managers/leaders and a habitual inclination to assign responsibility to others. Nonetheless, while there are difficulties there are also possibilities:

> ... prescriptions for facilitative leadership may struggle to break free from the constraints of pre-defined agendas. But even if flirtations with democratic and facilitative forms rarely deliver much in terms of genuine involvement, they indicate an organizational landscape that, for both normative and instrumental reasons, may be ready for more sincere initiatives. (Fryer, 2012: 39)

Fryer commends forms of leadership which aim to create unrestricted communicative communities, where there is freedom to make and dispute assertions, and where barriers that might distort communication are identified and dismantled. In order to make leadership practically legitimate, as opposed to rhetorically appealing, it needs to be communicatively authorized, where employees are engaged as responsible organizational citizens, in the selection, appraisal and retention of leaders.

It is necessary not to hold out naïve hopes for how readily such ideas will be adopted in a world where 'the maximization of commercial performance and the acquisition and retention of power have come to dominate organizational agendas' (ibid.: 26). It is also relevant to bear in mind how the realization of communicative action in organizations may work against what employees currently conceive as their interests with respect to the avoidance of managerial responsibility. Employees may resist or reject forms of *social* responsibility when they are adversely affected by moves to make firms and other employers more socially responsible and accountable for issues such as pollution and unsustainable consumption as well as quality of working life. Nevertheless, a critical focus upon distortions of communicative action as a framework for analysing and assessing leadership offers a possible way forward for its critical study.

 ## Summary

This chapter has explored the terrain of management studies which is most directly people-oriented. That said, mainstream strands of organization theory, human resource management and leadership are inclined to treat these topics as (reified) entities, and then seek to explicate their structural and aggregated aspects in a way that is abstracted from those most directly involved in reproducing and transforming their realities. From a CT perspective, employment conditions and the scope for employee influence are vital for understanding and transforming work organizations. How organizational structures and control mechanisms influence the preferences, feelings and self-definitions of individuals – managers and others – invites critical scrutiny. Corporate cultures, career-oriented HRM systems and leadership practices and ideologies all condition the formation of identities at work. Emancipation-oriented studies are committed to exposing and exploring the unnecessarily demeaning effects of contemporary organizational arrangements, including how forms of HRM and styles of leadership subordinate employees with the intent of moulding them into well adapted, passive and compliant, career-oriented subjects. A critical orientation to the areas of organization theory, HRM and leadership involves studying not only the role of an elite in the construction of prison-like organizations but also the active and frequently willing participation of less privileged employees in reproducing, as well as resisting, their own subordination. Leadership is not just imposed from above but is accomplished as an interactional process in which employees sometimes learn to define their role as 'followers'. This oppressive dynamic becomes a priority to explore – and to try to challenge and change.

 ## Notes

1   We do not provide coverage of finance, mainly because there is fairly little to draw upon within a Critical Theory tradition. For a brief review of some works of a broader critical relevance, see Hopwood (2009).

2   The most obvious example is the impact of Burrell and Morgan's *Sociological Paradigms and Organizational Analysis* (1979) upon the conceptualization of the other specialisms. See Chapter 2.

3   *Inter alia*, there have been studies that highlight the central role of power and politics (Clegg, 1989; Knights, 2009), class relations and control of the labour process (Braverman, 1974; Knights and Willmott, 1990), ambiguity, confusion and lack of rationality in organizations (Brunsson, 1985), the subjective and interpretative nature of social life and organizations (Czarniawska-Joerges, 1992), culture and symbolism (Alvesson, 2012a; Martin, 2002), and gender issues (Alvesson and Billing, 2009). The interested reader is encouraged to consult Knights and Willmott (2012) and Thompson and McHugh (1995) for overviews.

4   Fox (1974), for example, has interpreted the shift from 'unitarism' to 'pluralism' as a sophisticated ideology for 'maintaining the status quo of highly unequal power, wealth and privilege' (ibid.: 282). Widespread acceptance of the status quo, he contends, is more a reflection of the power of the few to shape the views and priorities of the many than it is an expression of unforced consensus (see Chapter 1). This is not just because employees are forced to earn a living by selling their labour. It is also because the powerful few have control of 'the many agencies of socialization through which conformist attitudes and values are shaped' (ibid.: 284; see also Chapter 3).

5   Pluralist analyses have been plundered by managerialists who argue that conflicts are functional, that they can be managed and, indeed, that they are of critical

importance for engineering more effective decisions. Limited forms of conflict in organizations are then represented as a healthy sign of 'pluralism' – a pluralism that legitimizes managerial authority and is actually or potentially functional for the affirmation of instrumental rationality (see Chapter 1).

6 For a discussion of diverse perspectives on ideas on eroticism, sexuality and pleasure in organizations, see Burrell (1984, 1992).

5

Critically Assessing Management Specialisms II

Marketing and Strategic Management

Marketing and strategic management are amongst the specialisms of management with the lowest resistance to managerialism. Where the social and behavioural sciences have been incorporated into these specialisms, they have been guided by this ideological orientation. Conventional wisdom is naturalized, and a scientistic approach to research is adopted which relies upon the pseudo-sophistication of quantitative measures. 'Thing-like' entities such as market segments, price decisions and distribution channels have mystified the social organization of markets and strategies. It is an approach that has served to mask their allegiance to senior management values and priorities, and has also yielded some measure of academic respectability; and, in this respect, the specialisms of marketing and strategic management have something in common with the specialisms of finance and entrepreneurship. In the latter areas, some critical studies have been appearing in recent years (see Froud and Johal, 2008; Jones and Spicer, 2005; Keasey and Hudson, 2007) and this is also the case for marketing and strategic management. Notably, in the marketing field there has been a rash of good, critical textbooks (e.g. Ellis et al., 2010; Saren et al., 2007). There has also been a growing attentiveness to how marketing and strategy are accomplished in practice, especially in the strategy-as-practice approach, as well as to their performative effects (Tadajewski and Brownlie, 2008). Accompanying this shift is an increased use of qualitative methodologies, including ethnography, that has produced a rather different and often challenging picture of the marketing and strategy specialisms compared to accounts based on the use of questionnaires and secondary sources. Once consideration is given to the context and practice of any area of management – whether it is entrepreneurship, leadership or marketing – there is an increased prospect of opening them up to explore contradictions as well as dissonance with idealized, managerialist accounts of their reality.

Marketing

Marketing is arguably the most visible and controversial of the management specialisms. Marketing ideologies and practices are most prominent within, and are
often scorned by, the media and in public debates where it tends to be reviled as
'spin' and manipulation. The academic status of marketing is also rather precarious.
Brown (1993: 28), for example, talks about 'marketing's perennial search for academic respectability' and of 'the discipline's lowly standing in the scholarly caste
system'. More salient are the widely expressed doubts about its contribution to the social
good of society: if goods and services are actually needed, then why is the (massive)
marketing of them necessary except to *create* a need (e.g. by associating a product
with a lifestyle) or to secure market share? The intense debates about, and critique
of, affluent consumption, and efforts to influence and control consumers, are salient
in other areas of social science as well as in public discussion. Yet they have little
presence in research and textbooks produced by marketing academics. With few
exceptions (e.g. Hunt, 1991; Skålén et al., 2008; Tadajewski, 2006, 2008) it is probably fair to say that, of all the management specialisms, marketing has been one of
the least self-reflective about its knowledge claims and, seemingly, is one of the
most self-satisfied. Its advocates appear to be highly receptive to their own hype.
As a discipline, marketing lacks theoretical sophistication and diversity, and is
seemingly contentedly trapped in a scientist universe of hypothesis testing and
construct measurement (Arndt, 1980, 1985; Burton, 2005). The question of its scientific status has been periodically raised – but then only, it would seem, to deliver
a positive answer, and thereby legitimize the claims of the discipline (Hunt, 1994).
Despite this, there are signs of a growing interest in critical and reflective work
among a small but growing number of marketing academics (see Saren and
Svensson, 2009; Saren et al., 2007; Tadajewski, 2010) and the establishment of the
journal *Marketing Theory*.

Mainstream academics claim that marketing is concerned with satisfying the
needs of customers (see also Chapter 3). Kotler (1976), for example, defines
marketing as 'human activity directed at satisfying needs and wants through
exchange processes' (ibid.: 5). This is a very broad and imprecise definition that
presents marketing as something akin to a charitable activity: seeking out and
ministering to the needs and wants of the population. Unacknowledged are its
performative effects – that is, its contribution to the identification and even the
creation of needs and wants (see Chapter 3). Kotler's definition of marketing also
accommodates and encourages its (colonizing) extension into diverse spheres of
social and economic life, not to say societal politics, where marketing and
branding increasingly penetrate political life (Ellis et al., 2010; Klein, 2000;
Morgan, 2003). We begin with a review of doubts that have been expressed about
marketing's key claims. We then focus upon the role of consumer marketing in
societies where we note how massive resources are committed to the management
of demand for products and services for which there would otherwise be little
call.

Marketing as the Science of Exchange Behaviour

Marketing theory and research remains staunchly positivistic in its disregard of the historical and political construction of its research 'objects'. According to Brown (1993: 28), the low and rather disreputable status of marketing, which is strongly associated with doubts about its claims to serve (rather than hoodwink) consumers, has meant that marketing specialists have long felt obliged to show how, by applying 'rigorous methods', their research is 'more scientific than science'. This move has then invited the critique that much marketing is conservative, passive, sterile and conceptually colonized by empiricism and micro-economic theory (Arndt, 1985). Certainly, marketing research and its leading journals remain heavily committed to the application and legitimation of such approaches. Their overriding concern has been the (scientistic) refinement and testing of instruments that are intended to measure the ever-increasing number of variables that supposedly enhance the capacity to predict the behaviour of consumers and other users. This view has been defended in terms of 'scientific realism' (e.g. Hunt, 1990), which pays little regard to the relationship between knowledge and wider issues, including history, culture and power (Brownlie, 2006; Willmott, 1996b).[1]

When seeking to rectify marketing's attachment to positivism, Arndt (1985) has suggested that ideas drawn from the non-functionalist paradigms identified by Burrell and Morgan (1979; see Chapter 2) can enable marketers to explore various neglected dimensions of marketing theory and practice, including subjective experiences, conflicts and liberating forces. In recent years, there has been a slowly growing interest in such approaches – notably, in interpretive marketing and consumer research (e.g. Belk et al., 1989; Hirschman, 1990; Ulver-Sneistrup, 2008). Studies of sales work and how consumption is promoted in sales interactions is one important area here (Korczynski, 2005). These less objectivistic (e.g. ethnographic) methods generate forms of knowledge that directly challenge the conventional wisdom by taking more direct account of the practical reasoning of consumers as they are targeted by marketing and sales efforts and decide which products and services they will buy. Yet, despite critique of the established positivist paradigm of marketing knowledge, alternative methodologies are only just beginning to influence the development of marketing theory and research.

In presenting itself as 'the discipline of exchange behaviour' (Bagozzi, 1975: 78), marketing excludes consideration of how 'exchanges' are mediated by asymmetrical relations of power. The appeal of a focus upon 'exchange' is that it readily implies that parties in exchange relations are equally subject to the forces of the market. No account is taken of how some individuals and groups are much better placed to 'play the market' than others, and indeed that many potential participants are effectively excluded from markets. An emphasis on 'exchange behaviour' displaces consideration of market failure. Baker (1987: 8) has proclaimed, in defence of marketing, that 'it is all about mutually satisfying exchange relationships for which the catalyst is the producer's attempt to define and satisfy the customer's need better.' Note here how the term 'defining' is being used. The marketer presents him/herself as the expert who can best discern and define the needs of the customer. There is an assumption that the marketer is a neutral helper who has no vested interest in shaping – in the stronger sense of 'defining' – customer needs. Identifying exchange as its central concept, marketing provides a deceptively simple, easy-to-understand formulation of the complexities of human interaction. It neglects to discuss how structures of domination and exploitation shape and mediate relationships.

To a certain extent some research on industrial marketing has begun to explore these issues (Tadajewski, 2006). For example, consideration has been given to the replacement of 'pure' exchange relations based on short-term contracts by longer-term collaboration in networks in a manner that partially obviates the limitations of intra-organization/market types of interactions. Case studies of network relationships between customers and suppliers in business-to-business settings sometimes include broader issues involving power, politics and conflict associated with difficult collaborations. This approach is more influential in Europe, and particularly Sweden, than in the USA. The attentiveness to political and conflictual dimensions, is, however, rather narrow and often driven by a managerial preoccupation with how the 'politics' could be minimized or smoothed over (see Chapter 1). The overall approach tends to be management-focused rather than critical or even interpretive. Still, as it offers an alternative to the marketing mainstream, and the richness of the empirical material renders it more open to reinterpretation from a critical standpoint, it is relevant to recognize the contribution of this case-based work. Our principal focus is in the area of consumer marketing as this is where most critical work in the field has been undertaken, and it is also most salient from a critical point of view.

In addressing the sub-field of consumer marketing, it is relevant to acknowledge that all relationships, including those that are personal and intimate, as well as those that involve the impersonal acquisition of goods or services, *can* be represented in the language of exchange. The issue is why this interpretive framework is favoured: what values does it assume and promote? Insofar as these relationships are increasingly targeted and influenced by marketing practices – which take it for granted that 'exchange forms the core phenomenon for study in marketing' (Bagozzi, 1975: 32) – they may indeed come to conform more closely to the 'truths' that such knowledge is sensed to convey (Foucault, 1977). A practical outcome of conceptualizing social interaction as exchange is, arguably, to depersonalize and commodify relationships as well as to disregard forms of domination and exploitation that underpin and circumscribe these relationships. In such relationships, individuals are routinely encouraged to represent, and relate to, each other as commodities in a marketplace – a development that exchange theory and associated discourses actively promote (see Chapter 2). The contemporary interest in branding and the encouragement of people to see themselves as a 'brand' illustrate this phenomenon (e.g. Lair et al., 2005). The metaphor management (marketing) as colonization project is illuminating here (see also McFall, 2004).

The concept of exchange is beguiling because, as we noted above, it suggests that each individual is free to pick and choose in the marketplace. The discourse of exchange appeals to a common-sense humanism and voluntarism that provides a central plank in marketing's professional ideology. Its promise is to recognize and expand, through the medium of market relations, the individual's sense of freedom and enjoyment. What this promise obscures, or at least fails to address, are the *social* relations of inequality that privilege or exclude participation in *marketized* transactions. Or, as Giddens (1979: 272) articulates this argument, the basic deficiency of exchange theory is that it 'does not incorporate power ... and tends to remain tied to a framework of utilitarian individualism'. Through the (ideological) concept of exchange, social interactions are portrayed and naturalized as processes of reciprocal manipulation between (egoistic) parties who individually derive benefit from such transactions.

Far from securing consumer sovereignty and satisfaction, it has been argued that many of the marketing methods celebrated in the academic literature frustrate or even undermine the realization of this ideal (Jonsson, 1979; Saren et al., 2007). Students of marketing are presented with theories and methods that claim to weaken or circumvent the will of consumers by inducing them to act in a habitual way (e.g. by encouraging brand loyalty), or in an impulsive way (e.g. by legitimizing a compulsion to consume). More specifically, Jonsson's (1979) examination of the contents of marketing textbooks reveals their advocacy of the following:

- The use of cosmetic product differences in order to make it difficult for the consumer to identify more substantive differences between products.
- The use of background music in order to distract the consumer, and make it more difficult for him or her to suggest counter-arguments to what the seller proposes.
- The appeal to the consumer's guilt feelings through a small gift, which makes the consumer feel inclined to buy as a response.

In sales, the trick is often to make customers feel that they are sovereign while the 'professional', effective salesperson strives to define the situation in a way that makes the purchase justifiable if not irresistible – in the words of the advert 'Because you are worth it'. While seemingly emphasizing sovereignty, the purchase places the customer in a position where a decision not to purchase would seem perverse (Korczynski, 2005). Two forms of enchantment in the sales process are important here:

> enchantment of sociality, in which the sales worker engenders within the customer an enchanting sense of liking and being well liked, and enchantment regarding the qualities of the product or service concerned. (2005: 75)

Jonsson (1979) contends that the satisfaction of consumers' given needs and wants is frustrated and counteracted by particular forms of marketing practice. His aim is the development of less manipulated, more autonomous patterns of consumption. However, by focusing only upon the tendency of marketing methods to undermine customer sovereignty, which is itself unproblematized, a limited critique of the process of marketing and consumption is presented. The problems that attend processes of consumption are not restricted to specific forms of marketing management, but include a broader social dynamic that is impelled by, and serves to fuel, consumer capitalism (Tadajewski and Brownlie, 2008).

A more penetrating critique must address the question of how consumers become aware of their preferences and how their decisions are shaped by social processes which include, but are not reducible to, the process of marketing products and services. As Morgan (2003) points out, it is necessary to move beyond a limited critique of marketing as creating problems by functioning as a hidden persuader (Packard, 1981) or even as a source of the mystification of product preferences, choices and needs. This critique must be complemented by a more far-reaching exploration of how people become produced as customers, with a value set and an existential orientation built very much around the purchase and consumption of goods and services in market relations. A penetrating and insightful exploration of this is provided by Klein (2000) in her best-seller *No Logo*. Klein shows how branding expands into, and penetrates, more and more sectors of society – cities, mass media, internet sites and airports have all become hoardings for signs of McDonald's, Starbucks, Nike, etc. Schools and the arts have also become advertising sites for soft drinks, fashion clothes and many other products. Watching a movie often means viewing a series of trailers and advertisements before being subjected to a string of product placements in the movie itself. The film *Sex and the City* earned the 'movie whore' award for the record number of products being promoted. All these marketing investments exert effects, otherwise they would not be made. Marketing has become so widespread and institutionalized that those seeking to avoid or resist its messages may feel socially and aesthetically inadequate in relation to others who are more receptive to such incitements to consume. Children and young people are particularly impressionable and therefore highly vulnerable to marketing campaigns (see McAlister and Cornwell, 2010; Schor, 2004) that effectively mobilize 'pester power' or peer pressure to brand their lives in the 'right' way.

In countering the fetish of consumerism, it is relevant to recall the existence of groups (e.g. environmentalists) that more or less explicitly question the rationality of continuously increasing consumption. Garrett's (1987) study of the effectiveness of marketing-policy boycotts against companies deemed to be operating unethically (e.g. polluting the environment, etc.) is indicative of one way forward for the academic field of marketing (see Lasn, 2000). Knowledge gained from 'adbusting' experience is of relevance not only for boycott organizers, but also for other potential targets of boycotts (companies) which may be encouraged to reform their practices in order to avoid such unwanted attentions. However, from a CT position, Garrett's study has a narrow focus on the effectiveness of boycotts. It does not, for example, address questions of how an interest in changing company policy is formed; and no distinction is made between normatively and communicatively anchored standpoints for identifying unethical policies or organizing boycotts. Nonetheless, this study is suggestive of ways in which a critical knowledge of marketing and consumerism can be forged, thereby enabling marketers to free themselves from narrow, technicist research and anodyne textbook accounts of their specialism. Klein (2000) moves further here, addressing anti-consumerist and, in particular, anti-branding activism. In Habermasian terms, her critique of branding is targeted at its coloniz-ation of the lifeworld by 'system' values that prioritize capital accumulation through the exchange of commodities governed by the regime of the branding system (see Chapter 2). However, as a pro-activist author, Klein has little patience for the delib-eration required to establish what Habermasian communicative rationality would regard as a sufficiently well-grounded position. Klein would doubtless contend that the extension of branding to every expanding sector of public and personal exis-tence, particularly in the US but increasingly on a global scale – with its implications for planetary sustainability as well as human physical and mental health – makes the validity and urgency of resistance to the insidious domination of 'brandwashing' clear and justifiable enough.

Marketing, Needs and Consumerism

As we have noted, most marketers – academics as well as practitioners – are inclined to assume that marketing theory and practice broadly serve the interests of custom-ers, and thereby contribute to the well-being of individuals and society. Intuitively, one might indeed expect that an increase in consumption would lead to an increase in satisfaction. Given the intensive bombardment of messages promising increased satisfaction through consumption, one could assume that this social construction of reality should have some reality-defining effects. But it does not seem to work like this. Especially when a comfortable material standard of living is already enjoyed, it is highly debatable whether increases in consumption bring about any lasting happi-ness or increased satisfaction. A large number of investigations in wealthy countries suggest that this is not the case (e.g. Kasser, 2002; Wachtel, 1983). Such studies indi-cate that levels of satisfaction do not increase when material living standards improve substantially. Fifty years after Galbraith (1958) published his book *Affluent Society*, most but not all sections of the population in the USA and Western Europe have become considerably more affluent. On average, their economy has grown by 2 per cent per year since the industrial revolution, meaning that the material standard of living doubled over 30–35 years. But there appears to be no equivalent increase in happiness and few signs of saturation.

One explanation of this paradox is that many so-called 'needs' that consumers strive to satisfy are unreflectively acquired. Needs for products and services may be induced by others – neighbours and friends as well as marketers – who are in the business of suggesting that our life, or sense of self-identity, is incomplete or impov-erished unless we fulfil the ascribed need, which may be material (e.g. a new car) or symbolic (a qualification). The point is that the creation of aspirations and the dissemination of ideas of what counts as a good or fulfilled life are crucial for understanding how the demand for products is managed. In this regard, Pendergrast (1993) notes that Coca-Cola's midfield signs at the playoffs of the 1990 Foot-ball World Cup reached a worldwide audience of 25 billion viewers, and that Coca-Cola invested $80 million on its 1988 Olympic promotions. 'Regardless of the sport – field hockey, basketball, volleyball, gymnastics, sumo wrestling, motor-cycle races – Coca-Cola sponsored it in almost every country in the world' (ibid.: 389). Such investment is justified because, without it, more people might start drinking tap water and/or other brands of sweetened, carbonated water, which would steal Coca-Cola's market share.

The investments in branding – attributing a specific set of meanings, values and emotions to products, services and the firms presenting these to the minds and hearts of the population – are huge and expanding (Klein, 2000). Marketing campaigns serve to reinforce the idea that the consumption of such goods is not only desirable and fashionable, but also entirely normal. The message is not that consumption satisfies a material need, for which there are many, less expensive substitutes, but that it does so in an exceptionally gratifying (identity-enhancing) way. Irrespective of how much we try to minimize being influenced by the daily bombardment of consumption propaganda, for populations in 'advanced' economies the sheer number and sophistication of messages promoting consumerist values is difficult to ignore or resist. Even if we are able to disregard the appeal of specific products, such as a particular soap or shampoo, the collective effect of marketing is to normalize mass consumption – to make it seem ordinary and inescapable. Mass media – even those just claiming to inform us (about new films, products, services, travelling, etc.) – provide subtle forms of solicitation as public space becomes cluttered and saturated by consumption-promoting messages. Exhortations to consume may be experienced as trivial, innocuous and perhaps frustrating, but they are arguably detrimental – not only in terms of unsustainability with regard to finite planetary resources but also in terms of mental health. Mass media associate satisfaction and fulfilment with consumption, yet the pleasures of consumption are transitory and, in the absence of critical reflection, simply reinforce a desire for increased consumption (Kasser, 2002; Schor, 2004).

Leiss (1978) has argued that mass consumption society – promoted by its greatest advocates, the marketers – induces numerous psychological problems: a fragmentation and destabilization of 'needs'; difficulty in matching 'needs' with the characteristics of goods; and a growing indifference to more basic needs or wants. When, for example, a company like Coca-Cola or Levi's associates its products with youth – or, at least, with people's 'need' to appear young – an imaginary relationship between needs (for warm clothing) and a particular brand of drink or jeans is produced and reinforced. The 'need' for clothing or drink becomes associated more closely with the image (and value) of glamour and youthfulness than it is with the use as protection against the elements or the relief of thirst. In such ways, commercial forces feed off the largely repressed fear of old age and death as they 'sell' the ideal of immortality (Willmott, 1995b).

The unfortunate effects of advertising, according to its critics, include the reinforcement of social (e.g. gender) stereotypes; the trivialization of language; the promotion of conformity, social competitiveness, envy, anxieties and insecurities; and disrespect for tradition by appealing to newness and youth (Pollay, 1986; see also debate between Holbrook, 1987, and Pollay, 1987, on this issue; and McFall, 2004). A focus upon consumption as a good in itself is productive of a moral vacuum, it is argued, which advertising simultaneously stakes a claim to fill. As desires are repeatedly aroused and exploited, people may become more cynical (e.g. they become used to incomplete information, half-truths or deceptions), irrational (e.g. they may become compulsive about consuming), greedy and narcissistic (see Chapter 3).[2] Other strivings and desires (e.g. individuality, solidarity) that are either in conflict with, or resistant to, the fuelling of possessive individualism and capital accumulation processes are deemed peripheral, naïve, or are in other ways marginalized. The propaganda of consumption, Lasch contends:

> addresses itself to the spiritual desolation of modern life and proposes consumption as the cure. It not only promises to palliate all the old unhappiness to which flesh is heir; it creates or exacerbates new forms of unhappiness – personal insecurity, status anxiety, anxiety in parents about their ability to satisfy the needs of the young. Do you look dowdy next to your neighbours? Do you own a car inferior to theirs? ... Advertising institutionalizes envy and its attendant anxieties. (1979: 73)

The satisfaction of having and exhibiting a brand that other people cannot afford acts as a means of social differentiation. It is accompanied by a largely sub-conscious feeling of satisfaction associated with superiority. Status motives are often denied, but nevertheless are crucial (Ulver-Sneistrup, 2008). Conversely, it is a source of dissatisfaction and aspiration for those who lack it. In effect, where a premium is placed upon the possession and/or consumption of goods, satisfaction is bought at the expense of others' dissatisfaction.

Advertising through the mass media (and, more recently, through more selective targeting, such as personalized mail shots and 'spamming'), plays a central role in the process of stimulating and legitimizing consumption (see Harms and Kellner (1991) for a discussion of Critical Theory and advertising). Through the use of sophisticated advertising and marketing techniques, the mass(ive) consumption of goods and services is routinely presented as *the* answer to widespread feelings of insecurity, inferiority, frustration, disorientation and meaninglessness. By inhibiting the development of more value-rational consumption (see below), consumerism is identified as the 'fix' that alleviates, albeit temporarily, the existential pain to which it needlessly contributes by offering a superficial and transient remedy. Of course, from a conventional marketing perspective, the transience and the reinforcement of feelings of dissatisfaction that it promises to mitigate are both prized effects as they keep the wheels of consumption and accumulation spinning.

As marketing becomes respectable and institutionalized, it becomes applied to an ever wider terrain of human existence. All social relations are potential targets of its discipline as market mechanisms become the preferred means of representing, monitoring and controlling social relations. The outcome, as Morgan has observed, is an increased

> monetization and commodification of social relations. In this world, marketing can tell us the 'price of everything, but the value of nothing'! Anything can be marketed.

It does not have to be the more obvious goods and services; it can be 'good causes', 'political parties', 'ideas'. The whole world is a market and we are consumers in a gigantic candy-store. Just sit back and enjoy it! (1992: 142–3)

The most important impact of marketing discourses and practices is not to make individuals buy *specific* products but their role in establishing and reinforcing the *generalized understanding* that consumption, which is increasingly customized and individualized, is entirely normal and unequivocally desirable. As Featherstone has observed:

Within contemporary consumer culture (lifestyle) connotes individuality, self-expression, and stylistic self-consciousness. One's body, clothes, speech, leisure pastimes, eating and drinking preferences, home care, choice of holidays, etc. are to be regarded as indicators of the individuality of taste and sense of style of the owner/consumer. (1991: 83)

The norm of individuality is one regulated by marketing institutions as strong associations are forged between images of individuality and consumption. Behind the right style and brand there is, paradoxically, a strong but unacknowledged force of conformism. Even, or perhaps especially, when consumption occurs at a cynical, 'knowing' distance, it involves a broad acceptance of the meaning of the products and services as manifest in the confected 'brand identity'; and, in particular, it involves an identification (or partial disidentification) with what the brand says about the 'individuality' of the consumer. Huge investments in products and services with a global presence presuppose and produce a homogenous market segment, one where the need to appear individual is satisfied through minor variations within a preconditioned responsiveness to mass communication and recipes for exercising the 'right individuality' that it prescribes.

In this light, marketing is identified as a powerful and seductive agency of social control. Its pervasive effect is to place mass consumption at the centre of our awareness and sense of self-identity so that we become dependent, like addicts, upon the consumption of commodities for maintaining our lifestyle/lifeworld – 'I Shop Therefore I Am' or 'Shop Til You Drop' as 1980s T-shirts ironically but smugly declared, in deadly humorous fashion.

Consumption, Status and Value Rationality

The message of much advertising and packaging, expressed overtly as well as subliminally, is that consuming is pleasurable and that it will establish and/or enhance the individual's social status and/or self-esteem. Goods and services are transformed from 'being primarily satisfiers of wants to being primarily communicators of meanings' (Leiss et al., 1986: 238). As marketing seeks to fix our attention upon its 'solutions' to our 'problems', it distracts and deflects attention from values and goods that are less readily satisfied through the marketplace – such as quality of work, more fulfilling personal relationships and ecological concerns such as air quality and water purity (Haug, 1986). All kinds of personal services become commodified, or mediated by the market – from 'chat lines' to computer dating agencies. And yet, however sophisticated the means of satisfying the needs ascribed to consumers become, the connection between consumption and satisfaction remains weak – such satisfaction is, at best, fleeting.

One explanation of the weak connection between consumption and satisfaction focuses upon the relative or positional character of consumer goods (Hirsch, 1976). Goods, it is argued, are not in themselves necessarily sources of positive satisfaction. Instead, what is important is what one owns, or what one consumes, *in relation to other people*. A person is likely to be more satisfied to own a bicycle in a village where everyone else has to walk than a person who owns a small car in a town where every other car is bigger. People very soon become accustomed to the possession of new goods, which they then take for granted so that their delivery of pleasure and satisfaction is short-lived. There is then a craving for something else – for example, ownership of a small car to replace the bicycle. Something similar is indicated by the concept of mimetic rivalry (Asplund, 1991). This phenomenon concerns people's inclination to value and want what other people want. It has also been suggested that much consumption by the middle and upper classes derives its value from being differentiated from the products and services consumed by other people from whom they seek to maintain some social distance (Hirschman, 1990). Satisfaction is thus largely a matter of distinguishing oneself from, and elevating oneself over, others – in terms of taste, prestige and, consequently, power (Bourdieu, 1984; Veblen, 1953). Status competition clearly fuels economic activity, but the number of people who can 'score' higher, or become better off, than the average is constant, so levels of satisfaction remain relatively unchanged while, arguably, levels of expectation and frustration tend to increase.

Marketing as cultural doping and mystification

A major problem with consumerism, and the social and ideological processes that support this ideal, is that it narrows and distorts processes of communication and self-formation. By inducing an emotional commitment to maintaining the flow of goods, and being dependent on its mass producing and distributing capacities, consumerism ties people to the present social order which is socially divisive and ecologically unsustainable. The problem is not that marketers' efforts to manage demand mystifies rational decisions so that people purchase the wrong things. Rather, the problem is that marketing produces people as consumers who, in effect, become addicted to the pleasures associated with the fantasy as well as the reality of the next purchase as they become heavily dependent on commodified products and services for meaning, well-being and feelings of security. Studies of the efforts of marketers to turn small children into consumers demonstrate the potent and intensive nature of this socialization process (McAlister and Cornwell, 2010; Schor, 2004).

Drawing upon Weber's (1978) ideal–typical distinction between four forms of action, we can say that marketing routinely promotes and legitimizes a preoccupation with either *affective* pursuits (e.g. shopping to get a psychological boost), or the *rational calculation* of material self-interest, with the intent of identifying and satisfying immediate subjective wants. Where affect dominates, consumers simply indulge whatever desire happens to flood their consciousness. Consumption is driven by forces (e.g. advertising) about which the individual consumer has limited conscious knowledge, and over which s/he is able to exert little rational control (i.e. in the extreme, what has been termed 'compulsive shopping disorder'). Where instrumentally rational action is dominant, the consumer is able to calculate which of many possible forms of consumption is likely to yield the greatest satisfaction. Unconstrained by ultimate values or predetermined commitments, the individual is 'free' to consume in all directions (see Chapter 2). As du Gay and Salaman (1992) have characterized the cult(ure) of the (instrumentally rational) customer, it is a world in which customers are constituted as seemingly sovereign, self-actualizing actors who are 'seeking to maximize the worth or their existence to themselves through personalized acts of choice in a world of goods and service' (ibid.: 623). As we noted earlier, there is a paradox in how ostensibly 'free' consumers are circumscribed and regulated by marketing and sales institutions where, for example, sales people avoid all indication that they are steering potential customers in a particular direction, but employ subtle means of ensuring that this freedom is exercised by making a purchase (Korczynski, 2005).

To these possibilities of affective and instrumental rationality, Weber (1978) counterposes *value rational* action. This involves the individual in orienting his or her choices to ultimate values. In contrast to the affective and instrumentally rational customer, the 'value rational' actor is guided/constrained by particular value commitments that necessarily focus and limit his or her pattern of consumption. They are evident where, for example, religious and ethical considerations play a role in economic behaviour (Etzioni, 1988). Such constraints are generally not good for business unless they can be incorporated into the consumption process – for example, by differentiating a product on the basis of being 'Fairtrade' or 'Organic'.

Marketing techniques rarely promote or serve the development of value-rational consumption although, of course, they may appeal to values in order to attract or develop a particular kind of customer who is prepared to pay a premium for specific (e.g. 'fairtrade' or 'organic') kinds of products or services. In general, however, the objective of marketers is to encourage individuals to maximize consumption, not to focus and constrain it within the confines of a specific value-orientation that automatically excludes the possibility of certain forms of consumption. The objective is not to encourage resistances to consumption but, rather, to enable potential customers to overcome any moral and rational reservations about buying products or services instead of doing without them or relying upon non-commodified alternatives. Presenting themselves as champions of the 'needs' of the consumer, marketers cast consumption within a quasi-therapeutic ethos that promises fulfilment through consumption (Fox and Lears, 1983). All constraints upon consumption (e.g. resistance to credit) are regarded as irrational and detrimental; appeals are made to erode the established norm of saving money by encouraging customers to spend it; suggestions are repeatedly made to the effect that a particular life(–style) is incomplete without the purchase of a product or service.

Identifying marketing as a contemporary character trait, Fromm (1976) talks about 'the marketing personality' who is preoccupied with presenting a self in a form that is desirable to others. Arguably, this kind of 'personality' or life-orientation has become widespread and institutionalized. Fromm examines how marketing values shape and 'possess' individuals who are 'without goals, except moving, doing things with the greatest efficiency; if asked *why* they must move so fast, why things have to be done with the greatest efficiency, they have no genuine answer, but offer rationalizations, such as "in order to create more jobs"' (ibid.: 147). How frequently are aspects of the status quo – such as the increasing differentials of salary between senior managers and other staff – justified in terms of the jobs that such managers are deemed to create? 'Marketing personalities', according to Fromm, always keep 'moving'; they never stop to reflect upon how their frenetic activity defeats the very purpose (e.g. need fulfilment) that it ostensibly professes to serve. They rarely manage to penetrate beyond rationalizations of their actions to reveal the sense of emptiness that is driving them to make themselves desirable to others, and to maintain a sense of accomplishing something.

More generally, Fromm (1976) describes the development in the Western world as a massive social experiment concerning whether materialism might be the answer to the perennial problems of human existence. His answer is, unsurprisingly, negative. All the evidence suggests that raising the material standard of living for the prosperous in rich countries is pointless in terms of any positive, enduring effect on satisfaction (see above); and that some social problems (e.g. pollution, exhaustion of resources) can get much worse. As affluence increases in a market society, social divisions tend to become more visible and acute. Though highly relevant for the theory and practice of marketing, issues and debates of this kind are conspicuously absent from marketing texts and journals. With the increasing awareness of environmental degradation and the closeness of its association with excessive consumption and materialism, this is, however, set to change.

The cultural doping and mystification metaphors, described in Chapter 3, are relevant here. An image of individuality is sold through the purchase of goods that signal the accessibility and pursuit of a particular – seemingly distinctive, yet fundamentally conformist – lifestyle. Consider a junk mail brochure distributed by a major UK electrical chain which used the following banner headline: 'Improve your Lifestyle with a Mobile Phone'. This was accompanied, seemingly without humorous intent, by a large photograph of a man engaged in the supposedly tranquil sport of fishing with a phone tucked in his breast pocket, threatening to disturb his peace at any moment! The intent, presumably, was to make a connection between a leisurely lifestyle and the possession of a mobile phone. (Or perhaps it was intended to appeal as a gift for those excluded by such pursuits who could then monitor those engaged in such activities.)

Critical marketing studies can usefully debunk the seductive images promoted by companies that supposedly cater for consumers. Consider McDonald's. This company has successfully promoted an image of being a highly desirable place to eat, especially for families. Yet, upon critical reflection, it is apparent that McDonald's requires customers to wait upon themselves (by giving orders, fetching the food and disposing of the mountains of cardboard and plastic containers) and to eat with their fingers. As Letiche and van Hattem have observed:

> The choices for employees and customers are very limited. Every aspect of the food and its presentation has been calculated. The hamburgers look large because they stick out, just a bit, from the buns; the portions of french fries look large because the stripes on the little carton boxes are drawn to create an illusion of length, etc., etc. Every dietary facet, dimension of presentation, aspect of preparation, has been measured and is controlled. Hereby McDonald's maximizes predictability – eating at one McDonald's is the same as eating at any other; time of the day or year plays no role. Every aspect of the experience is as uniform as is possible. To achieve this goal a very high level of control is exerted. The cooks cannot influence the taste of hamburgers; the drink dispenser, not the employee, measures how much Coke you get. The work is entirely de-skilled; there's no real cooking, just the 'heating up' of pre-prepared products. Customers are controlled via the uncomfortable seats which limit visits to twenty minutes, and the 'saccharine music' which drives 'punks' away. (1994: 12–13)

Arguably, McDonald's is popular not because of what happens to their customers but because they have successfully associated notions of speed, precision, uniformity and predictability with images of what is desirable (Ritzer, 2004). Its success is an outcome of inviting the customer to focus upon what McDonald's *can* offer (consistency, etc.) by disregarding and devaluing what it cannot (hand prepared food, personal service, non-disposable tableware). To be fair, McDonald's has been attempting to distance itself from the image that it acquired of being excessively regimented, standardized and unhealthy. This image was not good for business in an increasingly health-conscious era, and so there has been a partial makeover. Much of the 'old' McDonald's remains in order to retain its core clientele but much is also made of the 'new', less formulaic, 'innovative' and healthier elements in order to counteract negative publicity and potentially appeal to a changing or wider customer base, and ultimately to reassure shareholders that it is capable of moving with the times. That said, if health education, eating healthily and ethical farming were to be given as much emphasis (and marketing support) as fast consumption, it is likely that McDonald's would become a niche outlet rather than a dominant player.

Summary

Marketing is perhaps the sub-discipline of management on which Critical Theory (and related intellectual traditions) can make the deepest impact. For it is the specialism that directly touches the wider population of consumers, and yet until recently it has also been one of the specialisms where critical thinking is weakest although by no means absent (Tadajewski, 2010). In general, marketers have assumed the exist-ence of consumer needs and pointed to consumer demand as a way of justifying this assumption. Critical analysis, in contrast, is more concerned with the ideological, symbolic and psychoanalytical significance of consumption, arguing *inter alia* that the appeal of advertising and other forms of demand management feeds upon, and reinforces, infantile impulses and fantasies (Lasch, 1979); and that it is associated with various problems, such as:

- a widespread but flawed belief that consumption is the route to happiness, meaning, and the solution to most personal problems (see Fromm, 1955, 1976; Kasser, 2002; Marcuse, 1964);
- a displacement of feeling from the valuing of people to the valuing of objects, strongly reinforced by branding leading to products being ascribed a sacred meaning by many people (Klein, 2000);
- the creation and reinforcement of consumer identities, engendering to a precarious and vulnerable sense of self (Gabriel and Lang, 1995; Lasch, 1979);
- distorted political priorities, giving extra emphasis to private goods and neglecting public goods; the over-stressing of economic goals and downplaying of other ends such as peace and justice (Galbraith, 1958);
- ecological wastefulness and damage (Leiss, 1978).

The potential for critical thinking to foster an alternative to traditional marketing is strong (see Brownlie, 2006). As an academic discipline, marketing is about studying exchange relationships but it is not self-evidently concerned with developing a nar-row, managerialist focus on increasing demand by stimulating and controlling con-sumption. As we have indicated, a critical approach to marketing can bring fresh insights and provide a more penetrating appreciation of its wider ethical and social significance.

Strategic Management

Strategic management is one of the oldest *and* one of the newest of the management specialisms. It is old in the sense that owners and managers have always made key decisions – for example, about which business to be in, or about how human and material resources are to be deployed. But strategic management is also new because it is only comparatively recently that this responsibility has been labelled, studied and prized as 'strategic management' (Knights and Morgan, 1991). The contemporary preoccupation with strategic management, which rivals leadership (see above), has led one American management guru to remark about North Americans that 'We get off on strategy like the French get off on good food and romance' (Pascale, 1982, quoted in Wensley, 1987: 29). This remark might equally be directed at marketing – both areas are dominated by US scholars, and by US culture, for that matter. It is not surprising, therefore, that strategy and marketing are frequently grouped together within business schools even though, in principle, it would make equally good sense to locate strategic management alongside organization theory; and, indeed, recent developments have drawn more heavily upon theories of organization than upon its traditional basis in economics.

In the mainstream literature strategic management considers the competitive positioning of organizations in relation to the perceived opportunities and constraints posed by the (changing) contexts of their operation. From a managerial perspective, successful strategic management is about mobilizing resources in ways that strengthen the focal organization's command of its environment and/or weakens the position of competitors. Strategic management is generally identified with the work of senior managers (and their advisors); and it is most closely associated with the work of marketers and industrial economists. However, strategic management also encompasses the development of strategically conscious 'human resources' who are knowledgeable about, and committed to, the successful implementation of strategic plans – and, in this respect, there is an overlap with the 'strategic' aspirations of human resource management (see Chapter 4).

Orthodox Contributions to Strategic Management

Conventional approaches to strategic management are preoccupied with the rational identification of competitive advantage and the design of corporate structures, policies and business units. These approaches involve, *inter alia*, the identification and refinement of plans that are shaped through an analysis of the market structure of the firm, the resources at its disposal, and an appraisal of its actual and potential competitive advantages in comparison with its rivals (e.g. Porter, 1985). Plans may include the formation of strategic alliances and networks with other organizations or the pursuit of growth through acquisitions. Orthodox understandings of strategy and strategic management foster a mentality where the financial criteria are central and the development of a deeper understanding of businesses is downplayed (Mintzberg, 1990). This is most salient in the USA, where the use of case studies in education may lead students to believe that, based on a 20-page report, they can develop a strategy that will revive the fortunes of an ailing corporation. (For an interesting cross-cultural comparison with regard to strategy, see Whittington, 1993.)

Such thinking about strategic management tends to ascribe to the managers of corporations immense powers to identify sources of competitive advantage, and then to direct their businesses to secure the strategic objectives. This thinking assumes that 'environments' are predictable, and that long-term plans can be sensibly made and progressively implemented. Against this view, it has been argued that the scope for exercising strategic choice is severely constrained (or enabled) by the capabilities, or 'core competences', present within any given organization (Hamel and Prahalad, 1989). Strategy, it is argued, should be driven by the 'leveraging' of these competences, not by the identification of a niche that might be beyond an organization's capabilities.

It has also been objected that in mainstream thinking on strategic management, little account is taken of the unpredictability of events and the volatility of market forces. It is argued that many successful 'strategies' are more likely to 'happen' as a consequence of accident and good fortune, rather than as an outcome of rational planning. This view implies the strategic relevance of being alert and prepared to exploit new openings, and being willing to experiment with a range of options rather than carefully formulating a strategy and then systematically implementing it. But, against this view, it has been suggested that the scope for opportunism is severely constrained because firms are frequently grouped in similar populations lodged in shared market niches; and that, in practice, established routines and modes of response constrain the capacity to move into new niches (Aldrich, 1979; Hannan and Freeman, 1977). To this objection can be added the view that many markets are dominated by a few key players who alone command the resources sufficient to exclude new entrants; and that firms are deeply embedded in social systems and networks that at once impede and promote particular kinds of (strategic) thinking and action (Granovetter, 1985; Whittington, 1993).

Strategic Management as Process

Orthodox researchers concentrate on how to elaborate and refine highly idealized, *prescriptive models* of strategic management. This orientation has been challenged by research on how strategies are *practically organized* and realized (Golsorkhi et al., 2010; Jarzabkowski, 2005). It is common that the resulting pattern of activity may deviate – for organizationally sound reasons – from the intentions of those who originally formulated the strategic plans (Mintzberg et al., 1976). In a similar vein, Quinn (1980) has challenged the idea of strategy as a rationally ordered cycle of stages beginning with formulation and concluding with implementation, arguing instead that strategic management is, in practice, often a highly recursive and incremental activity.

From this processual perspective, strategic management is seen to be 'crafted' rather than planned (Mintzberg, 1987). The craft metaphor suggests a comparatively 'open' approach to strategy–making that is appreciative of the existence of recursive processes through which strategic *learning* is accomplished, and continuous adjustments are made. It suggests that the practicalities of strategic management involve fuzzy and intuitive processes of understanding in which managers 'learn about their organizations and industries through personal touch' rather than by reading 'MIS reports and industry analyses' (Mintzberg, 1987: 73). As Johnson has commented, such research suggests that:

> In the process of strategic decision-making there is a much greater reliance on management judgement and past experience than the evaluative techniques of the management scientist would suggest. ... What becomes clear is that the selection of strategy is primarily by means of management judgement and is likely to be bound up in a process of bargaining within the organization. *Solutions are not so*

much likely to be adopted because they are shown to be better on the basis of some sort of objective yardstick, but because they are acceptable to those who influence the decision or have to implement it. (1987: 29, emphasis added)

From this perspective, strategic management practice involves processes of negotiation or bargaining between parties in which decisions are reached that are 'subjectively' acceptable rather than 'objectively' rational. The practical accomplishment of strategic management calls for attention to '*the processes of knowing* – those processes that produce the rules by which an "organization" is managed and judged' (Smircich and Stubbart, 1985: 727, emphasis in original).[3] And when these processes are located in a wider institutional context, strategic management is related to (senior) managers' efforts to organize, secure or advance their sectional interests in relation to such factors as continued employment, promotion prospects, divisional or departmental empire building, etc. (see Chapter 1). Entrenched ideologies and practices may preclude the consideration of alternative strategies (Whittington, 1989; see also Huff, 1982). The very opportunity to identify, and choose between, alternative strategies is enabled/constrained by these patterns of thought or ideologies (Pettigrew, 1985; Wilson, 1982). This perspective accepts and illustrates the understanding that established assumptions or beliefs held by decision makers routinely shape processes of strategic management. But instead of regarding strategists' recipes and repertoires as forces that are given by the culture of the industry, attention shifts to consider how strategic recipes are socially constructed and reproduced through *relations of power*. The transformation of strategic decision making is intertwined with the changing of these relations (see, for example, Child and Smith, 1987).

'Systemic theorists' of strategy, as Whittington (1993: 28) has described them, contend that strategic management is guided by norms derived from 'the cultural rules of the local society. ... The internal contests of organizations involve not just the micro-politics of individuals and departments but the social groups, interests and resources of the surrounding context.' In other words, it is argued that in order to understand the exercise of managerial judgment, it is necessary to appreciate how strategic decision making is affected by the play of wider social forces – forces that are a condition as well as a consequence of organizational decision-makers' work.

However, processual and institutional studies of strategic management seldom relate the politics of strategic decision making to the wider historical and social contexts of managerial action (see Wood, 1980). There is a large and expanding literature on 'strategizing' and strategy-in-practice which examines how strategic work is actually conducted (Johnson et al., 2007; Whittington, 2006). Elements of this rapidly expanding literature contribute to de-mystifying dominant rationalistic notions of strategic management, but its micro-focus has shortcomings (see Clegg et al., 2011; Ezzamel and Willmott, 2010). In common with processual analysis reviewed above, organizational and sectoral contexts of decision making are largely taken as given in the analysis of the empirical material. The outcome is a recognition and trivialization of the politics of strategic management (see Alvesson and

Willmott, 1995; Levy et al., 2003). Insufficient account is taken of how managers are positioned by historical forces to assume and maintain a monopoly of strategic decision-making responsibility (see Chapter 1). And there is minimal concern to explore how managers' practical reasoning about corporate strategy is conditioned by politico-economic contexts and considerations that extend well beyond the boundaries of any particular organizational sector. There is little examination of how managerial values are laden with ideological assumptions about the 'facts' of strategic management. Corporate strategies are rarely assessed in terms of possible negative consequences for specific groups of employees and even less with regard to their wider impacts on society. To address such issues necessitates a shift from the study of strategic management as a process of *organizational* politics to a perspective that locates this process within the wider context of contemporary capitalist society. In particular, it is important to extend analysis beyond a consideration of how strategy is consequential for top managers' work, identity, status and communication tactics and its role in shaping internal organizational relations and power dynamics (Ezzamel et al., 2008), to consider how strategic management has material effects beyond the corporate sphere, (e.g. on consumers, the environment, regulatory regimes, national and international development and so on, see Clegg et al., 2011). This is of course particularly important for large, multinational firms, sometimes with an economy as huge as many nations, which are able to use considerable muscle in relationship to governments and international regulators.

Strategic Management as Domination

The common limitation of mainstream approaches to strategy, from a critical perspective, is their failure to analyse strategic management as a condition and consequence of wider, institutionalized forms of domination. This is most transparent in orthodox accounts of strategic management where managers are urged to perfect the (technocratic) rationality of their decision making. When surveying the orthodox literature, one is struck by the continuity between Frederick Taylor's mission to rationalize the design of shopfloor work and the efforts of strategic management theorists – such as Porter (1985), Hamel and Prahalad (1989) and even Pettigrew (1988) – to generate technocratic methods for building and sustaining a position of competitive advantage (see Chapter 1). As Fischer has noted:

> for technocrats, the solution is to replace the 'irrational' decision processes of democratic politics (group competition, bargaining, and compromise, in particular) with 'rational' empirical/analytical methodologies of scientific decision-making ... Nothing is more irrational to technocratic theorists than the disjointed, incremental forms of decision-making (typically described as 'muddling through') *that result from a political commitment to democratic bargaining and compromise.* (1990: 22, emphasis added)

It is, of course, precisely the 'disjointed, incremental' quality of decisions that advocates of the processual perspective valuably recall and illuminate. However, as we have stressed, when focusing upon the organizational politics of different individuals and groups of managers, processual analysts of strategic management largely take for granted the wider structures of domination. These structures include dominant discourses of strategy – processual as well as orthodox – that organizational members are induced to use in order to define and realize their purposes (Ezzamel and Willmott, 2008). We now discuss three aspects of domination in the theory and practice of strategic management: the colonizing effect of talk about strategies; practices associated with mergers and/or acquisitions which weaken or avoid competition; and the issue of power and accountability in strategic decision making.

Strategy talk

Debates about what strategy 'is', and how it should be understood properly, take place against the taken-for-granted assumption of the importance of the subject matter. The strategy industry includes a large number of writings – on everything from strategic human resource management to strategic information management – that contribute to the colonization of management thinking and practice by talk of 'strategic' relevance. It could, of course, be argued that the relationship between strategy talk and managerial practice is, like 'leadership' (see Chapter 3), very loose; but this does not prevent strategy from having a far reaching impact in the ideational world. (And, of course, upon the 'substantive' world which we address in the next subsection.) The colonizing tendency of strategy discourse produces peculiar effects – such as people saying 'strategically important' when by 'strategically' they simply mean important. In an academic seminar, one participant who was conducting research on strategic decisions confessed that by 'strategic', he just meant 'big' decisions. The term 'strategic' is bandied about to add rhetorical weight, misleadingly one might say, to managerial activity and academic research projects. One could argue that such name calling is innocent and trivial. And in some cases 'strategy' means little more than a positive-sounding labelling of what people think or claim they are doing. In a large R & D company, mid-level managers described themselves as 'occupied with the larger picture' and with 'strategies', even though they were far from the market, had no overall business responsibility, and were supposed to work strictly within a segment of an overall product development process (Alvesson and Sveningsson, 2003a). Strategy here seemed to be almost anything not directly operative or administrative. Such framing is increasingly common, and does little more than mystify managerial work – for managers and others. The strategy-as-practice literature tends to accept and reproduce a general tendency to label whatever managers think or label as strategy as an example of it, thereby endorsing the status and mystique of managerial work as somehow 'strategically important' (Ezzamel and Willmott, 2004).

Sometimes the expansion of strategy talk from the military to all sectors of organizational and everyday life has stronger political effects (Knights and Morgan, 1991). Like other discourses that have a colonizing impact, its weakening of alternative ways of framing issues and assessing values acts to inhibit rather than open up debate. Strategy talk frames issues in a way that privileges instrumental reason; it tends to give the initiative to those who successfully claim to be 'strategists'; it also has clear masculine connotations that reproduce and reinforce gender biases, although this may be diminishing, as today strategy, as an increasingly watered-down term, is less loaded with masculine meaning than it was a few decades ago (Alvesson and Billing, 2009).

When Mintzberg, for example, conceptualizes strategy as 'pattern in a stream of decisions' (1976), it could be said that such processes have little to do with strategy as more conventionally defined (i.e. a plan followed by implementation); or, indeed, that such formulations actively disrupt such conventional wisdom. Nonetheless, the uncritical quality of such formulations contributes to the construction of strategy as a highly significant phenomenon. Once the idea of strategy becomes established and widely accepted as a primary concern of competent organizational members, it can quickly become an important benchmark for guiding and legitimizing plans and actions. Among middle and senior managers at least, demonstrable knowledge of the existence, and significance, of 'internal' resources and 'external' constraints becomes a way of displaying competence and suitability for promotion. Strategy talk becomes an integral part of impression management for managers. In effect, the adoption of strategy talk also has self-disciplining effects as employees contrive to gain credibility and influence by demonstrating and promoting the relevance of their work for attaining objectives that are deemed to be 'strategic'. As Knights et al. (1991: 9–10) have noted, 'an effect of strategic discourse is to constitute the organization and the individual subject as self-consciously aware of the competitive struggle for power and to render them "open" to techniques of rational control and evaluation in its pursuit.'

To the extent that the discourse of strategy is successfully introduced and disseminated by a powerful, managerial elite, it serves to construct (or reinforce) the common-sense understanding that organizations are strategy-driven and that employees outside the strategic core should realize their own limited overview and understanding, and so subordinate themselves to the strategy. In turn, this understanding helps to encourage, as well as to justify, the introduction and development of new forms of management control (e.g. high performance teams) without careful scrutiny and discussions involving all those concerned. The hegemonic effect of disseminating knowledge and awareness of strategic management among employees may be to increase employee compliance. New techniques of control, and 'downsizing' the work force, are legitimized on the grounds that they are strategically necessary. Against 'non-traditional' students of strategy who continue to invoke and affirm the potency of the concept, one could argue that not only different talk about strategy is needed, but also less talk. Efforts to broaden strategy – as processualists and advocates of strategy-as-practice do – are positive insofar as they move 'strategy' away from an exclusive attentiveness to top management. A problem with strategy talk, however, is that it lends a managerial influence to whatever it addresses. Research on the process and practice of strategy can reinforce a managerialist tendency to make strategists the key actors in organizations. The value of addressing decisions about IT systems as 'strategy' (Samra–Fredericks, 2005) invite critical scrutiny. Today, the importance of 'strategy' has become self-evident, but this is an effect of the colonization of strategy talk.

Domination through concentration

Strategy calls for attention from critical thinking not just in terms of its ideational appeal, but also in terms of its substantive (material) consequences. Notably, actions inspired by strategic management ideas often reinforce concentrations of power and have negative effects for less powerful groups seen as outside the category of 'strategists' (Levy et al., 2003; Phillips and Dar, 2009). The espoused intent of strategic management is to weaken competitive pressure by finding niches, acquiring competitors, expanding vertically, etc. Growth and forms of 'strategic collaboration' are commended as means of securing economic power. Corporations also deploy their resources to stifle innovations which pose a threat to established patterns and interests (Frost and Egri, 1991), to influence government policies and to shape public opinion (Barley, 2007). An example of how corporate strategies exploit and control the use of mass media for purposes of marketing products and services is given by Rose, who notes how, in the USA:

> Hill and Knowlton, in 1986 the largest public relations firm, bought the lobbying company owned by Robert K. Gray. Five years later, not to be outdone forever, the public relations firm of Burson-Marsteller bought Black, Manafort, Stone and Kelly, also a lobbying firm. Prior to the purchase of lobbying companies designed to affect the outcome of the passage of laws in legislatures and the U.S. Congress, P.R. companies had endeavoured to affect opinion in mass market audiences through the stories they placed on television and in the print media. Various media conveyed their messages. After the acquisition of (the) lobbying firms, new thinking and new strategies for influencing the public sector were formulated. I should mention that both Hill and Knowlton and Burson-Marsteller were owned by even more massive advertising agencies and when they acquired lobbying firms, a fuller institutional and utilitarian conceptual order was made possible. *This is called 'integrated marketing'. Now advertising messages can be coupled to public relations campaigns and with lobbying efforts all directed out of the same firm with enormous resources.* (1993: 21–2, emphasis added)

Strategic management, encompassing mergers and acquisitions as well as product and organizational development, can be evaluated in terms of its consequences for establishing centralized economic power and suppressing public debate over key politico-economic issues. In general, strategy often aims at reducing competition and increasing corporate control over suppliers as well as markets (Whittington, 1993). As Levy et al. (2003) remark, when considering how Porter and the resource-based view have been busy advocating how a firm might actively build market barriers and sustain monopolistic structures: 'it was not without some justification, perhaps, that Microsoft argued in its anti-trust suit defence that it was merely pursuing the precepts of good business strategy' (ibid.: 95).

There are, therefore, strong reasons to evaluate corporate strategies less one-sidedly in terms of their contribution to corporate profits or executive prowess, and more in terms of a debate about the social good, including the ecological consequences of the exploitation and depletion of natural resources.

A particularly glaring weakness in most strategic business thinking is its exploitation and/or predatory neglect of the natural environment. In managerial thinking, analysis of 'the environment' is framed in terms of a combination of technological, economic and social factors, with – at least until recently – little attention being paid to nature. In effect, nature has been assumed to be a free good. This devaluation of the natural environment is rather perverse, given that so much organization theory draws more or less explicitly upon biological metaphors, such as organism and population ecology (see especially Chapter 3). However, more studies in strategic management are now paying attention to ecological issues (e.g. Jermier and Forbes, 2003; Shrivastava, 1993) in ways that urge a radical re-think of how decision-makers in companies relate their activities to ecological concerns – such as the effort to minimize the use of non-renewable supplies of energy and to support policies of sustainable growth. For example, Shrivastava (1993) talks about *ecocentric strategic management*, in which the corporation is seen as a part of a living natural environment. Instead of regarding the natural environment as separate from companies, and using it as a free receptacle for externalized costs (e.g. waste), an ecological orientation to strategic management demands that full account be taken of how corporate goals, production systems and products interact with ecological systems. Jermier and Forbes (2003) talk about 'holistic greening' in which there are efforts within organizations to 'institutionalize a system-wide environmentalist or ecocentric culture' (ibid.: 168). This is an important counter-position to increasingly popular strategies of 'ceremonial greening' and 'environmental management', where lip service and forms of 'greenwash' are favoured rather than genuinely eco-friendly design, production and distribution activities. As Jermier and Forbes (2003) point out, Critical Theory is well placed 'to critique green imposters and promote transformational green politics' (ibid.: 173).

Power and accountability in strategic management

The most entrenched obstacles to wider participation in strategic ('big') decision making – for consumers and citizens as well as immediate employees – are political, not natural or even technological, factors. Orthodox representations of strategic management take for granted institutionalized structures of power – of patriarchy and ethnicity as well as ownership. Processual studies tend to focus upon the local (i.e. organizational and sectoral) dimensions of their reproduction, to the neglect of societal embeddedness. From a critical perspective, the study of strategic management must investigate how processes of strategy making involve an exercise of power over how people interpret reality and develop opinions.

Most writers on strategic management take it for granted that processes of strategic decision making are necessarily and legitimately the monopoly of top management. By projecting solidarity of purpose and the universality of the interests of senior managers and stockholders, the discourse of strategy legitimates organizational hier-archy with its differential influence and rewards. The importance attached to strategy implies that employees who work outside the 'strategic core' of an organization make a lesser contribution, and therefore cannot be expected to participate, even marginally, in decisions for which others are responsible. It also supplies a rationale for differentiating the pay and conditions of 'core' and 'peripheral' employees. The appeal of asserting the status of an elite group of 'strategic managers' is perhaps great-est in advanced economies where manual labour is declining and traditional divisions between task execution and conception are loosened up (Levy et al., 2003). At the same time, there are examples of companies and social enterprises in which broader groups of employees participate in discussions and decisions on core issues in ways that depart quite radically from established, top-down conceptions of strategic man-agement (e.g. Parker et al., 2007; Raspa, 1986; Weisbord, 1987).

Participation, or at least some form of employee involvement, is not uncommon in many knowledge-intensive and professional service firms as well as organizations, including university departments and consultancy firms, where the networks of employees form a key resource which facilitates and constrains strategic options (Löwendahl, 1997). A shift to post-industrial, service organizations and methods of manufacturing that demand employee engagement and the responsibilization of work means that an increasing number of organizations rely upon the 'involvement' of many employees whose knowledge often spans a number of areas of expertise. Despite this, senior executives are, in practice, primarily accountable to their share-holders and are reluctant to loosen or dilute their managerial prerogative.

Some writers on strategic management have argued that a bottom-up orientation to strategic management should complement, and be fused with, the top-down direc-tion of strategic management (Bourgeois and Brodwin, 1984; Westley, 1990). But such proposals involve only middle managers and exclude low-level employees. And, although they commend a broadening of the representations of views and arguments beyond an elite of senior executives, the form of participation amounts to little more than consultation that is very much controlled by senior management. Of course, middle managers and other lower-level employees may well wish to exert influence upwards in order to reduce the negative impact of top managerial decisions on local conditions (Alvesson and Blom, 2011). But, so long as those at the top remain largely unaccountable to those at the bottom, it is difficult to imagine how processes of bottom-up influence, through forms of consultation, will bring about substantive changes to the structure of domination within organizations. Calls for a bottom-up orientation are nonetheless worth repeatedly making as they serve to highlight the contradiction of excluding from strategic decision-making processes those who are most immediately affected by the decisions made. Although senior managers may celebrate notions of 'corporate citizenship', their receptiveness to suggestions and feedback on the unintended as well as intended effects of their initiatives and actions may be highly partial. That is because their priority is to safeguard their reputation (and ego), and not to lay bare the unwelcome or negative effects of their decision making, or the lack of it. Strategic management that lacks involvement by those who have on-the-ground and up-to-date knowledge of the volatility of 'environments' risks acting in counter-productive ways and also losing their confidence, let alone their commitment. For the above reasons, 'participation' is likely to take the form, at best, of selective consultation geared to concerns with pre-empting or avoiding problems so as to positively influence career prospects and deliver to the bottom line.

From a critical perspective, a basic problem with established strategic management theory and practice is the assumption, noted earlier, that senior managers have a legitimate monopoly over strategic decision making; and that their expertise ensures the best means of generating and allocating technological and human resources. There is a neglect of the diversity of groups – citizens, consumers and employees among others – who may be positively or adversely affected by these decisions. Within orthodox and processual views of strategic management, these groups have relevance only for the implementation of strategic plans which may also be seen to depend upon their obedience or compliance (e.g. the receptivity of consumers to promotions that encourage them to purchase new products). The issue then becomes one of calculating how employee or customer support can be cost-effectively engineered, rather than how their concerns can best be appreciated or addressed.

This is not to say that 'everybody' can or should be involved in all forms of 'strategic decisions'. This is sometimes unrealistic and may be judged collectively to be counter-productive. Many people may not be interested in spending much time and energy to become sufficiently well informed to participate in complicated processes of decision making. The key point, however, is that this judgment should be made democratically, and not left to existing senior managers. They may have relevant skills and experience and therefore have a key contribution to make, but their participation should be democratically accountable. In the absence of top-down responsibility and accountability, there is a danger of senior managers living in a bubble of endless meetings, consultancy reports and Powerpoint presentations – a world of symbolism detached from the major parts of organizational activities. The difficulties of establishing and operating organizational democracies do not justify top managers being the only participants in strategic decision making. Forms of representative democracy where union representatives sit on boards of directors as in Scandinavia and Germany is an option, but also more 'internal' forms of participation are important and possible (e.g. committees with representations of different groups, or large open meetings, where everyone interested in an overall, strategic topic can participate).

It is, of course, tempting to be dismissive of approaches that encourage employee contribution to strategic management on the grounds that they seek to appropriate employee knowledge rather than respect it. Certainly, it is relevant to question whether bottom-up approaches to strategic management are motivated by a commitment to developing industrial democracy and open communication, rather than an instrumental concern to manage the contradictions of capitalist control without changing existing structures of domination (see Chapter 3). Nonetheless, moves to encourage genuine participation (and not mere consultation) by employees and other groups in processes of strategic management can be cautiously welcomed – especially when they openly recognize that orthodox, top-down, technocratic methods of managing strategy fail to address the social organization of productive activity. Participation is very welcome even if it is insufficient. The crucial issue is whether discussion and identification of goals, priorities, values, directions and means for accomplishing objectives is based upon a sufficiently broad set of social as well as economic criteria, and whether these criteria are themselves open to questioning and reconsideration. In short, the adequacy of decision making should be judged by democratic criteria. Saying this, it is also important to recognize that employees who participate in strategic decision making may be as eager as the most venal of capitalists to boost corporate efficiency in order to raise their pay, career options and other benefits at the expense of suppliers, customers and/or the environment. It is for this reason that the most important consideration is not participation *per se* but, rather, the democratic scrutiny of objectives, values, means and arrangements. Of central interest is the (e)quality of the communicative processes through which such questions are addressed and resolved. Do they permit and indeed encourage open questioning and criticism of objectives, values, etc. or do the processes inhibit and suppress it? We pursue these issues in Chapters 7 and 8.

Summary

Our discussion has challenged the narrow basis of both rational and post-rational (e.g. processual) approaches to strategic management. Critical approaches offer a range of alternative views, drawing attention to strategy as ideology (universalization of sectional interests), discourse (constituting certain identities and social relations) and political economy (producing material effects) (Phillips and Dar, 2009). Critical thinking can make a valuable contribution in moving us beyond the 'soft technocratic' framework of approaches where wider social and ethical questions are – conveniently – sidelined in the agenda of management, and where the legitimacy of placing decision making in the hands of an elite of self-appointed experts is unquestioned. Critical theory can here contribute to a resistance to the (over-)labelling of 'strategy' as anything 'important' or pretentious that is done by managers, thereby de-mystifying the inclination to boost the meaning of practices and contributions of managers. Apart from debunking the pretentious use of 'strategy', critical management studies may contribute to a broader consideration of the meaning and consequences of strategy in which the political aspects of strategy work and its effects on organizational relations and external groups (and nature) are better appreciated.

 Conclusion

Studies of marketing and strategic management typically assume that the development of knowledge is guided by a technical cognitive interest of improving means for the optimization of ends (see Chapter 2). This assumption is closely tied to the adoption of a top management perspective where the purpose of research is equated with the expertise of one constituency – senior executives. Reliance upon this assumption is more pronounced than in organization theory where there is comparatively greater openness to other cognitive interests in the production of knowledge and to a wider range of potential audiences as beneficiaries of such knowledge. It is therefore not surprising to find that those with a background in organization studies figure rather prominently in the critical literature on strategic management and, to a lesser extent, in that on marketing. This situation is likely to change as marketing and strategy specialists increasingly take a broader view of the nature and significance of the practices that comprise their respective domains of interest.

We have argued that marketing is not reducible to a study of exchange relations but is a major force of the contemporary age (see Willmott, 2010). It colours and shapes all kinds of relations and phenomena, from politics to art to private life. What makes the critical study of marketing so vital is its very strong culture and consciousness-creating effects. As Klein (2000: 4) notes, a number of corporations have 'made the bold claim that producing goods was only an incidental part of their operations ... what these companies produced primarily were not things, they said, but images of their brands. Their real work lay not in manufacturing but in marketing.' In other words, the hollowing out of corporations to become branding machines means that the satisfaction of needs gives way for the control of consciousness and affective responses.

Strategy as an area of knowledge and as a set of practices (and even more as claims around practices) has expanded rapidly and there is now an inclination to refer to almost anything as strategy and strategic. We are witnessing an explosion of references to strategic HRM, strategic IT, strategic marketing, strategic leadership, etc. This leads to a strengthening of managerialism where those who work outside 'strategy work' are regarded as less important and so more readily dispensable. In a seemingly strategy-driven world, alternative ways of organizing, developing an overview and gaining a sense of direction become devalued or lost. Here the need for critical work is pressing. There is a strong case for the development of empirically rich studies which take a broader approach than those that focus upon discourse or practice processes by paying attention to the wider material effects of strategic management activities.

Our discussion of marketing and strategic management has suggested how critical forms of analysis can foster new understandings of these specialisms. Such analysis is committed to developing ways of organizing that are more socially responsible with respect to marketing management and the identification and implementation of strategic objectives. Attention is then focused upon tensions and contradictions that harbour a potential for reconsidering goals, questioning means–ends assumptions and thereby enabling these specialisms to develop in an emancipatory direction.

 Notes

1 It would seem that in common with economists, politicians, business and union leaders, marketing academics are caught in a logic of action in which ends most readily associated with quantifiable measures are given priority

(Offe and Wiesenthal, 1980), despite the risks attached to this myopia, especially in terms of ecological catastrophes (Jermier et al., 1996; Shrivastava, 1993; Stead and Stead, 1992).

2 For example, a survey of 1,000 readers of *Company* magazine, reported in the *Observer* (on 16 October 1994), found that 'given the choice between having £2,000 to spend on clothes, a job promotion, going on holiday, falling in love and losing a stone in weight, more would choose to go shopping than any other option'.

3 Placing 'organization' in scare quotes indicates that the differentiation of the organization from its environment is a product of strategists' social knowledge rather than a reflection of empirical reality (for an elaboration of this argument in relation to discourse on strategy, see Knights, 1992).

6

Critically Assessing Management Specialisms III

Accounting, Information Systems and Operational Research

In common with the previous chapter, our purpose is to show how critical thinking can provide us with fresh understandings of the specialisms of management. When addressing accounting, operational research and information systems, we note that although quantification is strongly favoured there is a growing appreciation of the 'behavioural' conditions and consequences of the predominant use of quantitative-based techniques. We also consider how, in each field, critical thinking has been deployed to challenge orthodox methodologies and to advance an alternative to the received wisdom.

 Accounting

Accounting is conventionally viewed as a rather dry, unexciting field of management concerned with the technicalities of measuring and reporting economic values, as exemplified by the practices of bookkeeping and external reporting. It is understood to comprise the principles and methods used to record transactions and prepare statements about assets, liabilities, costs, profits, etc.

Within accounting, a basic division can be made between its internal provision of management information and external reporting. The former is concerned with methods favoured within particular enterprises to monitor and control costs associated with the accumulation or transfer of economic values. It is termed 'management accounting' because its principal function is the support of management decision making. Calculating and recording the cost of materials or machinery, or the unit cost of producing goods, are examples of the traditional, focal concerns of management accounting. Financial accounting, in contrast, is concerned with the preparation of information to relevant people outside the organization – notably creditors, shareholders and tax authorities. This information may also be relevant to other parties, such as employees seeking to improve the terms and conditions of the sale of their labour. As conventionally defined, the purpose of financial accounting is to supply a quantified report or picture – principally in the balance sheet and profit and loss account – of the financial standing of an organization. Despite an established division between management and financial accounting, they are interrelated as the former frequently provides the raw information from which financial accounts are derived; and those who audit financial accounts may make recommendations about the internal production of management accounting information.

The Behavioural Dimension of Accounting

On the face of it, accounting can appear to be a straightforward, mechanical activity, comparable to basic mathematics. Indeed, it is quite often gently ridiculed, not least by accountants themselves, as 'score-keeping' or 'bean-counting'. This metaphor suggests that accountants, as independent and impartial observers, simply monitor and record the scores in a game played by other players, and so do little to influence the course of play. However, the mundane, unproblematic appearance of accounting is deceptive. Despite an image of objectivity, accounting is founded upon contestable conventions; and the construction, meaning and implications of its figures are always subject to interpretation and challenge (Robson and Young, 2009).

To elaborate briefly upon the 'game' metaphor, it is relevant to note that players in business do not necessarily accept the current methods of keeping score (for a broader discussion of the use of metaphors, see Chapter 3). Players may seek to influence how the scoring is conducted and what is recorded. Not infrequently, the very playing of the game is influenced by how accountants keep score as the players identify the easiest way to make an impact upon the relevant, most visible performance measures. For example, the way that a budgeting system is designed and operated can have non-trivial consequences for the allocation of resources between specialisms of management, or upon how the performance of managers (in keeping to budget) is assessed. Once it is recognized that accounting principles and methods are 'mere conventions' that construct economic reality in particular ways, rather than as mirrors that faithfully reflect reality (Hines, 1988; Gray et al., 1997), it is clear that financial accounting standards which, in principle, reduce the scope for 'subjectivity' are produced through a process of debate and contestation in which there is always one (or more) rival way of proceeding from currently accepted methods. Effective lobbying can have very considerable implications for the levels of performance or profit that are recorded, as was discovered so dramatically when the easing of regulations by powerful lobbying groups rendered the global financial system vulnerable to systemic meltdown.

When the embeddedness of accounting in social and organizational contexts is recognized, it becomes possible to appreciate how techniques – such as budgeting or costing – are developed and applied within *organizational relationships* where different groups are engaged in a *political* process of supporting or resisting alternative ways of constructing and interpreting accounts. With regard to internal management accounting, this concern has been explored using what has been labelled a 'behavioural' perspective. Borrowing heavily from organization theory, this approach has studied *inter alia* the relationship between accounting techniques and the psychological and organizational variables that condition their development and use. For example, behavioural accounting research has studied how local conditions or 'cultures' selectively use accounting techniques such as budgeting (e.g. Ezzamel, 1994).

Within behavioural accounting, considerable attention has been focused upon the question of how different configurations of accounting practice are associated with variables (or contingencies) that are deemed to determine their effectiveness in improving organizational performance (Otley, 1999). An alternative, more sociologically informed approach has endeavoured to appreciate how accounting techniques – such as budgeting – are practically interpreted and negotiated in organizations (Baxter and Chua, 2003). This approach, which has strong affinities with the interpretive paradigm (see Chapter 2), has addressed how accounting practices are shaped and operated through the medium of organizational members' diverse values and priorities (Chua, 1988; see also special issue of *Critical Perspectives on Accounting*, 2008).

A broadly similar pattern is discernible in financial accounting. Here too, the socially constructed character of accounts has become an increasingly influential focus of study. Fuelled by the lack of effective accounting regulation, coupled to the development and complexity of international business, there has been considerable scope for an expansion of 'creative accounting' (Shah, 1998). Associated with such developments, there has been a growth in studies that examine how principles and methods of external reporting are determined and enforced.[1]

From these brief remarks, it can be seen that accounting is not inherently the dry discipline that it is often assumed to be. However, and without suggesting the existence of a conspiracy, accountants have little incentive to debunk or discourage this understanding. This is not just because their training urges them to believe in their objectivity and independence (Power, 1991), but because the conventional image of accounting as a technical, score-keeping activity inhibits critical scrutiny. So long as accounting appears to be a purely technical matter, concerned only with varieties of 'score-keeping', there seems to be very little of interest to catch the critical eye. It is therefore somewhat surprising to discover that, of all the specialist fields of management, apart from organization theory, accounting has been subjected to the most vigorous and extended critical examination (Ezzamel and Robson, 2009; Hopwood and Miller, 1994; Morgan and Willmott, 1993).

Towards a Critical Perspective on Accounting

We have already noted how, even among fairly 'mainstream' accounting academics, there has been a growing interest in understanding how accounting techniques and procedures are developed and used within the context of organizations and society. In a seminal paper, Burchell et al. (1980) note how accounting has come to occupy a dominant position in the functioning of modern societies. Among its many roles, accounting is seen to act as a definer, regulator and monitor of economic performance within private and public sectors. It is also an adjudicator in the distribution of resources, and a key contributor to national and corporate planning. Finally, it is a principal medium in the construction of organizational realities, including the attribution of a specific, quantifiable identity and self-understanding to employees (Miller and O'Leary, 1987).

Burchell et al. (1980) challenge the idea that accounting is a passive reflector – or scorekeeper – of economic reality, arguing that it should be recognized as both a product and a producer of socio-political processes. This view, which echoes our earlier emphasis upon the motivation of the players in relation to the activity of the so-called scorekeepers, is dramatically expressed in the thesis that the appropriate metaphor for accounting is *not* that of an 'answering machine' that simply records what is fed into it. Rather, the more relevant metaphor is that of the 'ammunition machine' that is developed and refined in struggles between different groups in the belief that accounting provides the 'fire-power' that can best advance their most cherished beliefs or privileges (ibid.: 15).

Burchell et al. (1980) associate accounting procedures with mechanisms of social and organizational control developed to deal with 'the conflictive nature of organizational life'. But they are decidedly vague on the question of how the politics of accounting should be analysed. Despite connecting accounting practices to Weber's (1968) discussion of the growing dominance of formal rationality, based upon quantitative measures of efficiency, the development of this rationality is disconnected from an appreciation of the political struggles through which accounting's contemporary influence has been promoted and resisted.

Since the early 1980s, the theoretical vacuum in critical accounting scholarship has been filled by a diversity of theories and perspectives that have presented a range of challenges to narrow, technicist treatments of accounting theory and practice.[2] In addition to Critical Theory, critical accounting academics have drawn upon structuralist Marxism (e.g. Tinker et al., 1982), labour process analysis (e.g. Armstrong, 1987) and Foucauldianism (e.g. Miller, 2008), as well as studies that are more synthetic or eclectic in orientation (e.g. Lehman, 1992).

Critical Theory and Accounting

Structuralist Marxism, labour process analysis and Foucauldianism all have some affinities with Critical Theory (see Chapter 2). They broadly share a radical change conception of society; where power and domination, rather than consensus and community, are at the centre of social and economic relationships – including the theory and practice of accounting (Gallhofer and Haslam, 2002).[3] Structuralist Marxism and orthodox labour process analysis anticipate a process of radical transformation, a change that is provoked by the exploitative and unstable structure of capitalist society and which is struggled for by the organized working class. Both Critical Theory and Foucauldianism, in contrast, have serious doubts about the revolutionary credentials and/or potential of the working class. Foucault urges us to recognize the indivisibility of knowledge and power, and to remain sceptical, if not pessimistic, about the prospects of a domination-free society (see Chapter 7). Critical Theory, in its Habermasian formulation at least, pins its hopes upon a more diffuse and sustained process of emancipatory change, guided by critical reason and non–distorted communication, which is propelled by the agency of diverse social movements (see Chapter 2).

Although comparatively small in number, at least when compared to studies of accounting informed by structural Marxism (e.g. Armstrong, 2002; Bryer, 1993, 2006) and Foucauldianism (e.g. Miller and O'Leary, 1987), there exists a body of accounting research that draws upon Critical Theory (CT). In the main, the influence of CT upon this scholarship has been confined to the work of Habermas, with little sustained interest being shown in the writings of Horkheimer, Adorno or Marcuse to enrich the radical critique of accounting (although see Broadbent et al., 1991). For example, Arrington and Puxty (1991) take up a recurrent theme of Habermas' analyses – that 'technical' work is inescapably grounded in the 'practical' or 'moral' realm of social relations (see Chapter 2) – to suggest that Critical Theory provides the most relevant and penetrating resource for remembering accounting as 'a form of moral action' (ibid.: 48; see also Neu et al., 2001; Sikka et al., 1997). Accounting, they argue, represents the social action of economic life through the '"delinguistified" media of money' (ibid.). As such, it is a very fertile ground for empirical enquiry into distortions in communicative rationality (see Chapter 3).

The hidden moral quality of accounting, Arrington and Puxty propose, can be revealed by undertaking studies that appreciate how, in practice, accounting information is routinely produced, mobilized and contested in the pursuit of particular values and interests. To this end, they commend the use of Habermas' discussion of formal pragmatics as a conceptual framework for reinterpreting existing research and guiding future studies of the empirical realm of accounting practice (see also Puxty, 1991). Their suggestion is that Habermas' ideas could be used to explore '*how* interests are in fact adjudicated in accounting and *how* particular accounting acts do and must transpire with both empowering and pathological consequences' (Arrington and Puxty, 1991: 51). In this way, accounting theory and practice are identified as an important empirical site for understanding and challenging how communications are shaped within, and distorted by, asymmetrical relations of power (see Power et al., 2003).[4]

The fullest case for using Critical Theory in accounting research has been made by Laughlin (e.g. Broadbent and Laughlin, 2003). It is argued that CT provides a powerful vehicle 'through which understanding about reality can be achieved and transformation of concrete institutions [can] occur' (Laughlin, 1987: 482). The particular merit of Critical Theory, Laughlin contends, is that it is directly geared to the practical concern to change the world without recourse to the simplifications and historicism of structuralist Marxism. Moving beyond earlier applications of Habermas' ideas that simply critique the limitations of alternative methodologies (e.g. Willmott, 1983), Laughlin advocates the development of a research programme based on Habermas' (1984, 1987) writings on universal pragmatics and juridification.[5]

Laughlin (1991) applies a Habermasian framework to explore accounting in the operation of steering mechanisms that facilitate and legitimize the colonization of lifeworld values and practices. Specifically, he commends the relevance of Habermas' distinction between the self-formative 'lifeworld', where norms and values concerning 'ends' (e.g. personal creeds) are dominant and, in contrast, formalized 'systems' where purposive-rational calculations about the effectiveness of 'means' (e.g. the design of jobs) are central, and where 'steering media' (e.g. the law) direct the development of the 'systems' – including their colonization of processes through which the norms and values of the lifeworld are developed and sustained (see Chapter 3).

For example, Laughlin shows how, in the case of European Railways, traditional engineering values – which identified engineering practice as the essential activity and skill of running railways – were challenged and marginalized by the increasing application of financial criteria in decision making about how the railway should be run. New forms of accountability, Laughlin argues, acted to undermine the established (lifeworld) engineering craft values of railway workers, in which 'financial considerations were secondary', as a much stronger emphasis was placed upon the design and operation of effective and profitable systems of management control (Dent, 1986: 27, quoted in Laughlin, 1991). In this example, the increasing deployment of accounting techniques in management decision making in European Railways is seen to have problematized and undermined the rationality of established values. Traditional operational and engineering concerns were translated into 'the profit calculus', and railway matters 'came to be reinterpreted through the accounting thereof' (1991: 228; cf. Broadbent et al., 1991, where a similar analysis is applied to the UK's National Health Service). The lifeworld of the railway (wo)men was disrupted and severely damaged, Laughlin argues, as systemic rules were imposed – in the form of abstract accounting measures and controls. Laughlin's key argument is that established accounting disciplines did not act neutrally to facilitate the reproduction or survival of the existing lifeworld by enabling its practices to become more efficient or effective. Rather, their introduction tended to be corrosive of established lifeworld values.

The European Railways example is helpfully contrasted by Laughlin (1991) with the case of the Church of England where, despite a continuing resource crisis, accounting was found to play a secondary role. In contrast to the railways, Laughlin argues, the lifeworld values of the Church have been largely preserved because, he suggests, in this context the corrosive potential of an accounting mentality has, to date, been successfully resisted. Other examples fall between these extremes, but nonetheless illustrate the tensions between norms and values concerning 'ends' and purposive-rational calculations about the effectiveness of 'means' – such as struggles by public sector workers in the UK, notably medics and teachers, to frustrate or circumvent the accounting logic of unit costs in an effort to protect and preserve welfare and educational values. (For a more developed analysis that focuses upon recent reforms in health and education institutions in the UK, where accounting is identified as an 'active partner' in the possible disintegration of established 'organizational lifeworlds', see Laughlin and Broadbent, 1993; Lodh and Gaffikin, 1997.)

More recently, Laughlin and Broadbent have turned their attention to building more prescriptive models which are drawn from Critical Theory. Rather than simply showing how particular expressions of accounting are inappropriate and are being resisted, as in their public sector work, they have tried to speculate on what enlightened and enabling accounting would look like. They have also used Habermasian work to build a critical evaluatory process for the public sector reforms that they have been analysing over the last few years (see Broadbent and Laughlin, 2003).

Information Systems

There is a considerable and increasing degree of overlap between the fields of accounting and (management) information systems, particularly as management accountants seek to extend the boundaries of their expertise (Earl, 1983). Management accounting systems provide information and, consequently, there are often struggles for control over the design and operation of management information systems. What is distinctive about Information Systems (IS) is its *computer-based* provision of information and its aspirations to provide information support for *all* management functions – from accounting to personnel.

Using computer power, it is theoretically possible to gain instant access to diverse sources of information – not only to changes in 'the environment' such as sales information on different products, but also information on every operation within the organization, including the performance of each department and even each employee. There is also enormous potential for the development of shared networks between organizations, although their realization and implementation is often impeded as well as promoted by competitive pressures (see Knights et al., 1993). The focus of IS to date has been principally upon the hardware and software of computer science, it has also become increasingly concerned with the 'behavioural context' and organizational media of IS applications. In this respect, it parallels developments within other areas of management practice.

The Behavioural Dimension of Information Systems

In principle, the IS specialism addresses the computer-based processes through which information in organizations is collected, stored, manipulated and accessed. Its objective is to apply computer and behavioural science to make this process more systematic and, in recent years, more 'user-friendly'. However, most effort in IS has been directed towards the abstracted modelling of information systems which are then imposed, as it were, upon organizations. In this process, the users of the systems were initially marginalized from processes of design and development on the grounds that they lack relevant IS expertise, and are therefore unable to make any relevant contribution (Murray and Willmott, 1993). This situation has gradually changed in response to the substantive irrationalities – that is, failures – of formally rational systems. To the extent that designers of the systems concentrate on the technology, to the neglect of the 'needs' of the users, the outcome is the development of cumbersome, user-hostile systems that do not work well in practice. The shift from mainframe operations to the client–server networking of PCs has hastened this development.

Problems encountered in making systems work have enhanced the credibility of behaviourally oriented IS research. Much of this work has been preoccupied with the effective integration of social and technical systems (e.g. Baskerville and Myers, 2002). As in the case of other management specialisms, this has shifted attention away from the technical and towards the interpretive examination of the behavioural dimensions of systems design (Walsham, 2006). *Inter alia*, the examination of the organizational politics of designing and implementing information systems has been stimulated (e.g. Curry and Guah, 2007); and an awareness of the struggles between different specialist managers over the control and use of these systems has increased (Doolin, 2004; Knights and Murray, 1994). However, in common with behavioural studies that have developed in other areas of management, interpretive treatments of issues of power have been criticized for failing to penetrate the institutional and ideological barriers to improved forms of communication and organization (see Elkjaer et al., 1992; Jasperson et al., 2002; McGrath, 2005).

Towards a Critical Perspective on Information Systems

An interest in the political and processual aspects of IS has grown as their non-benign use and effects have become better recognized and understood (Howcroft and Trauth, 2004, and contributions to Howcroft and Trauth, 2005). Instead of seeing IS simply as a means of providing more detailed, speedier and more reliable information, systems are increasingly viewed as changing and often tightening the ways in which activity within organizations is monitored and controlled (e.g. Button et al., 2003; Sewell and Wilkinson, 1992). To take a comparatively trivial example, the computerization of supermarket checkouts can supply immediate and reliable information about the sale of goods which assists the process of re-stocking. But this innovation also presents an opportunity for management to monitor the speed, accuracy and honesty of checkout operators. As the potential of IS as surveillance systems is recognized and exploited, a 'darker' side of their development and implementation becomes more evident.

Partly because IS is a new field and partly because it has been dominated by computer engineers and systems analysts who are often more interested in developing the power and elegance of their machines and methods, critical reflection upon the social and political significance of IS has been rather limited. An early but influential exception is Weizenbaum's *Computer Power and Human Reason* (1976; see also Dreyfus et al., 1986, and Edwards, 1997). Weizenbaum highlights the potential of IS to deny reason and extend the abuse of power. Weizenbaum highlights a number of possible social dysfunctions of our increasing dependence upon computer-produced information. Commenting upon the use of computers in the Vietnam War (let alone the Gulf War or Iraq War, where their use enabled TV spectators to attend to the conflict less as war involving massive loss of life, and perhaps more as something comparable to a game of virtual reality Space Invaders), Weizenbaum observes that:

When the American President decided to bomb Cambodia and to keep that decision secret from the American Congress, the computers in the Pentagon were 'fixed' to transform the genuine strike reports coming in from the field into the false reports to which government leaders were given access. George Orwell's Ministry of Truth had become mechanised ...

Weizenbaum continues:

Not only have decision-makers abdicated their decision-making responsibility to a technology they do not understand – though all the while maintaining the illusion that they, the policy makers, are formulating policy questions and answering them – but responsibility has altogether evaporated. ... The enormous computer systems in the Pentagon and their counterparts elsewhere in our culture have, in a very real sense, no authors. Thus, they do not admit of any questions of right or wrong, of justice, or of any theory with which one can agree or disagree. They provide no basis on which 'what the machine says' can be challenged. (Weizenbaum, 1976: 238–240)

Of course Weizenbaum is not denying that the 'fixing' of computers is done by human beings, not computers. Rather, he is arguing that computer power can and does exert an insidious influence upon how people – particularly powerful people – are able to think, make decisions and act. Though not inevitable, the effect of this power, he argues, tends to reinforce a myth of technological rationality and inevitability where moral choices between alternative ends become reduced to a decisionistic process that is exclusively concerned with the computer-assisted calculation of means (see Chapter 1). A major difficulty with IS, Weizenbaum argues, is the widespread technocratic understanding that a continuous expansion and refinement of computer systems is an inescapable part of human progress – progress that is driven ever onward by what appears to be the impersonal march of science (see Chapter 2).

Technological inevitability can be seen to be a mere element of a much larger syndrome. Science promised man power. But, as often happens when people are seduced by promises of power, the price exacted in advance and all along the path, and the price actually paid, is servitude and impotence. Power is nothing if it is not the power to choose. Instrumental reason can make decisions, but there is all the difference in the world between deciding and choosing. (ibid.: 259)

Weizenbaum's central point is that the development and use of computers has tended to reflect and reinforce an instrumental conception of reason in which making choices between competing ends (e.g. using computers or not using them; using them selectively in ways that preserve the status quo or using them in ways that question the status quo, etc.) is subordinated to making decisions about how their power, speed, reliability, etc. could be increased – often 'for the morally bankrupt reason that 'If we don't do it, someone else will'. (ibid.: 252–3)

Weizenbaum calls for the development of *critical* reason (as contrasted with instrumental reason) so that it becomes both possible and desirable to exercise human, democratic judgment about how computer power may be most effectively used for human purposes. Or, as Weizenbaum puts it: 'The alternative to the kind of rationality that sees the solution to world problems in psychotechnology is not mindlessness. It is reason restored to human dignity, to authenticity, to self-esteem, and to individual autonomy' (ibid.).

Of course, the meaning of 'dignity' or 'authenticity' is not uncontested. Just as it is problematic to reify the meaning of 'science' (see Chapter 2), the meaning of 'autonomy' is properly a subject for critical interrogation that reveals its embeddedness within a peculiarly modern conception of the individual (Knights and Willmott, 2002; Winograd and Flores, 1986; see also Chapter 7). However, if we are to follow the tradition of Critical Theory, it is to be stressed that this Enlightenment conception of the nature and rights of the individual is worth valuing and defending. At the same time, its defence must allow, rather than deny, a full recognition of its historical relativity.

Critical Information Systems

From the perspective of Critical Theory, the challenge of developing a more rational society is not principally a technical one, involving the design and implementation of more powerful systems of control (e.g. the development of management information systems). Rather, the challenge is fundamentally social and political. It involves the transformation of institutions so that computer power acts to facilitate emancipation rather than to preserve the status quo (see Stahl, 2008a, b). This challenge has been taken up by a small but growing number of IS specialists who have drawn upon CT, especially the work of Habermas, to develop a critical alternative to mainstream, instrumental forms of IS theory and practice (for overviews, see Brooke, 2002; Howcroft and Trauth, 2005; Lyytinen, 1992). With the possible exception of Zuboff (1988), IS specialists have tended to exclude consideration of Foucauldian insights. Indeed, as Willcocks (2006: 274) has noted, 'it is surprising to find Foucauldian methods and concepts discussed so little, let alone digested and used, in the information systems (IS) field'.[6]

The application of Critical Theory in IS has, however, yet to progress much beyond a critique of existing approaches to systems development. This has been done either by drawing upon Habermas' theory of knowledge-constitutive interests, as outlined in Chapter 2 (e.g. Lyytinen and Klein, 1985), or by commending Habermas' work on communication as a promising approach to the study of IS (Heng and de Moor, 2003; Lyytinen and Hirschheim, 1988). The critique of conventional IS has challenged its epistemological and ontological assumptions, along similar lines to the objections raised by Weizenbaum (see above). For example, when attacking the mainstream conception of information systems as scientistic, Klein and Lyytinen (1985: 143) argue that 'the separation of information systems goals from human purpose and the identification of data with measurable facts conceal the real nature of information systems as social communication systems'; and that, 'under scientism, science, rather than being a critical conscience and teacher of practice, becomes its myopic servant' (ibid.: 151; see also Klein, 2004).

To counter the dominance of instrumental, scientistic reason within IS, Klein and Lyytinen (1985) commend two changes in the orientation of the IS community. First, they argue for a broadening of the education and training of IS specialists so as to increase awareness of the relativity and poverty of 'the scientistic paradigm'. Teachers of IS are asked to recognize and honour a responsibility for grasping and disseminating a plurality of approaches to IS development, including those informed by Critical Theory. This education and training, Klein and Lyytinen contend, should incorporate a consideration of 'the ethical–moral position which legitimizes preferred tools and methods as "good" and which is to guide their application' (ibid.: 152).[7] Second, when turning to consider the practice of IS, Klein and Lyytinen invoke the Jeffersonian dictum that the powers of society are best put in the hands of the people. From this position, they urge that systems designers should engage in a dialogue with the users of IT, the users being not just those who operate IT within organizations but everyone who is an end-user. They note that the prevailing philosophy and practice of IS do not permit users to exercise discretion over the development and use of IT, and comment:

> if industry leaders cannot explain how their approach to system design differs from that practised in totalitarian societies (e.g. by being able to demonstrate how they design systems with the people for the people by the people), then the Western world is in trouble. (ibid.: 154)

Relatedly, it is suggested that movement in a Jeffersonian direction can be facilitated by industry leaders becoming more open to studies that provide insights into the practical, processual operation of IS.

A good indication of CT's potential for studying and transforming IS is to be found in the work of Hirschheim and Klein (1989), who draw upon the Burrell and Morgan paradigmatic framework (see Chapter 2) to identify the distinctive contribution of CT to IS development in comparison to other diverse approaches.[8] Habermas, Hischheim and Klein's (1989) basic argument is that the legitimacy of system objectives and design is ultimately dependent upon a process of free and open communication, guided by an appreciation of the presence and value of each of the three knowledge–constitutive interests identified by Habermas (1972) (see Chapter 2). In this formulation, the goal of IS design and development would be to enable:

> [the] institutionalization of an ideal speech situation which in turn validates a consensus about system objectives and modes of design and implementation. The ideal speech situation would legitimate a moving balance between the fundamental three objectives of information systems development, namely improved technical control, better mutual understanding and continued emancipation from unwarranted social constraints and psychological compulsions. (Hirschheim and Klein, 1989: 1209)

Hirschheim and Klein recognize that Habermas' conception of the ideal speech situation (ISS) (see Chapter 2) is indeed an ideal that may never be fully implemented;

and they also acknowledge that, in practice, people may be unwilling or unable to engage in open debate or change their behaviour. Nonetheless, they suggest that the ISS can be used as a benchmark for assessing the quality of IS design and legitimizing its implementation. A number of ways of mitigating socially unnecessary impediments to, and distortions of, rational discourse are suggested. These include the reorganization of systems development processes so as to encourage 'rational motivations to participate, share and elicit missing information'; the introduction of conferencing systems that 'motivate people to contribute their expertise'; and the design of information systems that would 'motivate people to communicate criticisms and radical change proposals by shielding them from the threats of the powerful' (ibid.: 1209; see also Richardson and Robinson, 2007).

This 'wish list' has yet to be translated into a series of empirical studies or methodologies of change (see, for example, Howcroft and Trauth, 2008; Stahl et al., 2010; Trauth and Howcroft, 2006). As Lyytinen (1992: 175) observed, 'more detailed and explicit critical studies of ID development' are required if CT is to penetrate the IS community as a viable research approach. In commending the relevance of Critical Theory to IS specialists, Lyytinen suggests that they could usefully pay greater attention to developments in other management disciplines where such work is rather more advanced, and where CT-influenced studies have borrowed from traditions and theorists whose work provides more assistance in researching concrete practices. Specifically, Lyytinen (1992: 175) identifies work developed within the specialism of operational research, to be discussed below, as relevant 'for elaborating a critical methodology of IS development' (see Alvarez, 2008).[9]

Operational Research

The origins of operational research (OR, which in North America is more commonly known as operations research) lie in military operations where mathematical models were developed in an effort to identify the most efficient method of deploying available weaponry, supplies and manpower (for summaries, see Molinero, 1992; Rosenhead, 1989). It is also the case that a number of the key figures in the early history of OR regarded its development as a scientific means of creating a planned, socialist society based upon the efficient husbandry and use of scarce resources (Mingers, 1992a). However, this early idealism has subsequently been marginalized within the discipline of OR, although it has experienced a modest revival in the form of 'community OR' (Molinero, 1992; Parry and Mingers, 2001). Commenting upon this history, Tinker and Lowe (1984) have observed how the discipline 'languishes in a morass of technical specialization; it lacks overall coherence and direction' (see also Tinker and Lowe, 1982), a view that has been echoed by Oliga (1996).

OR techniques have been most widely adopted by industry and government to develop more effective systems, such as those designed to improve logistics, stock control and manpower planning. In the process, as Mingers (1992a: 93) comments:

Messy and complex problems were reduced to that which the technique could handle, and people were just another component of the system like machines and money. OR's 'solutions' gained their legitimacy through their supposed scientificity as embodied in the idea of optimality.

However, disillusionment subsequently set in as the mathematical models developed by OR specialists were perceived to be remote from, and frequently irrelevant to, managing an increasingly complex and changeable world. A concentration upon the perfection of mathematical technique had the unintended effect of reducing OR's influence and contribution to managerial decision making. As a consequence, accountants and, more recently, information systems specialists have been identified as possessing more relevant (e.g. 'behavioural') knowledge and skills, and a more pragmatic orientation, for undertaking tasks that previously were the preserve of OR specialists (Bain, 1992).

'Soft' OR

The response of OR specialists has been divided. Some have been content to concentrate their efforts in limited fields where their models continue to have some purchase – such as in queuing theory or in stock control. Others have endeavoured to broaden OR methodology to encompass 'soft' factors that had been excluded from 'hard', quantified models (see Mingers, 2000a). A variety of approaches and techniques have been developed (reviewed in Mingers, 1992a), all of which share the concern to appreciate the interactive, messy nature of most real-world activities and problems. Of these, Checkland's (1981) 'soft systems methodology' (SSM) is perhaps the most theoretically sophisticated and influential.

SSM departs from 'hard' methodologies by arguing that systems models do not, and cannot, capture or map the world that they study. At best, they can provide one possible language for communicating about this world. The purpose of SSM is to appreciate and model how different actors working within a particular situation (e.g. a company or a department) interpret and communicate their sense of reality (e.g. Ledington and Donaldson, 1997; Ormerod, 1996). Whereas 'hard'-systems thinking analyses the world as something that is given, and is accessible through the use of methods that emulate those of the physical sciences, SSM studies this world as the continuously negotiated outcome of interactions between people who mobilize diverse interpretive frameworks (Mingers, 2000a). The 'messiness' of much problem-solving is understood in terms of shifting negotiations, where there is frequently no common and shared definition of what the problem is, or of the appropriateness of alternative solutions. The value of SSM, it is claimed, resides in its capacity to model the diversity and complexity of these interpretative frameworks and thereby to facilitate a process of dialogue by enabling different groups to appreciate how others see the world, with the anticipation that, by engendering greater mutual understanding, consensus will be reached on the nature of the problem and how it is to be effectively solved (see Callo and Packham, 1999).

In parallel with critiques developed in other specialisms of management, 'soft' thinking has been attacked for its failure to deal adequately with issues of power and conflicts of interest (Bergvall-Kåreborn, 2002). Lacking in SSM, its critics argue, is an understanding of how different interpretive frameworks are historically embedded in, and sustained by, relations of domination and exploitation (for a review, see Willmott, 1989). When this shortcoming is acknowledged, it is evident that attaining consensus between different groups is likely to require a radical transformation of these relations. Otherwise, whatever agreements may emerge are likely to be conditioned by the position of comparative dependence or autonomy of some groups in relation to others. Views will not be freely formed, developed or expressed. Since their meaning is embedded in the power relations from which they derive their plausibility and force, few 'communication problems' are likely to be fully resolved by modelling meanings in the way that SSM proposes.

Critical OR

Initially, critiques of the neglect of the material conditions of OR theory and practice came from the tradition of structuralist Marxism and labour process analysis (e.g. Hales, 1974; Rosenhead and Thunhurst, 1982). More recently, these have been joined, and perhaps overshadowed, by OR specialists who have commended CT as a resource for advancing critical OR theory and practice, as well as a critical realist formulation of OR (Mingers, 2000c). These critics have often taken some version of 'soft' thinking as a point of departure for advancing an approach that takes account of power and domination in processes of decision making. Jackson argues that,

> the kind of unconstrained debate envisaged (e.g. in Checkland's SSM) cannot possibly take place. The actors bring to the discussion unequal intellectual resources and are more or less powerful. ... The result of the inequalities of power is that the existing social order, from which power is drawn, is reproduced. (1982: 25)

So, from a critical perspective, the consensus identified or encouraged through the use of 'soft' methodologies is viewed with suspicion. Little confidence is placed in agreements reached since these are understood to take shape within asymmetrical relations of power that inhibit the open formation and expression of views. One of the most developed attempts to apply Habermas' ideas has been made by Ulrich (1988, 2007). Ulrich's contention is that all statements – such as those made by managers or public planners – are necessarily founded upon unjustified judgments about the world. The critical aim of his Critical Systems Heuristics (CSH) is to press those in positions of authority to make transparent, and thereby make available for further interrogation, the normative basis of their policies and statements. By employing reason 'polemically' to recall how all statements rest upon undeclared 'break-offs' of justification, it is intended that authorities become provoked into articulating the values and assumptions upon which their claims are based – the objective of CSH being to facilitate debate about the adequacy and legitimacy of these claims. Critical

Theory ideas are then transformed from 'a mere research program into a practical tool of critical social inquiry and design' (Ulrich, 1988: 155).

CSH itself makes no claim to enjoy privileged access to the truth. Its critical intent is not to reveal the falseness of others' claims by contrasting them with the truth of CSH. Rather, its objective is to develop the conditions in which a plurality of parties can be reminded that their diverse positions share a basis in some undeclared 'break-off' which can be clarified only by challenging their authority. In principle, Ulrich (1983: 74) argues, 'the polemical employment of reason secures to both sides an equal position for reasonable dialogue' (see Flood and Jackson, 1991b for an application and evaluation of CSH; and for a dismissive treatment of CSH and the claims of CT more generally, see Tsoukas, 1992 – of which more below). However, Ulrich's thesis is somewhat disingenuous since the *effect* of CSH, if not its intent, is to deconstruct the position of those whose authority is most widely accepted or deeply entrenched (see Willmott, 1989, 1995a). It is likely that these authorities will also feel, rightly or wrongly, that they have much to lose from a dialogue that tenaciously questions their claims. If, as Ulrich argues, statements are founded upon unjustified judgments, it is to be expected that authorities will strenuously resist efforts to make these more transparent. Emperors do not willingly admit their nakedness! Even if authorities are privately persuaded by the arguments of CSH, they are unlikely to give strong support to its public application (see Payne, 1992). An adequate critical study of management must squarely face up to the likelihood of this response (see Chapter 8 for a fuller discussion of CSH; see also Ulrich, 2001).

To overcome resistance to change, a methodology of emancipation informed by the insights of CT must openly acknowledge, and work with, the tensions and con-tradictions within power relations, as experienced by those who are privileged and underprivileged by these relations. For example, while recognizing that there will be resistance from those in positions of authority, it is necessary to appreciate how each 'side' is a victim and a perpetrator of unnecessarily oppressive social arrangements and cultural traditions. Mingers (1992a) reaches broadly similar conclusions when he suggests that Habermas' highly abstract formulation of the organization of power must be complemented by approaches that are more directly concerned with the study of concrete practices and processes, a view that is also expressed by Lyytinen (1992) in relation to IS.

Addressing the Backlash

Finally, before concluding this chapter, it is relevant to take note of the sweeping critique of critical systems thinking, and of Critical Theory more generally, advanced by Tsoukas (1992, 1993). Although Tsoukas directs his fire at the use of CT in OR, a similar salvo could be directed at its application in other realms of management studies reviewed in this and the previous chapters. We do not have the space here to summarize and challenge this critique at any length. And, indeed, we accept a num-ber of the criticisms that Tsoukas makes of the critical systems perspective – for example, a tendency to regard society as a coherent entity and an inclination to favour an essentialist conception of human beings (see also Chapter 7). We also agree that 'Total Systems Intervention' (Flood and Jackson, 1991a) falls well short of a commitment to emancipation required by CT. As Mingers (1992b) cuttingly observes, Flood and Jackson's *Creative Problem Solving* (1992) reads 'more like a management consultant's handbook than an emancipatory tool' (ibid.: 734).

The basic difficulty with Tsoukas' critique stems from his desire for certainties and a related unwillingness to accept the problematical status of all knowledge, including science (see below). His many complaints about the philosophical weakness of critical systems thinking would seem to arise from a faith in the separation of knowledge/ facts and opinion/values (see Chapter 2). This leads him, unsurprisingly, to challenge the claims and coherence of analyses that borrow heavily from Critical Theory. It also leads him to make quite wild claims, such as the assertion that those sympathetic to a critical systems perspective believe in, and seek the abolition of, the means–ends distinction, whereas, arguably, the ambition of CT is not to abolish this distinction but to scrutinize, clarify and secure the (communicative) rationality of means and ends.

CT does not claim that critical reason is, or ever could be, supreme or free-floating in the process of developing human societies but, rather, that it is of value in loosening the grip of power relations, such as patriarchy, that impede and distort open communication and rational societal development. A number of Tsoukas' (1992) criticisms, including his exposure of the comparatively unsophisticated formulation of power in much CT-guided research, can be accepted (see also Mingers, 1992a). But he fails to demonstrate that a more satisfactory conceptualization is incompatible with CT's assumptions and ambitions. With regard to his understanding of science, we have no quarrel with the contention that self-criticism has (in principle!) been 'the cornerstone of scientific inquiry' (ibid.: 654). Yet, paradoxically, this observation fails to appreciate how CT (and, for that matter, Foucauldian analysis) has persuasively challenged assumptions about the autonomy of the scientist's self, the constitution of this self within relations of power and domination, and the limited capacity or preparedness of scientists to reflect critically upon the discourses and practices that have provided defences of positivist science, such as those advanced by Popper (see Habermas, 1976).

Refusal to reflect critically upon assumptions (e.g. the autonomy or impartiality of scientists) that underpin his objections to CT leads Tsoukas to conclude that CT is no different in spirit, or in practice, from the established interpretive perspective found in assumptionist analysis (Mason and Mitroff, 1981), second-loop learning (Argyris and Schon, 1978) and soft-systems methodology (Checkland, 1981). Instead of seeking to appreciate how a critical perspective favours a dialogical and less imperious approach to assessing the plausibility of competing truth claims, Tsoukas (1992: 654) insists upon evaluating the claims of CT in terms of an unreflexive, self-congratulatory conception of 'methodological rigour' (although this stance is substantially moderated and revised in his later contributions to the field, e.g. Tsoukas, 2004). Tsoukas (1992) is disinclined, or unable, to recognize that the relationship between positivist/interpretivist and critical perspectives is not inherently zero-sum. While there are fundamental differences in the assumptions and values that constitute these perspectives (see Chapter 2), there is no particular difficulty for CT in engaging with the 'dominant rationalities' of management or in providing interpretations that are of interest and value to managers. To assume that managers are entirely indifferent, if not wholly antagonistic, to ideas which directly challenge received wisdom about their 'problems' is, in effect, to embrace an essentialism that takes inadequate account of the complex and contradictory positioning and constitution of managerial work (see Chapter 1 and Willmott, 1996a).

Conclusion

In this and the previous chapter, we have sought to highlight research into specialisms of management that draws upon critical thinking, and especially CT, to provide an alternative to orthodox ways of making sense of management. We have also sought to make apparent the continuities with, as well as the departures from, other 'behavioural' and 'soft' portrayals of management's various specialisms. In reviewing each field, we have sought to show how critical thinking contributes fresh ideas and inspiration to those who are disillusioned with the divisive and destructive consequences of established ways of organizing and managing. In each of the specialisms, we identified a small but active and growing number of researchers who engage critical thinking to question and to change orthodox theory and practice. It is our hope that recognition of their pioneering efforts in applying critical reason to advance the theory and practice of management will inspire others either to join them or, at least, to appreciate and debate their concerns.

Notes

1   In the Anglo-American context, at least, financial accountants as well as those who check their accounts (the auditors), have tended to favour very general principles. This affords them the flexibility to choose between a range of approaches so as to present the performance of the organization in the best possible light. On the other hand, the users of financial accounts (e.g. creditors and shareholders) and government regulators have favoured increased standardization in order to achieve greater ease of comparability between financial statements. The comparability argument is contested by providers of financial information who argue that organizations operate in highly diverse conditions, and that standardization necessarily favours some sectors, contexts and organizations to the disadvantage of others. Only flexibility, and the opportunity to choose between competing methods, they argue, allow a 'true and fair' picture to be provided.

2   In quite marked contrast to other management specialisms, leading 'critical' accounting scholars have been very active in encouraging non-accounting academics to bring their insights to accounting – a development that has been assisted by an exceptionally tight labour market for accounting academics and, arguably, by the professional aspirations of accountancy as a rigorous intellectual discipline.

3 Here it is also relevant to note the violent disagreements among Marxian and Foucauldian accounting academics about what counts as 'radical scholarship'. See, for example, Neimark's (1991) polemical critique of the radical potential and aspirations of Foucauldianism and the special issue of *Critical Perspectives on Accounting* (1994) that contains responses and a rejoinder.

4 To date such studies, which use the idea of the ideal speech situation as their basis, have not been undertaken within the field of accounting. An indication of what such analysis would look like can be found in Chapter 3.

5 Juridification refers to a process or situation where the law goes beyond its established function of providing a formal framework, in which autonomy is in principle supported and enabled, to specify 'the social processes, relationships and often the outcomes ... which are determined by a definable political agenda and purpose' (Laughlin and Broadbent, 1993: 339).

6 As Willcocks (2006) notes, the most substantial Foucauldian studies of IS have been undertaken by non-IS specialists. See, for example, Bloomfield et al. (1997).

7 To facilitate this process, they call for additional channels for the dissemination of non-scientistic research papers – for example, by having special issues in existing journals. In contrast to the field of accounting, IS has lacked a journal that actively stimulates and disseminates critical research. However, the appearance of *Information and Organization* (previously *Accounting, Management and Information Technology*) and the broadening of policy of the *Journal of Information Systems* and *MIS Quarterly* suggest that this position may be changing.

8 Each paradigm, they argue, is associated with a different conception of the systems analyst: as systems expert (functionalist), as facilitator (interpretive), as labour partisan (radical structuralist), and as emancipator or social therapist (radical humanist).

9 Lyytinen's interest in critical work developed within the field of operational research and is indicative of a degree of overlap between these fields (see also Jackson, 1992).

PART III

RECASTING CRITICAL THEORY AND MANAGEMENT

7

Recasting Emancipation in Management and Organization Studies

Taking initial inspiration primarily from Critical Theory (CT), the previous chapters have reviewed critiques and counterpoints of conventional wisdom in specialist fields of management and organization studies. In this and the concluding chapter, we engage additional traditions of critical analysis more directly to reflect upon the claims of CT, and we also explore its links with more progressive forms of management theory and practice. More specifically, in this chapter, we seek to re-evaluate Critical Theory's concept of emancipation – that is, the understanding that, through a process of critical self-reflection and struggle, people can become freed from diverse forms of domination. In Chapter 8, management practice receives more explicit attention.

We noted in Chapter 2 that major critiques of CT have come from orthodox Marxism and, more recently, from various forms of feminism and poststructuralist theory.[1] Orthodox Marxism regards CT as excessively cerebral and lacking an understanding of how transformations of consciousness emerge from the blood-and-guts process of class conflict and struggle. Indeed, CT is attacked for lacking any well-defined agency of emancipatory change. As Cleaver (1979) expresses the complaint, Critical Theory is preoccupied with ideological critique and is impotent when it comes to considering the development of working-class power. We noted in Chapter 2 how some versions of feminism are close to CT (Alvesson and Billing, 2009; Martin, 2003) – for example, the critique of the domination of instrumental reason – but CT is criticized for its neglect of gender issues and, at least in the Habermasian version, for pursuing a too narrow cognitivist agenda. Overlapping with (some forms of) feminism, but in contrast to Marxism, poststructuralism (PS), which we address at some length in this chapter, doubts whether the 'truths' assumed by CT's critique of ideology can be separated from relations of power. Relatedly, PS questions whether the autonomous subject who overcomes the oppressive, consciousness-distorting effects of power is a plausible agent of change. Taking these arguments seriously suggests a more cautious vision of emancipatory transformation in which fuller account is taken of how different forms of knowledge – including CT – have the potential to become new sources of domination and/or obfuscation.

The chapter is written in the form of a dialogue between management and organization studies (MOS), Critical Theory (CT) and Poststructuralism (PS). By engaging in a kind of conversation between these three orientations, we explore what space there may be for emancipatory projects. Our discussion circles around various topics that have been touched upon in the earlier chapters – power, knowledge, improvement, autonomy, ends, etc. After presenting a brief account of the idea of emancipation in management, we consider critiques that CT, particularly in the context of management and organization studies, must take seriously. Following this, we sketch a framework for a modified understanding of emancipation as a response to such critique. Finally, we have some suggestions for emancipatory research concerning ways of listening, writing and reading, where space is given to critical reflection and emancipation as well as to other, more traditional concerns.

Management and Emancipation

In previous chapters, we have explored various ways in which critical thinking can be mobilized to examine and critique contemporary developments in management and organization studies. Analyses of the administered society, the culture industries and the consumer society can, as Kellner (1989) argues, provide vital insights into peculiar combinations of streamlined rationality and intense irrationality, of organization and disorganization, and of crisis tendencies and efforts at crisis management. However, CT, and Habermas in particular, have been preoccupied with developing grand frameworks and broad-brush comments on contemporary society, and have been less inclined to pursue specific investigations of institutions and practices. A systematic examination of institutional and organizational forms which articulate social systems and social actions has been lacking, for example, with respect to the study of firms, hospitals, schools, unions, churches, cultural and ethnic associations, etc. Given Habermas' critique of the system's colonization of the lifeworld, one would have hoped for a keener interest in the institutions that host this colonizing – such as management and organizations. After all, systems media such as money and formal power do not accomplish anything in the abstract. They exert effects only through the institutions and practices that influence and organize the social world and people's life orientations. Here business and a business/consumerist logic are increasingly central, increasingly colonizing and penetrating all sectors of social and political life (Grey, 1999). In the absence of the study of business and management, Critical Theory can appear not a little esoteric, remote and irrelevant.

Within mainstream management and organization studies, two dominant attitudes to the idea of emancipation can be found. One immediate, 'hard-nosed' response is to dismiss any suggestion that work organizations, and management in particular, are – or could ever conceivably be – associated with an idea as fancy or radical as emancipation. The role of managers, this response insists, is "to ensure the survival/ growth/profitability of the organization"; and/or "to satisfy the immediate demands of shareholders/customers/(and to some extent) workers"; or, more cynically, "to keep the shareholders/customers/employees off the backs of managers". It has nothing to do with emancipation, which is a private matter or an issue for broader social and political movements (Armstrong, 2011). Emancipation is simply not an issue for, or responsibility of, managers – or a suitable topic for proper management research and education. This response may indeed be shared by employees for whom the firm's survival, growth and profitability – to secure jobs, wage increases and career possibilities – are most salient. Even when a person is eager to develop her/his autonomy at the workplace, s/he may feel rather differently about others' aspirations in this respect, if this obstructs corporate results or interferes negatively with the person's own job. In short, many managers and other employees may simply exclude any ideas of emancipation from their understanding of the nature and purpose of workplaces.

An alternative response to the idea of emancipation – and one that is closer to, yet still at considerable distance from, the position of CT (and of this book) – is that there is already a place for it within management theory. Modern management theory is seen to be enlightened in its concern to free employees from unnecessarily alienating forms of work organization. The jargon term for this concern is 'empowerment'. Advocacy of less alienating, more meaningful, emotionally engaging forms of work extends from Human Relations through Quality of Working Life (QWL) to Corporate Culture and contemporary conceptions of leadership (e.g. 'transformational leadership'), the 'high performance workforce' and so on. The espoused purpose and priority of such 'humanistic' management theory is to redesign material and symbolic conditions of work in 'enriching' ways that serve higher-order needs (e.g. self-actualization), improve job satisfaction and thereby generate productivity improvements. When management provides opportunities that are claimed to satisfy such higher-order needs, the 'emancipation' of employees from alienating conditions of work is said to be well advanced, if not pretty much complete. Much writing on the topic of leadership advances the idea that the manager (labelled a 'leader') is in the business of empowering, developing and even liberating the individual through support, coaching and providing guidelines. Indeed, the idea of 'servant leadership' has been proposed and has had some impact, at least at the level of talk (Sendjaya et al., 2008).[2]

Proponents of CT are inclined to regard humanistic management theory as a fatally naïve, ideologically polluted version of 'emancipation' that merits harsh critique. Our own work has sometimes expressed such a position (Alvesson, 1987; Willmott, 1993a). But even though it merits highly critical examination, a more nuanced appreciation of humanistic management theory is possible, and elements may even receive a *carefully qualified* welcome. To its credit, humanistic management theory begins to understand employees as subjects, albeit ones from whom more productive effort can be squeezed, gleaned and garnered (see Burawoy, 1979). In principle, at least, (some) employees are recognized to possess what are termed 'higher-order needs'; and a moral as well as a material value is explicitly placed upon managing people in a caring, responsible manner. That said, humanistic management theory is founded upon a narrow, managerialist conception of 'empowerment' where it is viewed as identical to providing employees with training and jobs that allow them to progress up 'the needs hierarchy'. Crucially, 'empowerment' is conceived as a passive process that is *bestowed* upon employees by progressive, enlightened managers.

In contrast, when informed by CT, genuine empowerment is understood to involve an active process (or struggle) for individual and collective self-determination. CT is sceptical about – though not necessarily implacably opposed to – the emancipatory claims and effects of top-down change even, and perhaps especially, when this change is couched in the language of 'empower-and-facilitate' rather than 'command-and-control'. The 'empower-and-facilitate' discourse is expressed, for example, in the idea of 'a SuperLeader – that is, a leader who leads followers to lead themselves through empowerment' (Houghton et al., 2003: 124). The idea that extraordinary individuals can, through their leadership, create 'improved' people who take care of themselves in ways prescribed by the leader is clearly at odds with CT ideals. *For CT, emancipation is not a gift to be bestowed upon employees but, rather, is an existentially painful collective process of confronting and overcoming socially and psychologically unnecessary restrictions* (see Ulrich, 2003). The latter include a broad range of phenomena extending from sexual and racial discrimination to dependency on a consumerist lifestyle for self-esteem, and the fear of failure in relationship to ideologies of careerism. Unnecessary restrictions also include taking for granted the necessity of existing structures, practices and values, excessive subordination to hierarchies and authorities, and allowing fashions, trends and 'eternal' truths to escape critical scrutiny. In the absence of struggle, seemingly progressive management interventions may have the effect of weakening employees' capacity to reflect critically upon their work situation and corporate priorities. Seemingly 'good' corporate values or caring forms of leadership may reinforce employee passivity and so leave managerial wisdom and superiority effectively unchallenged. An example of how critical self-reflection may be impeded by the application of humanistic management theory is when the so-called cascading-down of responsibility from managers to 'empowered' employees is accompanied by a (centralized) strengthening of corporate culture. Of course, redesigning work in ways that expand opportunities for exercising discretion can make work more enjoyable and/or meaningful, although it may also make it more pressured and all-consuming. It is therefore relevant to consider what inspires and drives such redesign projects. Are they propelled by a commitment to greater self-determination or are they driven by managers' desire to justify their existence, by pressures to raise productivity, flexibility, etc.? Leaving aside the intentions, what are the outcomes? Is there some increase in empowerment or is the outcome mainly greater intensification? Executives, consultants and human resources specialists appropriate and promote all kinds of appealing ideas in pursuit of performance improvements (Boltanski and Chiapello, 2007). Most crucially, it is necessary to assess whether the new ways of working and designs of organization encourage or impede opportunities for, and capacities of, collective self-determination.

For CT, emancipatory change involves a *continuing social process* of critical *self-reflection* and associated *self-transformation*. Emancipation is not to be equated with, or reduced to, piecemeal social engineering directed by a more or less benevolent managerial elite. Rather, CT's conception of the emancipatory project encompasses a broad set of issues that includes the transformation of gender relations, environmental husbandry, the development of workplace democracy, overturning the legacies of colonialism, etc. But, equally, we believe that it is a mistake to assume a zero-sum game between improvements in organizational performance and emancipatory movement. Even *within* the constraints of capital accumulation and the domination of instrumental rationality, the contradictory dynamics of modern organizations are capable of accommodating – and even selectively promoting – *some* degree of increased employee responsibility and autonomy.

Critiques of Critical Theory

Having briefly discussed CT in relation to humanistic management theory, we now consider a number of critiques of CT, partly connecting to issues we addressed in Chapter 2. Although we focus upon CT, elements of these criticisms are also applicable to many approaches within the broad tradition(s) of Critical Management Studies (CMS). We identify and discuss three types of problems with CT's ideal of social science as a facilitator of emancipation: 'intellectualism', 'essentialism' and 'negativism'. All potentially lead to the marginalization of CT within management and organization studies (MOS) and need to be addressed.

Intellectualism

Critical Theory assumes that human reason can be an emancipatory force, a force which is constrained and distorted by historical conditions that can be changed (see Chapters 1 and 2). These conditions – which include managerialism, consumerism, a fetish for economic growth, and organizations taking over almost all human functions – counteract the ability of human beings to act individually and collectively to determine their own priorities and shape their own destinies. Such conditions are understood to engender experiences of frustration and suffering that trigger processes of critical reflection upon these conditions and thereby stimulate struggles of emancipatory transformation. In practice, however, pain and frustration may be eased in other ways – for example, through immersion in work (workaholism or the pursuit of career) or through escapist involvement in forms of distancing and entertainment, which effectively reduce the individual to an object of passified 'ego administration'. As Fay has observed, stressing the suffering aspect:

> Critical social science arises out of, and speaks to, situations of social unhappiness, a situation which it interprets as the result both of the ignorance of those experiencing these feelings and of their domination by others. It is this experience of unhappiness which is the wedge a critical theory uses to justify its entrance into the lives of those it seeks to enlighten and emancipate. (1987: 83)

Reflecting further upon the claims of CT, Fay (1987) questions whether the sequence of *problematical conditions* → *suffering* → *critical reflection* → *emancipation* is as unproblematical as Habermas, for example, seems to suggest. Without denying that critical reason is a potent source of emancipatory force, Fay argues that its powers are 'inherently limited' by somatic – embodied – learning in which the sense and (socio) logic of the contemporary social order becomes deeply embedded in the body. In other words, Fay contends that we become physically habituated to, and highly dependent upon, the-world-as-we-experience-it. The somatic impulse, unmediated by critical reason, is to cling to and defend this world-as-experienced – almost regardless of how unsatisfactory or futile such action may be. The 'devil we know' is preferred to engagement in a demanding, uncertain and threatening process of transformation.[3] The inability to break away from ingrained habits and repressive institutions can be very strong, as illustrated by the (over)consumption that characterizes most people in 'post-affluent society' and the difficulties experienced in changing quite superficial habits and routines.

If human beings are 'historical, embodied, traditional and embedded creatures' (Fay, 1987: 83), the capacity to respond to rational, critical arguments may be quite limited, at least in the absence of major disruption or dislocation. The target here is the cognitive emphasis in CT. Given the strength of physical habituation to established practices, CT may encounter unassailable resistance to its message, let alone its ambition of promoting critical self-reflection or fostering emancipatory practice. As its critics have put it, the cognitivism and rationalism of CT are evident in its neglect of the sentient and emotional aspects of human action. Attentiveness to these aspects is necessary if it is accepted that change is fuelled and sustained by a passionate commitment to a cause (see also McIntosh, 1994). In its absence, an emphasis upon reflection, evaluation and freedom in social life may, moreover, lead only to recurrent self-questioning and suspicion of all social arrangements. Recurrent doubts about what one is doing, and of the optimality of the social order, are perhaps as likely to induce despondency and paralysis as they are to inspire a process of personal and social reconstruction.

In response to such criticism, it is first worth noting that while the critique of Habermas' 'cognitivism' and rationalism is fair, other leading proponents of CT, such as Horkheimer and Adorno (1947b), were themselves well aware of the limitations of human reason – to the point of despair, since they saw no way of dealing with this problem. Not surprisingly, a number of proponents of CT, including Fromm, Marcuse and, to a more limited extent, Habermas, have developed a strong interest in psychoanalysis, the antidote to any belief that the intellect is the master of the human being. Marcuse's *One-Dimensional Man* (1964), in which the idea of the psychoanalytically inspired notion of 'repressive tolerance' (Marcuse, 1969) was introduced, had contributed significantly to a late-60s questioning of dominant values (e.g. materialism and consumerism) and social arrangements (e.g. hierarchy). This was somewhat ironic as Marcuse had previously considered such dissent to have been all but disabled by modern, technocratic consciousness and a widespread identification with consumption as the principal means of happiness (see Appendix). As mentioned in Chapter 2, some of the earlier proponents of CT (e.g. Marcuse, Fromm) wrote in a way that triggered strong emotional responses to their ideas. Their writings appealed to more than the intellect by aiming to challenge and shake their readers out of their ignorance and complacency.

Our response to doubts about the transformative contribution of CT is to retain and foster a belief in the *limited* power of reason to question conventional wisdom and current practice, while, at the same time, asserting its vital contribution to processes of emancipation. Instead of understanding the power of reason either as something universal *or* as something that is peculiarly dominant in modern society, we are inclined – in the after-shock of the Holocaust, McCarthyism, the Gulags, the fiasco of Iraq, Islamic and other religious fundamentalisms, and the financial meltdown of 2008 – to regard the critical deployment of reason as a historical phenomenon that is more or less salient during different eras and in particular contexts. In our view, the contemporary means of sustaining, and perhaps reviving, the limited and depleted potency of critical reason is to adopt and develop the insights of diverse critical theories. And, in doing so, we commend less preoccupation with Grand Theorizing and more determination to learn from, and contribute to, localized practical concerns. Here it is important to consider how emotion, fantasy, anxieties about changes, local ways of sense-making, habits that are hard to break away from, and so on, can exert a limiting but not necessarily negative effect upon the powers of reason.

It is also relevant to appreciate how 'cynical consciousness' (Fleming and Spicer, 2003; Sloterdijk, 1984) is a pervasive characteristic of our time. It is important to recognize a tendency for us to grasp intellectually that something – such as global warming – is problematic, but then to compartmentalize this understanding as we continue to act in ways that are inconsistent with doing something about it, perhaps because that is easiest or most instrumentally rewarding for us. Many of us know, or at least believe, that we are creating and are increasingly facing huge ecological problems, but this understanding may have little bearing on what we consume or upon our travelling behaviour, even though these are major determinants of the impending catastrophe. Or, to give another example, I may realize that acting out a gender role is restrictive, but this does not stop me doing it or indeed deriving some enjoyment from rationalizing the dissonance by celebrating my awareness of it. By reassuring myself that a sophisticated understanding has been developed, the problematic behaviour is then not really a problem, as I know what I am doing although I act as if I do not (see Zizek, 1989). In this way, self-esteem is preserved through feeling smart and appearing well informed. Actions that deviate from espoused social and ecological ideals are rationalized by such formulae as 'this calls for political reforms, not private or business solutions' – which may be a credible assessment but it does not absolve us of responsibility for changing ourselves and trying to reform our organizations. Such criticism is paralleled in poststructuralist arguments against meta-narratives and totalizing critiques, to which we now turn.

Essentialism

The criticism of CT for being essentialist is directed at its inclination to advance all-embracing frameworks that necessarily reduce or 'totalize' the complexity and heterogeneity of phenomena so that they then 'fit' within a single, integrated vision. Capitalism, male domination, managerialism and bureaucracy are examples of phenomena that have received a totalizing and essentializing treatment by their critics. Poststructuralists, in particular, have complained about this tendency (Cooper and Burrell, 1988; Lyotard, 1984). A second issue, which is also central to the challenge of poststructuralism (PS), has been the assault on the idea of an autonomous subject. Against the 'essentialist' idea of an integrated, coherent, unified individual, PS echoes psychoanalytic insights into the precarious, mythical status of the unified individual – such as 'the worker' or 'the manager'. This critique assumes fragmentation, inconsistency, undecidability, variation and heterogeneity, and attends to the critical significance of this understanding. As Alvesson and Deetz (1996) observe of 'the worker':

> The 'essence' of the worker is not the properties the 'object' contains but sets of relational systems including the division of labour. The focus on the subject and object properties is the mistake: the attention should be to the relational systems which are not simply in the world but are a human understanding of the world, and discursive or textual. The meaning of 'worker' is not evident or present (contained there) but deferred by the sets of oppositions and junctions, the relations that make it like and unlike other things. (ibid.: 208)

A basic assumption of humanist thinking, whether in management theory or social philosophy, is that beneath the alienated, fragmented surface of human consciousness there is an autonomous individual striving to get out.[4] Or as Weedon (1988: 21) puts it, humanism 'presupposes an essence at the heart of the individual which is unique, fixed and coherent'. As we noted earlier, in humanistic management theory, there is a widespread assumption of a fixed set of needs which are satisfied when presented with opportunities for their fulfilment by management. As we also noted earlier, CT rejects the (bourgeois humanist) idea that human autonomy can be bestowed by management. Although modern individuals have been freed from earlier illusions (e.g. the divine right of kings), CT attends to how we remain ensnared by equivalent contemporary illusions. Amongst these are the idea that 'freedom' is fully realized by the opportunity to buy and sell commodities and that labour that can be emancipated by applying behavioural science to rationalize existing means of organization.

In order to justify its critiques of contemporary illusions and 'social unhappiness', CT draws upon a premise shared by *radical* humanist forms of analysis (see Chapter 2) that, at the core of individuals, is a (potentially) unified, autonomous subject (Knights and Willmott, 2002). This subject is understood to be currently bewildered by contemporary illusions and degraded by established routines. Amongst these are the managerialist programmes of 'empowerment' that are seen to impede, rather than facilitate, the full flowering of a value-rational society (see Chapter 2).[5] It is the assumption of an essential, currently alienated autonomy that is challenged by PS. Subjectivity, advocates of PS argue, is the product of diverse and contradictory discourses and practices through which individuals come to be (misleadingly) identified, and to (mis) identify themselves, as actually or prospectively autonomous subjects. More bitingly put, the assumption of autonomy is regarded as a residue of bourgeois humanism (Knights and Willmott, 2002). For PS, 'The individual is both the site for a possible range of subjectivity and, at any particular moment of thought and speech, a subject, subjected to the regime of meaning of a particular discourse and enabled to act accordingly' (Weedon, 1988: 34). In other words, the humanist idea that human beings possess an (alienated) essence or unity that is struggling to 'get out' is challenged by recalling how the subjectivity of individuals is multilayered, internally inconsistent and infused by diverse, competing discourses, including humanism, which lend to human beings a sense of identity. From this perspective, conceiving of subjects as essentially autonomous is an expression of a *particular* (humanistic) discourse and should not be attributed to some *universal* authority. Indeed, to do so is seen to risk becoming a prisoner of this discourse.

The criticism of essentialism extends to CT's, and especially Habermas', contention that, in principle, distortions can be removed from communication to differentiate fact from fiction or ideology. In contrast, PS contends that the true/false and alienation/emancipation dichotomies are rhetorical and, ultimately, are unsupportable. Foucault (1980) in particular has challenged the idea which is, perhaps misleadingly, claimed to be central to CT: that the relationship between 'knowledge' and 'power' is wholly negative; and, relatedly, that the ideological aspects of the former can be eliminated by removing the latter. Most if not all power relations, Foucault contends, incorporate elements that are 'positive' for, and valued by, those populations whose subjectivity they constitute (e.g. career ladders that serve to shape and reproduce many employees' sense of identity). The broader Foucauldian, poststructuralist point is that power is not just exercised by a powerful elite of, say, marketing executives, advertising specialists and media moguls who skilfully manipulate and control the baser needs or instincts of seemingly mindless automatons. People are not simply 'turned' into consumers or wage slaves but are active participants in capillary relations and processes of power that are irreducible to the power exercised by elites. Elements of this thinking are hardly in opposition to CT, but there is a stronger emphasis upon the contingencies of the 'intra-subjective' on discourses and (other) power mechanisms than in Habermas' work, and to some extent that of other CT thinkers. What is distinctive is the insistence by PS that there is no foundation for warranting claims that knowledge can be cleansed of power.

Foucault draws attention to how forms of knowledge, however enlightened, exert truth effects that are ambivalent if not contradictory in their consequences. For example, the idea that human reason has emancipatory potential can produce a form of social theory – namely, Critical Theory – that privileges abstract theorizing and critiques over fostering critical insights into mundane philosophies and practices. The Great Critical Intellectual can become a Father (cf. Lacan) that people unthinkingly subordinate themselves to, or seek to emulate. There is the risk that Critical Theorists believe that they 'know best' and so contrive to establish themselves as Authorities, and thereby impede the dialogue that they profess to promote. These risks should not be exaggerated (Habermas cannot easily be faulted here) but neither should they be neglected. The ideal for CT is to offer counter-pictures, stimulating critical reflection on frozen truths and social arrangements, opening these up for the possible develop-ment of more compelling interpretations.

Turning away from grand critiques of exploitation and domination, in which society or organizations are treated as a totality, PS has favoured a focus upon what Foucault terms the microphysics of power. By this is meant the diverse and intersect-ing ways in which power is exercised through shifting networks, relations and struggles where everyday norms (e.g. about what it is to be a 'subject' or to engage in ethical conduct) are acquired and played out. This approach appreciates the com-plex and precarious dynamics of social organization which, for example, encourage individuals to become 'normalized' – with regard to acquiring and exhibiting the desired traits of a leader, having the right motivation, being eager to acquire forms of 'personal development', etc. This approach avoids reducing the messy and often paradoxical qualities of management and organization to a product or expression of some single, unified power (such as capitalism, technocracy, top management, the State, unions – or even mass culture and consumptionist ideology). In turn, it opens up the possibility of appreciating the frailty and vulnerability of processes which, from a more essentialist and totalizing perspective, appear uniform, inevitable and/or unshakeable. What, from a more distant or abstracted position, may be categorized and dismissed as expressions of 'bourgeois ideology' or as a generator of 'false-consciousness' are appreciated as ambiguous phenomena that, upon closer examination, are more ambivalent in their formation and effects.

Negativism

A third, related complaint against CT concerns its 'negativism'. The point is much less of relevance for Habermas than for other key writers in the CT tradition. It is perhaps more relevant for the work of Foucault whose work on 'discipline and punish' and the Panopticon is selectively but widely cited in management and orga-nization studies. Foucault argues that power/knowledge is 'productive' and not just restrictive, and so power is ambivalent, as in the case of processes of regulation. Foucault's position that 'everything is dangerous', not that everything is bad, and that, in his words, 'we always have something to do. So my position leads not to apathy but to a hyper- and pessimistic activism' (Foucault, 1984: 343) – a self-critical stance that is reasonant with the position we commend in this and the following chapter.

Critical scrutiny of conventional beliefs and assumptions is, or is supposed to be, a principal task of all academic research and scholarship. When criticism is not accompa-nied by more constructive suggestions, however, it becomes an easy target for the charge of 'negativism'. When totalizing, forms of negativism can present a mirror image of the hype and one-dimensional technicism of much management theory. It is perhaps not entirely unfair to say that 'for CMS, the world of management is a violent and unending catastrophe of repression, dependence, humiliation and pain' (Spicer et al., 2009: 551). Milder versions of such a worldview, which are more common, can also be unhelpful and unnecessarily alienating, in terms of how the objects of the critique are represented, and also in terms of demonstrating the practical relevance of its concerns.

It is not unusual for far-reaching critiques to result in marginalization, if not ostra-cism or excommunication. The credibility of CT is especially stretched in the field of management studies, which is saturated with all forms of positivity, glossing, kow-towing and devotion to (the engineering rhetoric of) instrumental action and problem-solving (see Fineman, 2006). This limits the appeal and reception of all forms of scepticism – as contrasted with forms of cynicism that are more readily digested as they are comparatively unchallenging.

The case for CT is weakened when it is sensed to adopt a superior, 'holier than thou' attitude. It then becomes uncompassionate and, in effect, uncommunicative. CT becomes (unintentionally) monological when it is perceived to be engaged *exclusively* in 'knocking' and 'putting down' conventional wisdom rather than appreciating how *some* forms of management knowledge *may* have a potential role to play in the devel-opment of a more (value-)rational society. We are, of course, not saying that conven-tional managerial wisdom should be spared critical examination. But if any form of critical analysis is to reach a wider audience, there must be some preparedness to engage with mainstream ideas and practitioners in ways that are accessible if also unset-tling (see Chapter 8). Hardly any job or organizational activity, not even the one of the critical academic or writer, can be carried out solely through critical knowledge.

Outright dismissals of 'managerial ideology' may miss positive aspects of the con-tradictions and counter-tendencies within ideology (see Chapter 1). For example, in emphasizing the difference between the oppressive logic of management practices and the emancipatory ideals of CT, one may overlook or underestimate *partially* progressive potentials in certain theories. Here we have in mind the contribution of some neo-human relations, corporate culture and leadership philosophies in ques-tioning, but not really problematizing, the assumptions and prescriptions of more tra-ditional, rationalist theories of management and organization. Corporate culture and organizational identity management may have some potential to create community feelings within organizations which, in addition to increasing work satisfaction, may also lead to a degree of solidarity across hierarchical levels and facilitate internal dis-cussions about social arrangements and practices. Despite its weaknesses, practically as well as ethically (Willmott, 1993a), such thinking invites consideration of alterna-tives to excessively narrow conceptions of 'rationality' that govern more classical formulations of management theory. People issues are brought forward and a sensi-tivity to human feelings and wants, albeit superficial and instrumentally motivated, is encouraged. Saying this, we are under no illusions about how this sensitivity can be abused and colonized – for example, by strategies of human resource management that urge employees to 'be themselves' while at work (Fleming and Sturdy, 2009). But, equally, a reluctance to engage dialogically with mainstream, pro-managerial approaches contributes to the marginalization[6] of critical analysis whenever its pro-ponents, ourselves included, aggressively advance arguments that are excessively one-sided, negative and unconstructive.

Contemporary developments in management theory share with critical thinking a recognition of how a narrowly technical conception of rationality, exemplified by Taylorism and Fordism, inhibits creativity and innovation as it exerts a divisive and deadening effect upon human organization. Shared, too, is a belief that people will often respond to opportunities which expand their discretion or extend their capabilities. Instead of acknowledging and exploring these areas of overlapping understanding, there is a tendency for critical analysis to attend *exclusively* to the negative aspects and impacts of modern management theory – such as its mystification of autonomy and the domination of employees' hearts and minds, in addition to their bodies.

A Rejoinder to the Critiques of CT

We have noted how, wishing to avoid the shortcomings attributed to CT, a number of critical students of management have turned to PS, and especially to the writings of Foucault (e.g. Knights, 2009; Townley, 1993). Some of Foucault's denser writings can compete with the most abstract offerings of CT, but much of his work (e.g. Foucault, 1977, 1980), especially his numerous interviews, cannot be accused of excessive esotericism or intellectualism. But neither does Foucault leave his readers in a wildly optimistic state concerning the chances for liberation. Geertz (quoted in Hoy, 1986), for example, characterizes Foucault's exploration of discipline and governmentality as a story of 'the Rise of Unfreedom'. Despite an emphasis upon the 'positive' (i.e. productive, effect-shaping) quality of power, its disciplinary effects are seen, mistakenly by many commentators, to be all-pervasive. Reflecting upon the political thrust of Foucault's work, Rorty (1985: 172) remarks that Foucault 'forbids himself the tone of the liberal sort of thinker who says to his fellow-citizens: "We know that there must be a better way to do things than this; let us look for it together"'. Such criticism can be challenged for assuming that a consensus can be readily established, and also for seeming to subscribe to the elitist view that writers of Foucault's stature should produce a 'blueprint' of a better society for others to follow. Foucault, it is worth noting, was highly sceptical about such missions, as they tend to marginalize or suppress dissent which, arguably, is a distinguishing feature of a 'good society' and a 'better way' to be. He believed that the role of the intellectual is not to legislate but, rather, to explicate. However, many readers of Foucault, especially his more influential writings such as *Discipline and Punish* (1977), are left with the feeling that there is no direction that appears positive, no knowledge claim that does not include a constraining (disciplining, normalizing) power effect. The idea is to encourage resistance, but it is not so easy to identify any *particular* institutions or power that are especially worthy of critique or challenge, as the suggestion is that everything is, potentially, dangerous. That, it seems, is the price to pay for avoiding (ontological) certainty and an associated (epistemological) authoritarianism based upon the appeal to some ostensibly given and indisputable foundations (see Heath, 1995). *If* it avoids premature closure and totalizing analysis, then it may be a price worth paying so long as release from lingering, modernist desire for certainty does not foster cynicism and nihilism.

Readings of Foucault that emphasize the seemingly totalizing effects of 'disciplinary power', for example, are dismissive of elements of Foucault's writings that directly discredit such readings and, indeed, pay no attention to his own involvement in various struggles and campaigns to challenge forms of 'disciplinary power', such as his work with prisoners. Such actions would be futile if disciplinary power is totalizing. When commenting critically upon the value of critiques that rely upon the essentialist assumptions of 'Utopian schemes', of which Habermas' ideal speech situation is a possible example, rather than engaging more directly in analysis of the microphysics of modern institutions, Foucault observes that:

> It seems to me that the real political task in a society such as ours is to critique the working of institutions which appear to be both neutral and independent, to criticise them in such a manner that the political violence which has always exercised itself obscurely through them will be unmasked, so that one can fight them. (Foucault in Elders, *1974: 171*, cited in Rabinow, *1986: 6*)

The differences between CT and Foucault should not be exaggerated. As Foucault (1991) himself acknowledged when reflecting upon his intellectual development, in which he, quite late, became familiar with the Frankfurt School:

> At that point, I realized how the Frankfurt School people had tried ahead of time to assert things that I too had been working for years to sustain. ... When I recognise all these merits of the Frankfurt School, I do so with the bad conscience of one who should have known and studied them much earlier ... if I had read those works earlier on, I would have saved useful time, surely: I wouldn't have needed to write some things and I would have avoided certain errors. (ibid.: *117, 119*)

Equally, despite what are arguably misguided criticisms of Foucault's subjectivism and conservatism, Habermas (1989a: 294) is by no means dismissive of Foucault's analysis of power/knowledge relations, arguing that 'he did indeed provide an illuminating critique of the entanglement of the human sciences in the philosophy of the subject'. Our own inclination is to interrogate and mobilize Foucault's writing in a project that is proto-emancipatory in intent (see White, 1986), even though his ideas are not without ambiguity in this enterprise.

PS ideas inject a healthy dose of scepticism into the heady, intellectualistic realms of CT (as well as into the naïve optimism of MOS). Foucault shows us the value of undertaking genealogical analyses of mundane processes and institutions (e.g. prisons and prison-like organizations) in a way that sheds new light upon their widespread oppressive effects, and thereby contributes to the enrichment of critique. In his later writings, Foucault's focus shifts to the question of how to take 'care of the self' in conditions that are often hostile, if not oblivious, to such concerns. Yet, with the possible exception of an ethical stance, and in particular his discussion of *parrhesia*, which was emergent in his final work (*History of Sexuality*, vols 2 and 3 – see Foucault, 1985, 1986), the positive features of Foucault's writings should not distract us from the fundamental difficulty in Foucault's early and most influential writings: the absence of any *consistent* normative bearings (Willmott, 1994a) and how to grapple with this deficit. Associated with this aporia, perhaps, is Foucault's reluctance to relate his penetrating discussion of power/knowledge relations and the constitution of

subjects to political economy, the functions of the capitalist system and its consequences for ecology as well as for the distribution of wealth and opportunity. As
Dews (1986: 33) has argued, in defence of Critical Theory and of Habermas in particular, against PS critique:

> It is true that Habermas' work does not hold up a mirror to contemporary experiences
> of fragmentation, loss of identity, and libidinal release, in the manner which has
> enabled post-structuralist writing to provide the 'natural' descriptive vocabulary. ...
> But neither does it pay for its expressive adequacy and immediacy with a lack of
> theoretical and historical perspective.

This critical assessment, which is itself over-zealous in its complaint about the lack
of historical perspective, especially in relation to Foucault's historically informed
writings, is more directly relevant for the arguments of Lyotard (1984) and other
authors interested in 'deconstruction' and 'the postmodern condition'. Despite the
best of intentions, an emphasis upon the open, ambiguous character of language and
a preoccupation with texts can degenerate into an exclusive intra-academic enterprise that speaks of the postmodern but loses any firm moorings to contemporary
political economy. A tendency towards the unqualified dismissal of contemporary
society and its institutions in CT is paralleled in a rejection of what it terms 'grand
narratives', i.e. all forms of large-scale frameworks and projects which are said to be
'totalitarian' (Lyotard, 1984). On this particular point, some versions of PS are cul-
pable of harbouring their own 'essentialism', in which all sorts of 'grand narratives',
excluding PS of course, are viewed as essentially the same in an undiscriminating way
(see Kellner, 1988, and Alvesson and Sköldberg, 2009).

On balance, it may be concluded that, for all its problems, the progressive ideals
associated with the emancipatory project of CT makes its blend of positive/con-
structive and negative/critical elements somewhat less alien (e.g. to practitioners and
MOS, at least) than the more consistently 'uncommitted' and recurrently deconstructive inclinations of PS (Willmott, 1996c). However, if CT is to have greater
relevance for actors in 'ordinary' organizational settings, its tendencies towards intellectualism, essentialism and negativism outlined above must be addressed (Spicer
et al., 2009). After all, if a basic purpose of organizations (at least those considered in
this book) is work and production – and not primarily reflecting critically on, debating
and combating diverse forms of constraint and oppression – then critical studies of
management and organization need be sensitive to this. This, in our opinion, does
not necessitate the jettisoning of the idea of emancipation as a guiding value. Instead,
it reinvigorates debate by recalling how theory is embedded in practices, and so is
recurrently subject to change and contestation. As Parker (1995: 561) contends, 'If
truth is seen as temporary consensus then debate about values becomes central …
Where we go from there becomes a matter of moral and political choice.'

If social science is to avoid becoming a nihilistic enterprise in which the generation of knowledge is completely alienated or disassociated from the values which
inspire and guide its production, then a commitment to its emancipatory potential

must be retained and reconstructed. CT and PS both provide instructive counter-points to bourgeois ideas (e.g. about taking the dominant order and the human being it produces as unproblematic – Firat and Venkatesh, 1992; Sampson, 1989). We have suggested that differences between CT and PS provide relevant inspiration and fruitful points of tension when addressing possibilities of emancipation (Alvesson, 1996; Alvesson and Deetz, 2000; Deetz, 1992b; Willmott, 1994a).

 ## Reconceptualizing Emancipation

Moving away from CT's rather one-sided focus on 'grand critiques' of one-dimensional society or system colonialization of lifeworlds can be helpful in assisting the expansion of critical analysis of ordinary, everyday power relations and struggles. In this respect, there is a parallel here with Geertz's (1973) argument that the (anthropological) concept of culture should be cut down in size so that it covers less and illuminates more. The concept of emancipation may be scaled down in a way that avoids making excessively, or exclusively, grandiose claims. The ambition is not to discourage broader critiques, but instead to accommodate forms of analysis and critique that are more sensitive to local conditions and small-step approaches to emancipatory transformation. In this section, we present a reconceptualization of emancipation in which the emphasis is on smaller-scale, open projects. In managerialist language, this stance welcomes the progressive contribution of incrementalism as an expedient and imperfect alternative to an indefinite wait for the arrival of radical emancipatory change.

Micro-emancipation

When focusing upon possibilities for 'micro-emancipation', the multifarious activities, recipes for action and techniques developed within organizations are addressed not only as means of control but also as objects and facilitators of resistance and, thus, as potential vehicles of emancipation. In this formulation, organizational processes are understood to be uncertain, contradictory, ambiguous and precarious. Within systems of power and control there are invariably interdependencies, contradictions and 'loopholes' that can be exposed and exploited for purposes of critical reflection and emancipatory transformation. As Deetz (1992a: 336) expresses it: 'with every "positive" move in disciplinary practices, there is an oppositional one'. Control is conceptualized not only as discipline and restriction of the space for action, but also as a potential stimulus for critical thought and emancipatory practice. When viewed in this way, all sorts of control stratagems are understood to be mediated by, or unintentionally productive of, 'signs' or 'messages' that can trigger suspicion, resistance and critical reflections – that is, impulses which can provide the basis for micro-emancipatory change.

The dialectic of control and resistance has been noted and more fully explored by authors working outside of the tradition of CT (e.g. Edwards, 1979; Giddens,

1979; Ezzamel et al., 2001). They have analysed this dialectic principally as a succession of conflicts between major, integrated managerial control strategies and large-scale resistance (or aggregates of similar small-scale reactions) to dominant control forms. What we seek to emphasize here is the relevance and significance of a *type* and *expression* of emancipatory action that is less extensive in conception and focus. This might, for example, be the redefinition of a verbal symbol launched by management for a particular purpose. Instead of being a vehicle for managerial control and integration, a symbol – e.g. a notion such as 'quality' – can become a manifestation of irony and distance. Other examples are the idea of 'empowering' employees or the 'mission statement' ascribed to an organization (see, for example, Smircich, 1983a). Similarly, status symbols such as office space, luxury equipment, controlled access to privileged areas, etc. often reinforce formal hierarchy and feelings of superiority/inferiority and support careerism. But they may simultaneously and inadvertently draw attention to the arbitrary and political nature of corporate arrangements, thus nurturing scepticism rather than tighter discipline. There is often a thin line between an arrangement, a slogan or an action that exerts a disciplinary effect and the triggering of awareness of control being at play, alerting people to the exercise of control and, possibly, stimulating critical reflection. Sometimes an ironic comment or the reframing of an incident can take the sting out of something that otherwise would lead to subordination (Ezzamel et al., 2001).

Inherent in the concept of micro-emancipation is an emphasis on partial, temporary movements that break away from diverse forms of mundane oppression, rather than successive moves towards a predetermined state of liberation. This 'micro' view of emancipation differs markedly from the traditional conception of a one-way transformation of consciousness from 'false' to 'true', or as the crucial element in the shift from an oppressive social order. The emancipatory project is instead formulated as a precarious, endless enterprise of continuous struggling to increase the space for forms of critical reflection and progressive change as it counteracts the diverse, oppressive effects of established traditions, ingrained prejudices, the ego administration of mass media, consumerist pressures, etc. that combine to place socially unnecessary but nonetheless imposing limits on how the social world is understood and enacted. This formulation of the emancipatory project portrays it not as one large, tightly integrated programme, but rather as a myriad of projects, each limited in terms of space and time (and of success). To be clear, this is not to deny or displace a more extensive conception of emancipation. Instead, it is to recognize and even celebrate its more everyday articulations which, despite their mundanity, may trigger, escalate or snowball into more significant emancipatory actions.

An illustration

We will illustrate the idea of micro-emancipation with one example drawn from an 'information meeting' about reorganization at a Swedish industrial company (Alvesson, 1996). Present during this two-hour-long meeting were about a hundred junior and middle-level managers. The top manager opened the meeting with a rhetorical question – 'Why are you here?' To which he immediately replied, 'It is because you are the managers in this company.' By examining this opening gambit, we will suggest that such an unremarkable way of addressing the audience is far from innocent and is a suitable theme of micro-emancipation (see also Knights and Willmott, 1987).

Let us first say that it is not self-evident that the people present are 'managers', even though they have this title. If it were self-evident, it is doubtful that the top manager would have begun by defining the reality of the situation in this way. To identify and constitute someone as a manager is not just a question of appointing the person to a particular formal position. The identity and the ideology which characterize the appointee are also crucial (cf. Deetz, 1992a; Sveningsson and Alvesson, 2003; Therborn, 1980). It cannot be taken for granted that people who are appointed to such positions regard themselves *primarily* as managers, or that they are regarded as managers by others. A given person who has the title of department manager may regard him- or herself primarily as a subordinate, a member of a unit or a professional (e.g. an engineer), or perhaps also and even primarily as a member of a family, as a female, as middle-aged, as 'green', as a union member, and so on. Allegiance to, or identification with, the corporation cannot be taken for granted simply because an employee has been given the title – or occupies the office – of 'manager'.

Corporate management competes with other groups, categories and identities for each person's time, self-perception, attention and loyalty. Doubtless, from top management's point of view, 'managers' *should* regard themselves primarily as company people who are 'married to the job'. It is therefore important to maintain and reinforce this managerial identity. Management is, to a considerable and increasing degree, a matter of regulating the identity of people (Alvesson and Willmott, 2002). Contemporary management places a strong emphasis upon issues of organizational identity, corporate culture, corporate branding, etc. (see Hatch and Schultz, 2002; Kärreman and Rylander, 2008).

By identifying employees as managers, certain ideas and values about the job are accentuated – such as responsibility, loyalty, work morale, results orientation, etc. In effect, members of this audience are being urged to disregard or subordinate other identities and associated identifications. As Galbraith (1983) has pointed out, managers are more strictly controlled in many respects than other employees; for instance, they have to be more careful about their appearance and what they say. To establish and reinforce this subservience, it is necessary for top management to continuously constitute the people who are expected to take their 'managership' very seriously. It is expected that they will give priority to values, ideas, feelings and actions – including self-discipline – that are closely associated with being a 'manager'. When understood in this way, the senior manager's opening gambit at the meeting serves to remind his audience that they should interpret the reorganization through a (pro-)managerial interpretive framework, and not as a family member who, for example, fears the loss of employment or even as an ambitious opportunist who is poised to make use of the company as a vehicle for self-advancement.

Micro-emancipation, in this example, would include resisting or subverting stratagems deployed in efforts to shape and fix the identities and self-understandings of
staff. Micro-emancipation is facilitated as critical reflection assists the retention or
formation of an open attitude to the ascription of identity. That is to say, it enables
an appreciation of the negative (e.g. subordination to certain norms and self-
constraints) as well as the positive (e.g. status confirmation) aspects of the use of the
term 'manager'. Relatedly, rather than pointing at false consciousness – it is not simply
false to see oneself as manager – the constraints associated with an uncritical, institutionalized acceptance of a particular prescribed identity are the target. This is then
about loosening up and un-fixing the position and identity of 'manager' (expected
to see everything from a manager's point of view, e.g. identify with and be loyal to
top management) and then, at times (such as in the meeting referred to above), trying
to think about what is happening here more openly and independently (see Parker,
2004). Being referred to as 'a manager' – and being identified as a particular kind of
manager, a subordinate one, who is expected to implement the strategies of top
management – could then not automatically and self-evidently be accepted, but be
treated as a stimulus or provocation for thinking through alternative self-positionings.
These would involve both 'non-managerial' identities and various forms of managerial ones. The former would include those that are most significant outside of
working hours and the latter could include being a 'professional' responsible for a
specialist function, being in charge of, and primarily loyal to, subordinates ('my
people'), and seeing oneself as a mediator between senior and junior levels or as a
hired hand, being paid only for the delivery of the results and as expendable as any
other employee. It could also mean the experience of a right to participate in dialogues with senior managers, rather than just being informed about executive elite
decisions.

At the core of micro-emancipation in this example is resistance to the senior
manager's power technique of defining his audience in a certain way, and in imagining alternatives before reaching a 'grounded' – reflectively arrived-at – position.[7]
Of course, meaningful resistance requires not only a 'rational reconstruction' of the
top manager's opening gambit in which its mundanity and naturalness is decon-
structed to disclose its political positioning and oppressive effects. In addition,
it requires 'critique' – that is, a move from *intellectual insight* into the (political)
significance of the communication to a *change of practice* – which might, for
example, take the form of a renewed determination to detect, resist and subvert
organizational efforts to deny or marginalize employees' (including managers')
wider affiliations and associated (e.g. domestic, ecological) responsibilities. A small-
scale liberation may then be accomplished – as a response to a specific move of
power (attempted privileging and fixation of identity) and not as a more ambitious
call for transformation of the situation (and the organizational context) into full-
scale democratization. The democratization of institutions is consistent with
micro-emancipation but is not equivalent to it. Micro-emancipation is arguably an
important condition of broader and deeper social transformations and reduces
the likelihood of their reversal but even this requires a leap, however small, from

private sceptical questioning of managerialism to a commitment to subvert its operation.

The Costs and Paradoxes of Emancipation

In this light, the potential for emancipation is seen to reside in everyday life including life at work, involving recurrent struggles between the exercise of power with oppressive effects and resistance to its exercise. This reconceptualization of emancipation also acknowledges that resistance to forms of domination, such as the Taylorization of craft production or the post-Fordist empowerment of employees, can provide a possible starting point for emancipation. Such resistance may bring about some reversal of the intensifying features of humanistic management techniques. But emancipatory change may also be accompanied by a fall in earnings associated with a loss of productive capacity. Employees seeking to expand their autonomy and control over productive forces may be less efficient, with consequences for their sense of self-identity as well as their employment security. Similarly, women emancipating themselves from dominant socialization patterns and gender roles may reduce their interest in, and capacity for, caring and thereby diminish their contribution to the unpaid economy. Employees who free themselves from a work ethic may become less committed to, and less capable of, acting as 'socially responsible' organizational citizens. Not only capitalists but also client groups (e.g. hospital patients) may suffer.

The critical questioning of beliefs and values, including over-rosy conceptions of struggles for emancipation, may facilitate more systematic reflection and assist recognition and clarification of neglected desires (e.g. for education or health), ideas about fairness, etc. But such thinking may also estrange the individual from whatever tradition has formed his or her sense of meaning and purpose. It is possible that anxiety, identity loss and other severe problems may accompany (or impede) participation in processes of emancipatory transformation (Fay, 1987). Freedom is not without its anxieties and pains; and we may fear it for 'justifiable' reasons. Emancipation as a project in contemporary organizations is hardly equivalent to escaping a concentration camp – there are invariably some defensible reasons for feelings of doubt and uncertainty about what is right and wrong as well as reservations about what an emancipatory project may involve in terms of possible advantages and disadvantages.

It is naïve and unrealistic to ignore or gloss over the 'demands' and 'costs' associated with processes of emancipation. It is far too simplistic to assume that only 'irrationality', aside from the repressive power of an egoistic economic and political elite, stands in the way of liberation. Emancipation involves a trade-off between gains and losses, albeit that the losses may, with the benefit of hindsight, be regarded as inconsequential or even beneficial.[8] It is also naïve and reckless to deny that discipline, social control and constraints are central pillars of any civilization. The issue is how such pillars are constructed and maintained in a manner that minimizes socially unnecessary suffering, both mental and physical. Encouragement for emancipation must be guided with this in mind – the challenge being to counteract and minimize what is assessed to be socially harmful and unnecessary oppression, not any form of constraint or discipline. As we have stressed, people may have compelling reasons for refusing emancipatory invitations, including both fear of failure and fear of the effects of 'successful' emancipation, such as material disadvantage or loss of status. It is often easier, at least in the short term, to comply with authorities, to follow fashion, to adapt to dominant norms or to embrace pre-structured lifestyles. Deviating from workplace and professional norms, business recipes, career ladders, cultural forms of doing gender, etc. involves risk and provokes anxieties – for those who deviate as well as for those who may feel threatened by the norm-breaking. These fears can only be addressed if they are acknowledged, and not dismissively swept away as 'irrationality' or 'conservativism'. Effective and sustained micro-emancipatory moves depend as much upon a capacity to anticipate and address reversals as they do upon the transformative possibilities afforded by dramatic moments of crisis.

Unless we are to assume that some people are already fully emancipated, it must be recognized that an anti-emancipatory tendency runs through all projects – even those with the best intentions and which are preceded by careful reflection. The dynamics and dialectics of emancipation mean that a promising idea, or an intended effect, can be subverted in its practical application. Even if an intervention begins by opening up understanding, or facilitating reflection, it can end up locking people into fixed, unreflective thinking (Willmott, 1993b). Critique and liberation from old dogma is then followed by new dogma, as many social movements inspired by Marxism, for example, have shown over history. Somewhere in the process, a theory guided by critical, emancipatory intent turns into a reactionary force (see Horkheimer and Adorno, 1947a). So, the dark side of emancipatory projects must be acknowledged, if the 'net effect' of progressive projects is to stand an improved chance of being positive (Akella, 2008).

A note on emancipation myopia

Having argued for the virtues of emancipatory micro-projects as well as the ambiguities of emancipation – irrespective of scope and intention – we now sound a cautionary note about an over-reliance upon local projects of micro-emancipation. An emphasis upon struggles around local practices may leave wider sources of irrationality and oppression unchallenged. Here we are thinking of, for example, historically and culturally anchored gender stereotypes, the hegemonic role of the mass media, the exploitation of the environment, the technocratic domination of professional and managerial ideologies, etc. Efforts to make space for increased discretion and autonomy on the local level may result only in a narrow kind of liberation in which local difficulties are (temporarily) ameliorated but deeper problems, often rooted in economic and material conditions, escape attention and correction. One can justly argue that there is often a narrow focus on subjects and subjectivities in CMS and a shortage of interest in much more profound concerns such as environmental problems (Newton, 2009) and financial issues (Hopwood, 2009).[9] Without denying that micro-emancipatory moves alone are sufficient, or that they may displace more extensive demands, we regard them as precursors of more joined-up, 'macro' forms of emancipatory action. We acknowledge that in many cases micro-emancipation means little more than holding back or weakening the grip exercised by a particular practice, ideology or identity template so that change does not reach much beyond resistance. Yet, in other cases it may strengthen the capacity for direct action, for engaging in communicative action or for strengthening an oppositional stance on oppressive management processes.

With these important considerations firmly in mind, we believe that it is desirable to move away from a conceptualization of organizations either as a tightly integrated chain of practices exerting the logic of an iron cage, as cruder variants of CMS tend to do; or as settings in which fragmentary, uncoupled forms of micro-power and local struggles are at play, as ostensibly exemplified by critical studies with a 'weaker' critical edge. Instead, organizations can be viewed as loosely coupled orders harbouring elements of oppression and related opportunities for emancipation which are, to varying degrees, connected to, and are products of, the cultural and politico-economic contexts of their formation and reproduction. We are not prepared to trade off 'totalizing' thinking for myopia. Many of the most significant sources of oppression associated with environmental pollution, domination of multinational corporations, commercialization of all areas of life, and poverty are of a global nature. We do not welcome a dilution of critical analysis in studies – of discourse, identity, leadership, etc. – that offer illuminating interpretations of aspects of the world of work but lack even minimal concern to address their embeddedness in wider forms of oppression or to change them. Despite its insights, the PS turn in critical management theory risks marginalizing consideration of the bigger picture. That said, global problems are manifest in local mundane practices of production and consumption. Worldwide pollution and depletion of natural resources, for example, are contingent upon how people think about and relate to everyday decisions, such as the organizational consumption of non-renewable sources of energy. Close critical analysis of decision making in organizations, including that informed by PS, is to be encouraged when it provides insights into what impedes more enlightened practice and thereby provides a sounder basis for critique and transformation. For example, mundane decision making in organizations can have more or less ecologically damaging consequences. Here we have in mind decisions about transport, especially flights and car usage, the consumption of meat, procurement of non-green goods and machinery, etc. All these decisions are not only a matter of managerial responsibility as well as collective political will, nationally and internationally, but also a matter of individual actions. By focusing upon micro-power and micro-emancipation, analysis has more direct relevance to the *lived experience* of people who are continuously engaged in local decision making and associated struggles to improve working conditions, to become ecologically responsible, to counteract inequalities, to overcome divisiveness, etc. At the same time, and as we have repeatedly stressed, for such connections to be made these struggles must be appreciated as a medium and outcome of broader processes of transformation.

Emancipation: Types and Foci

To elaborate our reconceptualization of emancipation, we outline a more nuanced understanding of the nature and direction of emancipatory moves. To this end, a distinction is drawn between the type of emancipatory project and the focus of its interest. As with many such distinctions, its value is heuristic: in practice the different types and foci of emancipation merge into one another. Nonetheless, this framework provides a point of departure, and offers a stimulus for developing a more adequate conceptualization of some key dimensions of emancipatory projects. Our discussion of the framework is illustrated by reference to CT but a similar analysis could be applied to other traditions of critical analysis. The matrix in Figure 7.1 summarizes the types and foci of emancipation.

On the *horizontal axis* we distinguish everyday questioning of ideas and practices from a more extensive form of emancipatory project. *Questioning* is principally directed at challenging and critiquing dominant thinking. Dominant ideas and current social arrangements are met with suspicion and are scrutinized. The aim is to combat the self-evident and the taken for granted. This type of emancipatory project is primarily concerned with investigating and problematizing. Its intent is to doubt and resist authority (and its disciplining effects) without necessarily proposing an alternative agenda or set of prescriptions. At the other end of the continuum of emancipatory projects, a *Utopian* approach develops an overall 'vision' that frequently ignores or marginalizes the relevance of immediate, 'micro' problems. It should perhaps be stressed that the Utopian project does not necessarily present a recipe for 'the good life' or for programming behaviour in a narrowly specified direction: insofar as CT has a Utopian element, it is also overtly anti-authoritarian. CT aims only to counteract ideologies and social arrangements that obstruct human freedom, not to fill the latter with particular contents. In CT, the Utopian element takes the form of a counterfactual proposition (e.g. the unalienated individual or the ideal speech situation) that aims at opening up consciousness for

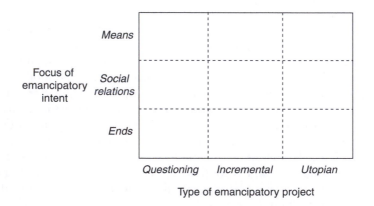

Figure 7.1   *Model summarizing types and foci of emancipation*

engagement with a broader repertoire of alternatives. Utopianism represents alternative thinking rather than the suggestion of a ready-made, 'better' alternative or the provision of recipes for action.

Between the questioning and Utopian types of emancipatory project, we identify *incremental undertakings* that favour and articulate a gradualist or reformist approach to emancipatory transformation. These often concentrate on participatory processes. Of course, questioning and incremental approaches may also involve a Utopian element. As we stressed earlier, the distinction between these approaches is heuristic; and it may be more helpful to think of them as dimensions of emancipation upon which more or less emphasis is placed in different emancipatory projects. Clearly, many forms of critique implicitly assume or anticipate an improved outcome, or an emancipatory change of direction. Even ideas about 'deconstruction' are, arguably, informed and influenced by an alternative set of ideas that claim to provide a more adequate account of how accepted understandings (e.g. about gender) are constructed (see, for example, Martin, 1990).

Turning now to consider the *vertical axis* of our matrix, by 'focus' we mean the primary object of emancipatory efforts. Here we make an analytical distinction between 'means', 'social relations' and 'ends'. Again, it is necessary to acknowledge the heuristic character of this distinction. *Means* is intended to refer to discourses and practices that are valued for their anticipated ability to make ends achievable. Emancipatory projects which address 'means' challenge the necessity and value of established methods of organization, including the hierarchical and fragmented division of labour, autocratic leadership styles, psychological testing, etc. – which, of course, have also been challenged, albeit in less penetrating ways, by humanistic management theory. The difference between them is that CT highlights the limits and complicity of humanism insofar as its neo-managerialism operates to reinforce practices that impede radical emancipatory transformations.

At the other end of the vertical axis, *ends* refer to the purpose of organizational or managerial activity. The emancipation of ends is concerned with unfreezing institutionalized priorities, thereby opening up debate about issues such as the practical value of economic growth, consumption, the quality of life and so on. The horizontal axis indicates the range of orientations, or emphases, that may inform such a focus. For example, a questioning approach might ask why it is that certain values and objectives are given priority over others. Alternatively, a Utopian conception of communication may be deployed to challenge the way in which particular ends have been selected and are defended by suggesting radically different values. An incremental orientation points towards ways in which (limited) opportunities for emancipatory change may be identified and pursued.

Finally, the inclusion of *social relations* as a focus of emancipatory intent draws attention to the social organization of privileges and power. Of course, social relations cannot be divorced from means or ends. Nonetheless, there is heuristic value in highlighting their significance. The focus on social relations is particularly attentive to how means and ends are embedded in structures of social relations. For example, an exclusive focus upon means, such as participatory styles of coordinating work for the attainment of ecologically sound production, does not necessarily touch upon issues like segmented labour markets, pay differences or other forms of class, gender or ethnic inequality. Actions directed against oppressive means and taken-for-granted ends do not exhaust the prospects for emancipation. It is possible to contemplate efforts directed at the emancipation of social relations from power asymmetries that would not significantly change ends and/or means. Workplace democracy or gender equality, for example, do not necessarily exclude high productivity as a taken-for-granted goal. Nor do they necessarily challenge an extensive division of labour (as long it is not gendered or otherwise socially divided) as the appropriate means.

Illustrating the Framework

Having discussed the elements of our heuristic framework, we now indicate how it may be used by comparing and contrasting approaches within management and organization studies (MOS) and CT. We start from the three foci and briefly explore types of emancipatory projects in relationship to each of these.

The primary focus of study in MOS is 'means'. Mainstream MOS is preoccupied with the refinement of means in a purely technical, non-emancipatory fashion (see Chapter 1). Sociotechnical and QWL movements, Corporate Culture, Performance Management, Value Management and so on may express aspirations to be emancipatory, at least in the sense of removing certain oppressive (e.g. close supervision) and wasteful (e.g. duplicating) practices. However, since an instrumental rationality pervades their recipes for change, such approaches are problematic in relationship to less compromised ideas about emancipation (Alvesson, 1987). Some weak emancipatory potential may be present, nonetheless, in the concern to remove overtly degrading and fragmenting forms of work. Since the questioning and Utopian elements of these approaches are largely absent, their emancipatory elements are viewed as, at best, incremental.

When it comes to emancipatory projects directed at changing social relations, there is greater variety in terms of the type emphasized. Some contributions to participation are, like most means-focused research, incrementally oriented, but they may also incorporate a more ambitious interest in modifying social relations (e.g. Gustavsen, 1985). Typically, the interest lies in facilitating wider workplace participation or even democracy, often through action research and sometimes in collaboration with unions (Sandberg, 1981). Such developments are generally intended to incorporate employees into organizations by enlisting their (increased) commitment to corporate objectives. Nonetheless, if approaches adopt a questioning, sceptical manner, they may present opportunities for pursuing demands for 'real' participation in decision making that extends to corporate responsibility (Scherer and Palazzo, 2007; Scherer et al., 2005). Most Marxist-inspired approaches (such as Braverman, 1974; Clegg and Dunkerley, 1980), in contrast, conceptualize emancipation as a matter of radically changing social relations. Their emphasis is typically Utopian (and often questioning). They push for a classless society in which the coordination of productive activity is based on consensual social relations but they tend to overlook or marginalize other sources of oppression and associated struggles. A promising alternative to these is a post-Marxist approach, which also takes issue with the soft-edged consensualism of Habermasian CT; assumes an 'agonistic pluralism' (Mouffe, 1999a; 1999b) in which democracy is understood to require and preserve ongoing conflicts between opposing views that fully acknowledge differences; and is suspicious of any consensus reached through a deliberative process – which it suspects of being the product of unacknowledged power politics rather than any unforced agreement (Kapoor, 2002; Edward and Willmott, 2008; in press).

Returning to CT-inspired authors and other radical humanists, they challenge the rationality of existing ends but are interested in the realization of the somewhat abstract goals of human freedom, creativity, rational dialogue, etc. They are generally concerned with ideology critique (e.g. the critique of scientism) that has a strongly questioning orientation (Alvesson, 1987; Mumby, 1988). Sometimes there is also an interest in more incremental projects, such as Forester's (1989) suggestions for the emancipation of planning practices from institutionalized forms of domination; or Spicer et al.'s (2009) proposal of a 'critical performativity', combining CT ideas with an appreciation of the constraints of the corporate world and more empathetic understanding of the situation, concerns and action possibilities of managers and others in organizations.

There are also more Utopian approaches, like Schumacher's (1974) ideas on small-scale, ethical production; Shrivastava's (1993, 1994a, 1994b) ideas on ecologically oriented ('ecocentric') management; or Burrell's (1992) ideas on pleasure as a driving force and end that can subvert its contemporary use as a source of profits (e.g. the leisure industry). In general, however, there has been some decline in the popularity of Utopian projects (see Parker, 2002).

As we argued earlier, it is extremely difficult, if not impossible and inadvisable, to maintain a hard and fast distinction between 'true' and 'false' emancipatory discourse and practice. We have stressed our scepticism about the possibility and value of 'purist' formulations of CT. We believe instead in fostering approaches that open up and explore – theoretically and practically – a space for emancipatory critique between the heady abstractions of CT and the glitzy hype of humanistic MOS. Our concern is to dispel the idealist fantasies, and associated disappointments, of the more fanciful claims of CT and MOS. In doing so, we think it is important to avoid conflating micro-emancipation with (pseudo-)humanistic versions of MOS in which conflicts between the material requirements and/or ethical sensibilities of human populations, on the one hand, and the priorities of capitalist corporations, on the other, are obscured through the presentation of a seductive package of humanistic management techniques (Potterfield, 1999). For other authors within humanistic MOS, all good things tend to go hand in hand – profitable firms invest heavily in people and create 'high-commitment organizations' (Huselid, 1995), transformational leadership results in a happy union between the individuals and organizations accomplished by the leader adopting the right style (Sashkin, 2004) and so on. It is 'just' a matter of adopting the right techniques and style.

We have suggested that the emancipatory contribution of both CT, PS and progressive elements of MOS can be enhanced if reflection upon the potential of its discourses and practices is not restricted to the narrow space of only one of the squares in Figure 7.1 above.[10] We have argued that emancipation, even in a micro-version, can and should encourage thinking and acting that transcend a singular type or focus, whether it is 'means', 'social relations' or 'ends'; 'questioning', 'incrementalism' or 'Utopianism'. The narrow targeting of a specific space within our matrix is to be avoided because it fragments and limits emancipatory practice. Here we might be misread as advocating a 'grand' approach to emancipation but, in our view, combating a narrow targeting of emancipation does not necessarily lead to 'grand critique' (of mega-phenomena like the market economy or even general critiques of HRM, organizational identity or corporate branding). Instead, it can become the connective space between a narrow, yet concrete, consideration of the micro-politics of emancipation and a broad, yet abstract, formulation of the historical and politico-economic conditions of change that we are seeking to disclose and occupy (Willmott, 2010).

Reorienting Emancipatory Studies

We have argued that the problems exposed by critiques of CT invite a reformulation of the idea of emancipation in social science in general, and in MOS in particular. An important element in such a project is the development of a new research strategy in which an overtly negative (hyper-critical) and Utopian version of Critical Theory – including its promise of fulfilling an emancipatory project of freeing people from 'ideologically frozen social relations' – is de-emphasized in favour of a more eclectic framework, which includes and is reconstructed by perspectives and voices other than those most closely allied to CT. Abstract, totalizing attacks on the prevalent social order (late capitalism, class society, managerialism, etc.) are then complemented by studies that explore and critique particular, local practices without losing sight of the relevance and potency of more 'global' issues and insights.

In the remaining pages of this chapter, we sketch a number of possible lines of development. Specifically, we consider: (a) the value of ethnography for emancipatory studies; (b) a new approach to writing and the transmission of ideas; and (c) new modes of reading in the interpretation of ideas. Our purpose here is not to propose an exhaustive list of possibilities or to claim their novelty. Instead, our more modest intention is to indicate and illustrate possibilities for micro-emancipation in the sphere of management and organization.

Listening

The conduct of ethnographic studies of organization presents an opportunity for employees to speak out in a way that can moderate and challenge the adequacy of more 'totalizing' and seemingly authoritative accounts of management and organization. Ethnography is a research process in which the researcher 'closely observes, records, and engages in the daily life of another culture ... and then writes accounts of this culture, emphasizing descriptive detail' (Marcus and Fischer, 1986: 18). In ethnography, the researcher is not just interested in behaviour and structures, but also, and quite often more so, in symbols and meanings (Rosen, 1991). *Critical* ethnography takes seriously the complexity, ambiguity and inconsistency of practice without falling into the empiricist trap of naturalizing the ideology, power and communications (including the ambiguity of language) that are central to the reproduction of management and organization.

Listening can be combined with an ethic of care (Jacques, 1992; Spicer et al., 2009). This involves attempting to provide space for respondents' views and feelings to be aired, but not naïvely accepted. It requires that researchers are able to subtly challenge and question these views. For CMS, this involves taking the voice of managers (leaders) and their subordinates (co-workers, followers) seriously. Before quickly jumping to a brutal dismantling or trashing of a manager's understandings and (mis-)deeds, it is vital to understand their worldview, including its complexities and ambivalences as well as its contradictions (Watson, 1994). This does not mean that researchers should become utterly immersed in this view, or unproblematically accept the manager's language and opinions. Rather, it means showing sufficient care in order to engage with, and make sense of, their actions. As well as respecting their practices, an ethics of care motivates a process of critical questioning of the means and goals espoused by the managers and others who are studied (Spicer et al., 2009).

While acknowledging the important contributions of interpretive ethnographies, the intent of a critical approach is to appreciate how meanings may carry privileged interests (Alvesson and Deetz, 2000) – such as the notion of 'partnership' within, or between, organizations which at once implies a degree of mutuality and can mystify institutionalized differences of power. An important challenge for the *critical* ethnographer is to place local actors' meanings, symbols and values within a wider political, economic and historical framework while, at the same time, minimizing any tendency for such a framework to squeeze the empirical material into a particular theory and language (a dominating voice), with the result that ill-fitting empirical material offers no stimulus for theoretical revision or refinement. By developing critical ethnography (and other ambitious, meaning- and context-sensitive studies) the politics of management and organization are more directly presented without obscuring the ambiguities and variations of local practice and the multiple ways in which management can be interpreted.

As a whole, CMS cannot be credited with a wealth of rich and convincing empirical studies. We agree with Fleming and Mandarini (2009) who point at CMS research having 'a more journalistic approach. Snippets of information and off-the-cuff remarks are preferred to get an "insider's view" of what may be actually happening in the corporation' (ibid.: 333). Nonetheless, there are some good examples of careful empirical research, including studies of organizational work that are informed by a broadly critical standpoint (e.g. Barker, 1993; Jackall, 1988; Knights and Murray, 1994; Kondo, 1990; Kunda, 1992). These studies yield some rich insights into the oppressive and self-defeating features of modern organizations. Critique is concretized, sometimes revised and developed, and brought to life through analysis of deeply qualitative data. In the process, a feeling for the specific situation and the understandings of managers and others involved is compellingly conveyed.

The risk of empirical work strongly guided by a narrow CMS agenda – in which the object of study is framed as a psychic prison, as patriarchical domination or as an iron cage from the outset – is that the researcher, in an elitist fashion, arrogantly imposes his or her truths or insights onto the corporate world. This may mean that instead of unsettling prevailing preconceptions and dogmas, the debunking of conventional wisdom conveys a sense of self-righteousness and superiority which seems, paradoxically, to be dismissive of, or poke fun at, the dilemmas and struggles of the people whose practices are the targets of critique. Unsurprisingly, the distanced and objectified orientation of some critical researchers is seen to be ethically problematic (Wray-Bliss, 2002). Of course, critical analysis demands a deflation of pretensions, including the claims and justifications of those who occupy positions of relative power and advantage. But this does not absolve it from being sensitive to their accomplishments and, in particular, to relate pretensions to historical and existential conditions (Knights and Willmott, 1989). Otherwise, critique is needlessly vulnerable to being interpreted and dismissed as arrogant, one-sided, axe-grinding, elitist and/or irrelevant. It then becomes self-defeating in its mission to facilitate emancipatory change.

One possibility is to undertake ethnographic studies that proceed from, and include, different critical perspectives and combine 'critical' and 'non-critical' perspectives. The more illuminating critical ethnographies depart from a blinkered approach in which the negative, self-defeating aspects of organizational work gain attention without acknowledging or exploring positive, productive features. Of course, we appreciate how a negative thrust can be valuable as a corrective to mainstream, functionalist accounts of organizational processes in which darker aspects are either undisclosed, naturalized or explained away by interpreting them as symptomatic of employee irresponsibility or managerial incompetence. But, equally, a refusal to acknowledge the micro-emancipatory aspects of 'non-critical' perspectives and interventions contributes to a marginalization of critical analysis, and also to reinforcing an unappealing sense of negativism, prejudice and one-sidedness. In focusing exclusively upon the negative, oppressive features of organizations, critical analysis can alienate readers who, potentially, are open to learning from its insights. It is possible, in principle at least, to emphasize the presence of contradictions and the potential for emancipation without ignoring or devaluing positive advances in the management of concrete organizational problems (e.g. compassionate leave, unforced pollution control) under contemporary conditions and restrictions. Such an approach presents one possibility for reducing the gap between CT and the more progressive elements of conventional MOS.

New Styles of Writing

The development of an empirically grounded, more accessible form of CT-informed research can also be facilitated by new styles of writing. Current ideas about writing and experimenting can provide challenging sources of inspiration for CT (see e.g. Clifford and Marcus, 1986; Jeffcutt, 1993; Van Maanen, 1988). An alternative is to toggle between 'practitioner-friendly' and 'critical-emancipatory' textual elements (see Knights and Willmott, 2007).

One could imagine a supplementary (or opposite) role of CT in writings which take a traditional approach to established topics. Emancipation can reside in the wings, taking centre stage in a text only when it has something of direct importance to say (Daft et al., 2010). Instead of focusing strongly on emancipation and critique in the overall approach, expressions of these impulses could be more selective. Stimulation of critical reflection is perhaps more likely when, instead of concentrating upon the production of devastating critiques of conventional wisdom, there is more exploration of competing interpretations. Through a process of 'critical signalling', portions of texts can point to problems by highlighting the linkages between management theory and capitalism, male domination, manipulation, distorted communication, privileged interests, repression, etc. The idea of emancipation then enters by stealth, in the form of disruptive asides in the text.

This possibility highlights the relevance of designing texts in ways that stimulate self-reflection (Alvesson and Sköldberg, 2009). Wherever possible, reflection should be encouraged not only upon the object of critique but also on the authority of the critique. Of course, this point – like many others in this chapter – is relevant not just for CT (and not least for mainstream MOS). The dangers of simply exchanging the authority of one account (e.g. MOS) for the authority of another (e.g. CT) must be recognized and resisted. If the selection and interpretation of teaching material illuminates problems and tensions that are widely encountered, and struggled with, it is perhaps less likely that the text will simply be 'banked' as another nugget of knowledge rather than applied, through a process of critical self-reflection, to illuminate and perhaps transform practice (Grey et al., 1996).[11]

Sometimes a text can be reinterpreted to draw out its more emancipatory implications. Take, for example, Pondy's (1983) discussion of myths and metaphors. He believes that myths are important because 'they place explanation beyond doubt and argumentation' (ibid.: 163). He also argues that 'in myth, the ordinary rules of logic are suspended, anomaly and contradiction can be resolved within the mythical explanation' (ibid.), and that myths therefore fulfil important managerial functions. Pondy's interpretation of myths and metaphors parallels the arguments of deconstructionists who seek to reveal how a sense of closure is accomplished by a text. In Pondy's case, closure is understood to be achieved through the use of metaphor as well as myth that effectively backgrounds or even excludes alternative, and potentially disruptive, representations of organizational reality. From the standpoint of CT, the presence of myths is oppressive where they impede rather than promote reflection, and thereby inhibit emancipatory change. However, from Pondy's managerialist standpoint, myths are uncritically embraced as tools of control on the grounds that 'attention to symbolic aspects is necessary for the effective management of organizations' (ibid.: 163).

Processes of emancipation value doubt; for doubt can open a space for critical self-reflection and transformation. In contrast, Pondy's commendation of a focus upon myths and metaphors has an anti-emancipatory thrust. His argument could encourage more critical thinking *if*, instead, he had suggested that: 'critical attention to symbolic aspects is necessary for the discovery of anomaly and contradiction, and – through that – the development of critical reflection among organizational participants'. This stance is entirely consistent with Pondy's thesis that myths and symbols obscure contradictions but it requires their reinterpretation in order to disclose their emancipatory relevance. Myths create closure which is (a) perhaps good, as too much doubt, anxiety and ambiguity is hard to bear and (b) perhaps bad, as this counters critical reflection and open-mindedness. A critical-emancipatory interpretation could follow, or be followed by, alternative kinds of understandings, including practical or even managerial, without any compulsion to integrate them (for an illustration, see Alvesson, 1996; Martin, 1992). By creating a series of tensions and/or (precarious) resolutions, a text can invite the reader to wrestle with alternative interpretations and thereby enable him or her to take from it what he/she will. Clearly, an anxiety about this approach, from a CT perspective, is that the reading will be dominated by common-sense interpretations that either dismiss its peculiarly open-ended character or lack the intellectual resources with which to challenge the wisdom of the conventional account. The counter-argument is that, as the text resonating with the reader's experience does not rely upon an all-guns-blazing critique of conventional wisdom, it may well have a more penetrating and enduring impact.

One can also work with the switching of style through invoking elements of irony. The major narrative style of CMS is undoubtedly the tragedy (Jeffcutt, 1993): the dark and gloomy side of organizations dominates and there is not much joy to be found in organizational life. Where there is, it is partial and the suspicion is that it reflects the operations of power exploiting emotions and pleasure. But tragedy can be combined, or at least be used interchangeably, with irony or satire. This represents another form of questioning of organization and management, one of unpacking the claims of rationality, control, order and forms of power/ideologies dominating the scene. Much research that lies somewhere between conventional MOS and CMS presents accounts of organization as out of control, irrational, messy, confusing, fragmented and ambiguous (e.g. Martin and Meyerson, 1988). Decision making is garbage can-like, and hypocrisy, symbolism, myths and confusion abound (Brunsson, 2003; March and Olsen, 1976; Meyer and Rowan, 1977). Managers and other people are shown to be sensitive to fashions and imitations. Exposing the often ridiculous, even farcical, nature of corporate life represents another, often highly effective form of questioning of organization and management, and provides a valuable antidote to forms of CMS analysis in which rationality, control, order and the dominance of power/ideologies tend to be assumed (Alvesson and Sveningsson, 2008; Jackall, 1988).

Combining less dark, more playful, even 'postmodernist' accounts of organization and management with more serious and cerebral CMS ideas offers a possible way of making the latter less one-dimensional, less gloomy and better attuned to key aspects of organization and management. A recent effort in this direction is Alvesson and Spicer's (forthcoming) suggestion of a 'stupidity-based theory of the firm'. Here it is proposed that organizations do not only rely on their knowledge-base but also on their stupidity-base: stupidity management fosters a willingness to shut off critical reflection as managers are seduced by the allure of leadership, prefer to follow fashion rather than exercise their own critical faculties, and refrain from asking questions about the meaningfulness of work and the social value of what their organization does.

Looking for Emancipatory Elements in Texts

Our third illustration of how a reconstructed concept of emancipation may be applied concerns the possibility of identifying emancipatory elements in management texts. As noted earlier, Critical Theory is inclined to dismiss ideas that are intended to enhance managers' capacity to raise the productivity of labour (such as Scientific Management, Human Relations, Corporate Culture and Organizational Identity). On occasions when these ideas are considered, it is their manipulative features that receive attention. Little consideration is given to their – admittedly limited – progressive qualities or the contradictory consequences of their application.

Yet, as we observed earlier in this chapter, common to a range of humanistic management theories – e.g. Relational Leadership (Ospina and Uhl-Bien, forthcoming), Corporate Culture (Kanter, 1983; Peters and Waterman, 1982) and Organizational Identity (Hatch and Schutz, 2004) – is a challenge to the adequacy of approaches that reduce human nature to a form of economic rationality. In each case, rationalistic theories are criticized for fostering forms of organization and job design that have the unintended consequence of inhibiting creativity and exerting a generally depressive effect upon morale and productivity. By acknowledging employees' creative capacities, and by expanding opportunities for them to respond to situations in innovative and 'responsible' ways, humanistic MOS theory (including high-commitment HRM and some forms of leadership) prescribes a move away from both the mechanistic application of bureaucratic rules and a reliance on formal hierarchy, to a process of influencing through persuasion and engagement. Instead of treating employees simply as economically rational appendages to the bureaucratic machine who are driven by monetary incentives alone, there is an attentiveness to mobilizing the sentiments of employees – for example, by seeking to promote flexibility and innovation within the parameters set by a few core values rather than a book of rules and procedures. The basic idea is that performance and competitive-ness can be increased by encouraging employees to identify with, and internalize, a limited number of superordinate corporate values:

> Let us suppose that we were asked for one all-purpose bit of advice for manage-ment, one truth that we were able to distil. ... We might be tempted to reply, 'Figure out your value system. Decide what your company stands for. What does your enter-prise do that gives everyone the most pride?' (Peters and Waterman, 1982: 279)

Here, 'pride' is linked to the appeal of the object – in this case, the corporation – with which employees are invited and enabled to identify. Organizational identification is promoted by endeavouring to manage organizational members' sense of their value.

> When a person's self-concept contains the same attributes as those in the per-ceived organizational identity, we define the cognitive connection as organizational identification. Organizational identification is the degree to which a member defines him- or herself by the same attributes that he or she believes define the organization. (Dutton et al., 1994: 239)

As we noted earlier in the example of the 'information meeting', a challenge for managers is to manage identity which includes 'the perceived organizational identity – a member's beliefs about the distinctive, central, and enduring attributes of the organization'. This identity can then 'serve as a powerful image influencing the degree to which the member identifies with the organization' (ibid.: 244). Such prescriptions can be interpreted as manipulative where self-esteem becomes a resource for securing competitive advantage, and also as ideological when it appears that there is an equivalence between corporate and employee values (see Chapter 1). Managers are advised to commit resources to identifying and nurturing, and if necessary creating, the values that guide, or will guide, corporate behaviour in ways that exploit the desire of employees to gain a sense of pride, and thus make them more willing to work hard and cooperatively (e.g. flexibly and creatively) for their employer.

It is not difficult to argue that the insecurity of employees is being exploited when a corporate image is internally marketed in order to convince them that their self-esteem can be boosted by identifying more closely with the superordinate values of the company for which they work. Yet, at the same time, such invocations implicitly invite employees to question the value of many established forms of organizational control. Generations of management gurus have repeated the mantra that people are more complex, and have greater potential, than is generally attributed to them (e.g. Peters and Waterman, 1982: Chapter 3). Instead of being expected to work accurately and productively in exchange for a wage, employees are urged to view their working lives as a series of opportunities to apply and develop their capacities to be innovative and to exercise discretion. Within the boundaries defined by the culture – which is the rub for Critical Theory (Willmott, 1993a) – 'people are encouraged to stick out, to innovate' (Peters and Waterman, 1982: 106). In turn, this ideology raises expectations about the quality of work and the treatment of employees by managers that can be difficult to fulfil when there are pressures from shareholders to deliver 'value', and pressures from competitors to reduce costs and/or improve quality. A perverse consequence of humanistic management theory can be intensified employee scepticism and disillusionment that extends to the ranks of management. In principle, this provides a basis for connecting lived experience with critical analysis that can make more compelling sense of such experience than the superficial diagnoses and associated prescriptions offered by mainstream theory.

Exposing the limitations and anti-emancipatory impulses of humanistic management theory is undemanding (Willmott, 1993a). A likely effect of its implementation, if unresisted, is to make corporations more illiberal, if not totalitarian, as managers hire and fire individuals on the basis of whether they demonstrate a sufficient deference towards their sacred values (Soeters, 1986) or what Dutton et al. (1994: 239) term 'organizational identification': 'you either buy into their values or get out' (Peters and Waterman, 1982: 77). Corporations remain shackled to the task of achieving profitable growth to which end the strengthening of corporate culture continues to be perceived as a relevant means. At the extreme, organizations become cult-like (Tourish and Pinnington, 2002) but a more common outcome is that they become more hypocritical in terms of a widening gap between what employees feel and how they present and report these feelings; and between what managers claim to value and the values embodied in their actions. Nonetheless, an emphasis upon creativity, innovation and discretion may open up some opportunities for questioning and challenging such gaps (see Wilkinson and Willmott, 1995b). Where the promises remain unfulfilled, there is a stimulus to reflect critically upon the rationality of organizations and the adequacy of their management. And to the extent that promises about creativity, etc. are partially realized, their likely effect is to constitute employees whose sights are, in principle, raised with regard to further opportunities to exercise 'autonomy' and 'responsibility'. Finally, a high level of identification implies a degree of commitment to the workplace which may encourage efforts to speak up or 'voice' demands, and to strive for improvements, grounded in employees' views of what is important and valuable about the organization.

To be clear, we are not saying that advocates of Corporate Culture or Organizational Identity and related management theories are in the vanguard of (micro-)emancipation. The anti-emancipatory elements are too salient and sometimes dominant; such theory concentrates solely on means, taking corporate goals and management prerogatives as given, and so cements the social relations through which they are reproduced (Stablein and Nord, 1985). Instead, we are saying that the (limited) recognition of human creativity and engagement, as well as the individual capacity to make choices and exercise discretion, etc., should be positively acknowledged. These espoused values provide a basis, albeit compromised and slender, for holding management accountable. Where 'empowerment', for example, is promised, there is a basis for sustained questioning of the ends and priorities of companies and quality of working life when these are seen to diverge from, or be in conflict with, the fulfilment of such espoused values. But, of course, this questioning is only possible when it is informed by an understanding of 'empowerment' that radically exceeds the scope and penetration of the managerialist spin placed upon it.

Summary and Conclusion

In this chapter, we have sought to initiate and develop a conversation between humanistic management theory, Critical Theory and poststructuralism. More specifically, we have explored the question of how the emancipatory impulse of CT may be expressed in the face of quite different theoretical and practical critiques from poststructuralist and practitioner positions. In opposition to some authors, we favour harnessing the insights of different traditions of critical thinking – early Frankfurt scholars, Habermas and Foucault, not either/or – but without denying or glossing over their differences or believing in the possibility of synthesizing their respective contributions. We believe that CMS is best served by being inspired by a diversity of critical inputs in a way that inspires recurrent critical reflection upon their respective contributions (Alvesson and Deetz, 2000; Alvesson and Willmott, 1992).

We have suggested that emancipation does not have to be conceptualized or realized only in the form of 'grand' projects. Instead, it may be partially and imperfectly fulfilled in everyday management and organizational practices. This view, we have argued, is consistent with a critical interpretation of humanistic management theory. It is a view that also resonates with the scepticism expressed by poststructuralism about all-embracing theoretical projects envisioning far-reaching, contradiction-free programmes of social improvement. Small steps and small wins may be a better tactic if one wants to accomplish something and thereby gain some momentum (Spicer et al., 2009). Encouraging a dialogue between CT and PS (e.g. the work of Foucault) can be supportive of less abstract understandings of management and organization that can make more accessible the often remote, philosophical arguments of CT. Indeed, this is a view that Habermas (1994) himself seems to endorse when he observes that:

> Foucault's microanalysis of power calls our attention to an invisible dialectic between the egalitarian tendencies of the age and those new unfreedoms that settled into the pores of simultaneously emancipated and systematically distorted communicative practices. (ibid.: 119)

Practical gains, however small, in terms of increased discretion and improved job satisfaction should be appreciated as such, and not simply be measured and found wanting in relation to Utopian visions of autonomy, creativity, non-gendered organizations and democracy – for such visions, as CT itself emphasizes, may have little meaning for the everyday life experiences, aspirations and struggles of many organizational participants. Positive aspects of contemporary organizational transformation should not be disregarded or dismissed when drawing attention to its more sinister and oppressive features.

Notes

1 We recognize that there are significant differences and tensions amongst leading proponents of Critical Theory – for example, between Adorno and Habermas (see Appendix). We are also aware that the poststructuralism label has been actively resisted by many of those to whom it has been applied, including Foucault. For us, the contribution of poststructuralism is more important than disputes over the use of this label. While Foucault's corpus as a whole cannot simply be identified with poststructuralism, his work on the relation between power, truth and subjectivity does have close affinities with key poststructuralist concerns.

2 Likewise, in the fields of equal opportunity and diversity, management is directed to counteract sex stereotypes, gender oppression and discrimination against ethnic groups in order to better use 'talents' irrespective of gender and ethnicity. It is questionable whether these developments result from a conviction about equality or a calculation about the nurturing and attraction of capable labour, a concern to comply with the law or simply a desire to cultivate a progressive image, especially in organizations that are in the public eye. Equal opportunity and diversity management are often chastised for being more about creating legitimacy than creating substantive changes (Alvesson and Billing, 2009; Prasad et al., 2011).

3 This criticism resonates with the observation, most forcefully articulated by Sloterdijk (1980), that ideology critique has become too weighty and solemn. By cutting itself off from 'the powerful traditions of laughter within *satirical* knowledge, which have their philosophical *roots* in ancient kynicism', they have come to assume 'a complete air of bourgeois respectability' (Sloterdijk, 1984: 202).

4 The intellectual origins of humanism can be traced to the Enlightenment, when 'Man', through the agency of reason, 'postulated the human, as opposed to a divine, construction of the ideal' (Dawe, 1979: 375).

5 Marcuse (1955), for example, identified human instincts at the core of human existence that would disrupt and transcend the totalizing control of advanced society. Currently, Habermas' more cerebral formulation of the core of human activity is dominant. Autonomy and solidarity are coupled to communicative action. Central here is anticipation of the speech act in a free dialogue in a non-authoritarian society where the potentials in language for questioning, checking and arguing are fully developed (see Chapter 2).

6 When combined with the intellectualism and essentialism in CT, its negativism may account for its marginal presence within, and impact upon, management theory and practice. This situation is partly attributable to the esoteric language employed within CT as well as to the dominance of values that are hostile to CT. Difficulties experienced in publishing critical management research in the most established journals, especially in the USA where the sciences of management and organization are – uncritically – assumed to be apolitical, mean that the contribution of CT continues muted but not entirely 'silenced'.

7   Contemporary critical researchers often favour the term 'resistance' rather than
    emancipation. We believe that this is symptomatic of a narrow focus upon
    responses to 'control'. Our notion of micro-emancipation overlaps with, but also
    goes beyond, what are identified as expressions of 'resistance'. For us, 'resistance'
    may amount to little more than a temporary challenge to specific forms of
    subject-defining force. For example, Thomas and Davies (2005) characterize the
    expression of a negative opinion to a policy as resistance. It offers some relief
    from, or subversion of, control but does not necessarily offer emancipation from
    it in the sense of a move to a more 'positive' state. On the contrary, a degree of
    'resistance' may be tolerated by managers in order to secure their control; and
    expressions of resistance by employees may simply enable them to preserve some
    measure of self-esteem without having to confront management or struggle for
    change. Emancipation, even micro-emancipation, in contrast, includes a degree
    of 'politicization' where resistance is linked, more or less intentionally, to the
    challenging and potential removal of practices which are felt to be oppressive.
    There is some measure of positive grounding, where an individual or a group
    has created some space for keeping constraining forces under control and some
    clarification of a reflectively or communicatively grounded position. Even if
    micro-emancipation emphasizes small moves and small wins in this context, the
    positive or active, humanistic element is more pronounced than in resistance-
    focused studies. The difference between micro-emancipation and resistance is,
    however, fine tuned, and some authors use the terms in rather similar ways.
8   Consider the probable outcome of enhanced ecological consciousness and
    greater freedom and creativity at work, which are two priorities that are likely
    to emerge from processes of critical reflection and emancipatory change. These
    may be accompanied by reduced wages and falling consumption, or even bank-
    ruptcy and unemployment.
9   To such charges, we plead guilty despite having drawn attention to their impor-
    tance for many years (Cooper et al., 1996; Sikka et al., 1998; Klimecki and
    Willmott, 2009; Ezzamel et al., 2008). An attentiveness to environmental con-
    cerns was prominent in the first edition of this book where we made repeated
    reference to ecological destructiveness as well as the social divisiveness of con-
    temporary management.
10 The argument against restricting the project of emancipation to one focus or
    type does not depart only from 'grand' versions of improvement and liberation.
    It is unsatisfactory, in our view, to exclude more mundane levels of incremental
    change – and thereby the concerns of organizational participants – from
    accounts of emancipatory transformation. That said it is equally unsatisfactory to
    improve means without critically considering the wider context of social relations
    or alternative ends. Without the latter, we can hardly talk about emancipation.
    Many (most?) forms of organization development and neo-human relations tech-
    niques fall victim to this criticism since they routinely abstract organizational
    behaviour from its context and/or reduce the analysis of context to the interac-
    tion of a set of conditioning variables. They typically take efficiency and profit

motives for granted and subordinate 'humanization' to these dominant goals (Alvesson, 1987). Similarly, as we argued in Chapter 2, ideas about women in management, for example, are inadequately understood when they are boiled down to the issue of equal access to career possibilities, without any consideration of the more profound relationship between gender relations and organizational arrangements and goals (Alvesson and Billing, 2009; Calas and Smircich, 1993, 2006). Emancipatory discourses and practices are partial and incomplete when they do not give full recognition to the role of macro-level forces – such as class, race and gender structures and associated ideologies of domination that pervade and legitimize the world of organization and management. Taking the idea of emancipation seriously – even when revised along the lines suggested here – does not leave the social totality unexamined, taken for granted or undisturbed but instead keeps a critical eye on how the social totality is imprinted at the micro-level (Willmott, 2010). Likewise, a focus on elements for micro-emancipation – such as the message of an advertisement appealing to the desire to feel young and beautiful – may, for example, strengthen a general questioning of how corporations and marketing create consumer-centred identities (see Chapters 3 and 5).

11 The banking concept of knowledge is drawn from Freire (1972). It is a notion which directly echoes Horkheimer's (1937: 222) critique of the Cartesian understanding of knowledge in which the 'essential unchangeableness between subject, theory, and object' is assumed.

8
Critical Theory and Management Practice

In Chapter 7 we argued for an approach, broadly informed by Critical Theory (CT) but not limited to it, that acknowledges and explores commonalities between CT and progressive elements in management and organization studies. In this chapter, we explore further the relevance and impact of CT for people working in organizations – academics and students as well as practitioners – who are potential agents of (micro-) emancipatory transformation. An important task and contribution of Critical Management Studies (CMS), we argue, is to promote a more systematic critical consideration of the contexts of organizational work.

Individual employees (or groups of these employees), including managers, are an important, but not an exclusive, audience for CMS.[1] Our image of these people, ourselves included, is not that of heroes or 'black belt' emancipatory warriors who have already achieved self-clarity and autonomy. Rather, we picture diverse individuals and groups struggling to 'get by' – to deal with everyday challenges and frustrations – in conditions that are psychologically demanding, and where managerial pressures, personal ambitions, the threat of unemployment and other considerations often militate against progressive, emancipatory forms of practice. Human frailties and imperfections, like indolence and opportunism, are not wholly attributable to a 'bad system' to be combated with ideology critique resulting in the creation of sound organizations in which only 'good' intentions and actions are to be found. Nonetheless, our assumption is that critical reflection can make a positive difference by enabling us to intervene productively in the daily struggle of living one's life, including managing one's work and organizational situations.

Because we explore some of the implications of critical thinking for different groups of practitioners and academics, this chapter is inevitably wide-ranging. We begin by situating this thinking within a discussion of alternative means of promoting social change. We then review alternative models of reflective practice before contemplating the possible consequences of critical thinking upon corporate employees. There we return to the argument, sketched in earlier chapters, that decisions are often complex and involve trade-offs between competing objectives and rationalities. As a consequence, there is frequently some space for exercising judgment and discretion in ways that can reduce unnecessary suffering associated *inter alia* with dependence and apathy, and can also expand autonomy and responsibility. However, such opportunities are not always seized; and we therefore address and discuss resistance to research and teaching that is critical of received wisdom. Finally, we reaffirm our view that there remain opportunities to debunk and transform oppressive conditions and exploitative relations.

Means of Promoting Progressive Social Change

Before dealing with the question of how Critical Management Studies (CMS) may inspire more reflective forms of organizational practice, we consider alternative means of putting into practice the ideals of contemporary critical thought. In principle, and without focusing particularly on Critical Theory (CT), we identify four means of promoting progressive reform:

1   *'Better', more enlightened forms of social engineering, including management and public administration.* Here it is assumed that modern, progressive forms of management may accomplish greater individual autonomy, community and/or self-fulfilment in organizations. Although intended principally to improve productivity, quality and flexibility, a number of contemporary management techniques and programmes (e.g. quality circles, Total Quality Management, certain forms of leadership) can encourage limited, local forms of participation and involvement, as we acknowledged in Chapter 7. There is some shading of this stratagem into point 4 below.

2   *Political reforms, often championed by leftist parties and movements, enshrined in legislation on consumer policy, worker safety, environmental protection, etc.* Through the introduction of regulations mediated by the legal system, constraints on corporations are applied, and examples of 'best practice' and 'good citizenship' are promoted, often in 'partnership' with industry. The emancipatory contribution of such reforms may be modest, at best, but they should not be dismissed out of hand as 'mere' appeasement or cynical PR.

3   *Political struggles pursued mainly outside the formal political system (e.g. by environmental protection groups or by members of the women's movement).* These struggles often aim to influence politico-legal systems, but they also routinely achieve other, more far-reaching effects that act to change understandings and attitudes in a progressive way. For example, more ecologically informed customers may make choices that induce manufacturers to produce 'cleaner' or more sustainable products; female (and male) employees may be strengthened by the women's movement in their resolve to resist traditional, gendered employment practices and divisions of labour.

4   *Forms of collective action and participation in the community or the workplace.* In some organizations (e.g. universities, cooperatives and knowledge-intensive firms), forms of participation, or at least 'networking', are to some degree institutionalized, as a consequence of their collegial development.[2] In comparison to the programmes identified in point 1, forms of local participation are not orchestrated from above, and can be productive of less hierarchical forms of organization. More far-reaching forms of involvement are usually conditional upon a change in the legal base favouring co-determination, sometimes backed up by co-ownership.

These four, overlapping means of progressive reform offer ways – that are more or less potent, and more or less co-optable – of challenging and counteracting ideologies and practices that impede and/or suppress the development of greater autonomy, responsibility and emancipatory transformation. CMS supports these kinds of reform directly through recognizing or suggesting alternative organizational designs (Parker et al., 2007), or indirectly through developing concepts, frameworks or empirical studies that supply background knowledge and inspiration for progressive change initiatives. At the very least, contributions to CMS serve to highlight the limitations and potentially regressive effects of apparently progressive reforms. They may, for example, contribute to the critical evaluation of participative modes of management by:

(a) highlighting the shortcomings of manipulative methods and techniques (e.g. their use in Total Quality Management – Wilkinson and Willmott, 1995a; McCabe et al, 1998);
(b) researching how organizations are involved in implementing progressive legislation and policies (e.g. Flood and Jackson, 1991a);
(c) studying progressive social movements and new organizational forms to assess their effects and suggest paths for future development (e.g. Grimes and Cornwall, 1987); or
(d) conducting research that is of direct relevance from the subordinates' or union's point of view (e.g. Brown and Tandon, 1983).

CMS scholars may also move outside of academia and use ideas and skills in politically conscious ways in order to reach out and have an impact on opinion formation by stimulating greater critical awareness.[3] We illustrate this in Box 8.1.

Box 8.1

A couple of years ago one of us published an article on the debate page of a major national tabloid newspaper on the problems of consumerism.

The article made the point that in affluent society, enormous amounts of resources, time and talent are invested by corporations to convince consumers to desire and purchase products. Much of this is non-obvious – for example, through product placement in mass media. Attention of the readers of the paper was drawn to the negative psychological effects on self-esteem and the environmental costs of this use of resources. The policy recommendation was to raise taxes on advertising and product-promotion type activities. In order to increase the chance of getting the text published and also to have a stronger effect, the author suggested to the editor that they could illustrate the article with

(Continued)

(Continued)

a photo from the then-popular movie *Sex and the City*. The picture and text would point out that the movie recently had received the International Film Whore Award for the extensive use of product placement in the film. Having done research on the media, there was an understanding of how they operate: an easy and eye-catching visual representation is seen as highly effective for attracting the attention of tabloid readers.

This example is of course comparatively minor and trivial. But compared to spending months writing an academic paper read by 20 or so people, it may be that spending a day and reaching perhaps 100,000 (although for only five minutes) may be a worthwhile exercise. It calls for some investment in learning how to write for the general public and for newspapers, and occasionally thinking through the broader implications of our work. Obviously, the internet presents further opportunities through blogging and hosting websites, including free access to electronic journals such as *Ephemera*. As Prem Sikka (2008), a 'critical accountant' who has engaged in this activity for many years, reflects 'the internet has created possibilities for fermenting emancipatory change through articles and blogs that can reach a wide variety of audiences. Through trenchant critiques and even humour, academics can ferment possibilities of change by informing, galvanizing and even infuriating some.' Being an academic – with knowledge and writing skills, legitimacy as an 'expert' of sorts, time to write and some independence in relation to social pressures – lends itself to this work.

One aspect of the above example – which may also apply to writing blogs and especially dealing with or even ignoring vitriolic responses to them – is the identity struggle of publishing in a medium or for elements of an audience for which one has limited respect. To engage in such activity may feel beneath one's dignity and status as a 'scholar'. In which case, the increasing pressures to publish, to provide students with 'customer friendly' service and to play a full part in dealing with the growing administrative burdens of academic life (associated with teaching and research-quality monitoring and accreditation) may displace such outward-facing activity; or it may provide a handy excuse for avoiding the risks to identity and reputation associated with such engagement. Reaching out to a wider audience currently receives little encouragement, prestige or reward within academia. Striving to have a broader social and political impact by communicating with other, often rather hostile, audiences demands a willingness to branch out from a narrow focus on intra-group self-confirmation.

CMS contributes to the four means of promoting change listed above. But its distinctive and far-reaching contribution as we indicated in Chapter 7 – resides in the capacity to stimulate and nurture reflection which encourages emancipatory thinking, communication and change, rather than detailed problem-solving or answering empirical questions. It is in the (re)formation of consciousness that CT can make a difference: by presenting challenges to what is taken for granted, including how empirical questions are framed; and by inspiring and supporting new forms of thinking and action. Reality 'out there' (identified as ecology, material structures, economic forces) is, of course, of great significance for the quality of life, since the pollution of air and water, for example, immediately degrades it. But, from a CT perspective, the key to reducing pollution (in this example) resides in changing how people think about, monitor and enact this reality. That is because *we can only communicate, critically evaluate and transform the 'quality' of this 'external reality' through our knowledge of it and our capacity to reflect critically upon it*. This is why communication, and the encouragement of critical reflection upon the (ideologically distorted) media and contents of communication, are a cornerstone in CT's project; and it is no less relevant for critical studies of management. Critical reflection invites some questioning of whether 'more' or ostensibly 'better' management is a rational response to failures of management. There may, for example, be widespread agreement that there is wastage and inflexibility in private and public sector organizations. But are additional targets, regulations, strategic planning, etc. the only, or even the most defensible, response to such problems? As Grey (2003: 11) has argued, when Management is viewed as the solution rather than part of the problem, it is time to appreciate how threadbare are the clothes worn by this Emperor. Indeed, Grey suggests that we should 'declare that the Emperor of Management is wearing no clothes', before he goes on to ask if such a view is '[i]mplausible, idealistic, impractical, ill-informed?' And, responding to his own question, Grey answers 'Let's hope so, for that is what the defenders of naked Emperors always say' (ibid.; see also Grey, 1999).

In this regard, CMS challenges the widely held assumption that technically oriented knowledge – such as the prescriptions commended by Business Process Reengineering or The Balanced Scorecard – is *practically* relevant and useful. An example is the advocacy of 'modern management' in post-colonial contexts. As Murphy (2008) has observed, the appeal of 'modernization' to the managerial elite is that it provides a justification for releasing social relations from the restrictive drag of traditional obligations. But, at the same time, the material and symbolic advantages enjoyed by managers in the Indian context, at least, rely upon a continuing 'subaltern servitude' (ibid.: 418) that supplies both domestic staff and cheap goods. For the managerial elite, modernization holds the prospect of gaining access to transnational employment and business relationships while continuing to benefit from an established system of hierarchy and social exclusion (e.g. caste discrimination which Murphy illustrates by reference to privatized Dalit human-excrement cleaners). A less managerial, more critical understanding of modernity incorporates a concern with social justice that implies the reduction, if not abolition, of entrenched inequalities and a spreading of 'the benefits of global insertion throughout society through redistributive taxation policy and broad-based social and economic development' (ibid.: 419).

Inverting conventional wisdom, CMS questions the relevance and defensibility of limiting management knowledge to what is technical and instrumental, including 'humanistic' techniques for engineering increased productivity (see Chapter 1 and 7). Reliance upon technical logic using calculations to select the optimal means of accomplishing ends marginalizes critical reflection and debate over the ends, often with fateful consequences when key contingencies, local or global, are disregarded (Thompson and Willmott, 2011). This approach is blind to how applications of technique seldom work in a straightforward manner. For example, the introduction of scientific management had the unintended consequence of acting as a recruiting sergeant for unions.

Some limitations of the technical knowledge model have recently been illustrated by a study of MBA (Masters in Business Administration) students (Sturdy et al., 2006). These students were told that only practically relevant and useful knowledge of direct applicability to their future careers was included in their course. Yet, five years later, none of the students could recall any examples of knowledge that they had actually used. Other, less technical and not directly applicable issues were seen as valuable, such as expanding their network of contacts and developing more of a 'helicopter view'. This example does not, of course, prove the value of critical reflection, but it does place in question its exclusion or marginalization from business school curricula on the grounds that technical knowledge is of proven importance or that it is of greater relevance because it contributes directly to 'better' management. What this example also illustrates is how MBA education is ostensibly de–politicized by presenting it as 'technical'. A strong emphasis upon technical knowledge acts to exclude (critical) analysis that questions the political neutrality of such knowledge and, more generally, doubts the impartiality of managerial work. Indeed, what could be more 'political' than the exclusion of critical reason by equating management with the exercise of value-neutral, technical expertise?

By engendering local forms of critical consciousness within organizations, including business schools, CMS can make a contribution to a broader movement of emancipatory transformation. Clearly, critique as a kind of intellectual pastime is of no practical value. The point of critique is not simply to better understand the world but to change it. That is to say, critique must take the form of praxis – in the sense of informing and guiding actions that are transformative (Foster and Wiebe, 2011). That said, critique is not directed at 'structures of domination' (ibid.) as if such 'structures' exist externally to the many mundane processes that, *inter alia*, limit critique to a kind of intellectual pastime. 'Structures of domination' include influences, compulsions, anxieties and imperatives that impede the translation of critique into emancipatory intervention and change. When complemented and enriched by poststructuralist (e.g. Foucauldian) analysis (see Chapter 7), critical studies incorporate consideration of 'the endless everydayness of small, insignificant claims and counterclaims (which) provide the full measure of the functioning of power in corporations' (Deetz, 1992a: 302). Facilitating and promoting change in actors' everyday orientations, with regard to gender or sexual orientation for example, is vital – not just for the improvement of local situations but for the contribution it can make to wider processes of emancipatory change. Yet, as we also emphasized in Chapter 7, micro-settings and interactions do not exist in a historical and socio-political vacuum. It is therefore necessary to challenge and seek to dissolve a tendency to divorce private troubles from public issues by appreciating how local tensions and frustrations form an integral part of the reproduction and potential transformation of the bigger picture.

Ideas for More Reflective Work Methods

CMS assumes that it would be highly desirable for organizations to be populated and managed by people who are critically minded and reflective. Only by applying these qualities is there any prospect of weakening the grip of reducing and ultimately removing the deleterious consequences of modern management – in terms of ego administration, pacification, conformism, wastefulness, pollution, etc. (see Chapter 1). Committed to the development of dialogically based micro-decisions and actions in everyday working life, CMS aims to stimulate and support reflection along a broad scale. So, while it may focus upon local forms of domination (e.g. distortions in communication found in micro-settings), it interprets these in relation to wider historical forces (e.g. patriarchy). To illustrate how CMS addresses emancipatory change within organizations, we briefly consider the contributions of Forester on planning, Fryer on leadership and the work of Payne on corporate ethics. In each case, critical thinking is applied to advance and facilitate pro-emancipatory principles for organizational work.

Forester – policy making

Forester (1985, 1993, 2003) has used Habermas' theory of communicative competence to argue that planning should be viewed as attention-shaping (communicative action), and not purely, or principally, as a means to a particular end (instrumental action). Close attention is paid to the subtle communicative effects that shape and mediate the planning process. Commenting upon its dynamics, Forester observes that:

> Actions as diverse as threatening, promising, and encouraging ... may be instrumentally oriented toward some end, but each is fundamentally and practically communicative too ... action *seeks ends and meaningfully communicates*: the most instrumental action without meaning would be simply *meaningless*, not even recognizable as an action. (1993: 24, emphasis in original)

Applying the theory of communicative action, Forester shows how each of Habermas' types of validity claim can be used to reveal distortions of communication, and thereby expose forms of domination (see also Chapters 2, 3 and 4). This research is guided by a concern to reduce communicative distortions through practical measures so as to remember the norms of comprehensibility, sincerity, legitimacy and truth[4] in face-to-face interactions, in organizational communications and in politico–economic relations. In this process, the following vision of local planning practice emerges:

> As we broaden our understanding of the planner's action (from technical to communicative), we come to understand the practical organizational problems planners face a little differently. We come to understand that problems will be solved not by one expert, but by pooling expertise and non-professional contributions as well; not by formal procedure alone, but by informal consultation and involvement; not predominantly by strict reliance on data bases, but by careful use of trusted 'resources', 'contacts', 'friends'; not through formally rational management procedures, but by internal politics and the development of a working consensus; not by solving an engineering equation, but by complementing technical performance with political sophistication, support-building, liaison work, and finally, intuition and luck. (Forester, 1985: 212)

Forester's research illustrates how, in practice, technical and practical rationalities are intertwined. Effective planning is not accomplished simply by undertaking the calculations of technical reason but is embedded in relations of power that render it possible and perhaps necessary to engage in informal consultations. In demonstrating how Habermas' theory of communicative action is relevant for interrogating routine practices of organizational work, Forester's analysis enables us systematically to raise and explore the critical issue of whether organizational communications are genuinely cooperative achievements or the product of strategic action in which force is overtly or covertly substituted for open discussion. Forester (1983) suggests that where conditions for questioning communications are impoverished or absent – with the result that organizational members have little or no possibility for challenging and debating demands made upon them – there are strong grounds for suspecting that the institutional framework of social norms is founded upon 'tyranny rather than authority, manipulation rather than cooperation, and distraction rather than sensitivity' (ibid.: 240). By exposing and analysing the way domination is institutionalized in mundane organizational work, critical analysis stimulates the process of challenging and transforming its rationality.

Habermas' ideas have also influenced the critical study of leadership, as briefly sketched in Chapter 4. Attributions of leadership tend to be viewed sceptically by CMS scholars, as something that reinforces hierarchy and discourages autonomy by assuming and legitimizing leader–follower distinctions and identities. Yet, arguably, leadership may be a relevant and legitimate quality when it is not imposed from above or taken for granted as an ideological prop of domination. Less hierarchical and more relational forms of leadership are possible (Uhl-Bien and Marion, 2007), in which the dialectical and dialogic nature of interactions between senior and junior employees is emphasized (Collinson, 2005). Ideally, the issue is neither to celebrate and exaggerate subordination to leaders, nor to deny that there may be situations and circumstances where it is reasonable to respect, and to some extent subordinate oneself to, people that have more knowledge, experience or a better overview

(Alvesson and Spicer, 2012a ; Sennett, 1980). Authority can be useful and productive – teachers, supervisors, senior colleagues and managers may have a well-grounded basis for acting as authorities or leaders *vis-á-vis* junior or less-knowledgeable people. A key issue is whether privileged access to scarce resources (e.g. knowledge) is mobilized and applied to cement a position of privilege or to facilitate emancipatory transformation. Knee-jerk denial or blanket rejection of authority as a way to combat hierarchical relations may obstruct a more well-grounded form of maturity and autonomy[5].

Fryer – leadership

Fryer (2012) contends that if people involved actively and freely decide to accept a particular form of leadership after careful reflection and communicative actions, then there is little basis for challenging such a democratic process. He commends certain social rules or ideals for making this possible. These include legitimizing leadership status by ensuring that (a) formal leadership positions are subject to ongoing communicative authorization; (b) there is formal, democratic participation in the selection, appraisal and retention of leaders; and (c) an explicit process should be available whereby challenges to a leader's own discursive fealty can be raised and considered. The central idea is that there are democratic mechanisms for making leadership accountable and also for leadership to incorporate efforts to create conditions for open communication that include stepping back from instrumental work practices in order to interrogate and challenge the factual and normative accuracy of key assertions.

   This model would mean that formal subordinates take responsibility for leadership and are involved in its 'meta-creation' and development. This does not imply that there is participation in leadership all the time and in every respect. A group may agree that a leader has considerable discretion in terms of making decisions and governing work, at least for a defined period and/or under certain conditions. In many situations such leadership may be regarded as one possible option, with other forms of coordination, guidance and support offering alternative and possibly better solutions. Careful reflection about a variety of resources and social forms for guidance and support – and not just leadership – may result in a group's active use of autonomy/self-management, group decisions and/or peer relations which might limit the demand for leadership (Alvesson and Blom, 2011). A critical view of leadership that includes a desire to have practical implications requires consideration not only of the unfortunate tendency to over-value leadership and place 'non-leaders' in a position of immaturity and dependence, but also of the benefits that arise from legitimate forms of asymmetry and authority. The ambivalence of leadership as a productive or repressive force needs to be fully acknowledged if it is to be handled in an informed and sensitive manner. Overdependence as well as counter-dependency on leadership can, in principle, be replaced by more mature and thoughtful, democratically grounded ways of assessing what kind of leadership, if any, is to be practised (Alvesson and Spicer, forthcoming).

Payne – ethical dialogue

Payne (1991) suggests the creation of settings in organizations in which diverse stakeholders are relatively free to discuss ethical issues. Without denying the restrictions and practical difficulties of achieving such an (ideal speech) situation, he commends a middle course 'between awareness of the impossibility of ever realizing the ideals of true participant autonomy and responsibility versus the dangers of readily accepting conventional organizational communication and meanings' (ibid.: 75). Payne's proposal takes the form of establishing an 'ethical dialogue group' within organizations that can serve an interpretive *and* critical role in raising issues and critical consciousness, rather than acting directly as a change agent. His justification for this separation between changing consciousness and transformative action – praxis – is that the latter activity calls for other skills and priorities; and, relatedly, that a focus upon the practicalities of managing change would tend to place constraints upon and/or prejudice processes of critical reflection. The modest role of the ethical dialogue group is to identify and explore stakeholder views and moral claims, and to propose a critical standard by which to improve theory and practice without direct and potentially restrictive regard for how such a critical standard might be applied.

An obvious limitation of Payne's proposals concerns the probable resistance by some stakeholders (e.g. investors and owners) to an institution – the ethical dialogue group – that may be perceived as posing some threats to their claims or to give equal or greater recognition to other stakeholders (e.g. employees, citizens) who do not necessarily share their values and priorities. As a consequence, latent forms of conflict that have been effectively suppressed by the denial of such 'dialogue' may come into the open. On the other hand, if this threat is not anticipated or anxieties are allayed, the separation of consciousness-raising from practical intervention may at least allow a critical questioning of existing priorities to be voiced, and, perhaps, a gradual incremental shift in understanding, policy and practice to be fostered (see Chapter 7). Even if the call for an ethical dialogue group fails to attract support or, when implemented, it becomes no more than a talking shop that immediately changes nothing, such a group, if established, may be of value in revealing how some stakeholders are more dominant, and unaccountable, in shaping processes of communication and decision making. Developing and maintaining critical awareness is the starting point for any progressive action, even though such action may not be the outcome. It is, however, important that the possibilities for practice are carefully scrutinized. Sometimes people 'cynically' comply with (unsatisfactory) conditions as they simply 'play the game', all the while believing their insights on the situation to be superior.

Employees who passively comply with authorities avoid the material and emotional costs associated with challenging and changing practices, but they also miss the opportunity to engage actively in struggles for change as well as reaping any benefit of new (less oppressive) arrangements. Where this takes the form of 'cynical consciousness', a kind of 'pseudo-liberation' occurs as a deceptive sense of rising above – or maintaining a distance from – mundane forms of exploitation and oppression, developing in stark contrast to their institutionalized subordination (Fleming and Spicer, 2003; Sloterdijk, 2004). This may be typical for our time – we are ecologically aware and realize that consumerism is not the road to happiness, but this does not prevent (most of) us from making huge ecological footprints or equating pleasure with the consumption of what money can buy. Such 'cynical consciousness' is by no means foreign to some advocates of CMS who are indistinguishable from many other academics when they play 'the journal publication game' without believing in its value, apart from benefits that it brings for career.

The contributions of Forester, Fryer and Payne are illustrative of attempts to show how critical thinking is relevant for facilitating change. Others have addressed the issue of creating preconditions for a dialogue in labour/management interaction in relation to the implementation of workplace reform (Gustavsen, 1985) and have suggested that Habermas' ideas of undistorted communication could inform programmes of organizational development (Herda and Messerschmitt, 1991). While we are broadly supportive of such initiatives, and accept that they may involve some compromising of 'purist' CT (see Chapter 7), translating the insights of CT into practical situations does risk the trivialization, dilution and domestication of its critical, emancipatory intent. Adaptation to pragmatic concerns carries with it the danger of deflecting attention from more fundamental issues (e.g. those concerned with the preconditions and quality of communication). Nonetheless, it is only by struggling to apply critical thinking that its relevance for understanding and transforming everyday, organization work can be appreciated and assessed. In turn, it is hoped that these efforts can be refined and developed to advance CMS in directions that are theoretically rigorous *and* practically relevant.

CMS as a Source of Inspiration for Working Life

Using critical thinking as a source of inspiration for the initiatives and stratagems outlined so far is, of course, not the only way in which it may influence organizational practice. As we argued in Chapter 1, CMS can also equip students, managers and other practitioners with fresh and challenging concepts, ideas and understandings that act as a counterweight to the interpretive frameworks that are prevalent in educational and corporate settings. As students and managers become acquainted with, and (hopefully) persuaded by, the insights and relevance of CMS, they may be drawn to develop practices that actively encourage the expansion of critical reflection, self-clarification and collective and individual autonomy. Among the possible consequences of the wider dissemination and engagement of critical thinking are more reflective career choices and managerial decision making that incorporate a broader spectrum of criteria so as to include, for example, effects upon democratic will-formation and the sustainable use of resources. Of course, the practical results of critical consciousness do not end here, but we identify these as highly pertinent areas for its application.

CMS and Career Choices

Given wider exposure to ideas with an affinity to CMS, it can be expected that people will become more discriminating in their choice of employers and careers, at least to the extent that options are available. The choice of employment is already shaped by values, irrespective of encounters with CMS: vegetarians are not inclined to work in slaughterhouses or for hamburger chains; many people would not actively seek work in the defence/war industry, etc. But, as critical reflection upon the ethical nature and implications of corporate activity develops, it can be anticipated that employees will become increasingly sensitized to, and discriminating about, the obvious and not-so-obvious dimensions of employment – ranging from gender policies and work environments to the social value and ethical acceptability of the products and services that they produce and distribute. Potential recruits may ask themselves, for example, whether particular products and services, and the jobs attaching to them, are vital or marginal or even negative for human well-being. In affluent and post-affluent societies, an increasing share of economic and organizational activity stands in a dubious relation to the social good. Even if few things are inherently negative – many people believe in the value of weapons, tobacco, alcohol, travelling, luxury and high-status goods – their production and use is often harmful. Here we are thinking of the 'pollution industry' (chemical plants, car, oil and flight companies), the 'killing industry' (weapons, furs, meat) and the 'status and self-esteem regulation industry' (highly symbolic branded goods, often producing gender stereotypes and low self-esteem among those not living up to the norms of a glamorous appearance). When considering such industries, we have reason to ask: 'Wouldn't the world be a better place if we discouraged them or, in some cases, worked to remove them?'

Instead of treating the labour market predominantly in an economically rational way, and instead of assuming that legal corporate activities are also morally just (or simply beyond ethical reach), CMS encourages a more sceptical and questioning attitude, including amongst those for whom options are severely restricted. Where critical consciousness develops, and it is not treated like an intellectual fashion accessory, people, and especially those with options in the labour market, may be more inclined to dedicate their labour to activities, companies and organizations that, upon reflection, are considered to be comparatively beneficial or, at least, to be engaging in work whose harmful effects are comparatively minor and temporary. Conversely, organizations whose contributions are perceived to be unequivocally damaging, in terms of their social and ecological impacts as well as their employment practices, become less attractive to consumers as well as to prospective employees. To the extent that human flourishing and sustainability become embraced more widely, there will be increased pressures upon organizations to emulate these values in order to attract customers and retain employees.

Of course, the attractiveness of an employer or a job is also greatly contingent upon concrete benefits such as job security, work climate and pay as well as career opportunities, just as price and convenience are likely to remain important to consumers. For employees, it is to be expected that the risk of unemployment and/or limited opportunities for advancement will continue to counteract and limit employee sensitivity to the ethical-political standing of different employers. It is also probably unrealistic to expect a sacrifice of family responsibilities to some higher, collective ideal (although some people willingly make such sacrifices). But, at the same time, it is relevant to recognize that altruism as well as egoism is contingent upon socio-cultural conditions (see Perrow, 1986, for a discussion of how different types of organizational conditions influence such orientations). In the sphere of higher education, for example, pressures of the market economy and a 'customer is king' ideology tend to promote a self-centred, instrumental consumptionist orientation to education which treats qualifications as purchasable commodities. But against this pressure is a counter-tendency towards a greater appreciation of the interdependent, synergistic nature of human activity, an emergent awareness that self-interested actions are frequently counterproductive for personal as well as social development, and an inclination to participate in the activities of pressure groups that campaign for change in relation to specific issues. This is perhaps most evident in growing ecological awareness, but to some extent also more broadly in anti-consumerist standpoints and rebellion against the excesses of materialism (e.g. Klein, 2000).

That said, it seems unlikely that unconditional altruism will, in the foreseeable future, provide a stable or reliable basis for occupational and career choice. That will mean that CMS remains highly relevant, and will continue to contribute to challenging and shifting established perceptions and priorities – for example, by focusing attention upon otherwise neglected or 'hidden' dimensions of corporations with regard to such matters as employee involvement, recruitment and promotion policies, environmental policies, etc. At the very least, exposure to CMS can unsettle conventional views on the relative importance of pay and consumption 'needs' in relation to other concerns – such as the ecological soundness or the social contribution of one's job. As we indicated in Chapter 5, 'consumptionism' is an unreliable source of happiness (Kasser, 2002). Critical insights into consumption may encourage, but obviously cannot dictate, new priorities in life.

It is necessary to acknowledge that CMS provides no ready-made answers or blueprints for action. Indeed, it encourages suspiciousness towards such authoritative (and frequently authoritarian) prescriptions, especially those that lack any democratic mandate. Its contribution is to encourage broader reflection upon what is rational and valuable; and, relatedly, to counteract ideals and discourses that pre-structure choice in accordance with narrow sets of ascribed needs and values. Unforeseeable developments as well as unintended consequences make it impossible to predict outcomes following a change of orientation resulting from exposure to CMS. Any such prediction is inconsistent with the understanding that action is mediated by processes of interpretation whose patterning and effects cannot be reliably calculated. The contribution of CMS is to unsettle the rationality of what is taken for granted and to develop a critical orientation that is not wrong-footed by unexpected events – and not to provide an alternative source of authority to be uncritically complied with. What the dissemination of CMS risks, of course, is the selective appropriation of its insights for purposes – more effective exploitation or domination – that it seeks to question and eradicate.

CMS and Decision Making

As we have argued in earlier chapters, contemporary corporate life produces and reproduces a number of social and environmental irrationalities. These include unsustainable growth, pollution and divisions of class, gender and ethnicity. In addition to these irrationalities and forms of domination and exploitation, there is an overemphasis on careers at the expense of meaningful work; an uncritical adaptation to managerially defined values, norms and beliefs; and the mass media construction of compulsive (consumer) 'needs' and identities. In counteracting these irrationalities, CMS can prompt those involved, who include managers and others (e.g. suppliers, consumers) engaged in the reproduction of corporate capitalism to: (a) consider the implications of these wider concerns for management; and (b) take them into account in decision making in the anticipation that unnecessary suffering will be eliminated and/or opportunities for emancipatory action will be increased.

One example of socially irrational decision making that can have devastating human and ecological consequences is the design and operation of unsafe systems which may result in major industrial accidents accompanied by injury or loss of life and, in the case of the nuclear industry, a toxic legacy for future generations. In many cases, such designs and accidents could have been avoided if only a more reflexive (and less commercially cavalier) approach to risk management had been adopted. It is all too easy and convenient to attribute blame for such accidents to careless individuals or rogue organizations. For, arguably, absence of reflection and care is symptomatic of a politico-economic system in which short-term advantage is sought, often fuelled by bonus payments and performance-related pay, without sufficient regard for the longer-term consequences, human and ecological (Willmott, 2011c). Lack of effective public oversight is partly a consequence of corporate lobbying (Crouch, 2011) but it is also a result of public apathy and weak democratic institutions. As Gephart and Pitter (1993) have argued, accidents are 'often seen to be caused by the failure of individuals to acquire, possess, or implement (relevant) skills or traits' (ibid.: 248), yet they are more plausibly interpreted as a manifestation of a web of social and economic relationships in which a blind eye is turned, more or less knowingly, to the risks inherent in particular activities. Analysing accidents in the oil and gas industries, Gephart and Pitter (ibid.) apply Habermas' (1976) ideas on the connection between economic, political, legitimation and motivation crises to argue that 'rational' decisions inadvertently produce major industrial accidents. A recent example is the nuclear meltdown at the Fukushima plant in Japan in 2011 which has been linked to regulatory capture by the nuclear industry (see Exhibit 1). Part of the problem is that risks inherent in the commercial pressures of capitalism[6] (e.g. to reduce costs and increase returns) are transferred from corporations, via the State, to individual citizens who either suffer directly the consequences of these pressures or, as taxpayers, pick up the tab for remedying their effects. The Challenger disaster – when the space shuttle exploded partly due to evidence of problems being denied – provided an exceptionally traumatic and shocking example of the effects of such pressures (Schwartz, 1990; Vaughan, 1997).

Exhibit 1   A Case of Suspected 'Regulatory Capture'

In 2010, Toru Ishida, the former director general of the Ministry of Economy, Trade and Industry (METI), which has responsibilities that include regulating nuclear industry, left the agency and joined TEPCO (the electricity utility that owns and operates the Fukushima nuclear plant) a few months later to become a senior advisor. He followed Susumu Shirakawa, another METI veteran who was a board member and executive vice-president at TEPCO until retiring in June 2010.

Regulatory capture may have contributed to the cascade of failures which were revealed after the tsunami receded. Regulatory capture may have also contributed to the current situation. Critics argue that the government shares blame with the regulatory agency for not heeding warnings, and for not ensuring the independence of the nuclear industry's oversight while encouraging the expansion of nuclear energy domestically and internationally. World media have argued that the Japanese nuclear regulatory system tends to side with and promote the nuclear industry because of *amakudari* (roughly translated as descent from heaven), in which senior regulators accept high-paying jobs at the companies they once oversaw. To protect their potential future position in the industry, regulators seek to avoid taking positions that upset or embarrass the utilities they regulate. TEPCO's position as the largest electrical utility in Japan led it to be the most desirable position for retiring regulators; typically the 'most senior officials went to work at Tepco, while those of lower ranks ended up at smaller utilities' according to the *New York Times*.

Source: Fukushima Daiichi Nuclear Disaster [Online]. Available at: http://en.wikipedia.org/wiki/Fukushima_Daiichi_nuclear_disaster#International_aftermath. Accessed 5 July 2011.

We are not (quite!) naïve or idealistic enough to believe that increased awareness among decision-makers of the negative consequences of their decisions will make them more willing to sacrifice profits and, by implication, their jobs or career prospects. Nor should we neglect the role of not just greedy individual capitalists but also shareholders representing broad public interests, such as pension funds, not being inclined to accept economic losses for what may be seen as unnecessarily and very costly risk minimization investments. But, to a considerable extent, irrationality and socially unnecessary suffering is a consequence of narrow, technocratic and economic thinking, often further degraded by corruption that simply ignores or conveniently downplays potential risks and disregards alternative priorities and forms of action that could be supported without even significantly damaging profits or jobs. Was it the case that savings made by BP (e.g. from outsourcing and poor risk management) which contributed to the Deepwater Horizon disaster (see Introduction and Chapter 1) were mainly responsive to demands to maximize shareholder value lubricated by bonus payments tied to share options (see BP Annual Report and Accounts, 2009)? The report into the accident, which killed 11 people and caused one of the biggest oil spills in history, concluded that 'The immediate causes of the Macondo well blowout can be traced to a series of identifiable mistakes made by BP, Halliburton, and Transocean that reveal such systematic failures in risk management that they place in doubt the safety culture of the entire industry' (National Commission, 2011: vii). But the report does not illuminate the conditions that nurtured this 'systematic failure' and discredited industry safety culture, including the conditions which fostered a very similar kind of regulatory closure to that which facilitated the expansion and indulgence of the nuclear industry in Japan (*Wall Street Journal*, 2010). Instead, the report lamely concludes that 'Better management by BP, Halliburton and Transocean would almost have certainly prevented the blow-out' (ibid.: 90).

Exhibit 2   The Case Against BP

BP continued cost-cutting policies that pre-dated the explosion at its Texas City refinery in 2005 that killed 15 workers, despite findings by multiple reports linking this strategy to the blast, the investors' lawyers said. 'In 2009 alone, defendants cut BP's operational costs by 15 percent', according to the complaint.

This reduction in budgets and manpower further undermined the company's ability to operate safely as personnel were stretched even thinner and resources that should have been devoted to maintenance, monitoring and addressing crucial safety failures in every aspect of the company's operations were diverted.

'Next Catastrophe'

Any reasonable director sitting on the BP board before the Deepwater Horizon disaster would have recognized that when it came to the next catastrophe, the question was not 'if,' but rather 'when' and 'how bad.'

The lawyers contend that a series of events and regulatory fines since the Texas City explosion should have convinced executives and managers of the need for policy changes. BP's neglect of company pipelines in Alaska caused a March 2006 rupture that spilled 267,000 gallons of crude oil at Prudhoe Bay and led to $20 million in civil and criminal fines against BP, according to the complaint.

(Continued)

(Continued)

The company's internal study into problems at the Alaskan pipeline operations, by Booz Allen Hamilton in March 2007, found that 'BP's top-down budget targets provided a "budget box" in which activities, materials and projects had to fit,' according to the complaint.

Safety Violations

Federal safety regulators fined BP more than $5 million for 'wilful' safety violations at its Ohio refinery from 2006 to 2010, the investor lawyers said. Federal regulators and prosecutors fined BP more than $150 million in combined civil and criminal penalties for safety and environmental violations at the Texas City plant and the company's failure to bring the site into compliance after the fatal 2005 blast, according to the complaint.

The lawsuit also asked that the defendants account for profits and benefits, including salaries, bonuses and stock options, obtained through their alleged misconduct.

Source: Adapted from Fiske and Calkins (2011)

Even though the market economy routinely condones wastefulness (e.g. packaging and disposability) and promotes a predatory attitude to nature, it is often feasible to develop designs and processes that are humanly and ecologically less destructive and not significantly less, and sometimes more, profitable. The problem is that the latter concerns are not strongly prioritized. The idea that there is only one 'best' (i.e. profitable) way of managing organizations has long since been debunked although its seductiveness has been affirmed by the pursuit of 'best practice' (Thompson and Willmott, 2011). Moreover, while, in principle, executives are incentivized by stock options and performance-related pay to maximize profits, in practice there is invariably uncertainty over how this can, or should, be accomplished, if only because different specialists frequently hold strongly divergent views about how resources are to be allocated.

Most managers and other people are not only concerned to make decisions that are 'good enough' (cf. Simon's (1945), concept of bounded rationality; see Chapter 1) but when addressing uncertainties are more inclined to make decisions that are expedient (in terms of *realpolitik*) in the context of prevailing relations of power and domination. Such decision making may include current views of what is morally justifiable as well as assessments of what direction is maximally profitable, with the latter often conditioning the scope of the former. Within corporate governance, for example, there is the core issue of top management acting in their own interest, or in the interest of shareholders, or in that of a wider constituency of stakeholders, although share options are intended to square this particular circle by ensuring that executives prioritize the concerns of shareholders. Sometimes top managers may also be interested in being, or at least appearing to be, 'good corporate citizens' in the eye of the public – for example, by pursuing corporate social responsibility initiatives. Such developments potentially deviate from the goal of maximizing corporate results but corporate social responsibility (CSR) initiatives are typically subordinated to the burnishing of corporate image in an effort to increase the attractiveness of the corporation to investors and the consumers of its brands, and thereby increase shareholder value (Banerjee, 2007). In which case, the pursuit of CSR does not compromise profit-making and the application of instrumental rationality to this end. On the contrary, social responsibility forms part of a 'business case' in which CSR is

> neutralized and pulled back from imaginary possibilities to the actually possible ... CSR is important [to companies] because it is one of the keys to opening up the future ... commoditization and CSR are not enemies but bedfellows ... the big future markets are in areas where the two meet and intertwine ...'many of today's most exciting opportunities lie in controversial areas such as gene therapy, the private provision of pensions, and products and services targeted at low income consumers in poor countries' ... The firms in the best position to open up these opportunities will be the ones perceived as socially responsible. (Hanlon, 2008: 160; see also Hanlon and Fleming, 2009)

While there are intense pressures upon executives to meet investor expectations, as well as huge personal incentives in the form of share options and other inducements to deliver value to shareholders, we deliberately leave open the question of precisely how managerial decision making is shaped and accomplished. It is reductionist and thus misleading, in our view, to account for managerial practice by (pre)conceiving of managers as calculation machines dedicated to perfecting instrumental reason in the service of profit maximization. Neither the myth of profit maximization being the only thing that counts, nor the reactionary Leftist resistance to all reform on the grounds that it extends the life of capitalism, should detract from efforts, including those made by executives, to address ways of reducing needless suffering and waste. That said, as the indented quote above indicates, good intentions are impeded as well as facilitated by the vested interest that corporations have in embracing forms of social responsibility.

To summarize, we have briefly explored three areas in which critical thought may have an influence on managerial decision making: (a) when there is scope for letting various values and criteria make a difference, and enabling other ideals to complement, if not replace, profit maximization; (b) when there is a non-competitive relation between business goals and other ideals; and (c) when decisions are sufficiently ambiguous to permit the inclusion of alternative means of achieving conventionally 'acceptable' outcomes. People who have developed a capacity to think critically and thereby challenge conventional wisdom are, we believe, better equipped to play an active part in shifting the balance from established priorities and objectives towards other, more socially and ecologically defensible goals. CMS can inspire and support a shift in which wider concerns put an imprint on the criteria and considerations governing executive decisions and actions. Despite the pressures of capitalism and its rewarding of rugged individualism, other values – in the form of 'common decency' and 'good intentions' – continue to exert an influence upon management practices. Even though there are many situations where it feels as if there is little or no choice to act, there is often the possibility of acting otherwise. And there are other occasions where values such as autonomy, participation and sustainability can be prioritized, even if it is at the expense of gaining a larger salary cheque or bonus, the fastest promotion or simply making the customer happy. To take a comparatively trivial example, when making a sale, a salesperson may draw attention to ecological considerations, if there is an ecologically more positive alternative within the range of products available, even if this risks annoying the customer or losing some sales. CMS at once supports and appeals to such 'socially responsible' orientations. But it is primarily concerned to encourage and advance more systematic ways of thinking and acting that go beyond, or better galvanize, individual conscience and interventions and associated piecemeal improvements.

The Reflective and the Unreflective Practitioner: Two Illustrations

We now illustrate elements of the preceding sections of this chapter by giving examples of very different orientations in terms of reflectiveness (see Reynolds, 1998). We highlight: (a) variations in terms of ways of relating to what we do, (b) the possibilities for reflection, and (c) the relevance of reflection (see also Rostis and Helms Mills, 2010).

   We take our examples from self-reports of the work of executives. The first case is taken from the book *Odyssey* (1988) by John Sculley, who subsequently was hired by Steve Jobs to become CEO at Apple (Kahney, 2010), where he describes his time as a top executive at Pepsi when the company was embroiled in the so-called 'Cola Wars'. The following is an extract from an important executive meeting:

> Like the other meetings, this one was a ceremonial event. We marked it on our calendars many weeks in advance. Everyone wore the unofficial corporate uniform: a blue pin-striped suit, white shirt, and a sincere red tie. None of us would ever remove his jacket. We dressed and acted as if we were at a meeting of the board of directors. (ibid.: 2)

During the meeting, Pepsi is declared to be Number One in the USA market. It had captured a 30.8 per cent share compared to Coca-Cola's 29.2 per cent. The executives were, to say the least, elated:

> It was one of those moments for which you worked your entire career. We always believed, since the early seventies, when *Pepsi* was widely viewed as the perennial also-ran, that we could do it. All of us started out with that objective, and we never took our eyes off it. (ibid.: 3)

John Sculley then goes on to disclose, with a touch of self-deprecation, his own attitude towards this enterprise:

> If I was brash or arrogant on my way to the top, it mattered little to me. I was an impatient perfectionist. I was willing to work relentlessly to get things exactly right. I was unsympathetic to those who couldn't deliver the results I demanded. (ibid.: 4)

> Winning to me, was an obsession. I was driven not only by the competition but by the force of powerful ideas. I demanded the best of myself. If I walked away from an assignment not totally consumed or absorbed to near exhaustion, I felt guilty about it. Dozens had failed at this regimen, but to me, Pepsi was a comfortable home. (ibid.: 7)

Sculley assures his readers that the rules at Pepsi were fair, even though executives who failed were quickly replaced ('either your numbers went up and continued to grow, or you began to comb the classifieds for a job elsewhere'). He and his colleagues (at that time, Pepsi appears to have been populated exclusively by male executives) 'didn't complain'. Being critical of the company was taken as a mark of personal failure to adjust and deliver (see also Jackall, 1988). Complaining was simply inappropriate behaviour among the Pepsi managers, who regarded themselves as

> the best of the best. In a corporation populated with bright, ambitious achievers ... they had proven ... they were intellectually and physically fit survivors in America's corporate Marine Corps. (ibid.: 2)

Sculley and his colleagues appear to have behaved like the members of a religious cult whose prospects of salvation were measured in the sales of sweetened water. Through rigid codes (e.g. dressing), and through carefully orchestrated rituals ('public hangings' for poor performance), discipline and conformity at Pepsi were tightly maintained, supported by a strong, almost comical sense of masculinity (the heroes of sweetened water selling). In this context, it became unreasonable, indeed mad, to ask: What is the purpose of the Pepsi Corporation? Does it accomplish anything socially valuable? For members of the 'corporate Marine Corps', work was self-evidently purposeful so long as more sweetened water was sold, and the ultimate prize was to outsell Coca-Cola. A person working for the Red Cross, saving people from starving to death; a member of a resistance group fighting a cruel dictator; or a researcher solving the mystery of cancer or Aids – these could not have been more committed than Sculley and his fellow executives were to increasing Pepsi's sales. The meaning of life was defined in terms of competitiveness – external as well as internal – through career progression and in the service of corporate growth and profitability. Friendship, family and other interests were pushed to the margins. Complaints, doubts or questioning were not tolerated, being viewed as forms of disloyalty and personal inadequacy. When working for Pepsi, the purpose of being Number One was self-evident and unquestioned. To doubt, or to become deflected from this purpose, was heresy.

The example is instructive not only because it gives some insight into the motivation of executives and the intense, self-enforced pressures upon them but also because it illustrates the dedication and perseverance that can be directed towards even the most trivial of goals. Consider, then, what energies could be mobilized in pursuit of more substantial values and significant objectives. At Pepsi, it would seem that reflection was restricted to perfecting the means of enhancing short-term competitive capacities. The sales figures were more significant than anything else – even the profitability of the corporation – since, although related, the cost of increasing market share may have outweighed any benefits accrued to shareholders. To raise questions about the priority given to sales, except to ask how they might be further increased, was inconceivable. Today, it would seem that sales are no less important but their generation is accomplished in large part through forms of product placement, sponsorship and, most recently, 'crowdsourcing' (see Exhibit 3).

Exhibit 3   Pepsi Ditches the Super Bowl, Embraces Crowdsourced Philanthropy Instead

Source: Schwartz, 2010

'Sorry, Super Bowl ad lovers. Instead of spending millions on commercials for this year's game, Pepsi is putting its cash in the Refresh Project, an online cause marketing campaign that asks readers how the company should give away its grant money.

Starting February 1, readers can vote to give grants to a number of health, environment, culture, and education-related organizations. Pepsi plans to give away multiple grants each month, including two $250,000 grants, 10 $50,000 grants, and 10 $25,000 grants. Visitors are also encouraged to submit their own organizations and grant ideas.

Is this just a cost-cutting move for Pepsi? Partially. Pepsi spent $33 million on Super Bowl advertising last year, and the Refresh Project will cost $20 million. Instead of blowing the cash on a single night of football, Pepsi's investment will attract visitors throughout the year. The project will also have the potential to reach an audience that might not check out Pepsi's famous Super Bowl commercials. Regardless of its motives, Pepsi's initiative is another step towards the mainstreaming of crowdsourced philanthropy'.

In defence of corporations like Pepsi, it may be objected that critical analysis draws attention only to the dark side of management. It is, indeed, the dark side that critical studies seek to illuminate and challenge, and not least because this is effectively hidden by the public face of corporations presented through advertising and PR activities. Whatever valuable contributions corporations like Pepsi make to the well-being of employees, customers and to the planet more generally (and, in the case of corporations like Pepsi, this contribution is rather difficult to detect) can be readily acknowledged. But it should not obscure or displace a willingness to consider what is occluded or marginalized within glossy, upbeat, uncritical accounts of their activities and effects. From a critical perspective, the demands placed upon (Pepsi) executives (by peer pressure as much as by any 'external force', notably shareholders) are not regarded as 'given' or 'inevitable' but, rather, are viewed as symptomatic of a capitalist economy in which a particular objective – the pursuit of profitable growth and/or market share – tends to take priority over all other concerns. Currently, enormous amounts of human effort are marshalled and expended in producing and selling goods, such as sweetened water, to inflate the egos of executives (as Sculley demonstrates) or to increase the returns of shareholders, instead of being devoted to activities that, by almost any criterion, would be of greater personal and social value. In a sense, executives and consumers are pawns in the game of increasing market share and maximizing profit as they come to believe – or can imagine no alternative to the consumer capitalist mantra that the good things in life are obtainable only by devoting their lives to, or spending money on – commodities whose desirability is constructed through an association with other pleasurable (e.g. identity enhancing) images (see Chapters 3 and 5).[7]

From this broader perspective, the senior executives at Pepsi and equivalent corporations, no less than the consumers of their products and services, can be viewed as victims as well as perpetrators of a mind-numbing fantasy that mystifies and displaces what, upon critical reflection, is of greater personal and social importance. This tension may be partially sensed by executives, consumers and others who struggle to comprehend the genesis of such irrationality because they do not have the relevant, critical resources for making sense of it. CT and associated forms of critical analysis, we have suggested, can provide such resources: CT can stimulate critique as well as inform it and guide initiatives oriented to personal and social change.

The account of Pepsi provided by John Sculley can be contrasted with an interview given by Harald Agerley, chairman of one of Denmark's largest industrial companies (published by the Danish daily newspaper *Information*, 14 October 1991). Agerley, who at the time was nearing retirement, describes how, for many years, his company invested heavily in the cleaning of waste, cutting down the usage of water and energy consumption, and reducing pollution from heavy metals, etc. Affirming our earlier observations about how such initiatives provide a 'key to opening up the future' where 'commoditization and CSR are not enemies but bedfellows' (Hanlon, 2008: 160), Agerley stresses the possibility and importance of greener strategies in business life. But, crucially, he also remarks that this is *not sufficient*, as he questions whether ecologically sound business practice is fully reconcilable with the profitable operation of corporations. Agerley also acknowledges how his own company has traded on a positive image (which, in common with other PR-savvy executives – such as Richard Branson, Chairman of Virgin – Agerley costlessly promotes by giving

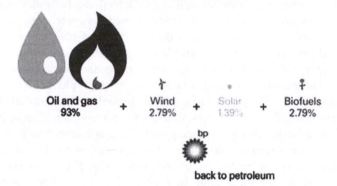

Figure 8.2   *BP wins Greenpeace Award for Worst Greenwash of 2008*

Source: www.greenpeace.org.uk

newspaper interviews). He argues that the commercial contribution of securing a favourable 'green' image is commercially important but also quite limited. The commercial payoffs of ecologically correct business policies, he suggests, are much exaggerated (because they rarely are worth the opportunity cost in terms of delivering requisite levels of profitable growth).

In Agerley's judgment, the idea that companies will reform their policies by being persuaded that ethical and ecological soundness is 'good for business' is seductive but ultimately chimerical. For substantial change to be achieved, he argues, governments must intervene to reform business practice. *Inter alia*, the following measures are identified: forcing companies to provide information about the ecological consequences of their products, taxing materials that are in short supply, increasing taxation on energy usage, and requiring companies to dispose of exhausted products. Unusually for a businessman (even one nearing retirement!), doubts are also publicly raised about the wisdom and sustainability of continuing economic growth, at least in the industrialized world. Given the standard of living enjoyed by a majority of people in the West, Agerley asks whether 'we have not arrived at a point where we should end our apparently insatiable hunger for more material goods'. He suggests that the West could sensibly produce more only if this were directed to the development of other countries.

When considering the reflections of Sculley and Agerley upon their business experiences, it is a little too easy to cast Sculley as an American 'devil incarnate' and Agerley as a European 'saint'. It is true that Sculley does not directly question Pepsi's mission or its business practices – including its cavalier treatment of staff ('improve or walk'). Nonetheless, his account is valuable in providing some insights into the values and priorities of major companies such as Pepsi Corporation. Even if Sculley does not directly relate life at Pepsi to the logic of capitalist enterprise, his account can stimulate critical reflection upon the purpose of such corporations and, in particular, the demands that are made upon their staff. In the case of Agerley, it is relevant to note that his company's success in decreasing pollution was in part a function of its previously high levels of energy consumption and pollution. It can also be argued that the views expressed by executives like Agerley (and amplified by ourselves), in which a different logic to that which currently dominates the world of business is advocated, are something of a luxury unless it can be shown that the application of deeply green policies, for example, will disproportionately benefit those who are currently most disadvantaged.

A Garbage-Can Model of Critical Thought

In earlier chapters, we have argued that decision making in modern organizations tends to be seen as an instrumentally rational process. Executives are obliged to wrap up their proposals in a rhetoric of rationality and to articulate their decisions in the ostensibly impartial language of efficiency and effectiveness (Adler et al., 2007; Meyer and Rowan, 1977). A rhetorical gloss of rationality, such as 'There is only one (rationally warranted) best way' and so 'There is no (reasonable) alternative', can belie the extent to which decision making is a 'non-rational' activity. Indeed, decision making has been likened to a 'garbage can' (March and Olsen, 1976) where decisions are frequently the product of more or less random, unsystematic and unpredictable processes.

From a critical standpoint, in contrast, decisions are seen to be infused by politics (see Chapter 1). March and Olsen do not directly address the politics of decision making but they do illuminate how decision-makers find themselves in a more complex, less stable world than the one described by standard theories of organization and organizational choice (see Chapter 3). The moment of choosing is, they suggest, '*a meeting place for issues and feelings* looking for decision situations in which they may be aired, solutions looking for issues to which they may be an answer, and participants looking for problems or pleasure' (ibid.: 25, emphasis in original).

When revisited from a critical perspective, two intertwined issues that arise in decision-making processes can be identified: those related to the sphere of instrumental rationality (efficiency, profits, etc.), and those falling within the politico-ethical sphere (ecology, democracy, autonomy, equality, etc.). Of course, these 'issues' are, in practice, fused, and the distinction is heuristic. The pursuit of efficiency, for example, is underpinned by a politico-ethical normative framework that ascribes legitimacy to this priority; the problems addressed and the solutions chosen may be more or less subordinated to an efficiency or profit maximization/satisficing logic; and the orientation of participants may be more or less democratic. Also, and as we have repeatedly argued, the *ambiguity* of many situations, as well as the anticipation of (adverse) outcomes, may stimulate critical reflection (Chia, 1994; Clegg et al., 2007), although anxieties associated with ambiguities may also inhibit such reflection. With these considerations in mind, it is possible to explore the extent to which a decision is more or less openly explored, or scrutinized, in communicative terms.

The iron grip of instrumental rationality is loosened when diverse considerations and values inform decision-making processes.[8] If we combine the notion of a *potentially* reflective and critical manager, as a person capable of instantiating critical discourse, with the ambiguity of decision processes, we can then posit 'critical reflection' as a fifth stream that runs alongside, or perhaps is a dimension of, the activities identified by March and Olson (that is, problems, solutions, participants and choice). When critical reflection intercedes with a particular problem (people/solution/choice/opportunity), it may inspire and guide efforts to influence a decision (see Forester, 1981, 1993).

It then follows that at least two kinds of links can be made between critical reflection and the four streams identified by March and Olson. The first concerns interpretation. Problems are normally open to many interpretations – upon which the possible solutions depend – which may be more or less technocratic or critically reflective. Deetz (1992a) speaks of the politics of representation, arguing that the language used to perceive and describe a phenomenon is of key importance. Critical interpretation can serve to highlight how 'favoured' representations routinely reproduce the prevailing pattern of domination as alternative representations are marginalized or suppressed (Mumby, 1997; see Chapter 4). In Chapter 7, we illustrated this point by using the example of a top manager explicitly identifying his audience as the managers of the company. The same goes for solutions: there are alternative solutions available for most problems, but conventions and institutionalized patterns of thought exclude or devalue such options. The contribution of critical thinking is to open up awareness of other possibilities for interpreting and acting upon streams of problems and solutions.

A second, related link to critical reflection concerns how 'the meeting place for issues and feelings' can trigger processes of critical reflection when found by a 'fifth' stream of activity (see Mumby and Putnam, 1992). Diverse politico-ethical dimensions of issues may then be discerned and addressed. These include domination, gender inequality, exploitation of personnel, environmental pollution, waste of resources, communication of misleading (dishonest) images to the public (e.g. through corporate branding, marketing strategies that have harmful social and psychological effects), acquisitions of companies to gain and exploit a monopoly position, leaders creating dependence amongst followers, and so on. The intervention of critical thinking enables decision-making situations to be interpreted in ways that are attentive to wider circumstances and effects, and not just to considerations that are most tightly coupled to established goals, such as growth or profits. Such thinking may be more sporadic than continuous, but it can also be cumulative to the extent that learning occurs in the process of addressing specific issues. For this to happen, however, established practices and routines of decision making must be at least partially disrupted or suspended. As Deetz (1992a: 29) has observed, the struggle to develop less destructive and divisive institutions is not 'against some powerful force out there that directs thought and action'. Rather, struggles for emancipatory change are with 'forgotten, hidden, misrecognized, suppressed conflict – the disciplinary power – of the momentary practice' (ibid.). The critical intent is to open up 'the micro-practices of closure' within and beyond corporations so that alternative courses of action can be recognized, considered and pursued.

Despite the restrictiveness of corporate discourse – which was illustrated earlier in Sculley's account of his experience of working at the Pepsi Corporation – there are often possibilities for deploying skilful means of unsettling conventional wisdom and stimulating critical reflection without suffering outright rejection. Disrupting the habitual tendency towards cognitive closure (closed-mindedness), to which Deetz points, is certainly not easy. It is possible to 'undo' embedded assumptions, thought patterns and institutional practices, as management gurus repeatedly assert, but this requires political will. There has been a good deal of 'reinvention' in organizations during the past two decades or more when corporations have de-layered, outsourced, restructured and so on. The challenge is to 'undo' in other directions – directions that are more democratic, less oppressive and more ecologically sustainable. To this end, advocates of change may talk the language of 'transformational leadership', 'empowerment' and 'constant change', and so appear to raise challenging questions of the status quo and to advocate radical agendas. Without nay-saying their efforts, it is vitally important to appreciate the limits and instrumentalism of such programmes. So often their purpose is to 'shake things up' in order to make actual proposals seem tolerably moderate and sensible in comparison.

In this context, recognizing and contributing to the existence of critical thinking in the contents of the 'garbage cans' of decision making is a worthwhile endeavour. That said, improving the odds for discursive openness and critical thought in corporations is not a panacea, and not least because there is a 'bigger picture'. That 'bigger picture' may, somewhat grandly, be termed 'global governance'. And, indeed, corporations themselves play an increasingly significant part in shaping the ideologies as well as in designing the procedures and delivering the processes of governance (Edward and Willmott, 2008; in press). Notably, their influence and reach, with respect to regulation and financial flows for example, increasingly rivals or exceeds that of many nation states (see Exhibit 4). Drawing upon Klein's (2007) analysis, Matten (2009: 568) observes how 'postwar Keynesian welfare state institutions have been weakened and privatized', not only in many advanced economies but in many developing and transitional economies as well; and how 'private corporations have become involved in delivering military services, homeland security, disaster relief, health care, and education' (see also Barley, 2007); and, finally, how especially in post-communist and developing countries, 'private corporations have become pivotal players with a degree of political influence that rivals, if not eclipses, the influence and power of governments' (Matten, 2009: 568–569). Of course, these very significant developments will come as little surprise to students of Critical Theory, who are inclined to regard liberal democracy more as a progressive conduit of capitalist development than as a force capable of effectively restraining its expansionary destructiveness (as has most recently been demonstrated by the regulatory failures leading up to the 2008 financial meltdown). For such reasons, it is relevant to connect the critical study of management to the wider context of global development and change (Scherer, Palazzo and Bauman, 2006; Scherer and Palazzo, 2011).

Exhibit 4   Growth and Distribution

- From 1960 to 1980, the rate of economic growth for all countries (excluding China) was somewhere between 3.2 per cent and 5.5 per cent. From 1980 to 2000, those numbers were somewhere between 2.6 per cent and 0.7 per cent. In other words, the general lot of economic growth has actually slowed during the age of globalization.
- From 1980 to the mid-1990s, there was dramatic economic growth in 15 countries, raising the incomes of about 1.5 billion people. Over the same time period, approximately 100 countries experienced a decline in economic growth, lowering the incomes of about 1.6 billion people. In 70 of those countries, the average income fell below the 1980 level. Thus, some countries got richer while others got poorer.
- According to data from the year 2000, 1 per cent of the world's richest adults own 40 per cent of global assets and the richest 10 per cent own 85 per cent of the world total.
- According to a 2007 study, the pay for the average American CEO was 364 times higher than the average American worker. In 1980, that difference was only 40 times higher.

Source: Adapted from Del Gandio (2008: 183)

Global Justice and Critical Management

The fall of the Berlin wall and the rise of China as a leading economic superpower make it even more apparent that the profit motive is the foremost, hegemonic driver of international economic expansion (Del Gandio, 2008; see also Exhibit 4). In this process, divisions between affluence and poverty have tended to become further widened and deepened (Castells, 2003), and ecological irresponsibility has hardly been curbed. Global economic growth has been accompanied by some changes of a potentially progressive character, such as internet-based communications. These, on balance, are to be welcomed and protected, although they are also used to communicate trivial and commercial messages and values, and internet-surfing hardly encourages intellectual depth. Partially progressive changes scarcely disguise or redress how capitalist expansion exploits and actually widens social divisions, as dramatically demonstrated by the fall-out from the global financial crisis of 2008 where the debt from which bankers made fortunes during the previous decade. This expansion also has been nationalized escalates ecological destruction, as demonstrated in the generation of elaborate carbon trading schemes that support business-as-usual instead of dealing with the issue head-on by intervening, through taxation and incentives, to reduce the burning of fossil fuels and to introduce renewable alternatives. This is an example of how 'the expansion of capital trumps actual public interest in protecting the vital conditions of life' (Foster and Clark, 2009). Political and economic elites have resisted advocating and introducing such measures, often disingenuously point-ing to the lack of public support as a fig-leaf to conceal their own investment in the status quo. For, clearly, 'any substantial transformation in social-environmental relations would mean challenging the treadmill of production itself, and launching an ecolog-ical-cultural revolution' (ibid.). This critique of the cancerous spread of contempo-rary capitalist development across the planet is, of course, shared by social movements whose objectives are congruent with those of critical students of management, and from which, in principle, much may be gained in mutual learning and sharing.

Consider, for example, how feminist ideas and modes of organizing have been central to the UN world conferences on women, the Latin American Feminist *encuen-tros* and also to NGOs providing popular education around women's human rights. As Ferguson (2006) argues, these developments point to the possibility of forging 'an alternative economy, an alternative politics and oppositional community networks that can flower into full-fledged movements against corporate globalization and a more robust moral vision of a better world'. In a similar register, but on an even wider terrain, it is possible to connect key elements in CMS to the aspirations of the Global Justice Movement which emphasize the importance of self-determination as an alternative to continued dependence upon corporate patronage or marginalization:

> We stand for the right of communities to control their own destinies and resources, whether that is an indigenous community preserving its land and culture or a neigh-bourhood deciding to keep its local hospital open. Enterprises and businesses must be rooted in communities and accountable to them. ... We also say that democracy, community, and true abundance are the real antidote to the despair that breeds terrorism, and the best means of assuring our global security. (Starhawk, 2000; see also Cavanagh and Anderson, 2002)

Affinities between the respective aspirations of CMS and the Global Justice Movement indicate the possibility of forging stronger, mutually enriching connec-tions between their respective concerns. Individual members of CMS already par-ticipate in movements that oppose corporate-led globalization – for example, by fostering a sustainability ethos that gives priority to biodiversity, water usage and carbon emission (e.g. Saravanamuthu et al., 2007). Extending such involvements and initiatives, there is the potential to develop closer institutional links – for example, by making connections between struggles for global justice and insights of CMS research into the operation of global institutions such as the World Bank, the Inter-national Monetary Fund, the G8, and the World Trade Organization.

Banerjee (2007: 102 *et seq.*), for example, highlights the exclusion of human rights and inclusion of property rights (TRIPS) in World Trade Organization agreements, noting how the WTO succumbed to lobbying by powerful transnational corpor-ations in the chemicals, pharmaceuticals and information technology industries. His analysis (ibid.: 105 *et seq.*) points to the damaging consequences of imposing a regime of intellectual property rights on indigenous knowledge. To address these concerns, Banerjee urges that greater attention be given to the range of social movements and organized collective efforts – which could include CMS as well as groups participating in the World Social Forum, for example – committed to addressing the most pressing contemporary problems of corporate social responsibility with respect to poverty, democracy and climate change.

To this end, it is relevant simultaneously to develop a close appreciation of the role and logic of 'global managerialism' as well as corporate and personal philanthropy (e.g. IBM, the Gates Foundation) in addressing yet also reproducing and legitimizing grossly unequal patterns of resource distribution presided over by global institutions. In another exemplary contribution to CMS scholarship, Murphy (2008) provides an empirically rich and disturbing analysis of the role of the World Bank in processes of global economic homogenization. More specifically, Murphy's study discloses how, as a dominant player within a complex of formal and informal transnational organizational networks (e.g. Davos, Bilderberg), the World Bank exports concertive control strategies into the international development domain. Through detailed, participant-observation case studies of the financing of the Karmet steel mill in Kazakstan and World Bank education initiatives in Niger and India, Murphy shows how global elites colonize their clientele through an appealing invocation of ostensibly de-politicized programmatic rhetorics of 'partnership', 'participation' and 'inclusivity'.

In such ways, critical thinking in CMS research reaches out beyond the conventionally and narrowly defined sphere of 'management studies' in ways that can provide resources for informed protests and progressive challenges to the operation of corporations as 'instruments of domination and exploitation' (CMS Division of the Academy of Management Domain Statement, available at http://group.aomonline.org/cms/About/domain.htm). By extolling and disseminating research in which corporations and managerialism are situated in a wider context (see Barley, 2007), there is an enhanced prospect of making connections between CMS research and resonant forms of activism, (e.g. Böhm and Brei, 2008). Forging such links can, moreover, help to 'connect the practical shortcomings in management and concerns of individual managers to the demands of a socially divisive and ecologically destructive system within which managers work' (CMS Division Domain Statement). In making these connections, critical management academics are involved in educating present and potential managers as well as a much wider audience who are affected, as citizens and consumers for example, by management practices that are guided and legitimized by particular, uncritical theories of organization, marketing, accounting and so on (see Chapters 2–6).

Situating CMS in the Context of Management Education and Research

We have stressed the importance of situating CMS in a wider context where links can be made to other movements for change, including participants in the Global Justice Movement. The primary focus of CMS, however, is managerial practice; and its distinctive contribution lies in enabling managers, managers-to-be and the many others affected by management to become acquainted with critical thinking about management. We indicated earlier how proponents of CMS can reach out to a wider audience through a number of channels but here we concentrate on how CMS may influence management education as well as research on management. Addressing this concern raises issues about the politics and practice of educational institutions and learning media as much as it does about the intellectual strength and student appeal of CMS.

Clearly much general education about management occurs through media to which management academics have limited access, and over which they exert very little direct control (see Grey, 2003; Sikka, 2008; http://www.nationaltheatre.org.uk/rss.php?id=15 for examples). Management education also occurs, formally or informally, 'in-house' within workplaces where CMS can have some influence when its advocates deliver courses or produce materials that are drawn upon for such purposes. In what follows, we restrict our discussion to the content and delivery of management education within educational establishments as this is the sphere where critical management academics currently exercise most influence. Much of what we have to say about this context has relevance for processes of education and training occurring within corporations (see Bierema, 2010). In each sphere, as Boje and Al Avkoubi (2009: 119) argue, education is a powerful vehicle for the development of a more just and enlightened world:

> Privileging a new political, economic, social and cultural system based on justice, human wellbeing, and respect of human dignity entails a new educational order that challenges well embedded assumptions and goes beyond the quick fixes.

A concern to raise the status and legitimacy of management education, primarily by founding it upon academic research rather than practitioner anecdotes, has resulted in business schools becoming 'academicized' (Khurana, 2007). An unintended consequence of situating business schools in universities has been the recruitment of staff who are interested in applying critical reason to a range of management specialisms, topics and issues in a way that is not confined to a managerial agenda or restricted to solving problems-as-identified-by-managers. While it is probably unrealistic to expect such critically inclined staff to exert a leading or dominant influence in their respective fields, some space has opened up for pursuing critical agendas in management and business degrees; and this has been considerably assisted in recent years by critiques emanating from disaffected authorities in the mainstream (e.g. Bennis and O'Toole, 2005; Ghoshal, 2005) as well as by a succession of corporate scandals and, most recently, by the failed management and meltdown of the financial system. The opportunities for disseminating more critical, or at least less managerialist, understandings of management has also expanded as management education has been offered to students in other disciplines, such as engineering and languages.

Some commentators have assessed the widespread increase of students entering higher education as a progressive force, making it less likely that employees will be inclined to subordinate themselves to capitalist exploitation. In this respect, a parallel can be drawn with the tendential emancipatory consequence of education in general in formenting demands for the revolutionary overthrow of oppressive regimes, as has recently been witnessed in the 'Arab Spring' (see Adler, 2002). Our own view is more sanguine. For us, the politically progressive consequences of higher education are debatable, not least because students in the field of business and management, at least, have already invested in the fantasy of a conventional managerial career, and so are perhaps less open to alternatives than students taking many other courses. Furthermore, as Boltanski and Chiapello (2007) have argued, critical insights into management may be recuperated to develop more sophisticated forms of control. With these circumstances in mind, we now consider the potential of CMS in shaping the future of management education.

Education as Agenda Setting

Management departments and business schools (hereafter 'business schools') are becoming key socializing agencies for the intelligentsia, or more accurately the middle-level technocracy, of advanced capitalist societies. By dint of their numbers alone, management academics exert an increasing influence – mainly over the students they teach but also in university committees. The remarkable growth of business schools means that their faculties are set to become increasingly influential in shaping the very meaning and future of education. Such opportunities are precious because, as we noted in Chapter 2, in contrast to traditional Marxism, education based upon a broader base of critical theory does not claim the support of any particular class or party (or unions). The implication is that all educational media become key channels for facilitating change. In this context, there are pressures upon all academics to endorse or passively accept the values and priorities of managerial elites. In the case of business academics, this compliance may be oiled by access to lucrative consultancy work and/or contributions to executive education programmes. But business academics also continue to enjoy some measure of 'academic freedom' which means that even their involvement in such programmes and/or the pursuit of consultancy can present opportunities for the introduction of elements of a critical approach. In many ways – by seizing the opportunity to develop and apply a range of professional and technical skills that facilitate access to executives, for example – critical management academics can address contradictions as a conscious force for change (Fenwick, 2005; Foster and Wiebe, 2011).

Working in business schools also presents opportunities to offer policy advice to decision-making centres in society (see Knights and Scarbrough, 2010). In turn, this can facilitate the dissemination of ideas that provide a more grounded illumination, illustration and critique of the operation of the 'purposive-rational subsystems' in contemporary society (see, for example, Sikka and Willmott, 1995). In a wide-ranging critique of aspirations to 'rebalance' the UK economy, Froud et al. (2010) note that problems of regional imbalance and dependence on public sector job creation outside the South-East region of the UK (which radiates out from London as its hub) can be traced at least as far back as the 1980s. To reverse the reliance upon the financial sector centred in the City of London and Docklands, and associated decline of British manufacturing, a series of sector specific tax privileges is proposed as incentives for manufacturers to expand output and invest in capacity and workforce skills (see Exhibit 5).

Exhibit 5   Land Value Tax

Strategies of relocation and new regional agencies could be backed up by the introduction of a land value tax which would go some way towards reducing the attractions of the South-East. Land value tax is an annual tax on the rental value of land (not on the property or infrastructure built upon it). Because land is difficult to hide in an offshore account, the tax is difficult to evade, and it provides an incentive for owners of vacant and under-used land to use their resource more productively or to make way for others who will. By definition a land value tax would therefore bear less heavily on those regions where land has little value, and it would work to divert economic activity away from the centre and into the regions. It could also be used as a substitute for other taxes on labour or firms in order to encourage investment in the regions where land values are lower. The tax could be used imaginatively to promote a range of local social and economic initiatives.

This is an example of how critical management academics can contribute directly to the process of dialogue in which policy is formed. In this process, their proposals are likely to come into conflict with aspects of a world that are hostile to CMS. Indeed, it would be uncanny if they did not. Resistance to CMS is fuelled not only by its challenge to conventional wisdom but also by deeply entrenched dependencies on the labour market, business, government and political elites. As we noted earlier, such dependencies can stimulate critical reflection and thereby facilitate a greater openness to the insights of CMS. But it may also frustrate processes of critical reflection when proposals are rejected on ideological grounds for being out of line with conventional wisdom (see Stepanovich, 2009). Even so, when making comparisons between the respective worlds of practising managers, policy-advisors and politicians on the one hand, and CT or CMS on the other, there is a danger of only identifying points of difference and overlooking possible points of *rapprochement* and commonality (see Chapter 7).

It should not be assumed that all prospective recipients of CMS are wholly immune to changing expectations and values in society. So, despite pressures to regard the status quo as given and legitimate, and for decisions to be viewed as being based upon impersonal, technically rational criteria, there is often some awareness, albeit disavowed publicly, of how the selection and application of these criteria are a product of political and ethical choice (see Chapter 2). Only in the world of 'decisionism', as Habermas (1974) characterizes it, is it assumed that the values currently dominating corporate activity are natural or lie beyond the reach of rational debate. So, despite much institutional and ideological resistance to its claims, the insights of critical thinking, often in very dilute form, are beginning to infiltrate the management sciences, as our review of the growing literature indicates (see especially Chapters 4–6) and as is more extensively demonstrated in the *Oxford Handbook of*

Critical Management Studies (Alvesson et al., 2009). This suggests that there is some overlap between the emergent concerns of practitioners and the perennial issues articulated by CT that have been taken up by critical students of management, albeit that their overlap is partial and precarious.

The wider dissemination of critical thinking is vital for championing and facilitating progressive forms of change without being didactic or overbearing. In principle, the approach most consistent with CT is one of dialogue, rather than monological lecturing, so that students are enabled to view themselves and their situation in a new and meaningful light (Grey et al., 1996). For teaching to be effective, it is certainly necessary, yet insufficient, for the teacher to be knowledgeable about CMS, and to be committed to its emancipatory agenda. Additionally, it is necessary to connect to the preoccupations, hopes and fears of students (Knights and Willmott, 2012). Bridging between the experiences and aspirations of students and the insights of critical thinking can be pursued in various ways but, in doing so, it is vital that tensions between critical thinking and the pressure to deliver results in an imperfect corporate world are acknowledged and appreciated (Dehler, 2009; Sinclair, 2007). Otherwise, CMS is destined to be a purely intellectual exercise, decoupled from possible change in organizations, and assuming the identity of a 'CMS' researcher may operate to stop rather than stimulate critical self-reflection (Perriton and Reynolds, 2004). Or, even worse, it may simply produce a reactionary reinforcement of the thinking that it strives to challenge. And, in this regard, the emergence of critiques of CMS are to be welcomed in aiding reflection and revisiting the rationale for, and direction of, the critical study of management (e.g. Thompson, 2005; Jones et al., 2006; Rowlinson and Hassard, 2011, see also Note 1).

During the past decade or so, the appearance and impact of relevant, critically oriented textbooks (e.g. Knights and Willmott, 2007; Linstead et al., 2009) and access to critical scholarship across a range of management specialisms (Alvesson and Willmott, 2011; Alvesson et al., 2009) are a significant development. Close-up studies allowing teachers to illustrate aspects of corporate life are also valuable for the development of CMS-inspired teaching (e.g. Bavington, 2010; see also Myers, 2008). What Spicer et al. (2009; see also Chapter 7) identify as five principles for critical performativity – including an ethic of care, a focus on potentialities and a more pragmatic and normative stance – may also inspire and guide critical management education, and thereby enable CMS to bear on, and influence, corporate practice through the students that are drawn to its agenda.

Nor should the contribution of hard-hitting, confrontational critiques, such as presented in the film *The Age of Stupid* or Klein's *No Logo* or *The Shock Doctrine*, be ignored. When the mass market equivalents of the worthy CMS article are not casually dismissed as too popular, too negative or as simply irrelevant, they can provide an invaluable antidote to the complacency of mainstream thinking. A possible way forward, then, is for CMS-guided education to include and alternate between radical, challenging ideas and their more pragmatic applications (Spicer et al., 2009). This proposal accommodates a spectrum of ways for introducing and applying critical thinking. Given the intellectual distance between conventional and critical forms of thinking, teachers who position their pedagogy in the broad tradition of CMS are probably more effective (and more consistent with the dialogical and self-directing philosophy of CMS) when they acknowledge a range of standpoints rather than attempting to impose a single framework that students are then left either to embrace or reject.

From Action Learning to Critical Action Learning

One area where conventional approaches to management education overlap with critical thinking is Action Learning (AL). AL encourages participation in the sharing of knowledge and constructively criticizing others' diagnoses and prescriptions (McLaughlin and Thorpe, 1993; Reynolds and Vince, 2004).[9] Moreover, this process is directed to, and by, self-development rather than a concern to learn about theories or models merely as a means of career advancement or for sitting examinations (see, for example, Vidaillet and Vignon, 2010).

An important feature of AL is its appreciation of, and sensitivity towards, some of the more troublesome and 'darker' aspects of organizational life. As McLaughlin and Thorpe (1993: 25) have observed, by openly sharing knowledge and constructively criticizing others' diagnoses and prescriptions, participants in AL groups '*can become aware of the primacy of politics, both macro and micro, and the influence of power on decision making and non-decision making, not to mention the "mobilization of bias"*' (emphasis added). In this reference to 'the primacy of politics' and 'the "mobilization of bias"', a connection is made between the embodied insights gained in processes of AL, with attention to the experiences of managing where priority is given to self-development rather than the acquisition of decontextualized knowledge, and ideas that we have explored in previous chapters (see also Fenwick, 2003). However, making this connection is by no means automatic as it depends upon the meaning and significance attributed to whatever discussions and 'confessions' emerge in AL processes.

We can illuminate the difference between AL and much traditional management education by considering three possible ways of responding to insights into 'the primacy of politics'. The *first* response is to regard such insights as another 'nugget of knowledge' about people, organizations and society that is irrelevant, except for career or other instrumental purposes, to self-development. A *second* response is to integrate the insights of Action Learning into the individual's *established* repertoires of knowing and acting. The insights then serve to increase, or refine, the individual's existing range of tools and techniques for pursuing current priorities which themselves are not subject to critical scrutiny. This response effectively disregards tensions or discontinuities between established knowledge, which had marginalized the significance of 'politics', and the new knowledge that accords it 'primacy'.

Finally, a *third* response explores the possibility that some forms of knowledge and learning are *systematically* encouraged, as other forms of knowledge and insight are routinely marginalized, devalued or suppressed. There is, in this response, a suspicion that such 'bias' may be symptomatic of the interplay of power and knowledge in society. Moreover, instead of assuming that the insight into 'the primacy of power' is irrelevant for, or that it can be integrated within, existing repertoires of knowing and acting, the third response involves reflection upon, and reassessment of, previously established priorities and their means of attainment (Voronov and Coleman, 2003). Of course, this reflection may be partial and temporary: it may not be sustained (Stepanovich, 2009). Nonetheless, it sows a seed of tension and doubt that may subsequently be regenerated.

Critical discourses on management resonate with AL's challenge to traditional approaches to learning and, more specifically, its capacity to facilitate and express an awareness of 'the influence of power on decision-making [and] the "mobilization of bias"' (McLaughlin and Thorpe, 1993: 25) with the insights into power generated by unplanned as well as organized forms of Action Learning. Where this awareness is raised and explored, there is a fusion of the respective agendas of AL and CMS. What we term Critical Action Learning (CAL) understands that 'the encouragement to think' is provoked by the contradictory forces that play upon everyday life; and that an attentiveness to 'the primacy of politics' enables explanations to be developed that are rationally more persuasive than those offered by traditional theory (see Table 8.1).

The emancipatory intent of CMS is to prompt and sustain critical reflection by challenging forces (e.g. patriarchy, consumerism, technocracy) that are productive of

Table 8.1   *An alternative approach to management education using a framework adapted from McLaughlin and Thorpe (1993)*

	Conventional Action Learning	Critical Action Learning
Worldview	The world is somewhere to act and change	The world is somewhere to act and change
	Self-development is very important	Self-development and social development are interdependent
	Curriculum defined by managers	Critical dialogue between researcher/teacher, managers and non-managerial (subordinates) leading to a communicatively grounded curricula
	Managers should be facilitated by a tutor to solve problems	Managers are potentially receptive to, and be facilitated by, the concerns of other groups, in addition to individual tutors, when identifying and addressing problems
Modus operandi	Experts are viewed with caution	Received wisdom, including that of experts, is subject to critical scrutiny through a fusion of reflection and insights drawn from critical social theory
	Models, concepts and ideas are developed in response to problems	Models, concepts and ideas are developed through an interplay of reflection upon practice and an application of ideas drawn from critical traditions

socially unnecessary suffering and/or inhibit critical reflection upon their rationality. CAL is the application of CMS to processes of education. In broad outline,[10] the process of Critical Action Learning involves the following moments which we illustrate by reference to our earlier account of John Sculley's experience at Pepsi (for a more extended discussion of these issues, see Kjonstad and Willmott, 1995).

1 An experience of tension (e.g. anxiety or doubt) or the identification of contradiction (e.g. success *and* unhappiness).
2 The interpretation of tension/contradiction as avoidable, i.e. as a social and political phenomenon rather than as a 'given' or a natural law.
3 Analysis of the tensions/contradictions, including the conditions that are understood to produce them.
4 Recurrent efforts to resolve tensions/contradictions through struggles to change their conditions of possibility. This includes strengthening the capacity to identify and analyse tensions/contradictions.
5 An experience of new tensions and/or the identification of contradictions arising from the process of struggle. Go back to point 2.

One way of reading Sculley's (1988) account of his time at Pepsi is as a confession, albeit a self-congratulatory one, that occasionally leaves the predictable terrain of books penned by 'heroic' senior executives. Sculley does commend the exceptional talents and quality of Pepsi executives, and thereby trumpets his own outstanding abilities. But he is also somewhat reflective about the Pepsi managerial culture in which 'everyone wore the unofficial corporate uniform', including 'a sincere red tie'. Sculley describes himself, ambiguously, as 'an impatient perfectionist' who was 'unsympathetic' to anyone who failed to perform to his standards. We interpret this narrative as one that is as suggestive of an admission of personal weakness as it is of macho strength. However partial,[11] Sculley's account of Pepsi may be, it is also expressive of *some degree* of critical reflection, no doubt assisted by gaining some distance from Pepsi following his appointment as CEO at Apple, a firm that he strongly celebrates in the book (see also Linzmayer, 2004, esp. Ch. XVI). Consider, more specifically, the following passage where Sculley (1988) draws attention to the experience of tension, in the form of guilt, that occurred whenever he was not totally consumed with, or absorbed by, his work:

> Winning to me, was an obsession. I was driven not only by the competition but by the force of powerful ideas. I demanded the best of myself. If I walked away from an assignment not totally consumed or absorbed to near exhaustion, I felt guilty about it. Dozens had failed at this regimen, but to me, Pepsi was a comfortable home.

Reflection upon his time at Pepsi leads Sculley to appreciate how his sense of identity and purpose had become totally invested in the Pepsi Corporation – to the extent that it had become his 'comfortable home'. With the benefit of hindsight, he acknowledges how he was captivated by the force of the powerful idea that Pepsi could become Number One in the USA market, even though his commitment to the realization of this idea resulted in expelling family, friends and other interests to the margins of his life. Slavish devotion to the success of the corporation led Sculley to give Pepsi the 'best' of himself, leaving only the residue for others.

Sculley's Odyssey can be read, and perhaps was intended, as a cautionary tale for executives (and academics like ourselves, for whom 'writing' or 'publishing' might be substituted for 'winning' in the above quotation from Sculley) who are vulnerable to the seductions of 'the powerful ideas', however absurd or trivial, generated within corporations, including academia. And, to this extent, the experience of tension is represented as an *avoidable* product of corporate seduction. Sculley's realization that slavish devotion to the corporation was not inevitable (even though it might have meant dismissal from 'America's corporate Marine Corps') gives a critical edge to what might otherwise have been a celebratory account of Pepsi culture. It makes it possible for Sculley to be self-deprecating about his ridiculous yet obsessive preoccupation with winning the 'Cola Wars' (the equivalent in academia being the 'Rating Wars' between different universities and departments, see Willmott, 1995a, 2011b).

However, revealing anecdotes are no more than an entertaining diversion if they are not accompanied by at least a modicum of critical analysis. *Odyssey* is a fairly entertaining read but description is largely uninformed by, or combined with, critical reflection. With reference to the 'primacy of politics', Sculley makes no connection between the pressures applied to Pepsi managers and the organization of capitalism as a politico–economic system in which demands for the commodification and exploitation of the sellers of labour to its corporations, including executives, are relentless. In effect, the 'bias' that is 'mobilized' in Sculley's narrative acts to naturalize capitalism and egoism, resulting in mindless careerism.[12]

In effect, the process of Critical Action Learning plateaus at stage 2 (see above). Further reflection is impeded as capitalism is naturalized and Pepsi executives are assumed to be sovereign individuals who freely chose to devote themselves to its objectives, as if they were uninfluenced by dominant cultural values which prize(d) growth, market share, profits and career advancement. There is scant appreciation of how a reduction in the tensions and contradictions described by Sculley is conditional upon struggles for social development as well as self-development. These struggles involve an effort to address directly whatever frustrations, unhappiness or sense of inadequacy fuels an obsessive (macho) concern with winning – an obsession that offers a socially acceptable, yet contradictory, means of escaping feelings of incompleteness and an associated sense of inadequacy. Moving beyond an ironic and ultimately quiescent accommodation to the status quo demands engagement in some form of Critical Action Learning in which the telling of a confessional tale is superseded by the more arduous task of self and social transformation.

From the perspective of CMS and CAL, much management education, and especially that provided by business schools, seems to be trapped in a self-affirming bubble. Executives and students are corralled within the equivalent of a gated community where they are protected from critical analysis and, more specifically, critical scrutiny of their practices. Occupying this bubble, they are largely spared from participating in 'difficult conversations' that link their activity directly to the outrageous and growing social divisions of wealth and opportunity nationally and globally, the mounting crises of energy and food, and of course the contribution to, and effects of, climate change. When they do have such conversations, it is on their terms and in a manner that simultaneously asserts and excludes the need for radical change (e.g. Hehir and Petrella, 2011), and marginalizes public scrutiny and minimizes accountability (see http://blogs.hbr.org/haque/2011/01/ten_things_youre_not_allowed_t.html, accessed 8 July 2011). CMS challenges the value of this myopic and self-serving response (see Nussbaum, 2010) by critically questioning the basis and adequacy of such managerialist 'fixes'.

Conclusion

Many management consultants, researchers and educators adhere to their task of presenting potential or existing managers with the techniques that are believed to enable them to enhance corporate and employee performance. Doubtless, this sense of mission would be unequivocally endorsed by Sculley, the driven Pepsi executive, when wearing his 'sincere red tie'. Conversely, the political and ethical significance of issues of ownership and managerial control are disregarded – or, at best, they are reserved for marginalized activities, such as the elaboration of codes of ethics (Willmott, 2011a) and brand-building forms of corporate social responsibility.[13] So, for example, ethical considerations are framed in terms of 'corporate responsibility' where the demonstration of responsibility is conflated with contriving and promoting an image of 'care' as a distinctive selling point – rather like bankers who wear smart suits to bestow a veneer of respectability upon their suave venality, and thereby lubricate the sale of their financial products. We have suggested that the irrationalities and contradictions associated with the theory and practice of management make it fertile ground for the application and development of critical thinking. Tensions within organizational practices and relations invite and can promote critical reflection, as established recipes for survival and success, both personal and collective, are found to be flawed and self-defeating (see Lee et al., 2008). Fresh ideas and perspectives are stimulated and more readily entertained when conventional wisdom fails, as it did most spectacularly in the global financial meltdown of 2008 (see Willmott, 2011a). When investigating the world of business, management and organization, the challenge is to show and explore how critical thinking has relevance for illuminating, interrogating and, hopefully, transforming the oppression, exploitation and suffering that unnecessarily tarnishes the modern world.

Critical Management Studies (CMS) are fuelled by the intent to 'analyze social conditions, to criticize the unjustified use of power, and to change established social traditions and institutions so that human beings are freed from dependency, subordination and suppression' (Scherer, 2009: 30). CMS examines and questions the commonsense thinking and established practices – including much of management theory and practice – that subordinate what is inherently of moral and political significance to what becomes framed as technical and instrumental. The normative quality of activities may be displaced or denied but it cannot be eliminated because, as Ray (1993: 25) has observed, 'even when actors are behaving in a purely instrumental fashion, in a market or in a bureaucracy, their communication must be bound by shared norms and beliefs which can be reconstructed and critically examined'. By undertaking analyses and disseminating research findings that are 'empirical, historically situated, phenomenologically cogent, normatively insightful' (Forester, 1993: 13), proponents of CMS contribute to the reconstruction of management education and practice.

If the emancipatory intent of CMS is to be fulfilled, a process of dialogue can be enabled by forms of critical management learning. To this end, CMS must move beyond abstract theorizing to critique and transform the mundane realities of management theory and practice – realities that extend from the supervision of work in the back office to meetings of the World Economic Forum. Authors like Klein (2000, 2007) and Sennett (1998, 2006) are, in this respect, exemplary in producing accessible and lively texts that mobilize critical insights to show the limitations of conventional wisdom to a wide audience. Applying critical reason to make sense of diverse aspects of management exposes the limitations and effects of managerialist thinking and its established practices as it confounds the rationality ascribed to them. In challenging received wisdoms, critical thinking necessarily encounters considerable resistance – which can be enlivening and inspiring, rather than threatening or disheartening (Sinclair, 2007). Many people recognize, at least privately if not in a managerial capacity, the value of questioning established truths, norms and practices, and they also have some inkling of how contemporary crises – financial, ecological, energy, food, migration – are bound up in contemporary managerial mantras about the desirability of growth, the imperative to increase shareholder value, the efficiency of markets, the restrictiveness of regulations, and so on. And that, in turn, the pursuit of managerial capitalism overseen by financial elites has produced private affluence, in the form of excessive consumerism, and a degradation of the public sphere. Resistance can be viewed as a carborundum for sharpening a capacity to cut through the bogus claims of conventional wisdom. Through a process of critique and transformation, the aspiration of CMS is to contribute to the development of a more equitable and sustainable future.

Notes

1   In contrast to the breadth of concerns explored within Critical Theory – such as legitimation crises within advanced capitalist states and Habermas' (1989b) identification of social and political movements outside of the workplace as the most promising source of modernization along non-capitalist paths (see also Chapter 2) – the focus of CMS is upon 'managing and organizing', which it addresses 'not as isolatable objects of study' but as 'socially embedded, economically engaged and politically disputed' (Letiche, 2006: 170). There is no reason why, in

principle, this focus should not include the organization of forms of resistance to, and transformation of, established institutions and practices.

2   This working principle is, however, always subject to erosion by divisive pressures, such as individual incentives; this as is clearly evident in continuing reforms of higher education where 'performance' is increasingly individualized (see Willmott, 1995a).

3   An exemplary case is Professor Prem Sikka, who has been conducting a critical dialogue with regulators, politicians and policy-makers on issues of accounting and financial regulation for the past 25 years. Much of the material and interventions relating to his activism, in which he has involved many politicians and campaigning groups, can be found at the website of the Association for Accountancy and Business Affairs (http://www.aabaglobal.org, accessed 21 November 2011). See also Sikka, 2008.

4   The *truth* claim concerns the veracity of the statement. When accepted, this claim has the effect of shaping the listener's beliefs. A *comprehensibility* claim concerns the clarity of the statement's expression which, when it is registered, shapes the listener's attention. A *sincerity* claim concerns the speaker's good faith. When accepted, this gains the listener's trust. Finally, there is a *rightfulness* claim. This concerns the appropriateness or legitimacy of the statement. When accepted, it facilitates the listener's cooperative involvement. See Chapter 2 for a fuller discussion.

5   See Sennett (1980) for an insightful and subtle treatment of the problem of authority, including the risk of a non-conscious negative bonding to authority figures through denial of dependency.

6   Gephart and Pitter (1993) acknowledge that industrial accidents also occurred in industrialized State socialist societies. Indeed, it is argued that the lack of separation between political and economic sectors in these economies made accidents more likely as they are more easily covered up by the State, and the citizenship has even fewer means of articulating its opposition to a repressive system that claims to represent the people while simultaneously exposing them to high and avoidable levels of risk.

7   In common with many other high-margin consumer products, soft drinks are heavily marketed by appealing to idealized images of youth, popularity, freedom, lifestyle, etc. (see Chapter 5). The fantastic quality of these images has been exposed by Pepsi's difficulties, at times, in promoting media heroes whose lifestyle is subsequently alleged to be tarnished by a real involvement in drugs and unorthodox relationships, in addition to (the by-now safely commodified and commercialized) rock and roll. More ambiguously, its advertising campaigns celebrate idealized versions of health and freedom. Partly in order to counteract adverse publicity, corporations like Pepsi routinely make substantial contributions to charitable organizations. For example, it has been claimed that donations by Pepsi (and Coca-Cola) to Save the Children has coincided with the latter organization's push for soda taxes as a way of counteracting childhood obesity. However, ideas about ageing, self-esteem and health education are not left untouched or undamaged by powerful campaigns showing (and celebrating)

young, beautiful, healthy people drinking sugared water as if it were the very elixir of life. Indeed, nothing particularly commendable would seem to flow from the enormous effort devoted by its executives to the Pepsi Corporation – in terms of personal development, healthier customers or other, comparable outcomes.

8   Of course, the logic of communicative rationality – undistorted dialogues grounding good decisions – may also be subverted by garbage-can processes and decisions. However, in the current situation, where instrumental rationality is dominant, ambiguity may more often favour efforts to loosen, if not counteract, its domination.

9   The following paragraphs have been extracted and revised from Willmott (1994b; 1997b).

10 It is potentially dangerous (and, indeed, not a little contradictory!) to provide a formula or blueprint for what is a complex and varying process of critical action learning. Nonetheless it can also be helpful for illustrating what may otherwise be viewed as a highly abstract notion.

11 The (nepotistic) fact that Sculley married the stepdaughter of Donald M. Kendall, the CEO and Chairman of PepsiCo from 1971 to 1986, does not figure prominently in his account.

12 The title of Sculley's book, *Odyssey*, alludes to the Homeric original discussed at length by Horkheimer and Adorno in *Dialectics of Enlightenment* (1947a/1979), two founders of Critical Theory (see Appendix), where it is deployed to illustrate the difficulties that attend the realization of critical reason. Sculley, in contrast, incorporates little direct reflection upon the significance of his experiences. The issue of how CMS should develop in its application of 'critical reason' has aroused considerable debate and controversy. See, for example, *Organization*, 2002; 2008; Wray-Bliss, 2004; Letiche, 2006; Akella, 2008; Tatli, forthcoming.

13 Here it might be objected that 'business ethics' is an established and expanding specialism within the field of management. We concur with this objection and see this specialism as a promising area for the development of an orientation informed by critical thinking (see Willmott, 1998; Ten bos and Willmott, 2001; Jones, Parker and Ten Bos, 2005; Wray-Bliss, 2009).

Appendix

Brief History of the Frankfurt School

Critical Theory (CT) draws its inspiration from a tradition of critical thought that emerged during the Enlightenment. At this time, knowledge based upon empirical investigation and philosophical reflection began to challenge established dogmas sanctified by religion (McCarthy, 1978; Schroyer, 1973). Key thinkers of the Enlightenment (e.g. Newton, Descartes) sought to set knowledge upon a more rational, (e.g. scientific) basis. The favoured form of this knowledge and 'rationality' was positivistic or *non-dialectical*. That is to say, reality was conceptualized as an ahistorical object-world that exists independently of the scientific methods that have the power to disclose and represent this world.

In the physical sciences, Einstein and especially Heisenberg have drawn attention to the limits of non-dialectical knowledge. In philosophy, Hegelian dialectics had earlier provided the first, Western problematization of Cartesian dualism. Hegel's critique was confined to the realm of ideas and was itself challenged by the 'young Hegelians' – notably Feuerbach and then Marx. They argued for the dialectical production, or reproduction, of social reality in which the material and ideal are intertwined and mutually constitutive. It is this left Hegelian stance that is the chief source of inspiration for Critical Theory (see Horkheimer, 1972).

Building upon the material dialectics of the left Hegelians, Critical Theory incorporates and addresses the major historical shifts and social and economic development of the intervening century. These include consideration of the worldwide expansion of capitalism, the rise of fascism, the degeneration of Marxism into Stalinism and Maoism – as well as critiques of mass society (Friedman, 1981). Intellectually, engagements with phenomenology and psychoanalysis have stimulated critical reflections upon the residues of materialism, determinism and rationalism in left Hegelianism (e.g. Fromm, 1970; Marcuse, 1955). This openness of CT to a range of intellectual traditions was initially prompted by a critical appreciation of the limits of orthodox Marxism, such as its failure to anticipate, and make coherent sense of, the development of welfare capitalism and the expansion of consumerism. The materialist correction of Hegelian idealism is seen to underplay the formative role of images and ideas – and of communication and consumption, more generally – in processes of socioeconomic development and domination (Habermas, 1979; Marcuse, 1964; see also Chapter 2).

The Early Years

The funding for what was to become known as the Frankfurt School was provided by Felix Weil, the son of a successful businessman. Attracted to leftist thinking when a student at Frankfurt University, Weil persuaded his father to make an endowment sufficient to employ researchers from a variety of disciplines – philosophy, sociology, economics, psychology. This private endowment enabled the Institute of Social Research, established in the early 1920s, to be more intellectually and politically independent than centres funded by the German State. So began a pioneering and exceptionally fruitful inter-disciplinary collaboration that continues to have far-reaching impacts, especially in Western Europe and North America.

After somewhat uncertain and shaky beginnings, the Institute established a clearer identity after Max Horkheimer was appointed as its Director. During the late 1920s and early 1930s, the Institute combined social science and philosophy into a politically and practically committed *social philosophy*. Its mission involved a sustained challenge to the orthodox assumption that social science can and should produce objective, value-free knowledge of social reality (see Chapter 2). Instead of feeling obliged to discover universal, invariant regularities and law-like patterns in social behaviour (or at least to dress up empirical findings in these terms), members of the Institute sought to show how seemingly 'given' patterns of activity (e.g. consumerism, authoritarianism) take shape within specific historical and societal contexts; and to argue that the methods of representing these patterns are themselves inextricably embedded within these contexts. Such patterns and methods, it was contended, should be perceived as a *dialectically constituted* moment in the historical movement of mankind – and not as the final form of society or of science. Underpinning this critique was an intent to engender reflection upon, and emancipation from, the contradictions and restrictions inherent in advanced capitalist societies. The 'politically and practically committed social philosophy', which was increasingly identified as the distinguishing feature of 'Frankfurt School' analysis, was directed at exposing and challenging the myths and irrationalities of modernity.

A strong thread of critique links the dialectical thinking of the Frankfurt School to that of the left Hegelians, whose most influential member was Marx (see Jay, 1973). However, its leading members were not activists in any Leftist political party, programme or movement. For Horkheimer and his colleagues, the erratic path of capitalist development, with its unexpected degeneration into fascism during the 1930s, made it doubtful, and even improbable, that the proletariat would emerge as the revolutionary agent of change. The industrial proletariat, they believed, had long since become divided and weakened – if, indeed, it ever had the capacity to overthrow capitalism and/or the vision to establish a genuinely socialist society. Nonetheless, members of the Institute identified themselves, perhaps rather romantically, with the emancipatory *intent* of the left-Hegelian tradition. But, instead of focusing upon the revolutionary potential ascribed to the proletariat, members of the Institute directed their attention to a more generalized sense of frustration, oppression and confusion that they associated with the contradictory claims, perverse priorities and divisive effects of modern capitalist societies. These feelings were seen to render many people and diverse groups potentially receptive to the revitalization of Enlightenment ideas about expanding their autonomy in relation to modern dogmas for which an important condition of possibility was the fostering of responsible citizenship.

Critiques of Totalitarianism

In the Germany of the 1930s, members of the Institute did not have to look far to find modern, capitalist institutions and ideologies that systematically suppressed and impeded the realization of autonomy and responsible citizenship. Focusing upon the rise of fascism in Europe and the increasingly authoritarian cast of the Soviet state, they asked: how could the critical reason which produced the Enlightenment become eclipsed by such irrational beliefs and ideologies? Horkheimer, Adorno, Fromm and others considered a large number of factors: from nationalist struggles that developed out of the crisis–ridden capitalist economy to oppressive social relations and forms of socialization that fostered the mass formation of authoritarian personalities (see Adorno et al., 1950; Fromm, 1941). Institutionalized nationalism, expressed as gross prejudice, was seen to be a condition and consequence of the development of authoritarian personalities. People with these personalities, it was argued, compulsively construct rigid and reified status hierarchies from which they derive a strong sense of identity and security. Obedient and loyal upwards, they are inclined to be intolerant and punitive downwards.

Such thinking was not welcome in the repressive climate of 1930s Germany. As the grip of the Nazis upon the German State and the activities of its intelligentsia tightened, many members of the Frankfurt School went into exile in the USA. In America during the 1940s and 1950s, they were exposed to, and deeply impressed if not traumatized by, the hyper–materialistic culture of the most advanced of the capitalist democracies. This experience of rampant consumer capitalism where responsible citizenship was worn away by competitive pressures stimulated renewed critical reflection upon the seductive power of market freedoms. Notably, Marcuse took an increasingly close interest in the (totalizing) impact of mass culture, especially in the industrialized production and distribution of news and entertainment. The mass media were seen to exert a numbing and homogenizing effect upon the consciousness of the population. There was a disturbing parallel with the mass psychology of fascism and state socialism in which normalized conformism inhibits or domesticates critical reflection. Accordingly, proponents of Critical Theory paid increasing attention to the power of the media, sponsored by business and/or the State, in shaping the population's ideas, beliefs and wants (Horkheimer and Adorno, 1947a; Marcuse, 1964). At the same time, the new culture industries were recognized to contain a *potential* to become positive sources of education, enlightenment and life-enhancing pleasure. The mass media were not regarded as *inherently* pacifying or 'evil' since, in principle, they could provide a powerful channel for challenging dogmas and raising consciousness, in much the same way that potential for using the internet and especially social networking sites is viewed today. However, the commercial and ideological priorities of consumer capitalism were seen by Marcuse and others routinely to displace, or at least marginalize, these emancipatory possibilities. The culture industry was found to operate primarily as an instrument of escapism and social control in which the values and power of social elites were celebrated and institutionalized.

Following the defeat of the Nazis, Horkheimer and Adorno returned to Germany while others, notably Marcuse and Fromm, remained in the USA. The horrors of the Nazi and Stalinist regimes starkly revealed the magnitude of human barbarism and irrationality. They had also demonstrated how science, technology and social organization could be harnessed to destructive and oppressive ends. In particular, the Holocaust, with its use of technologies of mass annihilation and its efficient dissemination of authoritarian ideology, demonstrated how the development of scientific knowledge is, at best, double-edged in its capacity to foster more rational forms of social and economic organization (Horkheimer and Adorno, 1947a, b). By the early 1950s, optimism about the chances of radical change in modern capitalist societies was draining away. Fascist regimes had been defeated but a new spectre now haunted the world, in the form of the Cold War and a seemingly unstoppable escalation of the nuclear arms race that threatened untold destruction. For Horkheimer and Adorno, in particular, it was difficult to comprehend how critical social science could facilitate, let alone justify, emancipatory change.

The Resurgence of Critical Theory

Marcuse, who remained in the USA, was somewhat less pessimistic about the possibilities of emancipation – even though he was broadly in agreement with Horkheimer and Adorno's prognosis of an ever-more 'administered world'. During the 1950s and early 1960s, Marcuse (1955, 1964) explored the shaping and sublimation of people's drives, instincts and wishes as capitalism developed into a mass consumer society. Through a radical reinterpretation of Freud, he identified negative (i.e. constructive) potentialities in the raw energy of libido (Marcuse, 1955), suggesting that deep instincts and drives – the pleasure principle of sexuality – could never be completely domesticated by the taboos and controlling forces of society. The biological anchoring of sexuality, Marcuse argued, meant that people could never be totally subordinated to the conformist-shaping powers of the mass media, business and government.

During the post-war 'boom' years of growth and comparative political stability, attentiveness to Marcuse's critical analyses of consumer capitalism or to his radical reinterpretation of Freud was confined to a small circle of intellectuals. Then, following the political radicalization of educated sections of the post-war 'baby boom' youth, Marcuse's analysis of consumerism and his attentiveness to sexuality were found to resonate deeply with the libertarianism of 1960s counter-culture. His ideas became influential in supporting and legitimizing the development of the New Left and associated movements (e.g. Students for a Democratic Society) as young affluent people became increasingly disaffected with what they regarded as the inane acquisitiveness and sham liberalism of Western society and also, if American men and women faced being drafted into a seemingly interminable Vietnam War. From the mid-1960s to the early 1970s, Marcuse's books – especially *Eros and Civilization* (1955) and *One-Dimensional Man* (1964) – were widely read (or at least were bought!) by hundreds of thousands of young people in the West. His thesis on the one-dimensionality of modern life – in which youth were trained and induced, as consumers and as producers, to become the fodder that fed the capitalist (military-industrial) machine – found a receptive audience among a generation who had become disillusioned with the life mapped out for them as cogs in 'the system'. Marcuse's message struck a chord with young people who had become dependent upon, yet were also bored with, consumer culture, and so were readily captivated by the easy pleasures and idealism of the 'flower power' phenomenon.

The wholly unexpected appearance of a mass audience for his ideas prompted Marcuse to review his opinion about the pacifying powers of the mass media and the prospects of liberation. The idea that the working class would become a collective agent for emancipatory transformation had, as we noted earlier, long been abandoned; and no plausible replacement had been found. Marcuse (1969) now contemplated the possibility that people on the margins of the mass consumer society – especially students and others who were seemingly less dependent, materially or psychologically, upon the flow of mass goods and services – might be capable of challenging and refusing its values and materialistic lifestyle. It can be said, with the benefit of hindsight, that Marcuse's hopes for radical change were wildly (and naïvely) optimistic – not least because he did not adequately appreciate the superficiality and faddishness of much experimentation with, and indeed consumerist orientation to, alternative lifestyles. He did not recognize the shallowness of the commitment to alternative values and institutions, and so did not anticipate how rarely these would be sustained beyond college years. On the other hand, amongst the leading members of the Frankfurt School, Marcuse can be credited with anticipating and facilitating growing expressions of 'revolt' from diverse groups – principally the peace, gay, feminist and environmentalist movements – that have inspired, championed and institutionalized social and cultural changes during the past 50 years. It is therefore somewhat surprising that Marcuse's ideas have not enjoyed sustained popular appeal. In contrast, there has been a continuing mass readership for the writings of Erich Fromm, whose gently radical humanism and willingness to address popular topics such as love and freedom, while minimizing explicitly political analysis, have appealed to people with an interest in personal development rather than to activists involved in emancipatory social movements.[1] It should be added that Fromm's writings are much more accessible than Marcuse's or indeed any of the other core members of the Frankfurt School.

Since the 1960s, the tradition of Critical Theory has been carried forward by Jürgen Habermas, who had been Adorno's assistant upon the latter's return to Germany (see McCarthy, 1978). In these early years, Habermas struggled to gain the respect and support of Horkheimer, who questioned Habermas' efforts to engage more directly with the practical politics of 1950s Germany. Throughout a long career, Habermas has consistently sought to reach a wider audience – notably, by giving many interviews (see, for example, Habermas, 1986) and by publishing newspaper articles concerning *inter alia* the reality and significance of National Socialism and the Holocaust,[2] the process of (re)unifying Germany, the meaning of the Gulf War (Habermas, 1994), the implications of 9/11 (Borradori, 2003) and the place of Islam in a post-secular society (Habermas et al., 2010).

Outside his native Germany, Habermas' influence has been largely confined to academia, as the deluge of secondary literature on Habermas bears witness,[3] and to which *Making Sense of Management* aspires to make a specialist contribution. In particular, Habermas has addressed directly the complaint repeatedly directed at the work of earlier Critical Theorists (e.g. Horkheimer, Marcuse), namely, that CT engages in mere moralizing as it lacks any rational basis for the normative standards and judgments that guide its critiques. To this accusation, some might add that this moralizing is propagated by privileged intellectuals who are simply nostalgic for a mythical past when humanistic ideas enjoyed some currency, and when academics exerted some influence. In response to this criticism, Habermas has sought to establish rational foundations for critique. His justification is based upon the conjecture that the structure of human communication at once anticipates and provokes an emancipatory impulse towards the development of a more rational society in which communication is no longer distorted by relations of power and domination (see Chapter 2). This 'quasi-transcendental' conjecture has, in principle, enabled Habermas to rebut the moralizing charge. More specifically, it is intended to provide a rational basis for supporting more optimistic assessments of possibilities for counteracting the negative features of the modern technological-capitalist society, such as those advanced by Fromm and especially Marcuse, as contrasted with the rather pessimistic prognoses offered by Adorno and by Horkheimer.

Regarded as one of the most original and influential of living Western social philosophers, Habermas has made the rationalization/technocratization of modern society – the domination of science, technology, administration and groups of experts over the lifeworld of its citizens (see Chapter 1) – the butt of his criticisms. As we argue throughout this book, modern forms of management and organization are media of such rationalization/technocratization and, so, are highly relevant targets of critique. The Habermasian emphasis upon the role of communication and the importance of unconstrained dialogue also resonates with broader contemporary 'turns' which emphasize the role and significance of language and discourse, including those that have occurred within the field of management and organization studies. Yet, the abstract and complex character of Habermas' major writings limits dissemination of his thinking to a wide audience, such as that reached by Marcuse (and Fromm), whose impassioned contributions engaged more directly with experiential issues such as consumption, freedom, sexuality, etc.

This concern to connect with everyday life and daily frustrations has been taken up by Habermas' most influential student, Axel Honneth. Indeed, Honneth has characterized his Hegelian-inflected focus upon 'the struggle for recognition' as 'an attempt to set Habermas' ingenious conception of [a communication theoretical turn] '"back on its feet"' (Honneth, 2003: 242). More specifically, he commends a shift *from* Habermas' (comparatively abstract or 'heady') explication of conditions (and claimed normative presuppositions) of communication as a basis for his discourse ethics *to* (comparatively earthy) experiences of mis-recognition – in the form of 'feelings of humiliation and disrespect' (ibid.: 245) – that, Honneth contends, engender social change. These immanent negations, he argues, are 'the engine of social change' (ibid.). And yet Honneth is lamentably silent on the question of whether, when and how such feelings are productive of developments that are progressive, rather than reactionary, in inspiration and effect.[4] So, questions remain open with regard to how emancipatory change occurs and also with regard to how emancipatory claims are to be justified. In this respect, at least, such openness points to the relevance, and perhaps inevitability, of immanent forms of critique and transformation that, being suspicious of the authority vouched in every positivity or normative framework, demand that full responsibility is taken for every act of resistance or revolt. To put this another way, ethics is prioritized over the (ostensibly authoritative) warranting of assumptions about epistemology and ontology.

Notes

1　Following an acrimonious exchange with Marcuse, principally over the latter's reading of Freud, Fromm distanced himself from the Frankfurt School (Willmott and Knights, 1982; see also Wiggershaus, 1994). Fromm, who was the first to combine the insights of Freud and Marx, challenged the Freudian emphasis upon sexuality and the death instinct. He also criticized Freud's crude materialism and patriarchal thinking. Fromm increasingly emphasized the importance and precariousness of the existential basis of human freedom (Fromm, 1961). For those who were sceptical about Marcuse's belief in the power of libido and/or Fromm's humanistic appeals, aesthetics (e.g. the work of writers like Kafka and Brecht) remained as a possible medium through which the sensibility and emancipatory praxis of the audience might be aroused (e.g. Adorno, 1967; Benjamin, 1973).

2　For an English language overview of the historian's debate on the Holocaust, see Holub, 1991, Chapter 7.

3　For overviews, many of which focus upon the work of Jürgen Habermas, see *inter alia* Bernstein, 1985; Finlayson, 2005; Friedman, 1981; McCarthy, 1978; and Thompson and Held, 1982. There are also a number of collections that contain illuminating articles on particular aspects of Critical Theory. See, for example, Bronner and Kellner, 1989; Fay, 1987; Kompridis, 2006; Sabia and Wallukis, 1983; Scheuerman, 2008; Wexler, 1991; Wheatland, 2009.

4　Honneth's ideas have yet to be widely taken up by critical students of management.

References

Adler, P. (2002) 'Critical in the name of whom and what?', *Organization*, 9: 387–395.

Adler, P., Forbes, L. and Willmott, H. (2007) 'Critical management studies', *Academy of Management Annals, 1: 119–179*.

Adorno, T. (1967) *Prisms*. London: Neville Spearman.

Adorno, T. (1973) *The Jargon of Authenticity*. London: Routledge.

Adorno, T.W., Frenkel-Brunswik, E., Levinson, D.J. and Sanford, R.N. (1950) *The Authoritarian Personality. New York: Harper*.

Akella, D. (2008) 'A reflection on critical management studies', *Journal of Organization and Management*, 14 (1): 100–110.

Aldrich, H.E. (1979) *Organizations and Environments*. Englewood Cliffs, NJ: Prentice Hall.

Alvarez, R. (2008) 'Examining technology, structure and identity during an Enterprise System implementation', *Information Systems Journal*, 18 (2): 203–224.

Alvesson, M. (1987) *Organization Theory and Technocratic Consciousness: Rationality, Ideology and Quality of Work*. Berlin/New York: de Gruyter.

Alvesson, M. (1995) *Management of Knowledge-Intensive Companies*. Berlin/New York: de Gruyter.

Alvesson, M. (1996) *Communication, Power and Organization*. Berlin: de Gruyter.

Alvesson, M. (2002) *Postmodernism and Social Research*. Buckingham: Open University Press.

Alvesson, M. (2004) *Knowledge Work and Knowledge-Intensive Firms*. Oxford: Oxford University Press.

Alvesson, M. (2010) 'Self-doubters, strugglers, storytellers, surfers and others: Images of self-identities in organization studies', *Human Relations*, 63 (2): 193–217.

Alvesson, M. (2011a) 'Leadership and organizational culture', in A. Bryman, D. Collinson, B. Jackson and M. Uhl-Bien (eds), *Handbook of Leadership Studies*. London: Sage.

Alvesson, M. (2011b) 'The leader as saint', in M. Alvesson and A. Spicer (eds), *Metaphors We Lead By: Leadership in the Real World*. London: Routledge.

Alvesson, M. (2012a) *Understanding Organizational Culture* (2nd edn). London: Sage.

Alvesson, M. (2012b) *The Triumph of Emptiness*. Oxford: Oxford University Press.

Alvesson, M. and Billing, Y. (2009) *Understanding Gender and Organization* (2nd edn). London: Sage.

Alvesson, M. and Blom, M. (2011) 'Less leadership?', Working paper, Department of Business Administration, Lund University.

Alvesson, M. and Deetz, S. (1996) 'Critical theory and postmodern approaches to organization studies', in S. Clegg, C. Hardy and W. Nord (eds), *Sage Handbook of Organization Studies*. London: Sage.

Alvesson, M. and Deetz, S. (2000) *Doing Critical Management Research*. London: Sage.

Alvesson, M. and Kärreman, D. (2007) 'Unraveling HRM: Identity, ceremony, and control in a management consultancy firm', *Organization Science*, 18: 711–723.

Alvesson, M. and Sköldberg, K. (2009) *Reflexive Methodology* (2nd edn). London: Sage.

Alvesson, M. and Spicer, A. (eds) (2011) *Metaphors We Lead By: Leadership in the Real World*. London: Routledge.

Alvesson, M. and Spicer, A. (2012a) 'Critical leadership studies', (forthcoming).

Alvesson, M. and Spicer, A. (2012b) '*A stupidity based theory of organizations*'. Unpublished paper. Lund University.

Alvesson, M. and Sveningsson, S. (2003a) 'Good visions, bad micro-management and ugly ambiguity: Contradictions of (non-)leadership in a knowledge-intensive company', *Organization Studies*, 24 (6): 961–988.

Alvesson, M. and Sveningsson, S. (2003b) 'The great disappearance act: Difficulties in doing "leadership"', *Leadership Quarterly*, 14: 359–381.

Alvesson, M. and Sveningsson, S. (2003c) 'Managers doing leadership: The extra-ordinarization of the mundane', *Human Relations*, 56: 1435–1459.

Alvesson, M. and Sveningsson, S. (2008) *Changing Organizational Culture*. London: Routledge.

Alvesson, M. and Thompson, P. (2005) 'Post-bureaucracy?', in S. Ackroyd, R. Batt, P. Thompson and P. Tolbert (eds), *Oxford Handbook of Work and Organization Studies*. Oxford: Oxford University Press

Alvesson, M. and Willmott, H. (eds) (1992) *Critical Management Studies*. London: Sage.

Alvesson, M. and Willmott, H. (1995) 'Strategic management as domination and emancipation: From planning and process to communication and praxis', in P. Shrivastava and C. Stubbart (eds), *Advances in Strategic Management*, vol. 11. Greenwich, CT: JAI Press.

Alvesson, M. and Willmott, H. (2002) 'Identity regulation as organizational control: Producing the appropriate individual', *Journal of Management Studies*, 39: 619–644.

Alvesson, M. and Willmott, H. (eds) (2011) *Major Works in Critical Management Studies*, Vols 1–4. London: Sage.

Alvesson, M., Bridgman, T. and Willmott, H. (eds) (2009) *Oxford Handbook of Critical Management Studies*. Oxford: Oxford University Press.

Argyris, C. and Schon, D. (1978) *Organizational Learning*. Reading, MA: Addison-Wesley.

Armstrong, P. (1987) 'The rise of accounting controls in British capitalist enterprises', *Accounting, Organizations and Society*, 12: 415–436.

Armstrong, P. (2002) 'The costs of activity based management', *Accounting, Organizations and Society*, 27 (1–2): 99–120.

Armstrong, P. (2011) 'From bourgeois sociology to managerial apologetics: A tale of existential struggle', in P. Armstrong and G. Lightfoot (eds), *"The Leading Journal in the Field": Destabilizing Authority in the Social Sciences of Management*. Available at www.mayflybooks.org.

Arndt, J. (1980) 'Perspectives for a theory of marketing', *Journal of Business Research*, 8: 389–402.

Arndt, J. (1985) 'On making marketing science more scientific: The role of observations, paradigms, metaphors and puzzle solving', *Journal of Marketing*, 49: 11–23.

Arrington, C.E. and Puxty, A.G. (1991) 'Accounting, interests and rationality: A communicative relation', *Critical Perspectives on Accounting*, 2: 31–58.

Arvidsson, A. (2006) *Brands: Meaning and Value in Media Culture*. London: Routledge.

Ashforth, B. and Mael, F. (1989) 'Social identity theory and the organization', *Academy of Management Review*, 14: 20–39.

Asplund, J. (1991) *Rivaler och syndabockar*. Göteborg: Bokförlaget Korpen.

Bagozzi, R. (1975) 'Marketing as exchange', *Journal of Marketing*, 39: 32–39.

Bain, G. (1992) 'The Blackett Memorial Lecture: The future of management education', *Journal of the Operational Research Society*, 43 (6): 557–561.

Baker, M.J. (1987) 'One more time – what is marketing?', in M.J. Baker (ed.), *The Marketing Book*. London: Heinemann in association with the British Institute of Marketing.

Banerjee, B. (2007) *Corporate Social Responsibility: The Good, the Bad and the Ugly*. London: Edward Elgar.

Bank, J. (1992) *The Essence of Total Quality Management*. London: Prentice Hall.

Baritz, L. (1960) *The Servants of Power*. Middletown, CT: Wesleyan University Press.

Barker, J.R. (1993) 'Tightening the Iron Cage: Concertive control in self-managing teams', *Administrative Science Quarterly*, 38 (3): 408–437.

Barley, S.R. (2007) 'Corporations, democracy and the public good', *Journal of Management Inquiry*, 16 (3): 201–215.

Baskerville, R.L. and Myers, M.D. (2002) 'Information systems as a reference discipline', *MIS Quarterly*, 26 (1): 1–14.

Bass, B.M. and Steidlmeier, P. (1999) 'Ethics, character, and transformational leadership behavior', *Leadership Quarterly*, 10: 181–217.

Bavington, D. (2010) *Managed Annihilation: An Unnatural History of the Newfoundland Cod Collapse*. Vancouver: University of British Columbia Press.

Baxter, J. and Chua, W.F. (2003) 'Alternative management accounting research – whence and whither', *Accounting, Organizations and Society*, 28: 97–126.

Bedeian, A. (1989) 'Totems and taboos: Undercurrents in the management discipline', *Academy of Management News*, 19 (4): 1–6.

Beech, N. (2008) 'On the nature of dialogic identity work', *Organization*, 15: 51–74.

Belk, R., Wallendorff, M. and Sherry, J. (1989) 'The sacred and the profane in consumer behaviour: Theodicy on the Odyssey', *Journal of Consumer Research*, 16 (June): 1–38.

Bell, D. (1974) *The Coming of Post-Industrial Society*. London: Heinemann.

Benhabib, S. (1992) *Situating the Self: Gender, Community and Postmodernism in Contemporary Ethics*. Cambridge: Polity Press.

Benhabib, S. and Cornell, D. (eds) (1987) *Feminism as Critique: Essays on the Politics of Gender in Late-capitalist Societies*. Cambridge: Polity Press.

Benjamin, W. (1973) *Charles Baudelaire: A Lyric Poet in the Era of High Capitalism*. London: New Left Books.

Bennis, W.G. and O'Toole, J. (2005) 'How business schools lost their way', *Harvard Business Review*, May: 96–104.

Benson, J.K. (1977) 'Organizations: A dialectical view', *Administrative Science Quarterly*, 22 (1): 1–21.

Berglund, J. (2002) *'De otillräckliga'* ('The insufficient'), PhD dissertation. Stockholm: Stockholm School of Economics.

Bergvall-Kåreborn, B. (2002) 'Qualifying function in SSM modeling – A case study', *Systematic Practice and Action Research*, 15 (4): 309–330.

Bernstein, R.I. (ed.) (1985) *Habermas and Modernity*. Cambridge: Polity Press.

Bierema, L.L. (2010) *Implementing a Critical Approach to Organization Development*. Malaba, FL: Krieger Publishing.

Billing, Y.D. and Alvesson, M. (1994) *Gender, Managers and Organizations*. Berlin/ New York: de Gruyter.

Bittner, E. (1965) 'The concept of organization', *Social Research*, 32: 230–255.

Bloomfield, B., Coombs, R., Knights, D. and Littler, D. (eds) (1997) *Information Technology and Organizations*. Oxford: Oxford University Press.

Böhm, S. (2005) *Repositioning Organization Theory: Impossibilities and Strategies*. London: Palgrave Macmillan.

Böhm, S (2007) 'Reading Critical Theory', in C. Jones and R. ten Bos (eds), *Philosophy and Organization*. London: Routledge

Boje, D.M. and Al Avkoubi, K. (2009) 'Critical management education beyond the siege', in S.J. Armstrong and C.V. Fukami (eds), *The SAGE Handbook of Management Learning, Education and Development*. London: Sage.

Boltanski, L. and Chiapello, E. (2007) *The New Spirit of Capitalism*. London: Verso.

Borradori, G. (ed.) (2003) *Philosophy in a Time of Terror: Dialogues with Jurgen Habermas and Jacques Derrida*. Chicago: University of Chicago Press.

Bottomore, T. (1984) *The Frankfurt School*. London: Tavistock.

Bourdieu, P. (1984) *Distinction*. Cambridge, MA: Harvard University Press.

Bourgeois, L. and Brodwin, D. (1984) 'Strategic implementation: Five approaches to an elusive phenomenon', *Strategic Management Journal*, 5: 241–264.

Boxall, P. and Steeneveld, M. (1999) 'Human resource strategy and competitive advantage: A longitudinal study of engineering consultants', *Journal of Management Studies*, 36 (4): 443–463.

Boxall, P., Purcell, J. and Wright, P. (2007) 'Human resource management: Scope, analysis and significance', in P. Boxall, J. Purcell and P. Wright (eds), *The Oxford Handbook of Human Resource Management*. Oxford: Oxford University Press.

BP Annual Report and Accounts (2009) *Directors' Remuneration Report*. Available at: http://www.bp.com/assets/bp_internet/globalbp/globalbp_uk_english/set_ branch/STAGING/common_assets/downloads/pdf/BP_Annual_Report_and_ Accounts_Directors_remuneration_report.pdf. Accessed 8 February 2011.

Braverman, H. (1974) *Labor and Monopoly Capital*. New York: Monthly Review Press.

Brief, A.P. (2000) 'Still servants of power', *Journal of Management Inquiry*, 9 (4): 342–51.

Broadbent, J. and Laughlin, R. (2003) 'Control and legitimation in government accountability processes: The private finance initiative in the UK', *Critical Perspectives on Accounting*, 14 (1–2): 23–48.

Broadbent, J., Laughlin, R. and Read, S. (1991) 'Recent financial and administrative changes in the NHS: A critical theory analysis', *Critical Perspectives on Accounting*, 2 (1): 1–29.

Bronner, S.E. and Kellner, D.M. (eds) (1989) *Critical Theory and Society: A Reader*. London: Routledge.

Brooke, C. (2002) 'What does it mean to be "critical" in IS research?', *Journal of Information Technology*, 17: 49–57.

Brown, L.D. and Tandon, R. (1983) 'Ideology and political economy in inquiry: Action research and participatory research', *Journal of Applied Behavioural Science*, 19: 277–294.

Brown, R. H. (1976) 'Social theory as metaphor', *Theory and Society*, 3: 169–197.

Brown, S. (1993) 'Postmodern marketing?', *European Journal of Marketing*, 27 (4): 19–34.

Brown, S. (1996) 'Art or science: Fifty years of marketing debate', *Journal of Marketing Management*, 12 (4): 243–267.

Brownlie, D. (2006) 'Emancipation, epiphany and resistance: On the underimagined and overdetermined in critical marketing', *Journal of Marketing Management*, 22: 505–528.

Brunsson, N. (1985) *The Irrational Organization: Irrationality as a Basis for Organizational Action and Change*. New York: Wiley.

Brunsson, N. (2003) *The Organization of Hypocrisy: Talk, Decisions and Actions in Organizations* (2nd edn). Copenhagen: Copenhagen Business School Press.

Bryer, R.A. (1993) 'The late nineteenth-century revolution in financial reporting: Accounting for the rise of investor or managerial capitalism?', *Accounting, Organizations and Society*, 18 (7–8): 649–690.

Bryer, R.A. (2006) 'Accounting and control of the labour process', *Critical Perspectives on Accounting*, 17 (5): 551–598.

Burawoy, M. (1979) *Manufacturing Consent*. Chicago: University of California Press.

Burawoy, M. (2004) 'Public sociologies: Contradictions, dilemmas, and possibilities', *Social Forces*, 82 (4): 1603–1618.

Burchell, S., Clubb, C., Hopwood, A., Hughes, I. and Nahapiet, J. (1980) 'The roles of accounting in organizations and society', *Accounting, Organizations and Society*, 5 (1): 5–27.

Burnham, J. (1941) *The Managerial Revolution*. London: Pitman.

Burns, J.M. (1978) *Leadership*. New York: Harper & Row.

Burns, T. and Stalker, G.M. (1961) *The Management of Innovation*. London: Tavistock.

Burrell, G. (1984) 'Sex and organizational analysis', *Organization Studies*, 5: 97–118.

Burrell, G. (1992) 'The organization of pleasure', in M. Alvesson and H. Willmott (eds), *Critical Management Studies*. London: Sage.

Burrell, G. (1994) 'Modernism, postmodernism and organizational analysis 4: The contribution of Jürgen Habermas', *Organization Studies*, 15 (1): 1–19.

Burrell, G. and Morgan, G. (1979) *Sociological Paradigms and Organizational Analysis*. London: Heinemann.

Burton, D. (2005) 'Marketing theory matters', *British Journal of Management*, 16: 5–18.

Butler, J. (2004) *Undoing Gender*. New York: Routledge.

Button, G., Mason, D. and Sharrock, W. (2003) 'Disempowerment and resistance in the print industry? Reactions to surveillance-capable technology', *New Technology, Work and Employment*, 18 (1): 50–61.

Calas, M. and Smircich, L. (1991) 'Voicing seduction to silence leadership', *Organization Studies*, 12 (4): 567–602.

Calas, M. and Smircich, L. (1993) 'Dangerous liaisons: The "feminine-in-management" meets "globalization"', *Business Horizons*, March–April: 73–83.

Calas, M. and Smircich, L. (2006) 'From the "woman's" point of view. Feminist approaches to organization studies', in S. Clegg, C. Hardy and W. Nord (eds), *Handbook of Organization Studies* (2nd edn). London: Sage.

Callo, V.N. and Packham, R.G. (1999) 'The use of soft systems methodology in emancipatory development', *Systems Research and Behavioral Science,* 16: 311–319.

Carroll, B. and Levy, L. (2008) 'Defaulting to management: Leadership defined by what it is not', *Organization*, 15 (1): 75–96.

Casey, C. (1995) *Work, Self and Society: After Industrialism*. London: Routledge.

Casey, C. (2002) *Critical Analysis of Organizations: Theory, Practice, Revitalization*. London: Sage.

Castells, M. (2003) 'The rise of the fourth world', in D. Held and A. McGrew (eds), *The Global Transformations Reader*. Cambridge: Polity Press.

Cavanagh, J. and Anderson, S. (2002) *What is the Global Justice Movement?* Available at: http://www.ips-dc.org/global_econ/movement.pdf. Accessed 9 December 2007.

Checkland, P.B. (1981) *Systems Thinking, Systems Practice*. London: Wiley.

Chia, R. (1994) 'The concept of decision: A deconstructive analysis', *Journal of Management Studies*, 31 (6): 781–806.

Child, J. (1969) *British Management Thought*. London: Allen and Unwin.

Child, J. (1972), 'Organizational structure, environment and performance: The role of strategic choice', *Sociology*. 6: 1–22.

Child, J. (2009) 'Challenging hierarchy', in M. Alvesson, T. Bridgman and H. Willmott (eds), *Oxford Handbook of Critical Management Studies*. Oxford: Oxford University Press.

Child, J. and Smith, C. (1987) 'The context and process of organizational transformation – Cadbury Limited and its sector', *Journal of Management Studies*, 24 (6): 565–593.

Chua, W.F. (1988) 'Interpretive sociology and management accounting research – A critical review', *Accounting, Auditing and Accountability Journal*, 1 (2): 59–79.

Clarke, C., Brown, A. and Hailey, V. (2009) 'Working identities? Antagonistic discursive resources and managerial identity', *Human Relations*, 62: 323–352.

Cleaver, H. (1979) *Reading Capital Politically*. Austin, TX: University of Texas Press.

Clegg, S. (1989) *Frameworks of Power*. London: Sage.

Clegg, S. and Dunkerly, D. (1980) *Organization, Class and Control*. London: Routledge and Kegan Paul.

Clegg, S., Carter, C., Kornberger, M. and Schweitzer, J. (eds) (2011) *Strategy: Theory and Practice*. London: Sage.

Clegg, S., Kornberger, M. and Rhodes, C. (2007) 'Organizational ethics, decision making, undecidability', *Sociological Review*, 55 (2): 393–409.

Clifford, J. and Marcus, G.E. (eds) (1986) *Writing Culture*. Berkeley, CA: University of California Press.

Collins, H. and Pinch, T. (1998) *The Golem: What You Should Know About Science* (2nd edn). Cambridge: Cambridge University Press.

Collinson, D. (1992) *Managing the Shopfloor: Masculinity, Subjectivity and Workplace Culture*. Berlin: De Gruyter.

Collinson, D. (2005) 'Dialectics of leadership', *Human Relations*, 58 (11): 1419–1442.

Collinson, D. (2006) 'Rethinking followership: A post-structural analysis of follower identities', *Leadership Quarterly*, 17: 179–189.

Collinson, D. (2011) 'Critical leadership studies', in Bryman, A., Collinson, D.L., Grint, K., Jackson, B. and Uhl-Bien. M. (eds), *The Sage Handbook of Leadership*. London: Sage.

Collinson, D. and Hearn, J. (1996) 'Breaking the silence: On men, masculinities and managements', in D. Collinson and J. Hearn (eds), *Men as Managers, Managers as Men*. London: Sage.

Collinson, D., Knights, D. and Collinson, M. (1990) *Managing to Discriminate*. London: Routledge.

Contu, A. (2009) 'Critical management education', in M. Alvesson, T. Bridgman and H. Willmott (eds), *Oxford Handbook of Critical Management Studies*. Oxford: Oxford University Press.

Cooper, D.E. (1990) *Existentialism: A Reconstruction*. Oxford: Basil Blackwell.

Cooper, R. and Burrell, G. (1988) 'Modernism, postmodernism and organizational analysis: An introduction', *Organization Studies*, 9 (1): 91–112.

Cooper, D., Puxty, A.G., Robson, K. and Willmott, H.C. (1996) 'Changes in the International Regulation of Auditors: (In)stalling the Eighth Directive in the UK', (1994) *Critical Perspectives on Accounting,* 7 (6) 589–613.

Costas, J. and Fleming, P. (2009) 'Beyond dis-identification: A discursive approach to self-alienation in contemporary organizations', *Human Relations*, 62: 353–378.

Costea, B., Crump, N. and Amiridis, K. (2008) 'Managerialism, the therapeutic habitus and the self in contemporary organizing', *Human Relations*, 61 (5): 661–85.

Critical Perspectives on Accounting (1994) Special Issue on Foucault and Accounting, 5 (1).

Critical Perspectives on Accounting (2008) Special Issue on The Future of Interpretive Accounting, 19 (6): 837–926.

Critical Perspectives on International Business (2010) Special Issue on Critical International Management and International Critical Management: Perspectives from Latin America, 6 (2/3).

Crook, S., Pakalski, J. and Waters, M. (1992) *Postmodernization: Change in Advanced Society*. London: Sage.

Crouch, C. (2011) *The Strange Non-Death of Neoliberalism*. Cambridge: Polity Press.

Curry, W.L. and Guah, M.W. (2007) 'Conflicting institutional logics: A national programme for IT in the organisational field of healthcare', *Journal of Information Technology*, 22: 235–247.

Czarniawska-Joerges, B. (1992) *Exploring Complex Organizations*. London: Sage.

Daft, R.L., Murphy, J. and Willmott, H. (2010) *Organization Theory and Design*. London: Cengage Learning.

Dalton, M. (1959) *Men Who Manage*. New York: John Wiley.

Davis, G.F. (2009) *Managed by the Markets: How Finance Re-Shaped America*. Oxford: Oxford University Press

Dawe, A. (1979) 'Theories of social action', in T. Bottomore and R. Nisbet (eds), *A History of Sociological Analysis*. London: Heinemann.

Deetz, S. (1992a) *Democracy in an Age of Corporate Colonization: Developments in Communication and the Politics of Everyday Life*. Albany, NY: State University of New York Press.

Deetz, S. (1992b) 'Disciplinary power in the modern corporation', in M. Alvesson and H. Willmott (eds), *Critical Management Studies*. London: Sage.

Deetz, S. (1993) 'Debate comment' in L. Putnam, C. Bantz, S. Deetz, D. Mumby and J. Van Maanen (eds) (1993) Ethnography versus critical theory, *Journal of Management Inquiry*, 2: 221–35.

Deetz, S. (1996) 'Describing differences in approaches to organization science: Rethinking Burrell and Morgan and their legacy', *Organization Science*, 7 (2): 191–207.

Deetz, S. (2003) 'Disciplinary power, conflict suppression and human resource management', in M. Alvesson and H. Willmott (eds), *Critical Management Studies*. London: Sage.

Deetz, S. and Mumby, D. (1990) 'Power, discourse, and the workplace: Reclaiming the critical tradition in communication studies in organizations', in J. Anderson (ed.), *Communication Yearbook*, Vol. 13. Newbury Park, CA: Sage.

Dehler, G. (2009) 'Prospects and possibilities of critical management education: Critical beings and a pedagogy of critical action', *Management Learning*, 40 (1): 31–49.

Delbridge, R. (2010) 'The critical future of HRM', in P. Blyton, E. Heery and P. Turnbull (eds), *Reassessing the Employment Relationship*. London: Palgrave Macmillan. pp. 21–40.

Delbridge, R. and Keenoy, T. (2010) 'Beyond managerialism?', *The International Journal of Human Resource Management*, 21 (6): 799–817.

Del Gandio, J. (2008) 'Global justice rhetoric: Observations and suggestions', *Ephemera*, 8 (2): 182–203.

Dent, J. (1986) 'Organizational research in accounting: Perspectives, issues and a commentary', in M. Bromwich and A. Hopwood (eds), *Research and Current Issues in Management Accounting*. London: Pitman.

Denzin, N.K. and Lincoln, Y.S. (eds) (2005) *The Sage Handbook of Qualitative Research* (3rd edn). Thousand Oaks, CA: Sage.

Dews, P. (ed.) (1986) *Habermas: Autonomy and Solidarity*. London: Verso.

Doolin, B. (2004) 'Power and resistance in the implementation of a medical management information system', *Information Systems Journal*, 14 (4): 343–362.

Dreyfus, H.L., Dreyfus, S.E. and Athanasiou, T. (1986) *Mind over Machine: The Power of Human Intuition and Expertise in the Era of the Computer*. Oxford: Basil Blackwell.

Drucker, P. (1977) *Management*. London: Pan.

du Gay, P. (1994) 'Colossal immodesties and hopeful monsters: Pluralism and organizational conduct', *Organization*, 1 (1): 125–148.

du Gay, P. and Salaman, G. (1992) 'The cult(ure) of the customer', *Journal of Management Studies*, 29 (5): 615–633.

Dutton, J., Dukerich, J. and Harquail, C. (1994) 'Organizational images and member identification', *Administrative Science Quarterly*, 39: 239–263.

Earl, M. (1983) 'Management information systems and management accounting', in D.J. Cooper, R. Scapens and J. Arnold (eds), *Management Accounting Research and Practice*. London: Institute of Cost and Management Accountants.

Edward, P. and Willmott, H. C. (2012) 'Discourse and normative business ethics', in C. Luetge (ed), *Handbook of the Philosophical Foundations of Business Ethics*. Dortrecht: Springer.

Edwards, P.N. (1997) *The Closed World: Computers and the Politics of Discourse in Cold War America*. Cambridge, MA: MIT Press.

Edwards, R. (1979) *Contested Terrain*. London: Heinemann.

Elkjaer, B., Flensberg, P., Mouritsen, J. and Willmott, H.C. (1992) 'The commodification of expertise: The case of systems development consulting', *Accounting, Management and Information Technology*, 1 (2): 139–156.

Ellis, N., Fitchett, J., Higgins, M., Jack, G., Lim, M., Saren, M. and Tadajewski, M. (2010) *Marketing: A Critical Textbook*. London: Sage

Emery, F. and Trist, E. (1960) 'Socio-technical systems', in F. Emery (ed.), *Systems Thinking*. Harmondsworth: Penguin.

Engelen, E., Erturk, I., Froud, J., Johal, S., Leaver, A., Moran, M., Nilsson, A. and Williams, K. (2011) *After the Great Complacence: Financial Crisis and the Politics of Reform*. Oxford: Oxford University Press.

Etzioni, A. (1988) *The Moral Dimension*. New York: Free Press.

Ezzamel, M. (1994) 'Organisational change and accounting: Understanding the budgeting system in its organisational context', *Organization Studies*, 15 (2): 215–240.

Ezzamel, M. and Robson, K. (2009) 'Accounting', in M. Alvesson, T. Bridgman and H.C. Willmott (eds), *The Oxford Handbook of Critical Management Studies*. Oxford: Oxford University Press.

Ezzamel, M. and Willmott, H. (1998) 'Accounting and employee remuneration in the new organization', *Accounting and Business Research*, 28 (2): 97–110.

Ezzamel, M. and Willmott, H. (2004) 'Rethinking strategy: Contemporary perspectives and debates', *European Management Review*, 1 (1): 43–48.

Ezzamel, M. and Willmott, H. (2008) 'Strategy as discourse in a global retailer: A supplement to rationalist and interpretive accounts', *Organization Studies*, 29 (2): 191–217.

Ezzamel, M. and Willmott, H. (2010) 'Strategy and strategizing: A poststructuralist perspective', in J.A.C. Baum and J. Lampel (eds), *The Globalization of Strategy Research* (Advances in Strategic Management, Volume 27). Bingley: Emerald (pp. 75–109).

Ezzamel, M., Willmott, H. and Worthington, F. (2001) 'Power, control and resistance in the factory that time forgot', *Journal of Management Studies*, 38 (8): 1053–1079.

Ezzamel, M., Willmott H. and Worthington, F. (2008) 'Manufacturing shareholder value: The role of accounting in organizational transformation', *Accounting, Organizations and Society*, 33 (2/3): 107–140.

Fairhurst, G. (2001) 'Dualisms in leadership research', in F. Jablin et al. (eds), *Handbook of Organizational Communication*. Thousand Oaks, CA: Sage.

Fay, B. (1987) *Critical Social Science*. Cambridge: Polity Press.

Fayol, H. (1949) *General and Industrial Management*. London: Pitman.

Featherstone, M. (1991) *Consumer Culture and Postmodernism*. London: Sage.

Fenwick, T.J. (2003) 'Emancipatory potential of action learning: A critical analysis', *Journal of Organizational Change Management*, 16 (6): 619–632.

Fenwick, T. (2005) 'Ethical dilemmas of critical management education within classrooms and beyond', *Management Learning*, 36 (1): 31–48.

Ferguson, K.E. (1984) *The Feminist Case Against Bureaucracy*. Philadelphia, PA: Temple University Press.

Ferguson, A. (2006) 'Women organizing for global justice', working paper, Center for Global Justice, University of Massachusetts. Available at: http://www.global-justicecenter.org/papers2006/ferguson2ENG.htm. Accessed 9 December 2007.

Fineman, S. (2006) 'On being positive', *Academy of Management Review*, 31 (2): 270–291.

Finlayson, G. (2005) *Habermas: A Very Short Introduction*. Oxford: Oxford University Press.

Firat, A.F. and Venkatesh, A. (1992) 'The making of postmodern consumption', in R.W. Belk and N. Dholakia (eds), *Consumption and Marketing: Macro Dimensions*. Boston, MA: PWS-Kent.

Fischer, F. (1990) *Technocracy and the Politics of Expertise*. London: Sage.

Fiske, M.C. and Calkins, L.B. (2011) 'BP's pursuit of cost-cutting led to Gulf Spill, lawyers say', Bloomberg, 5 Feb. Available at: http://www.bloomberg.com/news/2011-02-05/bp-mismanagement-led-to-explosion-spill-lawsuit-says-update1-.html. Accessed 8 February 2011.

Flax, J. (1990a) *Thinking Fragments: Psychoanalysis, Feminism and Postmodernism in the Contemporary West*. Berkeley, CA: University of California Press.

Flax, J. (1990b) 'Postmodernism and gender relations in feminist theory', in L.J. Nicholson (ed.), *Feminism/Postmodernism*. London: Routledge.

Fleming, P. (2009) *Authenticity and the Cultural Politics of Work*. Oxford: Oxford University Press.

Fleming, P. and Mandarini, M. (2009) 'Towards a workers' society? New perspectives on work and emancipation', in M. Alvesson, T. Bridgman and H. Willmott (eds), *Oxford Handbook of Critical Management Studies*. Oxford: Oxford University Press.

Fleming, P. and Spicer, A. (2003) 'Working at a cynical distance: Implications for power, subjectivity and resistance', *Organization*, 10: 157–179.

Fleming, P. and Spicer, A. (2007) *Contesting the Corporation: Struggle, Power and Resistance in Organizations*. Cambridge: Cambridge University Press.

Fleming, P. and Sturdy, A. (2009) '"Just be yourself!":Towards neo-normative control in organisations?', *Employee Relations*, 31 (6): 569–583.

Fleming, P. and Sturdy, A. (2011) 'Being yourself in the electronic sweatshop: New forms of normative control', *Human Relations*, 64: 177–200.

Flood, R.L. and Jackson, M.C. (1991a) *Critical Systems Thinking: Directed Readings.* Chichester: John Wiley.

Flood, R.L. and Jackson, M.C. (1991b) 'Critical systems heuristics: Application of an emancipatory approach for police strategy toward the carrying of offensive weapons', *Systems Practice,* 4 (4): 283–302.

Flood, R.L. and Jackson, M.C. (1992) *Creative Problem Solving: Total Systems Intervention.* London: John Wiley.

Forester, J. (1981) 'Questioning and organizing attention: Toward a critical theory of planning and administrative practice', *Administration and Society*, 13 (2): 161–205.

Forester, J. (1982) 'A critical empirical framework for the analysis of public policy', *New Political Science,* 3, (1–2): 33–61.

Forester, J. (1983) 'Critical theory and organizational analysis', in G. Morgan (ed.), *Beyond Method.* Beverly Hills, CA: Sage.

Forester, J. (ed.) (1985) *Critical Theory and Public Life.* Cambridge, MA: MIT Press.

Forester, J. (1988) 'The contemporary relevance of critical theory to public administration: Promises and problems', Working paper, Dept of City and Regional Planning, Cornell University.

Forester, J. (1989) *Planning in the Face of Power.* Berkeley, CA: University of California Press.

Forester, J. (1992) 'Critical ethnography: On fieldwork in a Habermasian way', in M. Alvesson and H. Willmott (eds), *Critical Management Studies.* London: Sage.

Forester, J. (1993) *Critical Theory. Public Policy and Planning Practice: Toward a Critical Pragmation.* Albany, NY: State University of New York Press.

Forester, J. (2003) 'On fieldwork in a Habermasian way: Critical ethnography and the extra-ordinary character of ordinary professional work', in M. Alvesson and H. Willmott (eds), *Studying Management Critically.* London: Sage.

Fosstenløkken, S.M. (2007) 'Enhancing intangible resources in professional service firms: A comparative study of how competence development takes place in four firms', PhD dissertation. Oslo: BI.

Foster, J.B. and Clark, B. (2009) 'The paradox of wealth: Capitalism and ecological destruction', *Monthly Review*, 61 (6). Available at: http://monthlyreview. org/2009/11/01/the-paradox-of-wealth-capitalism-and-ecological-destruction. Accessed 6 July 2011.

Foster, W.M. and Wiebe, E. (2011) 'Praxis makes perfect: Recovering the ethical promise of critical management studies', *Journal of Business Ethics*, 94: 271–283.

Foucault, M. (1977) *Discipline and Punish: The Birth of the Prison.* Harmondsworth: Penguin.

Foucault, M. (1980) *Power/Knowledge.* New York: Pantheon.

Foucault, M. (1985) *The Use of Pleasure.* Harmondsworth: Penguin.

Foucault, M. (1986) *The Care of the Self.* Harmondsworth: Penguin.

Foucault, M. (1991) *Remarks on Marx: Conversations with Duccio Tombadori*. New York: Semootext(e).

Fox, A. (1974) *Beyond Contract*. London: Faber and Faber.

Fox, R.W. and Lears, T.J. (1983) *The Culture of Consumption*. New York: Pantheon.

Fraser, N. (1987) 'What's critical about critical theory? The case of Habermas and gender', in S. Benhabib and D. Cornell (eds), *Feminism as Critique*. Cambridge: Polity Press.

Freire, P. (1972) *Pedagogy of the Oppressed*. Harmondsworth: Penguin.

Freud, S. (1917) *Introductory Lectures in Psychoanalysis*. Harmondsworth: Penguin.

Freundlieb, D. (1989) 'Rationalism v irrationalism? Habermas's response to Foucault', *Inquiry*, 31: 171–192.

Friedman, G. (1981) *The Political Philosophy of the Frankfurt School*. Ithaca, NY: Cornell University Press.

Fromm, E. (1941) *Escape from Freedom*. New York: Holt, Rinehart and Winston.

Fromm, E. (1955) *The Sane Society*. London: Routledge and Kegan Paul.

Fromm, E. (1961) *Marx's Concept of Man*. New York: Frederick Unger.

Fromm, E. (1970) *The Crises of Psychoanalysis*. Harmondsworth: Penguin.

Fromm, E. (1976) *To Have or To Be?* London: Abacus.

Frost, P. and Egri, C. (1991) 'The political process of innovation', *Research in Organizational Behaviour*, 13: 229–295.

Froud, J. and Johal, S. (2008) 'Questioning finance: A special issue of *Competition & Change*. Editorial', *Competition & Change*, 12 (2): 107–109.

Froud, J., Johal, S., Law, J., Leaver, A. and Williams, K. (2010) 'Rebalancing the economy (or buyer's remorse)', CRESC working paper series, Working Paper No.87, Centre for Research on Socio-Cultural Change (CRESC), Faculty of Social Sciences, the Open University. Available at http://www.cresc.ac.uk/publications/rebalancing-the-economy-or-buyersremorse. Accessed 12 February 2011.

Fryer, M. (2012) 'Facilitative leadership: Drawing Habermas' model of ideal speech to propose a critically sensitive way to lead', *Organization*, 19(1): 25–43.

Gabriel, Y. (2005) 'Glass cages and glass palaces: Images of organizations in image-conscious times', *Organization*, 12 (1): 9–27.

Gabriel, Y. and Lang, T. (1995) *The Unmanageable Consumer: Contemporary Consumption and its Fragmentation*. London: Sage.

Galbraith, J.K. (1958) *The Affluent Society*. Harmondsworth: Penguin.

Galbraith, J.K. (1983) *The Anatomy of Power*. New York: Simon and Schuster.

Gallhofer, S. and Haslam, J. (2002) *Accounting and Emancipation: Some Critical Interventions*. London: Routledge.

Garfinkel, H. (1967) *Studies in Ethnomethodology*. Englewood Cliffs, NJ: Prentice Hall.

Garrett, D. (1987) 'The effectiveness of marketing policy boycotts: Environmental opposition to marketing', *Journal of Marketing*, 51 (April): 46–57.

Geertz, C. (1973) *The Interpretation of Cultures*. New York: Basic Books.

Gemmill, G. and Oakley, J. (1992) 'Leadership: An alienating social myth', *Human Relations*, 45 (2): 113–129.

Gephart, R.P. and Pitter, R. (1993) 'The organizational basis of industrial accidents in Canada', *Journal of Management Inquiry*, 2 (3): 238–252.

Ghoshal, S. (2005) 'Bad management theories are destroying good management practices', *Academy of Management Learning & Education*, 4 (1): 75–91.

Giddens, A. (1979) *Central Problems in Social Theory*. London: Macmillan.

Giddens, A. (1989) 'Response to my critics', in D. Held and J. Thompson (eds), *Social Theory of Modern Societies: Anthony Giddens and His Critics*. Cambridge: Cambridge University Press.

Giddens, A. (1991) *Modernity and Self-Identity: Self and Society in the Late Modern Age*. Cambridge: Polity.

Gilligan, C. (1982) *In a Different Voice: Psychological Theory and Women's Development*. Cambridge, MA: Harvard University Press.

Goffman, E. (1959) *The Presentation of Self in Everyday Life*. Harmondsworth: Penguin.

Golsorkhi, D., Rouleau, L., Seidl, D. and Vaara, E. (2010) 'What is strategy-as-practice?', in D. Golsorkhi, L. Rouleau, D. Seidl and E. Vaara (eds), *Cambridge Handbook of Strategy as Practice*. Cambridge: Cambridge University Press.

Gore, J. (1992) 'What we can do for you! What can "we" do for "you"?', in C. Luke and J. Gore (eds), *Critical Pedagogy*. London: Routledge.

Gouldner, A. (1973b) 'The sociologist as partisan', in A. Gouldner (ed.), *For Sociology: Renewal and Critique in Sociology Today*. London: Allen Lane.

Gowler, D. and Legge, K. (1983) 'The meaning of management and the management of meaning: A view from social anthropology', in M.J. Earl (ed.), *Perspectives in Management*. Oxford: Oxford University Press.

Gramsci, A. (1971) *Selections from the Prison Notebooks of Antonio Gramsci*. London: Lawrence and Wishart.

Granovetter, M. (1985) 'Economic action and social structure: The problem of embeddedness', *American Journal of Sociology*, 91: 481–510.

Grant, D. and Oswick, C. (eds) (1996) *Metaphor and Organizations*. London: Sage.

Gray, R., Dey, C., Owen, D., Evans, R. and Zadek, S. (1997) 'Struggling with the praxis of social accounting: Stakeholders, accountability, audits and procedures', *Accounting, Auditing and Accountability Journal*, 10 (3): 325–364.

Grey, C. (1994) 'Career as a project of the self and labour process discipline', *Sociology*, 28: 479–497.

Grey, C. (1999) '"We are all managers now"; "We always were": On the development and demise of management', *Journal of Management Studies*, 36 (5): 561–585.

Grey, C. (2003) 'The strange case of management', *Fabian Review*, Autumn: 10–11.

Grey, C. (2008) *A Very Short, Fairly Interesting and Reasonably Cheap Book About Studying Organizations* (2nd edn). London: Sage.

Grey, C. and Mitev, N. (1995) 'Reengineering organizations: A critical appraisal', *Personnel Review*, 24 (1): 6–18.

Grey, C., Knights, D. and Willmott, H.C. (1996) 'Is a critical pedagogy of management possible?', in R. French and C. Grey (eds), *New Perspectives on Management Education*. London: Sage.

Grimes, A. and Cornwall, D. (1987) 'The disintegration of an organization: A dialectical analysis', *Journal of Management*, 13 (1): 69–86.

Grint, K. (1994) 'Reengineering history: Social resonances and business process reengineering', *Organization*, 1 (1): 179–201.

Gronn, P. (2002) 'Distributed leadership as a unit of analysis', *Leadership Quarterly*, 13 (4): 423–451.

Guest, D. (2002) 'Human resource management, corporate performance and employee wellbeing: Building the worker into HRM', *Journal of Industrial Relations*, 44 (3): 335–358.

Guest, D. and King, Z. (2004) 'Power, innovation and problem-solving. The personnel manager's three steps to heaven?', *Journal of Management Studies*, 41: 401–424.

Gustavsen, B. (1985) 'Workplace reform and democratic dialogue', *Economic and Industrial Democracy*, 6 (4): 761–780.

Habermas, J. (1971) *Towards a Rational Society: Student Protest, Science and Politics*. London: Heinemann.

Habermas, J. (1972) *Knowledge and Human Interests*. London: Heinemann.

Habermas, J. (1974) *Theory and Practice*. London: Heinemann.

Habermas, J. (1975) *Legitimation Crisis*. Boston, MA: Beacon Press.

Habermas, J. (1976) 'A positivistically bisected rationalism', in T. W. Adorno, H. Albert, R. Dahrendorf, J. Habermas, H. Pilot and K. R. Popper (eds), *The Positivist Dispute in German Sociology*. London: Heinemann.

Habermas, J. (1979) *Communication and the Evolution of Society*. London: Heinemann.

Habermas, J. (1982) 'A reply to my critics', in J. Thompson and D. Held (eds), *Habermas: Critical Debates*. London: Macmillan.

Habermas, J. (1984) *The Theory of Communicative Action, Volume 1: Reason and the Rationalization of Society*. London: Heinemann.

Habermas, J. (1985) 'A philosophico-political profile', *New Left Review*, 151: 75–105.

Habermas, J. (1986) *Autonomy and Solidarity: Interviews with Jurgen Habermas* (ed. P. Dews). London: Verso.

Habermas, J. (1987) *The Theory of Communicative Action, Volume 2: Lifeworld and System: A Critique of Functionalist Reason*. London: Heinemann.

Habermas, J. (1989a) *The New Conservatism: Cultural Critique and the Historian's Debate*. Cambridge: Polity Press.

Habermas, J. (1989b) *The Structural Transformation of the Public Sphere*. Cambridge: Polity Press.

Habermas, J. (1991) 'A reply', in A. Honneth and H. Joas (eds), *Communicative Action: Essays on Jurgen Habermas'* The Theory of Communicative Action. Cambridge, MA: MIT Press.

Habermas, J. (1992) *Postmetaphysical Thinking: Philosophical Essays*. Cambridge: Polity Press.

Habermas, J. (1994) *The Past as Future*. Cambridge: Polity Press.

Habermas, J. (2010) 'The "good life" – A "detestable phrase": The significance of the young Rawls's religious ethics for his political theory', *European Journal of Philosophy*, 18: 443–454.

Habermas, J., Brieskorn, N., Reder, M., Ricken, F. and Schmidt, J. (2010) *An Awareness of What is Missing: Faith and Reason in a Post-secular Age*. Cambridge: Polity Press.

Hales, C. (1993) *Managing Through Organization*. London: Routledge.

Hales, M. (1974) 'Management science and the second industrial revolution', *Radical Science Journal,* 1: 5–28.

Hamel, G. and Prahalad, C.K. (1989) 'Strategic intent', *Harvard Business Review*, 67: 63–76.

Hammer, M. (1994) 'Reengineering is not hocus-pocus', *Across the Board*, September, 31 (8): 45–47.

Hammer, M. and Champy, J. (1993) *Reengineering the Corporation: A Manifesto for Business Revolution*. London: Nicholas Brealey.

Hancock, P. and Tyler, M. (2009) *The Management of Everyday Life*. London: Palgrave Macmillan.

Hanlon, G. (2008) 'Rethinking corporate social responsibility and the role of the firm – on the denial of politics', in A. Crane, A. McWilliams, D. Matten and J. Moon (eds), *The Oxford Handbook of Corporate Social Responsibility*. Oxford: Oxford University Press.

Hanlon, G. and Fleming, P. (2009) 'Updating the critical perspective on corporate social responsibility', *Sociology Compass*, 2 (6): 1–12.

Hannan, M.T. and Freeman, J. (1977) 'The population ecology of organizations', *American Journal of Sociology*, 82: 929–964.

Hansen, M.T., Norhia, N. and Tierney, T. (1999) 'What's your strategy for managing knowledge?', *Harvard Business Review*, March–April: 106–116.

Harding, S. (1986) *The Science Question in Feminism*. Ithaca, NY: Cornell University Press.

Harms, J. and Kellner, D. (1991) 'Critical theory and advertising', in B. Agger (ed.), *Current Perspectives in Social Theory,* Vol. 11. Greenwich, CT: JAI Press.

Hartsock, N. (1984) *Money, Sex and Power: Toward a Feminist Historical Materialism*. Boston, MA: Northeast University Press.

Harvey, D. (1991) *The Condition of Postmodernity: An Enquiry into the Origins of Cultural Change*. Oxford: Blackwell.

Haslam, A. (2004) *Psychology of Organizations* (2nd edn). London: Sage.

Haslam, A. and Reicher, S. (2006) 'Social identity and the dynamics of organizational life', in C. Bartel, S. Blader and A. Wrzesniewski (eds), *Identity and the Modern Organization*. Mahwah, NJ: Lawrence Erlbaum.

Hatch, M.J. and Schultz, M. (2002) 'The dynamics of organizational identity', *Human Relations*, 55: 989–1018.

Hatch, M.J. and Schultz, M. (eds) (2004) *Organisational Identity: A Reader*. Oxford: Oxford University Press.

Haug, W.F. (1986) *Critique of Commodity Aesthetics*. Minneapolis, MN: University of Minneapolis Press.

Hearn, J., Sheppard, D.L., Tancred-Sheriff, P. and Burrell, G. (eds) (1989) *The Sexuality of Organization*. London: Sage.

Heath, J. (1995) 'The problem of foundationalism in Habermas's discourse ethics', *Philosophy and Social Criticism*, 21 (1): 77–100.

Hehir, P. and Petrella, T. (2011) *Business Worth Doing: A New Balanced Stakeholder System for the 21st Century*. Available at: http://www.bvgintl.com/wp-content/uploads/2011/03/BusinessWorthDoingDec2010S.pdf.

Heifetz, R. and Laurie, D. (1994) 'The work of leadership', *Harvard Business Review*, 75 (1): 124–134.

Held, D. (1980) *Introduction to Critical Theory*. London: Hutchinson.

Heng, M. and de Moor, A. (2003) 'From Habermas's communicative theory to practice on the Internet', *Information Systems Journal*, 13 (4): 331–352.

Herda, E.A. and Messerschmitt, D.S. (1991) 'From words to actions: Communication for business management', *Leadership and Organization Development Journal*, 12 (1): 23–27.

Hesketh, A. and Fleetwood, S. (2006) 'Beyond measuring the human resource management–organizational performance link: Applying critical realist meta-theory', *Organization*, 13: 677–699.

Heydebrand, W. (1980) 'A Marxist critique of organization theory', in W.M. Evan (ed.), *Frontiers in Organization and Management*. New York: Praeger.

Hines, R. (1988) 'Financial accounting: In communicating reality, we construct reality', *Accounting, Organizations and Society*, 13 (3): 251–261.

Hirsch, F. (1976) *Social Limits to Growth*. Cambridge, MA: Harvard University Press.

Hirschheim, R. and Klein, R. (1989) 'Four paradigms of information systems development', *Communications of the ACM*, 32 (10): 1199–1216.

Hirschman, E. (1990) 'Secular immortality and the American ideology of affluence', *Journal of Consumer Research,* 17 (June): 31–42.

Hochschild, A.R. (1983) *The Managed Heart: Commercialization of Human Feelings*. Berkeley: University of California Press.

Holbrook, M.B. (1987) 'Mirror, mirror, on the wall, what's unfair in the reflections on advertising?', *Journal of Marketing*, 51 (July): 95–103.

Holub, R. C. (1991) *Jurgen Habermas: Critic of the Public Sphere*. London: Routledge.

Honneth, A. (1991) *The Critique of Power: Reflective Stages in a Critical Social Theory*. Cambridge, MA: MIT Press.

Honneth, A. (2003) 'The point of recognition: A rejoinder to the rejoinder', in N. Fraser, A. Honneth, J. Golb and C. Wilke (eds), *Redistribution or Recognition? A Political-Philosophical Exchange*. London: Verso.

Hopper, T. and Powell, A. (1985) 'Making sense of research into the organizational and social aspects of management accounting: A review of its underlying assumptions', *Journal of Management Studies*, 22 (5): 429–465.

Hopwood, A. (2009) 'On striving to get a critical edge to Critical Management Studies', in M. Alvesson, T. Bridgman and H. Willmott (eds), *Oxford Handbook of Critical Management Studies*. Oxford: Oxford University Press.

Hopwood, A.G. and Miller, P. (eds) (1994) *Accounting as Social and Institutional Practice*. Cambridge: Cambridge University Press.

Horkheimer, M. (1937/1976) 'Traditional and critical theory', in P. Connerton (ed.), *Critical Sociology*. Harmondsworth: Penguin.

Horkheimer, M. (1972) *Critical Theory: Selected Essays*. New York: Herder and Herder.

Horkheimer, M. and Adorno, T. (1947a/1979) *The Dialectics of Enlightenment*. London: Verso.

Horkheimer, M. and Adorno, T. (1947b) *Eclipse of Reason*. New York: Oxford University Press.

Houghton, J.D., Neck, C.P. and Manz, C.C. (2003) 'Self-leadership and superleadership: The heart and art of creating shared leadership in teams', in C. L. Pearce and J. A. Conger (eds), *Shared Leadership: Reframing the Hows and Whys of Leadership*. Thousand Oaks, CA: Sage. pp. 123–140.

Howcroft, D. and Trauth, E.M. (2004) 'The choice of critical information systems research', in B. Kaplan, D.P. Truex, D. Wastell, A.T. Wood-Harper and J.I. DeGross (eds), *Information Systems Research: Relevant Theory and Informed Practice* (IFIP Advances in Information and Communication Technology). Boston: Springer.

Howcroft, D. and Trauth, E.M. (2005) *Handbook of Critical Information Systems Research: Theory and Application*. Cheltenham, Gloucestershire: Edward Elgar.

Howcroft, D. and Trauth, E.M. (2008) 'The implications of a critical agenda in gender and IS research', *Information Systems Journal*, 18 (2): 185–202.

Hoy, D. (ed.) (1986) *Foucault: A Critical Reader*. Oxford: Basil Blackwell.

Huff, A.S. (1982) 'Industry influences on strategic reformulation', *Strategic Management Journal*, 3: 119–131.

Hunt, S.D. (1990) 'Truth in marketing theory and research', *Journal of Marketing*, 40: 17–28.

Hunt, S.D. (1991) 'Positivism and paradigm dominance in consumer research: Toward critical pluralism and rapprochement', *Journal of Consumer Research*, 18 (1): 32–44.

Hunt, S.D. (1994) 'On rethinking marketing: Our discipline, our practice, our methods', *European Journal of Marketing*, 28 (3): 13–25.

Huselid, M.A. (1995) 'The impact of human resource management practices on turnover, productivity, and corporate financial performance', *Academy of Management Journal*, 38: 635–672.

Isle of Wight (nd) http://eduwight.iow.gov.uk/the_lea/personnel/images/GEN GUIDANCENOTESONHANDOFREDU.pdf, Accessed 18 November 2011.

Jackall, R. (1988) *Moral Mazes: The World of Corporate Managers*. New York: Oxford University Press.

Jackson, M.C. (1982) 'The nature of soft systems thinking: The work of Churchman, Ackott and Checkland', *Journal of Applied Systems Analysis*, 9: 17–29.

Jackson, M.C. (1992) 'An integrated programme for critical thinking in information systems research', *Journal of Information Systems*, 2: 83–95.

Jackson, N. and Willmott, H.C. (1986) 'Beyond epistemology and reflective conversation – towards human relations', *Human Relations*, 40 (6): 361–380.

Jacques, R. (1992) 'Critique and theory building: Producing knowledge "from the kitchen"', *Academy of Management Review*, 17 (3): 582–606.

Janssens, M. and Steyaert, C. (2009) 'HRM and performance: A plea for reflexivity in HRM studies', *Journal of Management Studies*, 46 (1): 143–155.

Jarzabkowski, P. (2005) *Strategy as Practice: An Activity-Based Approach*. London: Sage.

Jasperson, J., Butler, B.S., Carte, T.A., Croes, H.J.P., Saunders, C.S. and Zheng, W. (2002) 'Power and information technology research: A metatriangulation review', *MIS Quarterly*, 26 (4): 397–459.

Jay, M. (1973) *The Dialectical Imagination: A History of the Frankfurt School and the Institute of Social Research 1923–50*. Berkeley: University of California Press.

Jeffcutt, P. (1993) 'From interpretation to representation', in J. Hassard and M. Parker (eds), *Postmodernism and Organizations*. London: Sage.

Jermier, J.M. and Forbes, L.C. (2003) 'Greening organizations: Critical issues', in M. Alvesson and H. Willmott (eds), *Studying Management Critically*. London: Sage. pp. 157–176.

Jermier, J., Forbes, L., Benn, S. and Orsato, M.J. (1996) 'The new corporate environmentalism and green politics', in S.R. Clegg, C. Hardy, T.B. Lawrence and W.R. Nord (eds), *The Sage Handbook Of Organization Studies* (2nd edn). London: Sage. pp. 618–650.

Johnson, G. (1987) *Strategic Change and the Management Process*. Oxford: Basil Blackwell.

Johnson, G., Langley, A., Melin, L. and Whittington, R. (2007) *Strategy as Practice: Research Directions and Resources*. Cambridge: Cambridge University Press.

Jones, C. and Spicer, A. (2005) 'Disidentifying the subject: Lacanian comments on subjectivity, resistance and enterprise', *Organization,* 12 (2): 223–246.

Jones, O., Sharifi, S. and Conway, S. (2006) 'Accounting for *Organization*: round-up the usual suspects', *Critical Perspectives on Accounting*, 17 (2/3): 283-304.

Jonsson, E. (1979) *Konsten att lura konsumenten*. Stockholm: Rabén and Sjögren.

Kahney, L. (2010) 'John Sculley on Steve Jobs: The full transcript'. Available at http://www.cultofmac.com/63295/john-sculley-on-steve-jobs-the-full-interview-transcript. Accessed 21 November 2011.

Kalgaard, R. (1993) 'ASAP interview with Michael Hammer', *Forbes*, September: 69–75.

Kanter, R.M. (1983) *The Change Masters. Innovations for Productivity in the American Corporation*. New York: Simon and Schuster.

Kapoor, I. (2002) 'Deliberative democracy or agonistic pluralism? The relevance of the Habermas–Mouffe debate for third world politics', *Alternatives*, 27: 459–487.

Kärreman, D. and Alvesson, M. (2009) 'Resisting resistance: Counter-resistance, consent and compliance in a consultancy firm', *Human Relations*, 62 (8): 1115–1144.

Kärreman, D. and Rylander, A. (2008) 'Managing meaning through branding – the case of a consulting firm', *Organization Studies*, 29 (1): 103–125.

Kasser, T. (2002) *The High Price of Materialism*. Cambridge, MA: MIT Press.

Keasey, K. and Hudson, R. (2007) 'Finance theory: A house without windows', *Critical Perspectives on Accounting*, 18 (8): 932–951.

Keat, R. (1981) *The Politics of Social Theory: Habermas, Freud and the Critique of Positivism*. Oxford: Blackwell.

Keegan, A. and Boselie, P. (2006) 'The lack of impact of dissensus inspired analysis on developments in the field of human resource management', *Journal of Management Studies*, 43 (7): 1491–1511.

Keenoy, T. (1990) 'HRM: A case of the wolf in sheep's clothing', *Personnel Review*, 19 (2): 3–9.

Keenoy, T. (1999) 'HRM as hologram: A polemic', *Journal of Management Studies*, 36: 1–23.

Keenoy, T. (2009) 'Human resource management', in M. Alvesson, T. Bridgman and H. Willmott (eds), *The Oxford Handbook of Critical Management Studies*. Oxford: Oxford University Press. pp. 454–472.

Keenoy, T. and Anthony, P. (1992) 'HRM: Meaning, metaphor and morality', in P. Blyton and P. Turnbull (eds), *Reassessing Human Resource Management*. London: Sage.

Keleman, M. and Rumens, N. (2008) *An Introduction to Critical Management Research*. London: Sage

Kellner, D. (1988) 'Postmodernism as social theory: Some challenges and problems', *Theory, Culture & Society*, 5: 239–269.

Kellner, D. (1989) *Critical Theory, Marxism and Modernity*. Cambridge: Polity Press.

Kemmis, S. (2000) 'Exploring the relevance of critical theory for action research: Emancipatory action research in the footsteps of Jürgen Habermas', in J. Reason and H. Bradbury-Huang (eds), *Handbook of Action Research: Participative Inquiry and Practice*. London: Sage.

Kenny, K., Whittle, A. and Willmott, H.C. (2012) *Understanding Identity and Organizations*. London: Sage.

Kerfoot, D. and Knights, D. (1994) 'Empowering the "quality" worker: The seduction and contradiction of the total quality phenomenon', in A. Wilkinson and H.C. Willmott (eds), *Making Quality Critical*. London: Routledge.

Kets de Vries, M. (1994) 'The leadership mystique', *Academy of Management Executive*, 8 (3): 73–89.

Khurana, R. (2002) *Searching for a Corporate Savior: The Irrational Quest for Charismatic CEOs*. Princeton: Princeton University Press .

Khuruna, R. (2007) *From Higher Aims to Hired Hands: The Social Transformation of American Business Schools and the Unfulfilled Promise of Management as a Profession*. Princeton: Princeton University Press.

Kjonstad, B. and Willmott, H.C. (1995) 'Business ethics: Restrictive or empowering?', *Journal of Business Ethics*, 13: 1–20.

Klatt, L.A., Murdick, R.G. and Schuster, F.E. (1985) *Human Resource Management*. London: Charles Merrill.

Klein, H.K. (2004) 'Seeking the new and the critical in critical realism: Déjà vu?', *Information and Organization*, 14: 123–144.

Klein, H.J. and Lyytinen, K. (1985) 'The poverty of scientism in information systems' in E. Mumford, R. Hischheim, G. Fitzgerald and T. Wood-Harper (eds), *Research Methods in Information Systems*. Amsterdam: North Holland.

Klein, N. (2000) *No Logo*. London: Flamingo.

Klein, N. (2007) *The Shock Doctrine: The Rise of Disaster Capitalism*. London: Harmondsworth.

Klimecki, R. and Willmott, H.C. (2009) 'From demutualization to meltdown: A tale of two wannabe banks', *Critical Perspectives on International Business*, 5 (1–2): 12–140.

Knights, D. (1992) 'Changing spaces: The disruptive impact of a new epistemological location for the study of management', *Academy of Management Review*, 17: 514–536.

Knights, D. (2009) 'Power at work in organizations', in M. Alvesson, T. Bridgman and H. Willmott (eds), *Oxford Handbook of Critical Management Studies*. Oxford: Oxford University Press.

Knights, D. and Morgan, G. (1991) 'Corporate strategy, organizations, and subjectivity: A critique', *Organization Studies*, 12: 251–273.

Knights, D. and Murray, F. (1994) *Managers Divided: Organisation Politics and Information Technology Management*. Chichester: John Wiley.

Knights, D. and Scarbrough, H. (2010) 'In search of relevance: Perspectives on the contribution of academic-practitioner networks', *Organization Studies*, 31 (9/10): 1287–1310.

Knights, D. and Willmott, H.C. (1974/5) 'Humanistic social science and the theory of needs', *Interpersonal Development*, 5 (4): 213–223.

Knights, D. and Willmott, H.C. (1985) 'Power and identity in theory and practice', *Sociological Review*, 33 (1): 22–46.

Knights, D. and Willmott, H.C. (1987) 'Organizational culture as corporate strategy', *International Studies of Management and Organisation*, 17 (3): 40–63.

Knights, D. and Willmott, H.C. (1989) 'Power and subjectivity at work: From degradation to subjugation in social relations', *Sociology*, 23 (4): 535–558.

Knights, D. and Willmott, H.C. (eds) (1990) *Labour Process Theory*. London: Macmillan.

Knights, D. and Willmott, H.C. (2002) 'Autonomy as utopia or dystopia', in M. Parker (ed.), *Utopia and Organization*. Oxford: Blackwell. pp. 59–81.

Knights, D. and Willmott, H.C. (2007) 'Conceptualizing leadership processes: A study of senior managers in a financial services company', *Journal of Management Studies*, 29 (6): 761–782.

Knights, D. and Willmott, H.C. (eds) (2007) *Introducing Organizational Behaviour and Management*. London: Thomson Learning.

Knights, D. and Willmott, H.C. (eds) (2012) *Introducing Organization Behaviour and Management* (2nd edn). London: Cengage Learning.

Knights, D., Morgan, G. and Murray, F. (1991) 'Strategic management, financial services and information technology', Paper presented at the 10th EGOS Colloquium, Vienna.

Knights, D., Murray, F. and Willmott, H.C. (1993) 'Networking as knowledge work: A study of strategic interorganizational development in the financial services industry', *Journal of Management Studies*, 30 (6): 975–995.

Knorr Cetina, K. (1999) *Epistemic Cultures: How the Sciences Make Knowledge*. Cambridge, MA: Harvard University Press.

Kohn, M. (1980) 'Job complexity and adult personality', in N. Smelser and E.H. Erikson (eds), *Themes of Work and Love in Adulthood*. Cambridge, MA: Harvard University Press.

Kompridis, N. (2006) *Critique and Disclosure: Critical Theory between Past and Future*. Cambridge, MA: MIT Press.

Kondo, D. (1990) *Crafting Selves: Power, Gender and Discourses of Identity in a Japanese Workplace* (2nd edn). Chicago: University of Chicago Press.

Korczynski, M. (2005) 'The point of selling: Capitalism, consumption and contradictions', *Organization*, 12 (1): 69–88.

Kotler, P. (1976) *Marketing Management* (3rd edn). Englewood Cliffs, NJ: Prentice Hall.

Kunda, G. (1992) *Engineering Culture. Control and Commitment in a High-Tech Corporation*. Philadelphia, PA: Temple University Press.

Ladkin, D. (2010) *Rethinking Leadership: A New Look at Old Leadership Questions*. Cheltenham: Edward Elgar.

Lair, D., Sullivan, K. and Cheney, G. (2005) 'Marketization and the recasting of the professional self: The rhetoric and ethics of personal branding', *Management Communication Quarterly*, 18: 307–343.

Lakoff, G. and Johnson, M. (1980) *Metaphors We Live By*. Chicago, IL: University of Chicago Press.

Lasch, C. (1979) *The Culture of Narcissism*. New York: Norton.

Lasch, C. (1984) *The Minimal Self*. London: Picador.

Lasn, K. (2000) *Culture Jam: How to Reverse America's Suicidal Consumer Binge – And Why We Must*. New York: Quill.

Laughlin, R. (1987) 'Accounting systems in organizational contexts: A case for critical theory', *Accounting, Organizations and Society*, 12 (5): 472–502.

Laughlin, R. (1991) 'Environmental disturbances and organizational change pathways', *Organization Studies*, 12: 209–232.

Laughlin, R. and Broadbent, P.J. (1993) 'Accounting and law: Partners in the juridification of the public sector in the UK?', *Critical Perspectives on Accounting*, 4 (4): 337–368.

Ledington, P. and Donaldson, J. (1997) 'Soft OR and management practice: A study of the adoption and use of soft systems methodology', *Journal of the Operational Research Society*, 48 (3): 229–240.

Lee, H., Learmonth, M. and Harding, N. (2008) 'Queer(y)ing public administration', *Public Administration*, 86 (1): 149–167.

Legge, K. (1978) *Power, Innovation, and Problem-Solving in Personnel Management*. London: McGraw-Hill.

Legge, K. (1995) *Human Resource Management: Rhetorics and Realities*. London: Macmillan.

Legge, K. (1999) 'Representing people at work', *Organization*, 6 (2): 247–264.

Lehman, C. (1992) *Accounting's Changing Roles in Social Conflict*. New York: Markus Wiener.

Leigh, A. (1994) 'How to reengineer hearts and minds', *Management Consultancy*, May: 51–54.

Leiss, W. (1978) *The Limits to Satisfaction*. London: Marion Boyars.

Leiss, W. (1983) 'The icons of the marketplace', *Theory, Culture & Society*, 1 (3): 10–21.

Leiss, W., Kline, S. and Thally, S. (1986) *Social Communication in Advertising: Persons, Products and Images of Well-being*. New York: Methuen.

Letiche, H. (2006) 'Critical Management Studies (not) in The Netherlands', *Critical Perspectives on International Business*, 2 (3): 170–182.

Letiche, H. and van Hattem, R. (1994) 'Fractalization of the knowledge worker', Paper presented at Knowledge, Work, Managerial Roles and European Competitiveness Workshop, ESC, Lyon, 30 November–3 December.

Levy, D.L., Alvesson, M. and Willmott, H. (2003) 'Critical approaches to strategic management', in M. Alvesson and H. Willmott (eds), *Studying Management Critically*. London: Sage. pp. 92–110.

Linstead, S., Fulop, L. and Lilley, S. (2009) *Management and Organization: A Critical Text*. London: Palgrave Macmillan.

Linzmayer, O.W. (2004) *Apple Confidential 2.0: The Definitive History of the World's Most Colorful Company: The Real Story of Apple Computer, Inc.* San Francisco: No Starch Press.

Locke, R. (1989) *Management and Higher Education Since 1940*. Cambridge: Cambridge University Press.

Lodh, S. and Gaffikin, M. (1997) 'Critical studies in accounting research, rationality and Habermas: A methodological reflection', *Critical Perspectives on Accounting*, 8: 433–474.

Löwendahl, B. (1997) *Strategic Management in Professional Service Firms*. Copenhagen: Copenhagen Business School Press.

Luhmann, N. (1982) *The Differentiation of Society*. New York: Columbia University Press.

Lukacs, G. (1971) *History and Class Consciousness*. London: Merlin.

Luke, C. and Gore, J. (eds) (1992) *Feminism and Critical Pedagogy*. London: Routledge.

Lukes, S. (1982) 'Of gods and demons: Habermas and practical reason', in J.B. Thompson and D. Held (eds), *Habermas: Critical Debates*. London: Macmillan.

Lyotard, J. -F. (1984) *The Postmodern Condition: A Report on Knowledge*. Manchester: Manchester University Press.

Lyytinen, K. (1992) 'Information systems and critical theory', in M. Alvesson and H.C. Willmott (eds), *Critical Management Studies*. London: Sage.

Lyytinen, K. and Hirschheim, R. (1988) 'Information systems as rational discourse: An application of Habermas' theory of communicative action', *Scandinavian Journal of Management Studies*, 4 (112): 19–30.

Lyytinen, K. and Klein, H. (1985) 'The critical theory of Jurgen Habermas as a basis for a theory of information systems', in E. Mumford, R. Hirschheim, G. Fitzgerald and T. Wood-Harper (eds), *Research Methods in Information Systems*. Amsterdam: North Holland.

MacIntyre, A.E. (1981) *After Virtue: A Study of Moral Theory*. London: Duckworth.

Management Learning (2006) Debate Section, 37 (1): 7–42.

March, J.G. and Olsen, J.P. (1976) *Ambiguity and Choice in Organizations*. Bergen: Universitetsforlaget.

March, J. and Simon, H. (1958) *Organizations*. New York: John Wiley.

Marcus, G. and Fischer, M. (1986) *Anthropology as Cultural Critique*. Chicago, IL: University of Chicago Press.

Marcuse, H. (1955) *Eros and Civilization*. Boston, MA: Beacon Press.

Marcuse, H. (1964) *One-Dimensional Man: Studies in the Ideology of Advanced Industrial Society*. Boston, MA: Beacon Press.

Marcuse, H. (1969) 'Repressive tolerance' in R.P. Wolff, B. Moore and H. Marcuse (eds), *A Critique of Pure Tolerance*. Boston: Beacon Press.

Marshall, J. (1984) *Women Managers. Travellers in a Male World*. Chichester: Wiley.

Marshall, J. (1993) 'Viewing organizational communication from a feminist perspective: A critique and some offerings', in S. Deeta (ed.), *Communication Yearbook*, Vol. 16. Newbury Park, CA: Sage.

Martin, J. (1990) 'Deconstructing organizational taboos: The suppression of gender conflict in organizations', *Organization Science*, 11: 339–359.

Martin, J. (1992) *Cultures in Organizations: Three Perspectives*. New York: Oxford University Press.

Martin, J. (2002) *Organizational Culture*. Thousand Oaks, CA: Sage.

Martin, J. (2003) 'Feminist theory and critical theory: Unexplored synergies', in M. Alvesson and H. Willmott (eds), *Studying Management Critically*. London: Sage. pp. 66–91.

Martin, J. and Meyerson, D. (1988) 'Organizational cultures and the denial, channeling and acknowledgement of ambiguity', in L. Pondy et al. (eds), *Managing Ambiguity and Change*. New York: Wiley.

Marx, K. (1976) *Capital*, Vol. 1. Harmondsworth: Penguin.

Mason, R.O. and Mitroff, I. (1981) *Challenging Strategic Planning Assumptions*. New York: John Wiley.

Matten, D. (2009) 'Review essay: "It's the Politics, Stupid": Reflections on the role of business in contemporary nonfiction', *Business & Society*, 48 (4): 565–576.

Mayo, E. (1949) 'Hawthorne and the Western Electric Company', in D. Pugh (ed.), *Organization Theory*. Harmondsworth: Penguin.

McAlister, A.R. and Cornwell, T.B. (2010) 'Children's brand symbolism understanding: Links to theory of mind and executive functioning', *Psychology and Marketing*, 27 (3): 203–228.

McCarthy, T. (1978) *The Critical Theory of Jürgen Habermas*. London: Hutchinson.

McFall, L. (2004) *Advertising: A Cultural Economy*. London: Sage.

McGrath, C. (2005) 'Doing critical research in information systems: A case of theory and practice not informing each other', *Information Systems Journal*, 15 (2): 85–101.

McIntosh, D. (1994) 'Language, self and lifeworld in Habermas' theory of communicative action', *Theory and Society*, 23: 1–33.

McKenna, R. (1991) 'Marketing is everything', *Harvard Business Review*, Jan–Feb: 65–79.

McLaughlin, H. and Thorpe, R. (1993) 'Action learning – A paradigm in emergence: The problems facing a challenge to traditional management education and development', *British Journal of Management*, 4 (1): 19–27.

McSweeny, B. (2006) 'Do we live in a post-bureaucratic époque?', *Journal of Organizational Change Management*, 19: 22–37.

Meisenhelder, T. (1989) 'Habermas and feminism: The future of critical theory', in R.A. Wallace (ed.), *Feminism and Sociological Theory*. Newbury Park, CA: Sage.

Merchant, C. (1980) *Ecological Revolutions: Nature, Gender and Science in New England*. Chapel Hill, NC: University of North Carolina Press.

Meyer, J. and Rowan, B. (1977) 'Institutionalized organizations: Formal structure as myth and ceremony', *American Journal of Sociology*, 83: 340–363.

Miller, P. (2008) 'Calculating economic life', *Journal of Cultural Economy*, 1 (1): 61–74.

Miller, P. and O'Leary, T. (1987) 'Accounting and the construction of the governable person', *Accounting, Organizations and Society*, 12 (3): 235–261.

Mills, A. and Tancred, P. (eds) (1992) *Gendering Organizational Analysis*. London: Sage.

Mingers, J. (1992a) 'Technical, practical and critical OR – Past, present and future?', in M. Alvesson and H.C. Willmott (eds), *Critical Management Studies*. London: Sage.

Mingers, J. (1992b) 'What are real friends for? A reply to Mike Jackson', *Journal of the Operational Research Society*, 43 (7): 732–735.

Mingers, J. (2000a) 'Variety is the spice of life: Combining soft and hard OR/MS methods', *International Transactions in Operational Research*, 7 (6): 673–691.

Mingers, J. (2000b) 'An idea ahead of its time: The history and development of soft systems methodology', *Systemic Practice and Action Research*, 13 (6): 733–755.

Mingers, J. (2000c) 'The contribution of critical realism as an underpinning philosophy for OR/MS and systems', *Journal of the Operational Research Society*, 51 (11): 1256–1270.

Mingers, J. and Willmott, H.C. (2011) 'Moulding the one-dimensional academic: The performative effects of journal ranking lists', Working paper, University of Kent.

Mintzberg, H. (1975) 'The manager's job: Folklore and fact', *Harvard Business Review*, July–Aug: 49–61.

Mintzberg, H. (1976) 'Planning on the left side and managing on the right', *Harvard Business Review*, 54: 49–58.

Mintzberg, H. (1987) 'Crafting strategy', *Harvard Business Review*, July–Aug.: 66–75.

Mintzberg, H. (1990) 'The design school: Reconsidering the basic premises of strategic management', *Strategic Management Journal*, 11: 171–195.

Mintzberg, H., Raisinghani, D. and Theoret, A. (1976) 'The structure of "unstructured" decision processes', *Administrative Science Quarterly*, 21: 246–275.

Molinnero, C.M. (1992) 'Operational research: From war to community', *Socio-Economic Planning Sciences*, 26 (3): 203–212.

Morgan, G. (1980) 'Paradigms, metaphors and puzzle solving in organization theory', *Administrative Science Quarterly*, 25: 605–622.

Morgan, G. (1992) 'Marketing discourse and practice: Towards a critical analysis', in M. Alvesson and H. Willmott (eds), *Critical Management Studies*. London: Sage.

Morgan, G. (1997) *Images of Organisation* (2nd edn). Thousand Oaks, CA: Sage.

Morgan, G. (2003) 'Marketing and critique: Prospects and problems', in M. Alvesson and H. Willmott (eds), *Studying Management Critically*. London: Sage.

Morgan, G. and Willmott, H.C. (1993) 'The new accounting research: On making accounting more visible', *Accounting, Auditing and Accountability Journal*, 6 (4): 3–36.

Mouffe, C. (ed.) (1999a) *The Challenge of Carl Schmitt*. London: Verso.

Mouffe, C. (1999b) 'Deliberative democracy or agonistic pluralism?', *Social Research*, 66: 745–758.

Mumby, D. (1988) *Communication and Power in Organizations: Discourse, Ideology and Domination*. Norwood, NJ: Ablex.

Mumby, D. (1997) 'The problem of hegemony: Rereading Gramsci for organizational communication', *Western Journal of Communication*, 61 (4): 343–375.

Mumby, D.K. and Putnam, L.L. (1992) 'The politics of emotion: A feminist reading of bounded rationality', *The Academy of Management Review*, 17 (3): 465–486.

Mumford, M., Scott, G., Gaddis, B. and Strange, J. (2002) 'Leading creative people: Orchestrating expertise and relationships', *Leadership Quarterly*, 13: 705–750.

Murphy, J. (2008) 'Management in emerging economies: Modern, but not too modern?', *Critical Perspectives on International Business*, 4 (4): 410–421.

Murray, F. and Willmott, H.C. (1993) 'The communication problem in information systems development', in P. Quintas (ed.), *Social Dimensions of Systems Engineering*. London: Ellis Horwood.

Myers, M.D. (2008) *Qualitative Research in Business & Management*. London: Sage.

Naess, A. and Rothenberg, D. (1991) *Ecology, Community and Lifestyle*. Cambridge: Cambridge University Press.

National Commission on the BP Deepwater Horizon Oil Spill and Offshore Drilling (2011) *Deep Water: The Gulf Oil Disaster and the Future of Offshore Drilling*. Available at: http://www.oilspillcommission.gov/sites/default/files/documents/ DEEPWATER_ReporttothePresident_FINAL.pdf. Accessed 8 February 2011.

Neimark, M. (1991) 'The King is dead. Long Live the King!', *Critical Perspectives on Accounting*, 1 (1): 103–114.

Neu, D., Cooper, D.J. and Everett, J. (2001) 'Critical accounting interventions', *Critical Perspectives on Accounting*, 12 (6): 735–762.

Newell, S., Robertson, M., Scarbrough, H. and Swan, J. (2002) *Managing Knowledge Work*. London: Palgrave.

Newton, T. (2009) 'Organizations and the natural environment', in M. Alvesson, T. Bridgman and H. Willmott (eds), *Oxford Handbook of Critical Management Studies*. Oxford: Oxford University Press.

Nichols, T. and Beynon, H. (1977) *Living with Capitalism: Class Relations and the Modern Factory*. London: Routledge and Kegan Paul.

Nicholson, L.J. (ed.) (1990) *Feminism/Postmodernism*. London: Routledge.

Nussbaum, D. (2010) 'The death of Davos Man – The death of Davos', *Business Week*, 31 January [Online]. Available at: http://www.businessweek.com/innovate/ NussbaumOnDesign/archives/2010/01/the_death_of_davos_man--the_death_ of_davos.html.

Oakland, J. (1989) *Total Quality Management*. London: Heinemann.

Observer (16 October 1994).

Offe, C. and Wiesenthal, H. (1980) 'Two logics of collective action: Theoretical notes on social class and organizational form', in M. Zeitlin (ed.), *Political Power and Social Theory*, Vol. 1. Greenwich, CT: JAI Press.

Ogbonna, E. and Wilkinson, B. (1990) 'Corporate strategy and corporate culture: The view from the checkout', *Personnel Review*, 19 (4): 9–15.

Oliga, J. C. (1996) *Power, Ideology, and Control*. Boston: Springer.

Ormerod, R.J. (1996) 'Information systems strategy development at Sainsbury's supermarkets using "soft" OR', *Interfaces*, 26 (1): 102–130.

Ospina, S. and Uhl-Bien, M. (eds) (forthcoming) *Advancing Relational Leadership Theory: A Conversation among Perspectives*. Greenwood: Information Age Publishing.

Otley, D. (1999) 'Performance management: A framework for management control systems research', *Management Accounting Research*, 10 (4): 363–382.

Packard, V. (1981) *The Hidden Persuaders*. Harmondsworth: Penguin.

Palanski, M. and Yammarino, F. (2009) 'Integrity and leadership: A multi-conceptual framework', *Leadership Quarterly*, 20: 405–420.

Palmer, I. and Hardy, C. (2000) *Thinking about Management*. London: Sage.

Parker, M. (1995) 'Critique in the name of what? Postmodernism and critical approaches to management', *Organization Studies*, 16 (4): 553–564.

Parker, M. (ed.) (2002) *Utopia and Organization*. Oxford: Blackwell.

Parker, M. (2004) 'Becoming manager: Or, the werewolf looks anxiously in the mirror, checking for unusual facial hair', *Management Learning*, 35 (1): 45–59.

Parker, M., Fournier, V. and Reedy, P. (2007) *The Dictionary of Alternatives*. London: Zed Books.

Parry, R. and Mingers, J. (2001) 'Community operational research: Its context and its future', *Omega*, 19 (6): 577–586.

Pascale, R.T. and Athos, A.G. (1982) *The Art of Japanese Management*. Harmondsworth: Penguin.

Payne, S.L. (1991) 'A proposal for corporate ethical reform', *Business and Professional Ethics Journal*, 10 (1): 67–88.

Payne, S.L. (1992) 'Critical systems thinking: A challenge or dilemma in its practice', *Systems Practice*, 5 (3): 237–249.

Pendergrast, M. (1993) *For God, Country and Coca-Cola*. London: George Weidenfeld and Nicolson.

Perriton, L. and Reynolds, M. (2004) 'Critical management education: From pedagogy of possibility to pedagogy of refusal?', *Management Learning*, 35 (1): 61–77.

Perrow, C. (1986) *Complex Organizations: A Critical Essay* (3rd edn). New York: Random House.

Peters, T.J. and Waterman, R.H. (1982) *In Search of Excellence*. New York: Harper and Row.

Pettigrew, A. (1973) *The Politics of Organizational Decision-Making*. London: Tavistock.

Pettigrew, A. (1985) *The Awakening Giant: Continuity and Change at ICI*. Oxford: Blackwell.

Pettigrew, A. (1988) 'Longitudinal field research on change: Theory and practice', Paper presented to the National Science Foundation Conference on Longitudinal Research Methods in Organizations, Austin, TX.

Pfeffer, J. (1977) 'The ambiguity of leadership', *Academy of Management Review*, 2 (1): 104–112.

Pfeffer, J. (1981) *Power in Organizations*. Boston, MA: Pitman.

Pfeffer, J. (1994) *Competitive Advantage Through People*. Boston: Harvard Business Press.

Phillips, N. and Dar, S. (2009) 'Strategy', in M. Alvesson T. Bridgman and H. Willmott, (eds), *Oxford Handbook of Critical Management Studies*. Oxford: Oxford University Press.

Pine, B.J. (1993) *Mass Customization: The New Frontier in Business Competition*. Boston, MA: Harvard Business School Press.

Pollay, R.W. (1986) 'The distorted mirror: Reflections on the unintended consequences of advertising', *Journal of Marketing*, 50 (April): 18–36.

Pollay, R.W. (1987) 'On the value of reflections on the values in "the distorted mirror"', *Journal of Marketing*, 51 (July): 104–109.

Pondy, L.R. (1983) 'The role of metaphors and myths in organization and in the facilitation of change', in L.R. Pondy, P.J. Frost, G. Morgan and T.C. Dandridge (eds), *Organizational Symbolism*. Greenwich, CT: JAI Press.

Porter, M.E. (1985) *Competitive Advantage: Creating and Sustaining Superior Performance*. New York: Free Press.

Poster, M. (1989) *Critical Theory and Poststructuralism: In Search of a Context*. Ithaca, NY: Cornell University Press.

Potterfield, T.A. (1999) *The Business of Employee Empowerment: Democracy, Ideology and the Workplace*. Westport, CT: Quorum Books.

Power, M. (1990) 'Modernism, postmodernism and organizations', in J. Hassard and D. Pym (eds), *The Theory and Philosophy of Organizations: Critical Issues and New Perspectives*. London: Routledge.

Power, M.K. (1991) 'Educating accountants: Towards a critical ethnography', *Accounting, Organizations and Society*, 16 (4): 333–353.

Power, M.K. (1999) *The Audit Society: Rituals of Verification*. Oxford: Oxford University Press.

Power, M., Laughlin, R. and Cooper, D. (2003) 'Accounting and critical theory', in M. Alvesson and H. Willmott (eds), *Studying Management Critically*. London: Sage. pp. 132–156.

Prasad, A., Prasad, P. and Mir, R. (2011) '"One mirror in another": Managing diversity and the discourse of fashion', *Human Relations*, 64 (5): 703–724.

Prichard, C. and Willmott, H.C. (1997) 'Just how managed is the McUniversity?', *Organization Studies*, 18 (2): 287–316.

Puxty, A.G. (1991) 'Social accountability and universal pragmatics', *Advances in Public Interest Accounting*, 4: 35–45.

Quinn, J.B. (1980) *Strategies for Change: Logical Incrementalism*. Homewood, IL: Irwin.

Rabinow, P. (ed.) (1986) *The Foucault Reader*. Harmondsworth: Penguin.

Rasmussen, D. (1990) *Reading Habermas*. Oxford: Blackwell.

Raspa, R. (1986) 'Creating fiction in the committee: The emergence of the Saturn Corporation at the General Motors', *Dragon*, 4: 7–22.

Ray, L.J. (1993) *Rethinking Critical Theory: Emancipation in the Age of Global Social Movements*. London: Sage.

Reed, D. (1999) 'Stakeholder management theory: A critical theory perspective', *Business Ethics Quarterly*, 9 (3): 453–483.

Reed, M. (1984) 'Management as a social practice', *Journal of Management Studies*, 21 (3): 273–285.

Reed, M. (1990) 'From paradigms to images: The paradigm warrior turns postmodern guru', *Personnel Review*, 19 (3): 35–40.

Reynolds, M. (1998) 'Reflection and critical reflection in management learning', *Management Learning*, 29 (2): 183–200.

Reynolds, M. and Vince, R. (2004) 'Critical management education and action-based learning: Synergies and contradictions', *Academy of Management Learning & Education*, 3 (4): 442–456.

Richardson, H. and Robinson, B. (2007) 'The mysterious case of the missing paradigm: A review of critical information systems research 1991–2001', *Information Systems Journal*, 17 (3): 251–270.

Riesman, D. (1950) *The Lonely Crowd*. New Haven, CT: Yale University Press.

Ritzer, G. (1996) *The McDonaldization Thesis*. Thousand Oaks, CA: Sage.

Ritzer, G. (2004) *The Globalization of Nothing*. Thousand Oaks, CA: Sage.

Roberts, J. (1984) 'The moral character of management practice', *Journal of Management Studies*, 21 (3): 296–302.

Robson, K. and Young, J. (2009) 'Socio-political studies of financial reporting and standard-setting', in C.S. Chapman, D.J. Cooper and P.B. Miller (eds), *Accounting, Organizations and Institutions: Essays in Honour of Anthony Hopwood*. Oxford: Oxford University Press.

Roderick, R. (1986) *Habermas and the Foundations of Critical Theory*. London: Macmillan.

Rorty, R. (1985) 'Habermas and Lyotard on postmodernity', in R.J. Bernstein (ed.), *Habermas and Modernity*. Cambridge: Polity.

Rose, N. (1990) *Governing the Soul: The Shaping of the Private Self*. London: Routledge.

Rose, D. (1993) 'Private rhetoric for the public sphere', Paper presented to the 11th EGOS Colloquium, Paris, July.

Rosen, M. (1985) 'Breakfast at Spiro's: Dramaturgy and dominance', *Journal of Management*, 11 (2): 31–48.

Rosen, M. (1991) 'Coming to terms with the field: Understanding and doing organizational ethnography', *Journal of Management Studies*, 28: 1–24.

Rosenhead, J. (1989) 'O.R.: Social science or barbarism?', in M.C. Jackson, P. Keys and S.A. Cropper (eds), *Operational Research and the Social Sciences*. New York: Plenum Press.

Rosenhead, J. and Thunhurst, C. (1982) 'A materialist analysis of operational research', *Journal of the Operational Research Society*, 33: 111–122.

Rostis, A. and Helms Mills, J. (2010) 'A pedagogy of the repressed: Critical management education and the teaching case study', *International Journal of Management Concepts and Philosophy*, 4 (2): 212–223.

Rowlinson, M. and Hassard, J. (2011) 'How come the critters came to be teaching in business schools? Contradictions in the institutionalization of Critical Management Studies', *Organization*, 18 (5): 673–689.

Sabia, D.R. and Wallukis, J. (eds) (1983) *Changing Social Science: Critical Theory and Other Critical Perspectives*. Albany, NY: State University of New York Press.

Salaman, G. (2011) 'Understanding the crises of leadership', in J. Storey (ed.), *Leadership in Organization: Current Issues and Key Trends*, (2nd edn). London: Routledge.

Sampson, E. (1989) 'The deconstruction of self', in J. Shotter and K. Gergen (eds), *Texts of Identity*. London: Sage.

Samra-Fredericks, D. (2005) 'Strategic practice, "discourse" and the everyday interactional constitution of power effects', *Organization*, 12 (6): 803–841.

Sandberg, Å. (ed.) (1981) *Forskning för Förändring* (Research for Change). Stockholm: Centre for Working Life.

Saravanamuthu, K., Flanagan, J. and Howie, H. (2007) *Toolkit for Developing Sustainable Practices* [Online]. Available at: http://www.searchsa.com.au/kala/Toolkit.htm. Accessed 10 December 2007.

Saren, M. and Svensson, P. (2009) 'Critical marketing', in M. Alvesson, H. Willmott and T. Bridgman (eds), *The Oxford Handbook of Critical Management Studies*. Oxford: Oxford University Press.

Saren, M., Maclaran, P., Goulding, C., Elliott, R., Shankar, A. and Catterall, M. (eds) (2007) *Critical Marketing: Defining the Field*. Oxford: Elsevier.

Sashkin, M. (2004) 'Transformational leadership approaches: A review and synthesis', in J. Antonakis, A. Cianciolo and R.J. Sternberg (eds), *The Nature of Leadership*. Thousand Oaks, CA: Sage.

Scarbrough, H. (1998) 'Path(ological) dependency? Core competence from an organizational perspective', *British Journal of Management*, 9: 219–232.

Scherer, A.G. (2009) 'Critical theory and its contribution to critical management studies', in M. Alvesson, T. Bridgman and H. Willmott (eds), *The Oxford Handbook of Critical Management Studies*. Oxford: Oxford University Press.

Scherer, A.G. and Palazzo, G. (2007) 'Towards a political conception of corporate responsibility – Business and society seen from a Habermasian perspective', *Academy of Management Review*, 32 (4): 1096–1120.

Scherer, A.G., Palazzo, G. and Baumann, D. (2005) 'Global rules and private actors – Towards a new role of the transnational corporation in global governance', *Business Ethics Quarterly*, 16: 505–532.

Scheuerman, W.E. (2008) *Frankfurt School Perspectives on Globalization, Democracy, and the Law*. London: Routledge.

Schneider, S. (1999) 'Human and inhuman resource management: Sense and non-sense', *Organization*, 6 (2): 277–284.

Schor, J. (2004) *Born to Buy*. New York, NY: Scribner.

Schroyer, T. (1973) *The Critique of Domination: The Origins and Development of Critical Theory*. New York: George Braziller.

Schumacher, E.F. (1974) *Small is Beautiful*. London: Abacus.

Schwartz, A. (2010) *Pepsi Ditches the Super Bowl, Embraces Crowdsourced Philanthropy Instead*, Fast Company, 4 January [Online]. Available at: http://www.fastcompany.com/blog/ariel-schwartz/sustainability/pepsi-ditches-super-bowl-embraces-crowdsourced-philanthropy-inste.

Schwartz, H. (1990) *Narcissistic Process and Corporate Decay*. Albany, NY: State University of New York Press.

Sculley, J. (with J.A. Byrne) (1988) *Odyssey: Pepsi to Apple ... A Journey of Adventure, Ideas, and the Future*. New York: Harper and Row.

Sendjaya, S., Sarros, J.C. and Santora, J.C. (2008) 'Defining and measuring servant leadership behaviour in organization', *Journal of Management Studies*, 45 (2): 402–424.

Sennett, R. (1980) *Authority*. New York: Vintage Books.

Sennett, R. (1998) *The Corrosion of Character*. New York: Norton.

Sennett, R. (2006) *The Culture of the New Capitalism*. New Haven: Yale University Press.

Sewell, G. and Wilkinson, B. (1992) '"Someone to watch over me": Surveillance, discipline and the just-in-time labour process', *Sociology*, 26: 271–289.

Shah, A.K. (1998) 'Exploring the influences and constraints on creative accounting in the United Kingdom', *European Accounting Review* [Online]. Available at: http://www.informaworld.com/smpp/title~db=all~content=t713696487~tab=issueslist~branches=7 – v77:1 83 – 104.

Shamir, B., House, R.J. and Arthur, M.B. (1993) 'The motivational effects of charismatic leadership: A self-concept based theory', *Organization Science*, 4: 577–593.

Shrivastava, P. (1993) 'Crisis theory/practice: Towards a sustainable future', *Organization Environment*, 7: 23–41.

Shrivastava, P. (1994a) 'CASTRATED environment: GREENING organizational studies', *Organization Studies*, 15 (5): 705–726.

Shrivastava, P. (1994b) 'Greening business education', *Journal of Management Inquiry*, 3 (3): 235–243.

Sievers, B. (1986) 'Beyond the surrogate of motivation', *Organization Studies*, 7 (4): 335–351.

Sikka, P. (2008) 'The internet and potentialities of emancipatory change', *Critical Perspectives on International Business*, 4 (1): 75–82.

Sikka, P. and Willmott, H.C. (1995) 'The power of "independence": Defending and extending the jurisdiction of accounting in the UK', *Accounting, Organizations and Society*, 20 (6): 547–581.

Sikka, P., Willmott, H.C. and Mitchell, A. (1998) 'Sweeping it under the carpet: The role of accountancy firms in money laundering', *Accounting, Organizations and Society*, 23 (5/6): 589–607.

Sikka, P., Willmott, H.C and Puxty, T. (1997) 'Practicing accounting', *Critical Perspectives on Accounting*, 8 (1/2): 149–165.

Simon, H. (1997/1945) *Administrative Behavior: A Study of Decision-making Processes in Administrative Organizations* (4th edn). Chicago: Free Press.

Sinclair, A. (2007) 'Teaching leadership critically to MBAs: Experiences from heaven and hell', *Management Learning*, 38 (4): 458–472.

Skålén, P., Fougère, M. and Fellesson, M. (2008) *Marketing Discourse: A Critical Perspective*. London: Routledge.

Sloterdijk, P. (1980) *Critique of Cynical Reason*. London: Verso.

Sloterdijk, P. (1984) 'Cynicism – The twilight of false consciousness', *New German Critique*, 11 (3): 190–206.

Smircich, L. (1983a) 'Organizations as shared meanings', in L.R. Pondy, P.J. Frost, G. Morgan and T.C. Dandridge (eds), *Organizational Symbolism*. Greenwich, CT: JAI Press.

Smircich, L. (1983b) 'Concepts of culture and organizational analysis', *Administrative Science Quarterly*, 28: 339–58.

Smircich, L. and Stubbart, C. (1985) 'Strategic management in an enacted world', *Academy of Management Review*, 10 (4): 724–736.

Smith, V. (1990) *Managing in the Corporate Interest: Control and Resistance in an American Bank*. Berkeley, CA: University of California Press.

Soeters, J. (1986) 'Excellent companies as social movements', *Journal of Management Studies*, 23: 299–312.

Spicer, A., Alvesson, M. and Kärreman, D. (2009) 'Critical performativity: The unfinished business of critical management studies', *Human Relations*, 62 (4): 537–560.

Stablein, R. and Nord, W. (1985) 'Practical and emancipatory interests in organizational symbolism: A review and evaluation', *Journal of Management*, 11 (2): 13–28.

Stahl, B.S. (2008a) *Information Systems: Critical Perspectives*. London: Routledge.

Stahl, B.S. (2008b) 'The ethical nature of critical research in information systems', *Information Systems Journal*, 18 (2): 137–163.

Stahl, B.C., McBride, N. and Elbeltagi, I. (2010) 'Development and emancipation: The information society and decision support systems in local authorities in Egypt', *Journal of Information, Communication and Ethics in Society*, 8 (1): 85–107.

Starhawk (2000) *Turning the Trolls to Strategy for the Global Justice Movement* [Online]. Available at: http://www.starhawk.org/activism/activism-writings/trollstostone.html.

Stead, E. and Stead, J.G. (1992) *Management for a Small Planet*. Newbury Park, CA: Sage.

Steffy, B. and Grimes, A. (1986) A critical theory of organization science, *Academy of Management Review*, 11: 322–336.

Steffy, B. and Grimes, A. (1992) 'Personnel/organizational psychology – A critique of the discipline', in M. Alvesson and H. Willmott (eds), *Critical Management Studies*. London: Sage.

Stepanovich, P.L. (2009) 'The lobster tale: An exercise in critical thinking', *Journal of Management Education*, 33 (6): 725–746.

Steyaert, C. and Janssens, M. (1999) 'Human and inhuman resource management: Saving the subjects of HRM', *Organization*, 6: 181–198.

Stirner, M. (1907) *The Ego and His Own*. London: Libertarian Book Club.

Storey, J. (2001) 'Human resource management', in J. Storey (ed.), *Human Resource Management*. London: Thomson.

Storey, J. (2011) 'Signs of change: "Damned Rascals" and beyond', in J. Storey (ed.), *Leadership in Organization: Current Issues and Key Trends*, (2nd edn). London: Routledge.

Sturdy, A.J., Brocklehurst, M., Winstanley, D. and Littlejohns, M. (2006) 'Management as a (self) confidence trick – Management ideas, education and identity work', *Organization*, 13: 841–860.

Susman, G. and Evered, R. (1978) 'An assessment of the scientific merits of action research', *Administrative Science Quarterly*, 23: 582–608.

Sveningsson, S. and Alvesson, M. (2003) 'Managing managerial identities', *Human Relations*, 56: 1163–1193.

Sveningsson, S. and Larsson, M. (2006) 'Fantasies of leadership: Identity work', *Leadership*, 2 (2): 203–224.

Tadajewski, M. (2006) 'The ordering of marketing theory: The influence of McCarthyism and the Cold War', *Marketing Theory*, 6 (2): 163–199.

Tadajewski, M. (2008) 'Incommensurable paradigms, cognitive bias and the politics of marketing theory', *Marketing Theory*, 8 (3): 273–297.

Tadajewski, M. (2010) 'Critical marketing studies: Logical empiricism, critical per-formativity and marketing practice', *Marketing Theory*, 10 (2): 210–222.

Tadajewski, M. and Brownlie, D. (2008) 'Critical marketing: A limit attitude', in M. Tadajewski and D. Brownlie (eds), *Critical Marketing*. West Sussex: Wiley.

Tadajewski, M., Maclaran, P., Parsons, E. and Parker, M. (2011) *Key Concepts in Critical Management Studies*. London: Sage.

Taylor, F.W. (1911) *Principles of Scientific Management*. New York: Harper and Row.

Teece, D. (1998) 'Capturing value from knowledge assets: The new economy, markets for know-how, and intangible assets', *California Management Review*, 40 (3): 55–79.

Tett, G. (2010) *Fool's Gold: How Unrestrained Greed Corrupted a Dream, Shattered Global Markets and Unleashed a Catastrophe*. London: Abacus.

Therborn, G. (1980) *The Power of Ideology and the Ideology of Power*. London: Verso.

Thomas, A. (1993) *Controversies in Management*. London: Routledge.

Thomas, R. and Davies, A. (2005) 'Theorizing the micro-politics of resistance', *Organization Studies*, 26 (5): 683–706.

Thompson, J. and Held, D. (eds) (1982) *Habermas: Critical Debates*. London: Macmillan.

Thompson, M. and Willmott, H.C. (2011) 'The runaway train of best practice: Organizational routines, standardization, and the pathology of box-ticking', Working Paper.

Thompson, P. (2005) 'Brands, boundaries and bandwagons: A critical reflection on Critical Management Studies', in C. Grey and H.C. Willmott (eds), *Critical Management Studies: A Reader*. Oxford: Oxford University Press.

Thompson, P. and McHugh, D. (1990) *Work Organizations: A Critical Introduction*. London: Macmillan.

Thompson, P. and McHugh, D. (1995) *Work Organizations: A Critical Introduction* (2nd edn). London: Macmillan.

Thompson, P., Warhurst, C. and Callaghan, G. (2001) 'Ignorant theory and knowl-edgeable workers: Interrogating the connections between knowledge skills and services', *Journal of Management Studies*, 38 (7): 923–942.

Tinker, A.M. (1985) *Paper Prophets: A Social Critique of Accounting*. Eastbourne: Holt Saunders.

Tinker, A.M. (1986) 'Metaphor or reification: Are radical humanists really libertarian anarchists?', *Journal of Management Studies*, 24 (3): 367–382.

Tinker, A.M. and Lowe, E.A. (1982) 'The management science of the management sciences', *Human Relations*, 35 (4): 331–347.

Tinker, A.M. and Lowe, E.A. (1984) 'One-dimensional management science: The making of technocratic consciousness', *Interfaces*, 14 (2): 40–56.

Tinker, A.M., Merino, B. and Neimark, M. (1982) 'The normative origins of positive theories', *Accounting, Organizations and Society*, 7 (2): 167–200.

Tourish, D. and Pinnington, A. (2002) 'Transformational leadership, corporate cultism and the spirituality paradigm: An unholy trinity in the workplace?', *Human Relations*, 55: 147–152.

Townley, B. (1993) 'Foucault, power/knowledge and its relevance for human resource management', *Academy of Management Review*, 18 (3): 518–545.

Townley, B. (1999) 'Practical reason and performance appraisal', *Journal of Management Studies*, 36 (3): 287–306.

Trauth, E.M. and Howcroft, D. (2006) 'Critical empirical research in IS: An example of gender and the IT workforce', *Information Technology & People*, 19: 272–292.

Tsoukas, H. (1992) 'Panoptic reason and the search for totality: A critical assessment of the critical systems perspective', *Human Relations*, 45 (7): 637–657.

Tsoukas, H. (1993) 'Analogical reasoning and knowledge generation in organization theory', *Organization Studies*, 14 (3): 323–346.

Tsoukas, H. (2004) *Complex Knowledge: Studies in Organizational Epistemology*. Oxford: Oxford University Press.

Uhl-Bien, M. (2006) 'Relational Leadership Theory: Exploring the social processes of leadership and organizing', *The Leadership Quarterly*, 17 (6): 654-676.

Uhl-Bien, M., Marion, R. and McKelvey, B. (2007) 'Complexity Leadership Theory: Shifting leadership from the industrial age to the knowledge era', *The Leadership Quarterly*, 18 (4): 298–318.

Ulrich, W. (1983) *Critical Heuristics of Social Planning*. Berne: Werner-Haupt.

Ulrich, W. (1988) 'Systems thinking, systems practice and systems philosophy: A program of research', *Systems Practice*, 1 (2): 137–163.

Ulrich, W. (2001) 'The quest for competence in systemic research and practice', *Systems Research and Behavioral Science*, 18 (1): 3–28.

Ulrich, W. (2003) 'Beyond methodology choice: Critical systems thinking as critically systemic discourse', *Journal of the Operational Research Society*, 54: 325–342.

Ulrich, W. (2007) 'Philosophy for professionals: Towards critical pragmatism', *Journal of the Operational Research Society*, 58 (8): 1109–1113.

Ulver-Sneistrup, S. (2008) *Status-Spotting – A Consumer Cultural Exploration into Ordinary Status Consumption of 'Home' and Home Aesthetics*. Lund: Lund Business Press.

United Nations (2010).

Van Maanen, J. (1988) *Tales of the Field: On Writing Ethnography*. Chicago: University of Chicago Press.

Van Maanen, J. (1991) 'The smile factory', in P.J. Frost, L.F. Moore, M.R. Louis, C.C. Lundberg and J. Martin (eds), *Reframing Organizational Culture*. Newbury Park, CA: Sage.

Vaughan, D. (1997) *The Challenger Launch Decision: Risky Technology, Culture and Deviance at NASA*. Chicago: University of Chicago Press.

Veblen, T. (1953) *The Theory of the Leisure Class*. New York: New American Library.

Vidaillet, B. and Vignon, C. (2010) 'Bringing back the subject into management education', *Management Learning*, 412: 221–241.

Voronov, M. and Coleman, P.T. (2003) 'Beyond the ivory towers: Organizational power practices and a "practical" critical postmodernism', *The Journal of Applied Behavioural Science*, 39 (2): 169–185.

Wachtel, P. (1983) *The Poverty of Affluence: A Psychological Portrait of the American Way of Life*. New York: Free Press.

Walby, S. (1986) *Patriarchy at Work*. Cambridge: Polity Press.

Wall Street Journal (2010) 'Regulators accepted gifts from oil industry, report says', by Stephen Powers, 26 May [Online]. Available at: http://online.wsj.com/article/SB10001424052748704026204575266112115488640.html?mod=WSJ_hpp_MIDDLENexttoWhatsNewsSecond. Accessed 5 July 2011.

Walsham, G. (2006) 'Doing interpretive research', *European Journal of Information Systems*, 15 (3): 320–330.

Watson, T. (1977) *The Personnel Managers*. London: Routledge.

Watson, T. (1994) *In Search of Management*. London: Routledge.

Watson, T. (2004) 'HRM and critical social science analysis', *Journal of Management Studies*, 41: 447–467.

Watson, T. (2007) 'Organization theory and HRM', in P. Boxall, J. Purcell and P. Wright (eds), *The Oxford Handbook of Human Resource Management*. Oxford: Oxford University Press.

Watson, T. (2008) 'Managing identity, identity work, personal predicaments and structured circumstances', *Organization*, 15: 121–143.

Weber, M. (1948) *From Max Weber: Essays in Sociology*. London: Routledge and Kegan Paul.

Weber, M. (1949) *The Methodology of the Social Sciences*. New York: Free Press.

Weber, M. (1968) *Economy and Society: An Outline of Interpretive Sociology*. New York: Bedminster Press.

Weber, M. (1978) *Economy and Society*, 3 Vols. New York: Bedminster Press.

Weedon, C. (1988) *Feminist Practice and Poststructuralist Theory*. Oxford: Basil Blackwell.

Weisbord, M. (1987) *Productive Workplaces*. San Francisco, CA: Jossey-Bass.

Weizenbaum, J. (1976) *Computer Power and Human Reason – From Judgement to Calculation*. New York: Freeman.

Wensley, R. (1987) 'Marketing strategy', in M.J. Baker (ed.), *The Marketing Book*. London: Heinemann in association with the British Institute of Marketing.

Western, S. (2008) *Leadership: A Critical Text*. Thousand Oaks, CA: Sage.

Westley, F. (1990) 'Middle managers and strategy: Microdynamics of inclusion', *Strategic Management Journal*, 11: 337–351.

Wexler, P. (ed.) (1991) *Critical Theory Now*. London: The Falmer Press.

Wheatland, T. (2009) *The Frankfurt School in Exile*. Minneapolis: University of Minnesota Press.

White, S.K. (1986) 'Foucault's challenge to critical theory', *American Political Science Review*, 80 (2): 419–432.

White, S. (1988) *The Recent Work of Jürgen Habermas*. Cambridge: Cambridge University Press.

Whittington, R. (1989) *Corporate Strategies in Recession and Recovery: Social Structure and Strategic Choice*. London: Unwin Hyman.

Whittington, R. (1993) *What is Strategy – and Does it Matter?* London: Routledge.

Whittington, R. (2006) 'Completing the practice turn in strategy research', *Organization Studies*, 27 (5): 613–634.

Wiggershaus, R. (1994) *The Frankfurt School: Its History, Theories and Political Significance*. Cambridge: Polity Press.

Wilkinson, A. and Willmott, H.C. (eds) (1995a) *Making Quality Critical*. London: Routledge.

Wilkinson, A. and Willmott, H.C. (1995b) 'Introduction', in A. Wilkinson and H.C. Willmott (eds), *Making Quality Critical*. London: Routledge.

Willcocks, L.P. (2006) 'Michel Foucault in the social study of ICTs: Critique and reappraisal', *Social Science Computer Review*, 24 (3): 274–295.

Willmott, H.C. (1983) 'Paradigms of accounting research', *Accounting, Organizations and Society*, 8 (4): 389–405.

Willmott, H.C. (1987) 'Studying managerial work: A critique and a proposal', *Journal of Management Studies*, 24 (3): 249–270.

Willmott, H.C. (1989) 'OR as a problem situation: From soft systems methodology to critical science', in M.C. Jackson, P. Keys and S.A. Cropper (eds), *Operational Research in the Social Sciences*. New York: Plenum Press.

Willmott, H.C. (1990) 'Beyond paradigmatic closure in organizational enquiry', in J. Hassard and D. Pyrn (eds), *The Theory and Philosophy of Organizations: Critical Issues and New Perspectives*. London: Routledge.

Willmott, H.C. (1992) 'Postmodernism and excellence: The de-differentiation of economy and culture', *The Journal of Organizational Change Management*, 5 (1): 58–68.

Willmott, H.C. (1993a) 'Strength is ignorance; slavery is freedom: Managing culture in modern organizations', *Journal of Management Studies*, 30 (4): 515–552.

Willmott, H.C. (1993b) 'Breaking the paradigm mentality', *Organization Studies*, 14 (5): 681–720.

Willmott, H.C. (1994a) 'Theorising human agency, responding to the crisis of (post) modernity', in J. Hassard and M. Parker (eds), *Towards a New Theory of Organizations*. London: Routledge.

Willmott, H.C. (1994b) 'Management education: Provocations to a debate', *Management Learning*, 25 (1): 105–136.

Willmott, H.C. (1995a) 'Managing the academics: Commodification and control in the development of university education in the UK', *Human Relations*, 48 (9): 993–1028.

Willmott, H.C (1995b) 'Death: So What? Sociology and Sequestration', *Sociological Review*, 48 (4): 649–665.

Willmott, H.C. (1996a) 'A metatheory of management: Omniscience or obfuscation?', *British Journal of Management*, 7: 323–327.

Willmott, H.C. (1996b) 'On the idolization of markets and the denigration of marketers: Some critical reflections on a professional paradox', in D. Brownlie, M. Saren, R. Wensley and R. Whittington (eds), *Rethinking Marketing*. London: Sage.

Willmott, H.C. (1996c) 'Re-cognizing "the other": Reflections on a new sensibility in social and organization studies', in R. Chia (ed.), *In the Realm of Organization: Essays for Robert Cooper*. London: Routledge.

Willmott, H.C. (2003) 'Organizational theory as a critical science', in H. Tsoukas and C. Knudsen (eds), *The Oxford Handbook of Organizational Theory*. Oxford: Oxford University Press. pp. 88–112.

Willmott, H.C. (2010) 'Creating "value" beyond the point of production: Branding, financialization and market capitalization', *Organization*, 17 (5): 517–542.

Willmott, H.C. (2011a) 'Identities in organizations: Dynamics of antipathy, deadlock and alliance', mimeo, Cardiff Business School, Cardiff University.

Willmott, H.C. (2011b) 'Making sense of the financial meltdown–An extended review of *The Spectre at the Feast: Capitalist Crisis and the Politics of Recession*, *Organization*, 18: 239-260.

Willmott, H.C. (2011c) 'Journal list fetishism and the perversion of scholarship: Reactivity and the ABS list', *Organization*, 18(4): 4429–442.

Willmott, H.C. (2012) 'Spirited Away: All mouth and no trousers' in P. du Gay and G. Morgan (eds), *New Spirits of Capitalism? On the Ethics of the Contemporary Capitalist Order*. Oxford: Oxford University Press.

Willmott, H.C. and Knights, D. (1982) 'The problem of freedom: Fromm's contribution to a critical theory of work organization', *Praxis International*, 2 (2): 204–225.

Wilson, D. (1982) 'Electricity and resistance: A case study of innovation and politics', *Organization Studies*, 3 (2): 119–140.

Wilson, J. F. and Thomson, A. (2006) *The Making of Modern Management: British Management in Historical Perspective*. Oxford: Oxford University Press.

Winograd, T. and Flores, F. (1986) *Computers and Cognition: A New Foundation for Computer System Design*. New York: Ablex.

Wolfram Cox, J., LeTrent-Jones, T.G., Voronov, M. and Weir, D. (eds) (2009) *Critical Management at Work: Negotiating Tensions Between Theory and Practice*. Cheltenham, UK: Edward Elgar.

Wood, S. (1980) 'Corporate strategy and organizational studies', in D. Dunkerley and G. Salaman (eds), *International Yearbook of Organization Studies*. London: Routledge and Kegan Paul.

Wray-Bliss, E. (2002) 'Abstract ethics, embodied ethics: The strange marriage of Foucault and positivism in labour process theory', *Organization*, 9 (1): 5–39.

Wray-Bliss, E. (2009) 'Ethics: Critique, ambivalence and infinite responsibilities (unmet)', in M. Alvesson, T. Bridgman and H.C. Willmott (eds), *The Oxford Handbook of Critical Management Studies*. Oxford: Oxford University Press.

Ybema, S., Keenoy, T., Oswick, C., Beverungen, A., Ellis, N. and Sabelis, I. (2009) 'Articulating identities', *Human Relations*, 62 (3): 299–322.

Yukl, G. (1999) 'An evaluation of conceptual weaknesses in transformational and charismatic leadership theories', *Leadership Quarterly*, 10: 285–305.

Zizek, S. (1989) *The Sublime Object of Desire*. London: Verso.

Zuboff, S. (1988) *In the Age of the Smart Machine*. New York: Basic Books.

Index

Page references to Notes will have the letter 'n' following the note, while references to Figures will be in *italics*